Audubon

IN EDINBURGH

Published by
NMS Publishing
a division of NMS Enterprises Limited
National Museums of Scotland
Chambers Street
Edinburgh EH1 1JF

with the assistance of

The Royal College of Surgeons of Edinburgh
Nicolson Street
Edinburgh EH8 9DW

British Library Cataloguing in Publication Data
A catalogue record of this book
is available from the British Library.

ISBN 1 901663 79 5

Design by NMS Enterprises Limited – Publishing

Printed and bound by Keyline of Newcastle Limited, United Kingdom

CONTENTS

'Pileated Woodpecker', plate 111 of *The Birds of America* by John James Audubon. (Reproduced by kind permission of the President and Council of the Royal College of Physicians and Surgeons of Glasgow)

HRH The Duke of Edinburgh

MOST people with an interest in natural history will be aware of the magnificent bird pictures painted by John James Audubon for his four massive volumes on *The Birds of America*. Perhaps less well known – at least I was unaware of it – is that many of the first engravings of Audubon's paintings were done in Edinburgh and that, in the production of the accompanying five-volume letterpress *Ornithological Biography*, he was greatly assisted by William MacGillivray, conservator of the museum of the Royal College of Surgeons of Edinburgh. It appears that it was MacGillivray's friendship with Audubon and his admiration for his work which inspired MacGillivray to start on a similar, but sadly uncompleted, work on the birds of Britain.

This book records an important period in the life of probably America's most famous bird artist and the friendship which developed between him and William MacGillivray at a time when Edinburgh was enjoying its Golden Age. Their collaboration produced one of the great classics among bird books. I think the Royal College of Surgeons of Edinburgh and the National Museums of Scotland deserve great credit for supporting the publication of *Audubon in Edinburgh*.

'Heron' by Audubon's friend and associate William MacGillivray. (© The Natural History Museum, London)

ACKNOWLEDGEMENTS
John Chalmers

I HAVE been collecting material for this book over a period of 20 years and during this time have received generous help from many sources. I would like to thank especially the many librarians, curators and archivists who have tolerated without complaint my many requests for assistance. The following institutions and their staff have been of particular value: Natural History Museum, London; National Library of Scotland; Edinburgh University Library; National Museums of Scotland; Royal College of Surgeons of Edinburgh; Royal College of Physicians of Edinburgh; Scottish National Portrait Gallery; National Gallery of Scotland; Royal Scottish Academy; Perth City Library; Aberdeen University Library; Aberdeen City Library; Mitchell Library, Glasgow; Mitchell Library, Sydney; and the College of Charleston. Special mention must be made of the outstanding help received from the splendid Audubon Museum in Henderson, Kentucky and from the staff of the Edinburgh Room of the City Library, Edinburgh.

The National Museums of Scotland have kindly allowed me to reproduce some of their Audubon engravings and other illustrations from their library and museum exhibits. Charles D Waterston, Alan Simpson, Andrew Kitchener, Robert McGowan and Geoffrey Swinney, past and present members of the staff of the National Museums of Scotland, have drawn my attention to relevant material in the museum archives.

Professor David Simpson has generously allowed me access to his extensive library which has been the source of many of the illustrations of Edinburgh and Scotland at the time of Audubon.

I am most grateful for the support of Donald Macleod, vice-president of the Royal College of Surgeons of Edinburgh, who suggested that the college become a partner in the publication of this book.

The Royal College of Physicians and Surgeons of Glasgow generously gave permission to reproduce many of the Audubon illustrations from their copy of *The Birds of America*. The support and endorsement of both the Royal College of Physicians and Surgeons of Glasgow and the Royal College of Surgeons of Edinburgh towards this publication has been particularly gratifying.

Of the many individuals who have given help and valuable criticism I would like to thank particularly Mrs Charles E Winters of Bethesda, Maryland, a descendant of Audubon and an authority on his oil paintings. Don Boarman, curator of the Audubon Museum in Henderson, was a fund of information. John Waterton of Edinburgh gave me much information about his forebear Charles Waterton and Dr A J O Taylor of Edinburgh kindly allowed me to reproduce his pencil sketch by Audubon of the turkey cock. Lt. Col. Angus A Fairrie and Mrs Jane MacGillivray gave me valuable information regarding William MacGillivray's family history.

Michael Devlin has done much of the photography, for which I am most grateful; any apparent deficiences in reproduction of the illustrations are due to the quality of the original material and not to his unfailing skill.

No one writing about Audubon can fail to be indebted to the scholarly biographies by Frances Hobart Herrick and Alice Ford and I readily acknowledge the great help which I received from these seminal works, to which I make frequent reference in my text. The writings of Christine E Jackson and Jessie M Sweet have also provided a valuable resource.

I am most grateful to the Scottish Society of the History of Medicine for a contribution of £500 from the Douglas Guthrie Fund to assist my research into William MacGillivray.

Cara Shanley, editor, and Lesley Taylor, director of publishing, NMS Enterprises Limited, have given unstinting support and encouragement without which the project could not have reached fruition. I owe them a great debt of gratitude.

Inevitably, pursuing my interest in Audubon and MacGillivray over many years has involved other members of my family and I thank them most warmly for their forbearance and willing help. My daughter, Alison Milne, has been a kindly critic and corrector of manuscript and her husband Gordon has frequently rescued me from computer failure and frustration.

My wife, Gwyneth, has given constant support, encouragement and advice and it is with the greatest pleasure that I dedicate this book to her.

Audubon's Links with the Royal College of Surgeons of Edinburgh

ONE Edinburgh institution which played an important role in assisting John James Audubon to complete his life's work was the Royal College of Surgeons of Edinburgh. In order to explain this link it is necessary to give some background of this venerable institution, which is now approaching its quincentenary.

In 1505 the Barber Surgeons of Edinburgh were recognised by the town council as a Craft Guild, with its principal role the maintenance and promotion of the highest standard of surgical practice. A Royal Charter conferred by James IV of Scotland in the following year confirmed its status. Since that time it has developed from small beginnings into one of the leading centres of surgical training and governance with over 14,000 fellows throughout the world.

At the time of Audubon's first visit to Edinburgh in 1826, the city was enjoying its Golden Age, flourishing in the afterglow of the Enlightenment. Splendid new buildings had been erected, including the New College of the university and the Royal Institution at the foot of the Mound, and the new town was expanding northward. Intellectual societies abounded, numerous scientific and literary journals were produced, and the theatre and the arts were well supported.

The Royal College of Surgeons was in a period of transition. The 'Old' Surgeons' Hall which it had occupied since 1697 was in a state of disrepair and was inadequate to house the museum which was about to be greatly augmented by the conditional donation of the collection of Dr John Barclay and the purchase of the collection of Sir Charles Bell. In 1832 the splendid building designed by William Playfair was opened, with its largest apartments designed to accommodate the museum, which at that time was the main teaching facility. Robert Knox, the anatomist who is unfortunately remembered mainly for his unwitting(?) association with Burke and Hare rather than for his outstanding contributions to comparative anatomy and his brilliance as a teacher, was appointed as the first full-time conservator of the museum in 1826. He resigned in 1831 after disagreements with the curators and council.

William MacGillivray, who had spent the previous ten years as an assistant to the Edinburgh University professor of natural history Robert Jameson, was appointed as Knox's successor in the face of intense competition. Liberated from the rather oppressive influence of Jameson, MacGillivray flourished and his ten-year tenure at the college was a period of intense creative activity during which, in addition to supervising the transfer of the museum contents to the new building, arranging their display and cataloguing them to the complete satisfaction of the college council, he wrote no less than nine books and many articles on a wide variety of natural history topics. It is during this period that he became associated with Audubon and this led to the links between Audubon and the college.

Much of their collaborative effort would have taken place within the confines of the college. Audubon must have been a frequent visitor, for he donated 30 specimens to the museum which contained many ornithological specimens among its collection of comparative anatomy, and there is little doubt that he made use of the college facilities such as the museum and the library to help him with his work. MacGillivray taught him how to dissect birds, which he regarded as an essential requirement for their proper classification, while Audubon encouraged MacGillivray to complete his paintings for *Birds of Britain* and provided him with some of the specimens which he used as his models. MacGillivray's paintings which feature largely in this book were completed during his time as conservator of the College Museum.

Such was their friendship and mutual respect that Audubon named two birds after MacGillivray and MacGillivray named one of his sons after

SURGEON'S HALLS & UNIVERSITY BUILDINGS, EDINBURGH. 10,250. G.W.W.

Audubon. The relationship extended to their families, who shared excursions to the Scottish countryside.

While Audubon went on to fame if not fortune in his lifetime, MacGillivray, although succeeding to the chair of natural history in Marischal College in Aberdeen, has until recently suffered undeserved neglect and obscurity. As conservator he served the college with great loyalty and diligence, and during this most productive period of his life he found the time and energy to make major contributions in the field of natural history. His association with Audubon brought mutual benefit. The Royal College of Surgeons of Edinburgh is pleased to acknowledge the contribution of one of its greatest servants towards the completion of Audubon's *magnum opus*.

Photograph (c.1890) of the Royal College of Surgeons (on the right) and the University of Edinburgh (on the left) – the two institutions with which Audubon was most involved during his time in Edinburgh. (From the G W Wilson Archive, Aberdeen University)

Portrait of John James Audubon, painted in Edinburgh by John Syme (1826). Owned originally by James Wilson of Woodville, and now in the White House Collection, Washington DC. (© White House Historical Association)

The Scottish Associates of John James Audubon

THE seeds of this book were sown when as a schoolboy in America I was introduced to ornithology by my American cousins, Robbie and Ernie Livingstone, who in April 1941 pointed out to me both the Audubon and MacGillivray warblers on a memorable 'bird walk' near Portland, Oregon. My interest in John James Audubon, the French-American ornithologist, was rekindled when I discovered that he had spent several years in Edinburgh, his 'fair Edina' – a city which he grew to love, and where he had been associated with two institutions, Edinburgh University and the Royal College of Surgeons of Edinburgh, that have also played a part in my life. My researches into Audubon led me to discover William MacGillivray (1796-1852), a much neglected Scottish natural historian.

Many books have been written about Audubon, and his superlative bird paintings have been reproduced so often that most readers will have at least a passing familiarity with him and his works. None of the biographies, however, concentrates on the Edinburgh period which was to prove a turning point in his life. It was in Edinburgh that the first engravings of his great work *The Birds of America* were made by William Home Lizars; and it was in this city that he was introduced to William MacGillivray, who collaborated with Audubon over many years in the writing of his *Ornithological Biography*, the five-volume book which accompanied the paintings. The two men, so different in their characters and personalities, developed a warm friendship and mutual respect and their association is the central theme of this book.

Both men kept journals, although unfortunately many of Audubon's were destroyed in a warehouse fire in New York in 1845 and MacGillivray's in a fire in Australia. Some are preserved, however, as is much of their prolific correspondence. These sources provide a vivid description of Scotland and Edinburgh and its personalities in the period from 1826 to 1840. I have tried, in writing this book, to paint a contemporary picture of Edinburgh based upon their writings.

The period from 1730 to 1830 is sometimes referred to as Scotland's 'Golden Age'; during this time Scotland in general and Edinburgh in particular produced an outstanding number of 'men of genius and learning'. Among these were David Hume the philosopher, Adam Smith the economist, William Cullen the physician, James Hutton the geologist, Joseph Black the chemist, James Watt the inventor, Robert and James Adam the architects, Alan Ramsay and Henry Raeburn the painters, Sir Walter Scott the author and many others in the fields of law, science and the arts. This created an atmosphere of intellectual activity unmatched in the western world. Scotland produced many more scientists per head of population during the first half of the nineteenth century than any other country, most of them receiving their education in Edinburgh.[1]

There is no doubt that this stimulating environment was the influence which led Audubon to make Edinburgh his European base, and many of the eminent personalities of the time will be encountered through Audubon's journals and letters. It is also fortunate that several outstanding illustrators produced drawings and paintings of the environs of Edinburgh during that period and I have borrowed extensively from the works of Shepherd, Swarbrick, Ewbanks, Lizars and others to recall the scenes that would have been familiar to Audubon, many of which remain little changed to this day. I hope that readers will not only learn something of the personalities described, but will also get a sense of life in Edinburgh during the early nineteenth century. Like Audubon, 'I wish to make a *pleasing* book as well as an *instructive* one'.[2]

There were many other Scottish influences on Audubon's career, including the Scottish weaver Alexander Wilson who is regarded as the father of American ornithology, Robert Jameson, professor of natural history at Edinburgh University, Patrick Neill who persuaded Audubon to persevere when he was prepared to abandon his ambitious plans while in a mood of deep depression, and William Home Lizars who did Audubon's first engravings and introduced him to Edinburgh's Society. Audubon acknowledged that without the welcome and support that he received in this country his work 'might like an uncherished plant, have died'.

I have left it largely to the subjects of the book to speak for themselves by relying heavily on their own writings. I have also included brief accounts of the subsidiary characters – all of whom are of considerable interest in their own right and perhaps deserve fuller treatment. I hope that the bibliography will enable those who are interested to delve further into the lives of these characters.

It would be impossible to restrict the book exclusively to the Scottish influences in Audubon's career. To understand his complex character it is necessary to give some details of his background, but I have tried to keep these to a minimum so as to avoid ground which has been covered by others. Furthermore, Audubon's visits to Edinburgh between 1826 and 1839 were interrupted by journeys to other parts of Britain, to Paris and to America. For the sake of continuity these diversions are briefly mentioned.

Audubon's journals were written for his wife Lucy and not intended for publication. They were often written hastily after a long day's work, with little attention to spelling or grammar. However, the spontaneity and sincerity of the journals gives them particular charm and I have kept the original spelling, capitalisation and punctuation, usually without the tedious intrusion of 'sic'.

Notes

1   Birse, R M *Science at the University of Edinburgh 1583-1993.*
2   Letter of Audubon to Swainson, 2 Oct 1830, cited in Herrick, F H *Audubon the Naturalist* vol. II, p. 102.

Audubon's Early Life | 1

JEAN Jacques Audubon (later anglicised to John James) was born in 1785 in Santo Domingo, now Haiti. His father, Captain Jean Audubon, was a French sailor, merchant and slave dealer who had acquired a sugar plantation on the island. His mother, Jeanne Rabin, was a French servant from a neighbouring estate who died soon after his birth. In 1789 an uprising of slaves made life in Santo Domingo hazardous so Audubon's father abandoned his property and returned to his home in Nantes in France with Jean Jacques and his half-sister Rosa. Captain Audubon's wife, Anne Moynet, who had remained in France, received the two illegitimate offspring of her husband and brought them up with as much devoted care and tenderness as if they had been her own children. They were both formally adopted in 1794.[1]

France at that time was in the throes of the Revolution. Nantes, which had espoused the Republican cause, was the site of some of the bloodiest incidents. In 1793 it was besieged by an army of loyalists from La Vendee but managed to fend off the enemy. Later that year an extreme Revolutionist, Jean Carrier, carried out a fearful purge of royalist sympathisers in the city resulting in the death of about nine thousand of the populace. Audubon senior was a staunch Republican and served his cause in a variety of capacities both on land as a commissioner and at sea in command of Republican vessels. In one engagement he defeated an English privateer, the *Brilliant*, forcing it to surrender an American merchantman which it had captured.[2]

In the midst of this unrest young Audubon's education was inevitably interrupted. He attended school in Nantes when the disturbances allowed but showed little aptitude or interest in the academic subjects, although he acquired proficiency in violin-playing, dancing and fencing which was to serve him well in later life. From his earliest days he showed a great interest in natural history which was to remain a life-long obsession. As a boy he seized every opportunity to escape to the countryside to observe, collect and draw the wildlife.

> My father being mostly absent on duty, my mother suffered me to do much as I pleased; it was therefore not to be wondered at that, instead of applying closely to my studies, I preferred associating with boys of my own age and disposition, who were more fond of going in search of bird's nests, fishing, or shooting, than of better studies. Thus almost every day, instead of going to school where I ought to have gone, I usually made for the field, where I spent the day; my little basket went with me, filled with good eatables, and when I returned home, during either winter or summer, it was replenished with what I called curiosities, such as bird's nests, bird's eggs, curious lichens, flowers of all sorts, and even pebbles gathered along the shore of some rivulet.[3]

The young Audubon's early efforts at drawing did not reveal the talents which he subsequently developed. He himself recognised this and later wrote:

> My pencil gave birth to a family of cripples … the worse my drawings were, the more fruitful did I see the originals. To have been torn from the study would have been as death to me. My time was entirely occupied with it. I produced hundreds of these rude sketches annually; and for a long time … they made bonfires on the anniversaries of my birth-day.[4]

Audubon in later life claimed to have spent some time in the studio of Jacques Louis David, France's greatest artist of the time, famed for his dramatic paintings of Revolutionary scenes and for his portraits of Napoleon. There is no evidence to support this claim and much reason to doubt it, for there is no mention of Audubon's attendance in David's records and Audubon was never happy with the medium of oils to which he would undoubtedly have been exposed in David's *atelier*. Audubon not infrequently spread, or at least did not attempt to quell, romantic tales which added colour and respectability to his origins and background. It seems probable, however, that he developed his unique artistic skills by his own efforts, uninfluenced by the work of others.

Although Audubon senior was an ardent admirer of Napoleon, he did not wish his son to be conscripted into Napoleon's army. In 1803 the young Audubon, then aged 18, was sent to America to live at Mill Grove, a farm near Philadelphia that his father had acquired when he left Santo Domingo. The farm was tenanted by a Quaker family with whom Audubon lived and from whom he received an allowance 'sufficient for the expenditure of a young gentleman'. It was intended that he should learn English and establish himself in business.

Although his upbringing in France had been anything but harsh, Audubon revelled in his new-found freedom from family ties. He did what most young men given free rein and an adequate allowance would have done: 'I spent much Money … as Happy as the Young Bird; that having Left the Parents sight carolls Merily.' He entered fully into the social life of the community: '… not a ball, a skating match, a house or a riding party took place without me.' He bought the best horse and hunting equipment available and dressed himself in fine silks and satins. A contemporary wrote:

> Today I saw the swiftest skater I ever beheld; backwards and forwards he went like the wind, even leaping over large airholes fifteen or more feet across … and this evening I met him at a ball, where I found his dancing exceeded his skating; all the ladies wished him as a partner; moreover, a handsomer man I never saw, his eyes alone command attention.[5]

This period at Mill Grove was the happiest of Audubon's life. He met and eventually married Lucy Bakewell, the daughter of a prosperous neighbouring farmer. The Bakewell family had recently arrived from England. Audubon at first was reluctant to exchange hospitality with them for he had no fondness for the English, his father having been twice imprisoned and twice wounded as a result of naval actions against the British. Audubon said,

Mill Grove as it is today. It is now a museum dedicated to Audubon.

'As a lad I had a great aversion to anything English or Scotch.' Lucy's charm overcame his prejudices and soon cordial relationships were established. Little could they have foreseen, during this carefree period of their courtship, the hardships and poverty that they were to face in the years to come.

As Audubon did not take an active part in the running of the farm, he continued with his nature studies and paintings of birds. At Mill Grove he carried out possibly the earliest experiments in ringing or banding of birds in order to study their migrations. Lucy's brother describes Audubon's activities and appearance at that time:

> On entering his room, I was astonished and delighted to find that it was turned into a museum. The walls were festooned with all kinds of bird's eggs …. The chimney piece was covered with stuffed squirrels, racoons, and opossums; and the shelves around were crowded with specimens, among which were fishes, frogs, snakes, lizards, and other reptiles … many paintings were arrayed on the walls, chiefly of birds …. He had also a trick in training dogs with great perfection, of which art his famous dog, Zephyr, was a wonderful example. He was an admirable marksman, an expert swimmer, a clever rider, possessed of great activity, prodigious strength, and was notable for the elegance of his figure and the beauty of his features, and he aided nature by a careful attendance to his dress. Besides other accomplishments he was musical, a good fencer, danced well and had some acquaintance with legerdemain tricks, worked in hair, and could plait willow baskets.[6]

No wonder Lucy fell for such a dashing and talented young man.

The idyll at Mill Grove was all too soon to come to an end. Lead ore had been discovered on the farm and in an attempt to exploit the development of a mine other business partners were brought in. The enterprise failed and animosities arose among the investors in the scheme. Audubon returned briefly to France to report on the unsatisfactory state of affairs to his father, but he returned again to America in 1806 with a friend, Ferdinand Rozier, as business partner. The two young men were supplied with funds by their parents in order to develop business interests and to resolve the difficulties over Mill Grove, which they did by selling the residual Audubon share of the estate.[7]

After a brief introduction to the world of commerce at the counting house of Bakewell relatives in New York, Audubon and Rozier travelled in 1807 to Louisville where they hoped to establish a trading store. Louisville at that time was a bustling port on the Ohio River with a population of 1300, many of French origin. Once settled there Audubon returned to the east to marry Lucy and escort her to his new home. This consisted of rooms in the Indian Queen, a hotel with very basic facilities – a marked contrast to the comfort and genteel lifestyle to which she was accustomed. It was to be the first of the many hardships which Lucy was to endure in her new life. There their first son, Victor Gifford Audubon, was born on 12 June 1809.

Characteristically Audubon continued to pursue his obsession with nature and his hobby of painting, neglecting his responsibilities at the store for which he could generate little enthusiasm, much to the annoyance of his partner, Rozier. The store, wrote Audubon,

> … went on prosperously when I attended to it; but birds were birds then as now. And my thoughts were ever and anon turning toward them as the objects of my greatest delight. I shot, I drew, I looked on nature only; my days were happy beyond human conception, and beyond this I really cared not … I seldom passed a day without drawing a bird, or noting something respecting its habits, Rozier meantime attending the counter.[8]

It was in the store one day in March 1810 that an event occurred which was to prove critical in Audubon's life. A stranger, Alexander Wilson, entered with the objective of obtaining subscribers to his publication *American Ornithology*. This chance meeting, which is considered more fully in Chapter 3, made Audubon aware, possibly for the first time, that his bird paintings might have a commercial value. Henceforth his avocation gradually became his vocation. For the next 25 years he dedicated his life with even greater intensity to completing a portfolio of paintings of the birds of America, with a view to eventual publication.

The store in Louisville did not prosper and in 1810, soon after Wilson's visit, Audubon and Rozier loaded a flat boat and took their stock 125 miles down the Ohio River to the village of Henderson where the Audubon family set up home in a log cabin. Again business was poor and within a year the two would-be traders set off with their goods on a perilous winter journey up the Mississippi River to St Genevieve. As ever Audubon filled the time while waiting for the ice to break up by shooting and sketching new specimens for his portfolio. Soon relations between Audubon and Rozier were becoming strained. Rozier complained that 'Audubon had no taste for commerce, and was continually in the forest', while Audubon declared that 'Rozier cared only for money'. Clearly their partnership could not continue. They decided at St Genevieve to part company. Rozier remained there and became a prosperous merchant with a large family, while Audubon returned to Henderson to rejoin his patient and long-suffering Lucy and their young son.

The next eight years in Henderson was a reasonably settled period for the Audubon family. Their second son, John Woodhouse, was born on 30 November 1812. Although times were hard due to the war with England, the store was moderately successful. Audubon bought land, and together with his brother-in-law Thomas W Bakewell and other partners, built a steam grist and sawmill. Unfortunately after a brief period of success the mill failed in 1819. Audubon, never a businessman, was let down by his partners and was arrested and gaoled in Louisville for debt. He was released by declaring himself bankrupt and finally left Henderson 'with every particle of property I held, to my creditors, keeping only the clothes I wore on that day, my original drawings, and my gun'. Among the items disposed of were Lucy's wedding silver and dinnerware. This was one of the lowest periods in Audubon's life, for in addition to his business failures two infant daughters had died. He wrote, 'I can scarcely conceive that I staid there 8 years and passed them comfortably for it undoubtedly is one [of] the poorest spots in the Western Country ...'.[9]

Before the business collapsed in Henderson, the Audubons were visited by George Keats (1797-1841), brother of the poet John, and his young Scottish wife Georgina. The Keats stayed with the Audubons for a time as paying guests and George was persuaded by Audubon to invest a small legacy which he had received in the purchase of a steamboat on the Ohio River. The boat apparently sank – whether before or after the financial settlement is unclear. The financial loss had repercussions which distressed brother John. He wrote to George and Georgina in September 1819:

Your present situation I will not suffer myself to dwell upon – when misfortunes are so real we are glad enough to escape them, and the thought of them. I cannot help thinking Mr Audubon a dishonest man – Why did he make you believe that he was a Man of Property? How is it his circumstances have altered so suddenly? In truth I do not believe you fit to deal with the world: or at least the American mold .... Those Americans will I am afraid still fleece you ... it appears to me you have as yet been somehow deceived. I cannot help thinking Mr Audubon has deceived you. I shall not like the sight of him – I shall endeavour to avoid seeing him[10] (see Chapter 6, p. 52).

It is unlikely that Audubon deliberately deceived George. More probably he was himself deceived and let down by others. At this period of his life he was beset with debts and failures due to poor judgement and lack of business sense. Nonetheless, John Keats' dislike of the Audubons persisted. In a letter to Georgina of 13 January 1820 he wrote:

I was surprised to hear of the State of Society [sic] at Louisville, it seems you are just as ridiculous there as we are here – threepenny parties, halfpenny Dances – The best thing I have heard of is your Shooting, for it seems you follow the Gun. Give my compliments to Mrs Audubon and tell her I cannot think her either good looking or honest – Tell Mr Audubon he's a fool ....

Despite his unfortunate introduction, George remained in America and for a time became a successful and influential businessman in Louisville. Curiously he entered into a business partnership there with Audubon's brother-in-law William Bakewell, again in connection with shipping, and once again the business failed and

'Black Billed Cuckoo', plate 32 from *The Birds of America*. This is one of the paintings done by Audubon at Oakely. Joseph Mason was responsible for the magnolia background. Audubon wrote, 'he now draws flowers better than any man probably in America'. (Reproduced by kind permission of the President and Council of the Royal College of Physicians and Surgeons of Glasgow)

he was faced with bankruptcy at the time of his early death in 1841. Certainly these contacts with the Audubon family did not bring the Keats good fortune.

During the next five years Audubon travelled extensively in the eastern states, constantly seeking new specimens to complete his portfolio. The faithful Lucy, who never faltered in her belief in his talents and in the successful outcome of his project, worked as a teacher or governess to provide a home for the boys and financial support for her husband. Audubon obtained occasional work in a variety of menial jobs and had some success painting crayon portraits at $5 each, but most of his time was devoted to the relentless effort to complete his task. During the summer of 1821 he was invited to the plantation of Oakley near St Francisville in Louisiana, owned by a Scotsman, James Pirrie. Audubon was engaged to tutor Pirrie's daughter, but still had much time to devote to his own paintings. During this period he produced some of his finest work, assisted by the young Joseph Mason[11] who accompanied him at that time. Unfortunately, due to a misunderstanding involving Pirrie's daughter, Audubon had to leave rather hurriedly after five

months. The next three years were spent travelling in the eastern states from the Great Lakes and Niagara Falls to his old haunts along the Ohio and Mississippi rivers, sometimes in the company of his son Victor, but mainly on his own and usually in conditions of extreme hardship and poverty. During this period he met George Lehman,[12] a German-Swiss landscape painter whom he was later to employ to assist with the backgrounds of about 40 paintings (in 1831). Occasionally he would visit Lucy who had been invited to set up a private school on the estate of Captain Robert Percy near St Francisville, which she was to conduct for five years. Audubon spent the summer of 1823 there teaching the Percy children music and drawing, but once more had to make a hasty departure because of some circumstance involving one of the Percy daughters (see Chapter 6, note 12).

A friend described Audubon and his activities at this time:

Audubon was one of the handsomest men I ever saw. In person he was tall and slender, his blue eyes were an eagle's in brightness … his hair a beautiful chestnut brown, very

5

glossy and curly. His bearing was courteous and refined, simple and unassuming …. He was very sociable – being the center of attraction in every circle in which he mingled …. After spending short times with his family he would start out again on his lonely journey in the woods, alone and on foot …. While he was wandering the forest his noble wife was working in order to assist him …. Every time he returned home he found his wife fading and drooping and he could not help but compare her to a beautiful tobacco plant cut off at the stem and hung up to wither with head hanging down, as he put in his quaint way of using similes.[13]

By this time Audubon's collection of bird paintings had accumulated to the extent that he was considering their publication, but he was discouraged by a hostile reception in Philadelphia, orchestrated by the champions of Alexander Wilson who saw Audubon as a potential rival. George Ord (1781-1863)[†] in particular, a man of considerable power and influence, developed a consuming and pathological hatred of Audubon (this is a recurring theme in subsequent chapters). Audubon was advised that the only hope of achieving his objective lay in Europe.

My wife was receiving a large income – nearly three thousand dollars a year – from her industry and talents, which she generously offered me to help forward their publication; and I resolved on a new effort to increase the amount by my own energy and labour. Numerous pupils desired lessons in music, French, and drawing …. I received a special invitation to teach dancing, and a class of sixty was soon organized …. I placed all the gentlemen in a line reaching across the hall, thinking to give the young ladies time to compose themselves …. How I toiled before I could get one graceful step or motion! I broke my bow and nearly my violin in my excitement and impatience! …. The ladies were next placed in the same order and made to walk the steps; and then came the trial for both parties to proceed at the same time, while I pushed one here and another there, and all the while singing myself, to assist their movements …. Lessons in fencing followed …. The dancing speculation fetched two thousand dollars and with this capital and my wife's savings I was now able to foresee a successful issue to my great ornithological work.[14]

Thus provided, in May 1826 he was able to set sail for Britain. However, before continuing with Audubon on his travels it is appropriate at this point to give an account of Alexander Wilson – the first important Scottish influence in his life.

Notes

†   Denotes more information in the Biographical Profiles section of this book (see p. 205).

1   Not surprisingly, Audubon was rather reticent regarding his parentage and allowed several accounts to circulate. In one of these his mother was a beautiful and wealthy Spanish lady whom his father had married in Louisiana. He even allowed a more romantic rumour to circulate – that he was the Dauphin of France, the son of Louis XVI and Marie Antoinette, who had escaped from the Temple prison on 3 July 1793 (there were many pretenders to this title!). Credit is due to Audubon's biographer Herrick for establishing the true circumstances of his birth. (Herrick, F H: 'Audubon and the Dauphin', in *The Auk* [1937], 54: 476-99.)

2   Audubon's father, Captain Jean Audubon, had several contretemps with the British. In 1758 at the age of 14, while serving as a boy on his father's ship, he was captured by the British and held prisoner in England for five years. In 1779, when captain of his own ship, he was again captured by the British and held as a prisoner in New York for a year. As a result Captain Audubon developed an intense antipathy towards the British which his son shared at first, but this mellowed as a result of his contacts with the Bakewell family and others of British origin whom he met in America.

3   Audubon, M R: *Audubon and His Journals*, vol. I, p. 12.

4   Audubon, J J: *Ornithological Biography*, vol. I, p. viii.

5   Cited in Durant, M and Harwood, M: *On the road with John James Audubon*, p. 4.

6   Buchanan, R *The Life and Adventures of John James Audubon*, pp. 16-17.

7   Mill Grove exists today as a museum and wildlife sanctuary dedicated to the memory of Audubon. It is the only surviving residence of Audubon in the United States.

8   Cited in Durant and Harwood, loc. cit., pp. 34-5.

9   *Journal of John James Audubon 1820-1821*, p. 12.

10   Rollins, H E (ed.): *The Letters of John Keats 1814-1821*, p. 185 (Cambridge University Press, 1958).

11   Joseph Mason (1808-42) was aged 13 when Audubon engaged him as a pupil and assistant, and they travelled together for nearly two years. Mason proved an apt student and became an excellent artist, creating the floral backgrounds for at least 57 of Audubon's paintings (although his name does not feature on the engravings). He parted from Audubon on 23 August 1822. Audubon wrote: 'My friend, Joseph Mason, left me today, and we experienced great pain at parting. I gave him paper and chalks ... and the double barrelled-gun ....' Mason later became a floral artist in Philadelphia, but little is known of his subsequent life.

12   Audubon engaged the help of a number of assistants over the years in addition to Mason. George Lehman provided the background for at least 40 paintings between 1829 and 1834. Maria Martin (sister-in-law and later second wife of Audubon's great friend John Bachman) provided the floral settings for about 20 paintings. Lucy is known to have painted one bird and Audubon's two sons, Victor Gifford and John Woodhouse, helped increasingly towards the end of the project and made a large contribution to his next and last publication, the *Viviparous Quadrupeds of America*. Havell made alterations to 134 of the drawings. Audubon sometimes asked him to insert a suitable background.

13   Cited by Durant, M in *The Bicentennial of John James Audubon*, p. 107.

14   Buchanan, R: *The Life and Adventures of John James Audubon*, pp. 98-9.

2 | Alexander Wilson: Audubon's First Scottish Influence

ALTHOUGH Alexander Wilson (1766-1813) died soon after his historic meeting with Audubon, there is no doubt that he had a profound and continuing influence on Audubon's affairs. Perhaps for the first time Audubon was made aware of the possible commercial potential of his own paintings.

Alexander Wilson was born in the Scottish town of Paisley, which was then the third largest city of Scotland. He was baptised by John Witherspoon (1723-94), a distinguished cleric born in Gifford near Edinburgh. Witherspoon had been minister of Paisley New Church but he subsequently emigrated to America to become president of Princeton College, New Jersey, in 1768. He was elected the Congressional representative of New Jersey and as a leading figure in the American Revolution he was one of the signatories of the Declaration of Independence,

which he helped Thomas Jefferson to draft.

Wilson's father had pursued a chequered career as a smuggler and distiller of illicit whisky before settling down as a weaver – weaving was then the principal industry of Paisley. By the time of Wilson's birth his father had acquired respectability and later he could afford to send the boy to Paisley Grammar School. However, Wilson's formal education ended at the age of ten when his mother died and the family fortunes declined. He left home to work on a farm where he was described as a 'very careless herd, letting the kye transgress on the corn, being very often busied with some book'.[1]

Aged 13, Wilson was apprenticed as a weaver to his brother-in-law, William Duncan. He never enjoyed weaving and, although on completion of his three-year apprenticeship he worked in a desultory way for his father and others, Wilson

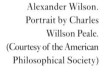

Alexander Wilson. Portrait by Charles Willson Peale. (Courtesy of the American Philosophical Society)

Far right: Memorial plaque of John Witherspoon mounted on a wall in the village of Gifford, East Lothian. The inscription reads: 'In honoured memory of the Reverend John Witherspoon, D.D. LL.D. only clergyman to sign the American Declaration of Independence. The first Moderator of the Presbyterian General Assembly in America and President of Princeton University. Born in the manse of Yester, Gifford Feb 5th 1723.'

like Audubon, escaped to the countryside whenever possible, where he acquired a skill with the gun and a talent for poaching. He relieved the boredom of the loom by reading and memorising the works of the great poets such as Milton and Pope, and by developing his own talent as a poet which was later to contribute to his downfall.

In his late teens Wilson resumed working for his brother-in-law who had now moved to Queensferry near Edinburgh, and he spent most of the next four years as a pedlar travelling around Scotland selling his wares. The pedlar, or packman, was at that period a useful and welcome member of society, at least among the humbler classes. Much of the population lived remote from the nearest town and with limited opportunities for travel. The pedlar was the bearer not only of much needed goods but of news and gossip from far afield. It was not an easy or financially rewarding existence, however. 'I have this day measured the height of a hundred stairs, and explored the recesses of twice that number of miserable habitations; and what have I gained by it? only 2 shillings of worldly pelf.'[2]

Wherever he travelled, Wilson, in his constant quest to expand his knowledge, went out of his way to explore places of interest and to meet the local characters, particularly those of a literary bent. Mostly he lived rough, sleeping out in the open or in barns, although when sales were good he indulged in the luxury of an inn. His poetic endeavours also continued and he attempted to sell books of his poems as well as his wares. An example of his style at that time is given in a poem which he wrote to introduce himself to his customers.[3] The first verse reads:

> Fair Ladies, I pray for one moment to stay,
> Until with submission I tell you,
> What muslins so curious, for uses so various
> A poet has here brought to sell you.

Wilson kept a journal during his travels as a pedlar that gives interesting glimpses of his life and times. At Musselburgh in 1789 he noted that 'the game of golph is much practiced by parties of gentlemen; and is, in my opinion, a more healthy than entertaining amusement'.[4] Benjamin Rush (1745-1813),[†] who also encountered golf for the first time in Edinburgh,

Golf on Leith Links, from Grant's *Old and New Edinburgh*. Leith Links and the nearby Musselburgh Links are arguably the oldest golf courses in the world.

reckoned that a man who played golf 'would live ten years longer for using this exercise once or twice a week' and hoped to introduce it to America.

During his travels Wilson admired the Bass Rock, which he described as

> … rising out of the sea to the dreadful height of 600 feet Prodigious numbers of Solan geese [gannets] build among the cliffs of the rock. The method used to catch their young is somewhat dangerous. As soon as it is perceived that the young are arrived at their proper bigness … the climber has a rope fixed round his middle with a feather pillow bound on his breast, to prevent sharp pointed crags from wounding him in his ascent or descent. Being thus secured, he is let down over the verge of the rock, till he come to the nests of the geese, while flying and screaming around him in vast multitudes … deploring the loss of their unfortunate young. A considerable number of boats are stationed below, ready to receive the fowls, as soon as he drives them from their holes …. The birds unable to support themselves, and falling from such a height, are so stunned, that before they can recover themselves, they are snatched from the sea and secured. This method they yearly repeat, sending those caught to Edinburgh, where they are generally sold at two shilling each.[5]

Audubon and MacGillivray were to visit the Bass Rock in 1835 (see Chapter 13, p. 166).

Engraving of the Bass Rock by Myles Birket Foster (1825–99).

species of pleasure more generally pleasing, or made more welcome to the human heart, than flattery. Flattery is the food of vanity, and vanity is the daughter of ignorance. To know ourselves, is the only method to exclude vanity and the certain way to despise flattery.

Wilson was moved by the beautiful setting of Edinburgh, just as Audubon was to be 40 years later. When walking along the shoreline at Musselburgh, Wilson noted:

> The sea was smooth as glass, and interspersed with a considerable number of large vessels, moving lazily along on the tide, while their white canvass glittered in the sun. The sea-fowl clamoured from every quarter, and a vast number of fishing-boats from different places, were scattered about a mile from the shore, intent at their occupation. Behind us, Arthur's Seat rose towering to the heavens. To the west and north, was seen the mountains of Fife, and to the east the most conspicuous were North-Berwick-Law and the Bass, rising a little above the mainland. The melody of birds on the one hand, the solemn sounding of the sea along the pebbly shore on the other joined to the wide watery prospect that spread before us, formed a most enchanting enter-tainment, that at once delighted the eye, charmed the ear, and conveyed a tide of rapture to the whole soul.[8]

In 1786 Robert Burns published his first book of poems in the Scottish dialect. Its impact was enormous and inspired a legion of amateur poets throughout Scotland to try to emulate his genius. Wilson became a great admirer and his own poetry was profoundly influenced. He was extremely flattered when one of his poems, 'Watty and Meg', which he published anony-mously, was considered by many to be the work of Burns and sold 100,000 copies. The poem is an account of the relationship between a dissolute husband and nagging wife. Eventually there is a reconciliation and the poem ends:

> Down he threw his staff, victorious;
>   Aff gaed bonnet, claes, and shoon;
> Syne below the blankets, glorious,
>   Held anithir Hinnymoon!

At Burntisland, a village on the north shore of the 'Frith' [sic] of Forth, Wilson describes what must have been one of the first catamarans: 'a strange vessel, called the EXPERIMENT … measuring about one hundred feet in length being almost two distinct vessels under one deck, but with two keels, two rudders, and five masts, and seems to have been the monstrous production of some mathematician's delirious pericranium.'[6]

While in Dalkeith near Edinburgh, Wilson was determined to meet the Duchess of Buccleugh, but was refused entry to the palace. During the annual town fair which coincided with his visit, he approached the Duchess as she made her habitual tour of the stalls and tried to entice her to see his wares. 'She paused for a moment and saying in a tone which pierced me to the soul, "I don't want any of the things," turned with her attendants to the next stall. You whose souls are susceptible of the finest feeling … think what I felt on this occasion.'[7]

The journal is interspersed with reflections and homilies which reveal Wilson's thoughts, such as:

> I am persuaded, that the humble, parsimonious peasant, eats his simple meal with as much satisfaction, rises refreshed from his simple meal with as much cheerfulness, and expe-riences more real happiness, peace of mind and bodily health, than those overgorged superiors, who treat their dependants as slaves, and look down on them as beings made of an inferior mould …. There is no

While Burns had concentrated largely on rustic and romantic themes, Wilson adopted the rapidly developing industrial scene as his chief subject. To his later regret he ignored his father's admonition: 'Sandy, I see you have some talent about you, but my advice is, never to use it to wound the feelings of others.' 'The Hollander, or Light Weight' was a thinly veiled attack on a local merchant well known for his tendency to cheat the weavers when buying their cloth. Although not named, the object of the attack was readily identifiable and took out a summons against Wilson for criminal libel and incitement to unrest. The trial for some reason was abandoned. One of the offending verses will suffice to give the gist of the poem and to show the influence of Burns:[9]

Shall black Injustice lift its head,
　　An' cheat us like the devil,
Without a man to stop its speed,
　　Or crush the growin' evil?
No; Here am I, wi' vengeance big,
　　Resolv'd to ca'm his clashing;
Nor shall his cheeps, or pouther't wig,
　　Protect him frae a lashin.

Wilson's attempts to sell his book of poems met little success. Burns had set the standard with which lesser poets could not compete. This failure, coupled with financial difficulties, induced a depressive illness which lasted some months. In a letter to his life-long friend Thomas Crichton he wrote at this time:

Such, my dear sir, are the thoughts that for ever revolve through my breast – such the melancholy reflections of one lost to every beam of hope, – and such, amid the most dismal, the most complicated horrors of distress! Driven by poverty and disease to the solitudes of retirement, at the same period when the flush of youth, the thirst of fame, the expected applause of the world, and the charms of ambition, welcomed him to the field. Had I but one hope more left of enjoying life and health, methinks I could cheerfully suffer the miseries that now surround me; but, alas, I feel my body decay daily, my spirits and strength continually decrease, and something within tells me that dissolution, – dreadful dissolution, – is not far distant.

No heart can conceive the terrors of those who tremble under the apprehension of death. This increases their love of life, and every new advance of the king of terrors overwhelms them with despair.[10]

It would be hard to find a better description of the agonies of depression.

As Wilson recovered, he adopted a more positive and realistic attitude: 'I find the decree of my fate running thus – Renounce poetry, and all its distracting notions, descend to the labourers vale of life, there attend the dictates of prudence, and toil or starve.'[11] Despite this resolution, as his spirits recovered, he resumed his writings. A second book of his poems met with some success.

The last decade of the eighteenth century was a period of unrest. The French Revolution was in progress and the sentiments which inspired it did not pass unnoticed in Scotland, and in particular in Paisley, where the effects of the Industrial Revolution were becoming apparent in the weaving industry. Disputes arose between the journeymen and master weavers and Wilson became involved with a group of agitators, leading to an event which would change the course of his life. In his biography of Wilson, Sir William Jardine (1800-4)[†] explains this aberration, which was totally at variance with Wilson's real disposition and the whole tenor of his former and after life.

The general depression of trade, occasioned by the wars incident to the French Revolution, threw into idleness many of the young operatives, who began openly to promulgate revolutionary principles …. It was Wilson's misfortune to have formed an intimacy with some of these, who, knowing his talents, prevailed on him to revile and satirize the conduct of those who were most offensive to their view of liberty, or of the propriety of conduct as masters …. Ever ready to redress what he imagined wrongs, [Wilson] produced a number of poetical squibs which held up the subjects of popular dislike to contempt and ridicule.[12]

One of these poetical 'squibs' alleged fraudulent dealing on the part of a wealthy and respected Paisley merchant. The merchant,

Thomas Paine, champion of the underprivileged and author of the *Rights of Man*.

William Sharp, was sent a copy of the poem, together with an anonymous letter informing him that the poem would be published within three days unless he paid five guineas to suppress it. Wilson, because of his previous poems of similar character, was suspected of being the author and was arrested. He acknowledged that the blackmailing letter was his but would not admit to writing the poem, which nevertheless was clearly in his style. Later, however, he admitted authorship. A sample verse reads:

> Wha cou'd believe a chiel sae trig
> Wad cheat us o' a bodle?
> Or that sai fair a gowden wig
> Contained sae black a noddle?
> But Shark beneath a sleekit smile
> Conceals his fiercest girning;
> And like his neighbours of the Nile,
> Devours wi' little warning.[13]

It is difficult to imagine that such a puerile diatribe could be taken seriously, but such was the atmosphere of unrest at the time that Sharp demanded the arrest of Wilson for his 'highly libellous, incendiary and dangerous publications'. Wilson was ordered to pay damages of £50 to Sharp and was fined a further £10. Sixty pounds in those days was equal to a year's income and Wilson could not pay. He was therefore jailed for several periods between May 1792 and January 1794 for the original offence and subsequent contempts of court. In later life Wilson was to regret these 'sins of my youth, and had I taken my good old father's advice they never would have seen the light of day'.[14]

In 1793 the government, alarmed by the news from France, carried out a vicious campaign against all who might be regarded as potential agitators, among whom the Paisley weavers figured prominently, being better educated and organised than most and generally familiar with Thomas Paine's *Rights of Man*. The rebellious Wilson was a great admirer of Paine. In 1792 he wrote a poem mock-ing the Church, in which he includes the following verse:

> The 'Rights of Man' is now weel kenned,
> And read by mony a hunder;
> For Tammy Paine the buik has penned,
> And lent the Courts a lounder;
> It's like a keeking-glass to see
> The craft of Kirk and statesmen;
> And we' a bauld and easy glee,
> Guid faith the birky bears them.

Fifteen years later Wilson, while in New York, visited the 'Celebrated author of the *Rights of Man* .... In the only decent apartment of a small indifferent looking frame house, I found this extraordinary man, sitting wrapt in a night gown .... Paine's face would have excellently suited the character of *Bardolph*; but the penetration and intelligence of his eye bespeak the man of genius and of the world ... he examined my book, – desired me to put down his name as a subscriber ....'[15] Paine's death soon after this visit terminated the contract.

At the instigation of Henry Dundas (1742-1811), the Lord Advocate (later Viscount Melville), the agitators were harshly dealt with. Some were executed and others sent to the penal colonies on the most trivial of pretexts. It is possible that the fact of Wilson being in jail during that period might have spared him from such a fate. In the summing up of the trial of Thomas Muir, who had been accused of making seditious speeches and circulating the *Rights of Man*, the notorious 'hanging judge' Lord Braxfield said that the 'Government in this country is made up of the landed interest, which alone has a right to be represented; as for the rabble, who have nothing by personal property, what hold has the nation of them? What security for the payment of their taxes? They may pack up all their property on their backs, and leave the country in the twinkling of an eye.'

On regaining his freedom Wilson, being one of Braxfield's 'rabble', decided that he had no future in Scotland. He had broken off contact with his long-standing friend Martha MacLean, the subject of many of his romantic verses, possibly because he realised that his irregular lifestyle was incompatible with marriage, and his relationships with his other friends had become strained by his constant appeals for money. In 1794, at the age of 28, Wilson emigrated to America, disembarking in the land of opportunity with a flute and fowling piece but virtually penniless.

A fellow Paisley weaver and poet, Robert Tannahill, marked the event with a poem on the *Emigration of Alexander Wilson to America*, from which the following verses are taken:

He bravely strave gainst Fortune's stream
While Hope held forth ae distant gleam,
Till dasht and dasht, time after time,
    On Life's rough sea,
He weeped his thankless native clime,
    And sail'd away.

The patriot bauld, the social brither,
In him war sweetly join'd thegither:
He knaves reprov'd without a swither,
    In keenest satire;
And taught what mankind owe each ither
    As sons of Nature

Since now he's gane, an Burns is deid,
Ah! wha will tune the Scottish reed?

Her thistle, dowie, hings its heid,—
    Her harp's unstrung,—
While mountain, river, loch, and mead,
    Remain unsung.

In America, Wilson obtained a variety of jobs, first as a copper engraver, then reverting to weaving, which he gave up as soon as possible to become a pedlar. Although his own formal education had been brief, he was better educated than most and for several years became a schoolteacher. He taught first at Elwood School in Milestown near Philadelphia, which he had to leave hurriedly – possibly as a consequence of an indiscreet love affair. He was succeeded in this post by his nephew William Duncan who had accompanied him to America. Duncan was, in his turn, succeeded by the Rev. John Bachman (1790-1874),[†] who will appear again as a close friend and collaborator of Audubon. In 1802 Wilson obtained another teaching job at the village of Kingsessing on the Schuylkill River, then four miles from Philadelphia and only 20 miles from Mill Grove where Audubon arrived the following year. He was to spend four years there, possibly the happiest period of his life, due largely to the friendship of his neighbour William Bartram (1739-1823).[†]

Bartram had inherited an outstanding botanical garden established by his father John Bartram (1699-1777)[†] on the banks of the Schuyl-kill River. In Wilson's time the school and garden were in the country, but gradually the district became absorbed into the expanding Philadelphia. Thirty years later Audubon, during a visit to the area,

Above, left: William Bartram. Portrait by Charles Willson Peale. (Courtesy of the Independence National Historical Park Collection, Philadelphia, USA)

Above: Alexander Wilson's schoolhouse at Kingsessing. From *Poems and Literary Prose of Alexander Wilson*, volume 1 (p. ix), edited by A B Grossart.

Bartram's composite drawing of toad flax, ruby throated humming bird and stone crab. (Plate 20 from the Forthergill Collection in the Natural History Museum, London. © The Natural History Museum, London)

Below: 'Crossbills and Buntings' by Wilson, plate XXXI from *American Ornithology*.

… passed poor Alexander Wilson's school-house and heaved a sigh. Alas poor Wilson! would that I could once more speak to thee, and listen to thy voice. When I was a youth, the woods stood unmolested here, looking wild and fresh as if just from the Creator's hands; but now hundreds of streets cross them, and thousands of houses and millions of diverse improvements occupy their place: Barton's [*sic*] garden is the only place which is unchanged.[16]

The Bartram home and part of the garden are still preserved within the city.

William Bartram was an enthusiastic naturalist who had compiled a list of 215 American birds. He was a talented artist. Many of his paintings are held in the Natural History Museum, London, and some have been published.[17]

He communicated his enthusiasm for ornithology to Wilson who, at the age of 38, commenced the study of American birds which was to preoccupy him for the rest of his short life. At last his chequered and restless career was to take on a new and intense purpose. With single-minded determination and the constant encouragement of Bartram, who taught him how to paint, he set about producing an illustrated account of all known American birds. His paintings are sometimes criticised on the

'Water rail and woodcock', by Wilson, plate XLVIII from *American Ornithology*.

grounds that they represent the birds in rather lifeless profile, usually several birds to a page for reasons of economy, and in random order as they came to hand. What Wilson's paintings may have lacked in artistic pose and arrangement, however, is more than compensated for by their accuracy, some critics even considering them to be more exact than those of Audubon. Wilson's paintings and the accompanying text are a remarkable achievement for a man who had no prior knowledge or training in natural history or painting, and minimal resources to finance his endeavour.

Wilson had one distinguished predecessor – Mark Catesby (1682-1749), who was born in England of a wealthy land-owning family. Catesby visited the New World for two periods of several years, engaged at first in collecting and sending back to Britain seeds of newly discovered plants. During his travels he recorded and painted the unfamiliar plant and animal life of all kinds which he published in his *Natural History of Carolina, Florida, and the Bahama Islands* (1731-43), including descriptions of 109 birds. Catesby engraved the illustrations himself and showed remarkable ability. The original paintings were purchased by King George III and remain in the Royal Collection. Catesby's travels exhausted his inheritance, however, and although his book was widely acclaimed and published in several languages, he died in poverty.

Wilson was rather dismissive of Catesby's work, which he had studied in Bartram's library. In a letter to President Thomas Jefferson, who was also a keen naturalist, he wrote of his 'design of publishing a new Ornithology of the United States of America, so deficient in the works of Catesby, Edwards and other Europeans'.[18] Given the times and conditions under which Catesby worked, this criticism is rather unfair, particularly as the artistic merit of his work bears comparison with that of Wilson.

In contrast to his rather primitive painting style, Wilson's writings reveal his natural gift for clear and expressive prose. Indeed, his written descriptions are sometimes more vivid than his paintings and are occasionally coloured by his irresistible inclination to express himself in verse – a delightful variation from the usual texts on ornithology. The early editions of the *Encyclopaedia Britannica* state with regard to Wilson's writings that 'passages occur in the prefaces and descriptions which, for elegance of language, graceful ease, and graphic power, can scarcely be surpassed'. Wilson's description of the migrations of the passenger pigeon gives an example of his graphic style:

But the most remarkable characteristic of these birds is their associating together, both in their migrations, and also during the period of incubation, in such prodigious

Above: 'Blue jay and Bay-leaved Smilax' by Catesby, who was the first naturalist to paint composite pictures of birds and plants. The plants were not necessarily associated with the habitat of the birds. From *Catesby's Birds of Colonial America* by Alan Feduccia. (© University of North Carolina Press, 1985. Used by permission of the publisher)

Above, right: 'Greater Prairie-Chicken' by Catesby. This bird is now almost extinct. The flower is the shooting star.

numbers as almost to surpass belief, and which has no parallel among any other of the feathered tribes on the face of the earth …. I have witnessed these migrations in the Gennesee country, often in Pennsylvania, and also in various parts of Virginia, with amazement; but all that I had then seen of them were mere straggling parties when compared with the congregated millions which I have since beheld in our western forests, in the States of Ohio, Kentucky, and the Indiana territory. These fertile and extensive regions abound with the nutritious beech-nut, which constitutes the chief food of the wild pigeon. In seasons when these nuts are abundant, corresponding multitudes of pigeons may be confidently expected …. Their roosting places are always in the woods, and sometimes occupy a large extent of forest. When they have frequented one of these places for some time, the appearance it exhibits is surprising. The ground is covered to the depth of several inches with their dung; all the tender grass and underwood destroyed; the surface strewed with large limbs of trees, broken down by the weight of the birds clustering one above another; and the trees themselves, for thousands of acres, killed as completely as if girdled with an axe. The marks of this desolation remain for many years on the spot ….

As soon as the young were fully grown, and before they left the nests, numerous parties of the inhabitants from all parts of the adjacent country, came with waggons, axes, beds, cooking utensils, many of them accompanied by the greater part of their families, and encamped for several days at this immense nursery. Several of them informed me that the noise in the woods was so great as to terrify their horses, and that it was difficult for one person to hear another speak without bawling in his ear. The ground was strewed with broken limbs of trees, eggs, and young squab pigeons, which had been precipitated from above, and on which herds of hogs were fattening. Hawks, buzzards, and eagles were sailing about in great numbers, and seizing the squabs from their nests at pleasure; while, from twenty feet upwards to the tops of the trees, the view through the woods presented a perpetual tumult of crowding and fluttering multitudes of pigeons their wings roaring like thunder, mingled with the frequent crash of falling timber; for now the axe-men were at work, cutting down those trees that seemed to be most crowded with nests, and contrived to fell them in such a manner, that, in their descent, they might bring down several others; by which means the falling of one large tree sometimes produced two hundred squabs, little inferior in size to the old ones, and almost one mass of fat.[19]

Wilson observed a migration which extended one mile in width and took four hours to pass overhead, and calculated that it contained more than 2,230,000,000 pigeons, each consuming half a pint of mast daily! It seems extraordinary that such a successful species could become extinct about a century after these observations were made – the last passenger pigeon died in Cincinnati Zoo in 1914 aged 29. This was largely as a result of destrucion of the pigeons' habitat by man.

(A passenger pigeon which had strayed to Scotland was shot in Fife on 31 December 1825 and shown at a meeting of the Wernerian Society in Edinburgh on 14 January 1826.)

As Audubon was to do some time later, Wilson took every opportunity to explore the countryside to study and shoot birds for identification and drawing. In his travels he covered thousands of miles throughout the eastern states from the Canadian border to Florida, mostly on foot and under conditions of considerable hardship. He described one of these journeys, to the Niagara Falls, in a narrative poem called 'The Foresters', which was widely admired at the time. The following extract contrasts the scant poetic output in the New World with the Old.

> Yet Nature's charms that bloom so lovely here,
> Unhailed arrive, unheeded disappear;
> While bare bleak heaths, and brooks of half a
>   mile
> Can rouse the thousand bards of Britain's Isle.
> There scarce a hillock lifts its little head,
> Or humble hamlet peeps their glades among,
> Our western world, with all its matchless floods,
> Our vast transparent lakes and boundless woods,
> Stamped with the traits of majesty sublime.
> Unhonoured weep the silent lapse of Time,
> Spread their wild grandeur to the
>   unconscious sky,
> In sweetest seasons pass unheeded by;
> While scarce one Muse returns the songs
>   they gave,
> Or seeks to snatch their glories from the grave.

In 1806 Wilson obtained a well-paid job as assistant editor for a new edition of Abraham Rees's *New Cyclopaedia*. This job not only gave him financial security but allowed him the opportunity to commence publication of his own work. His employer, publisher Samuel Bradford,

'Passenger Pigeon' by Wilson, plate XLIV from *American Ornithology*.

undertook to finance 200 sets of Wilson's proposed *American Ornithology*, provided that Wilson obtained that number of subscribers. One of the earliest subscribers was President Thomas Jefferson.

The total cost of Wilson's proposed ten volumes was $120 – a considerable sum in those days and well beyond the means of all but the very wealthy. Eventually, however, Wilson obtained 250 subscribers and the financial viability of the work was assured. One of his subscribers was William Morton, the wealthy president of an insurance company in Lexington, Kentucky, and son of the Earl of Morton of Dalmahoy near Edinburgh, at whose home Audubon was to spend some time 20 years later.

Wilson spent his remaining years totally dedicated to his project and successive volumes were produced under extreme difficulty. He described himself as a 'volunteer in the cause of Natural History, impelled by nobler views than those of money'. The task was enormous – long journeys to collect and paint his material, supervising the publication and trying to attract subscribers all at the same time. In these days there were few roads and the great rivers of the midwest, the Ohio and the Mississippi, afforded natural thoroughfares much used by both Wilson and Audubon in their travels. Wilson rowed himself down the Ohio River during the spring of 1810 in his rowing boat the *Ornithologist*. He described the journey in a letter to his engraver Alexander Lawson (1772-1846),[†]from which the following is an extract:

I rowed twenty odd miles the first spell, and found I should be able to stand it perfectly well. About an hour after night, I put up at a miserable cabin fifty two miles from Pittsburg, where I slept on what I supposed to be corn stalks, or something worse; so preferring the smooth bosom of the Ohio to this brush heap, I got up long before day, and, being under no apprehension of losing my way, I again pushed out into the stream. The landscape on each side lay in one mass of shade; but the grandeur of the projecting headlands … was charmingly reflected in the smooth glassy surface below. I could only discover when I was passing a clearing by the crowing of cocks, and now and then, in more solitary places, the big-horned owl made a most hideous hollowing, that echoed among the mountains. In this lonesome manner, with full leisure for observation and reflection, exposed to hardships all day, and hard berths all night, to storms of rain, hail, and snow – for it froze severely almost every night – I persevered, from the 24th of February to March 17 when I moored my skiff safely in Bear Grass Creek at the rapids of the Ohio after a voyage of seven hundred and twenty miles. My hands suffered the most; and it will be some weeks yet before they recover their former feeling and flexibility.[20]

During this journey, Wilson continued as ever to record the behaviour of birds and obtain new specimens. He wounded a Carolina parakeet and took it aboard the *Ornithologist*. The bird, named Poll, quickly became tame and was his companion for many months until it came to an untimely end in the Gulf of Mexico (see Chapter 3, p. 24). When he reached Louisville at the falls of the Ohio River, Wilson could take his rowing boat no further and checked into the Indian Queen Tavern where the Audubon family was living.

It was in Louisville that the chance meeting with Audubon took place which was to have such a profound influence on Audubon's future.

Later that same year (1810) Audubon also described a journey down the Ohio in a rowing skiff, but with more company and comfort. The journey started where Wilson had stopped in Louisville, and continued to Henderson.

When my wife, my eldest son (then an infant), and myself were returning from Pennsylvania to Kentucky, we found it expedient, the waters being unusually low, to provide ourselves with a Skiff, to enable us to proceed to our abode at Henderson …. We procured a mattrass, and our friends furnished us with ready prepared viands. We had two stout Negro rowers, and in this trim we left the village of Shippingport.[21]

He described an idyllic journey: the weather was warm and the autumn colours at their best. Game such as turkey, grouse and teal were abundant and they lived well. The peace of their travel was disturbed only by encountering an enthusiastic set of Methodists who were holding a noisy annual camp in a forest. Audubon comments with regret on the changes which had taken place in the environment of the river since the European colonisation.

When I … call back to my mind the grandeur and beauty of these almost uninhabited shores; when I picture to myself the dense and lofty summits of the forest … unmolested by the axe of the settler; when I know how dearly purchased the safe navigation of the river has been by the blood of many worthy Virginians; when I see that no longer any aborigines are to be found there, and that the vast herds of elks, deer, and buffaloes which once pastured on these hills and in these valleys … when I reflect that all this grand portion of our Union, instead of being in a state of nature, is now more or less covered with villages, farms, and towns, where the din of hammers and machinery is constantly heard … that hundreds of steam-boats are gliding to and fro … forcing commerce to take root and to prosper at every spot; when I see the surplus population of Europe coming to assist in the destruction of the forest, I pause and wonder ….[21]

Shippingport on the Ohio River, drawn by Audubon's Edinburgh friend Captain Basil Hall using the camera lucida technique. Engraved by W H Lizars. Shippingport, a suburb of Louisville, was the staging post on the Ohio where through traffic was blocked by waterfalls. A canal was being constructed to bypass the falls at the time of Hall's visit. From *Travels in North America* by Basil Hall.

[His wonderment could scarcely have conceived the further destruction of nature which has taken place since his time!]

In the year 1810 when these two journeys were undertaken, the first steam paddle-steamers were introduced into the Ohio and Mississippi rivers. Audubon, in an article which he published in Edinburgh in 1831,[22] described the remarkable transformation which this innovation made. Before the age of steam, a barge travelling from New Orleans upstream to the Ohio Falls would have taken three to five months, whereas with steam power the journey could be undertaken in nine days.

Wilson was also acutely aware of the effects of advancing civilisation.

When the population of this immense western Republic will have diffused itself over every acre of ground fit for the comfortable habitation of man – when farms, villages, towns and glittering cities … overspread the face of our beloved country … then, not a warbler shall flit through our thickets ….[23]

Wilson's engraver, Alexander Lawson, was another expatriate Scot who became a great friend and supporter, although his engravings did not do full justice to Wilson's paintings in the opinion of Elliott Coues (1842-99), an ornithologist of a later generation.[24] Lawson needed constant prodding and close supervision and had recurring problems with his colourists – just as Audubon was to experience in his turn. The task of engraving and hand-colouring the many illustrations was formidable. One of Lawson's colourists, Charles Robert Leslie, however, showed particular talent and was encouraged by Wilson and others to go to England to study art. He became one of Queen Victoria's favourite painters.

By now Wilson's reputation was becoming established and he succeeded in getting help and support from many quarters. William Bartram, his original mentor, continued to give constant advice and encouragement; and his niece, Nancy, became one of Wilson's colourists. This once-penniless emigré from Scotland had become the friend and correspondent of a wide range of influential Americans including President Jefferson, the explorer Meriwether Lewis,[25] Thomas Paine, author of the *Rights of Man*, and Charles Willson Peale, the painter and founder

Portrait of George Ord. (Courtesy of the American Philosophical Society)

of a natural history museum in Philadelphia, an important source of specimens for Wilson's studies.

Towards the end of his life Wilson wrote:

The publication of my *Ornithology*, though it has swallowed up all the little I had saved, has procured me the honour of many friends, eminent in this country and the esteem of the public at large; for which I have to thank the goodness of a kind father, whose attention to my education in early life, as well as the books then put into my hands, first gave my mind a bias towards relishing the paths of literature and the charms and magnificence of nature. These … particularly the latter, have made me a wanderer in life … and have been the sources of almost all my enjoyments.[26]

His most ardent friend and supporter was George Ord, who was inspired by Wilson to develop an interest in ornithology and who accompanied him on some of his expeditions. Ord was the son of a wealthy ship chandler and rope-maker. On his father's death he became head of the firm, but seems to have been able to afford to spend most of his time as a hunter and natural historian.

Wilson was elected a member of the American Philosophical Society, founded in 1743 by Benjamin Franklin, and of the Academy of Natural Sciences of Philadelphia, founded in 1812, a year before Wilson's death. Election to these two most prestigious scientific societies in

was buried in the Old Swedes Church in Philadelphia, as was his champion Ord who died later,
friendless and embittered, aged 82. Wilson's
early death denied him the satisfaction of the
fruits of his labour, although he is rightly remembered as the father of American ornithology.
His was the first attempt at a comprehensive
and definitive account of all the birds of America,
which included 48 new species described for the
first time. After Wilson's death his *American
Ornithology* became a bestseller, running to many
editions and revisions by Ord, Prince Charles
Lucien Bonaparte (1803-57)[†] and others. Two
editions were published in Edinburgh; one by
Professor Robert Jameson[27] and another by
Captain Thomas Brown. A third was published
in London by Sir William Jardine; and in this
edition the engravings were prepared from
Lawson's originals by William Home Lizars
(1788-1859),[†] who also did the first engravings
of Audubon's *Birds of America*.

A year before his death Wilson wrote to his
father:

America gave him great and justified satisfaction.
George Ord, as founding secretary of the Academy
of Natural Sciences and later secretary and
president of the American Philosophical Society,
was able to block Audubon's membership to
both societies for many years. His antipathy
towards Audubon, which began in 1824 and
persisted to his death, will be considered more
fully in Chapter 11.

When Wilson died of exhaustion and overwork in 1813 aged 47, having completed eight
of the intended nine volumes, Ord undertook
the task of completing the last with Charles
Willson Peale's youngest son, Titian Ramsay
Peale, aged 17, painting some of the plates. Ord
became Wilson's executor and fiercely defended
his memory against any criticism.

Wilson was attended during his last illness
by Dr Charles Caldwell (1772-1853), one of the
subscribers to *American Ornithology*. By curious
coincidence Caldwell provided a tenuous link
between Wilson's death and his early life, when
he was christened by the Reverend John Witherspoon. Caldwell had been involved in a bitter
dispute with Dr Samuel Stanhope Smith, the
son-in-law of the same John Witherspoon who
had succeeded him as president of Princeton.

Wilson died, as he had lived, in poverty and

> The difficulties and hardships I have encoun-
> tered in life have been useful to me. In youth
> I had wrong ideas of life. Imagination too
> often led judgment astray. You would find
> me much altered from the son you knew me
> in Paisley, – more diffident, of myself, and
> less precipitate, though often wrong ….

The inhabitants of Paisley, Wilson's home
town which he had left in disgrace in 1794,
came to recognise him as one of their most
famous sons and erected a statue in his memory.
The statue, carved by John Mossman, can be seen
today in the grounds of Paisley Abbey. George
Ord, who made a pilgrimage to Paisley in 1855,
gave a contribution of $300 towards its cost.

Typically Wilson expressed his dying wish in
a poem, from which the following verses are taken:

> But let the dewy rose,
> The snowdrop and the violet, lend perfume
> Above the spot where, in my grassy tomb
> I take repose.
>
> Birds from the distant sea
> Shall sometimes hither flock on snowy wings,
> And soar above my dust in airy rings,
> Singing a dirge to me.

Notes

1   Wilson, A: *Poems and Literary Prose,* vol. I, p. xx.

2   Ibid p. 16.

3   Ibid p. 4.

4   Ibid p. 5. Golf was then a very popular sport in Scotland among the better off, particularly in the vicinity of Edinburgh. The Links of Leith and Musselburgh had been used for this purpose since the early seventeenth century. King James VI was a keen player and Charles I, when playing on Leith Links, had to abandon his game on receiving news of insurrection in Ireland. Andrew Duncan Sr described a game of golf which he played with Sir Henry Raeburn in 1823: 'I am proud to say, that even in the 80th year of my age, I was his antagonist on the Links .... I called at his painting rooms, after concluding the business I had allotted for the day. After he had also finished his business, we walked together to Leith Links. There, removed from the smoke of the city of Edinburgh, we conjoined, with pleasing conversation, a trial of skill at a salutary and interesting exercise, to which we had both a strong attachment.' After the game they enjoyed a temperate meal and a social glass at the Golfer's Hall (Goff-House – the club house on Leith Links), but ' ... in little more than ... a month I had to perform the melancholy duty of accompanying his dead body to a grave'. From *A Tribute of Regard to the Memory of Sir Henry Raeburn* (1824), cited in *Golf a Royal and Ancient Game,* (R & R Clark, Edinburgh, 1875). Raeburn died aged 58, three years before Audubon's first visit to Edinburgh. Andrew Duncan died in 1828 aged 84. Raeburn painted a portrait of his friend Duncan which now hangs in the Royal College of Physicians in Edinburgh.

5   Ibid p. 9.

6   Ibid p. 13.

7   Ibid p. 25.

8   Ibid p. 32.

9   Ibid vol. II, p. 62.

10 Ibid vol. I, pp. 50-1.

11 Ibid p. 55.

12 Jardine, Sir William (ed.): 'Life of Alexander Wilson' in *American Ornithology* (A Wilson and C L Bonaparte) (1876), pp. ix-cv.

13 Wilson, A: op. cit., vol. II, p. 57.

14 Cited in *A Biographical Dictionary of Eminent Scotsmen* (1870 edn).

15 Hunter, C: *The Life and Letters of Alexander Wilson,* p. 287.

16 Audubon, L: *The Life of John James Audubon,* p. 393. Audubon confused William Bartram with Benjamin Smith Barton (1766-1815), professor of botany in Philadelphia and associate of William Bartram. Barton had studied medicine in Edinburgh.

17 Ewan, J (ed.): *William Bartram Botanical and Zoological Drawings, 1756-1788* (The American Philosophical Society, 1968).

18 Hunter, C: *The Life and Letters of Alexander Wilson,* p. 249.

19 In the section on the passenger pigeon in *American Ornithology* by Alexander Wilson (various editions).

20 Wilson, A: op. cit., vol. I, pp. 178-90.

21 Audubon, J J: *Ornithological Biography,* vol. I, pp. 29-32.

22 Audubon, J J: 'Improvements in the Navigation of the Mississippi', in *Edinburgh Literary Journal* 5, pp. 194-5 (1831).

23 Wilson, A: *American Ornithology,* vol. V, pp. vii-viii.

24 Coues, E: 'Behind the Veil', in *Bulletin of the Nuttall Ornithological Club* (1880), 5: 193-204. Elliott Coues (1842-99) trained as a doctor and held the chair of anatomy at Columbia University, but his main interest was in ornithology. He was editor of the *Bulletin of the Nuttall Ornithological Club* and its successor *The Auk.*

25 Meriwether Lewis, who with William Clark had established the Lewis and Clark route to the Pacific coast (1803-5), befriended Wilson and had given him permission to make use of any of the specimens which he had collected during his explorations. Lewis subsequently was made governor of part of the Louisiana territory. In 1809 he died in mysterious circumstances. Wilson, a year later, while undertaking his travels down the Ohio and Mississippi rivers, made a diversion to the house where Lewis had died and obtained from the owner a detailed and gruesome account of his death, which was apparently the result of self-inflicted pistol shots to the head.

26 Cited in *A Biographical Dictionary of Eminent Scotsmen* (1870 edn).

27 Two Edinburgh editions of Alexander Wilson's *American Ornithology* with Bonaparte's additions were published, one by Jameson in 1831 in four volumes without illustrations. Jameson's edition received a scathing review in the *Edinburgh Literary Journal* (vol. VI, 1831), from which the following extract is taken: 'It is with sincere regret that we submit these strictures upon the editorial conduct of one whom we respect so much as Professor Jameson – the man who has made natural history what it is in Edinburgh. Truth, however, obliges us to say, that he has discharged his task in a most slovenly and imperfect manner .... the book itself, which in spite of editorial negligence, must remain one of the most delightful books that has been offered to the public.' The reviewer is anonymous but clearly knew about birds. Could it have been MacGillivray?

3 | The Meeting of Audubon and Wilson

THE meeting between Audubon and Wilson in March 1810 was important for two reasons. First, there is little doubt that Wilson's *American Ornithology*, which Audubon saw then for the first time, sowed in Audubon's mind the idea of publishing his own paintings. Second, it gave direction and purpose to his later work. The differing accounts of the meeting given by the two men later became a contentious issue which assumed an unreasonable importance. Audubon's account of the meeting, written 21 years later in his *Ornithological Biography*, was as follows:

One fair morning, I was surprised by the sudden entrance into our counting-room of Mr. Alexander Wilson, the celebrated author of the *American Ornithology* of whose existence I had never until that moment been apprised …. How well do I remember him …. His long, rather hooked nose, the keenness of his eyes, and his prominent cheek-bones, stamped his countenance with a peculiar character. His dress, too, was of a kind not usually seen in that part of the country; a short coat, trousers, and a waistcoat of grey cloth. His stature was not above the middle size …. He … immediately proceeded to disclose the object of his visit, which was to procure subscriptions for his work. He opened his books, explained the nature of his occupations, and requested my patronage.

I felt surprised and gratified at the sight of the volumes, turned over a few of the plates, and had already taken a pen to write my name in his favour when my partner rather abruptly said to me in French, 'My dear Audubon, what induces you to subscribe to this work? Your drawings are certainly far better, and again you must know as much of the habits of American birds as this gentleman'. Whether Mr Wilson understood French or not, or if the suddenness with which I

paused, disappointed him, I cannot tell; but I clearly perceived that he was not pleased. Vanity and the encomiums of my friend prevented me from subscribing. Mr. Wilson asked me if I had many drawings of birds. I rose, took down a large portfolio, laid it on the table, and shewed him … the whole of its contents …. His surprise appeared great, as he told me he never had the most distant idea that any other individual than himself had been engaged in forming such a collection. He asked me if it was my intention to publish, and when I answered in the negative, his surprise seemed to increase. And, truly, such was not my intention; for, until long after, when I met the Prince of Musignano [Charles Lucien Bonaparte] in Philadelphia, I had not the least idea of presenting the fruits of my labours to the world. Mr Wilson now examined my drawings with care, asked if I should have any objections to lending him a few during his stay, to which I replied that I had none … I had made an arrangement to explore the woods in the vicinity along with him, and had promised to procure for him some birds, of which I had drawings in my collection, but which he had never seen.

It happened that he lodged in the same house with me but his retired habits, I thought exhibited either a strong feeling of discontent, or a decided melancholy. The Scotch airs which he played sweetly on his flute made me melancholy too, and I felt for him. I presented him to my wife and friends, and; seeing that he was all enthusiasm, exerted myself as much as was in my power, to procure for him the specimens which he wanted. We hunted together and obtained birds which he had never before seen …. I did not subscribe to his work, for, even at that time, my collection was greater than his. Thinking that perhaps he might be pleased to publish the results of my researches, I offered them to him, merely on condition that what I had drawn, or might afterwards draw and send to him, should be mentioned in his work, as coming from my pencil. I at the same time offered to open a correspondence with him, which I thought might prove beneficial to us both. He made no reply to either proposal, and … left Louisville … little knowing how much his talents were appreciated in our little town, at least by myself and my friends.[1]

Wilson, who wrote long and detailed letters to his engraver, Lawson, during his travels, did not mention meeting Audubon in Louisville, but his friend and champion, Ord, published in the 1814 edition of the *American Ornithology* what purported to be extracts from Wilson's diary which was then in his possession. While staying at the Indian Queen Tavern at Louisville, Wilson wrote:

March 20. 1810. Set out this afternoon with the gun; killed nothing new. People in taverns here devour their meals; many shopkeepers board in taverns; also boat-men, land-speculators, merchants, etc. No naturalists to keep me company.

March 23d. I bade adieu to Louisville, to which place I had four letters of recommendation and was taught to expect much of everything there; but neither received one act of civility from those to whom I was recommended, one subscriber, nor one new bird: though I delivered my letters, ransacked the woods repeatedly and visited all the characters likely to subscribe. Science or literature has not one friend in this place.

After reading Audubon's account of the meeting, Ord reacted angrily and published a fuller account of the extract from Wilson's diary in the 1828 edition of *American Ornithology* which differs considerably from the version given above, adding: 'March 21. Went out shooting this afternoon with Mr. A. Saw a number of Sandbill Cranes, Pigeons numerous', and to the entry for March 23 he now adds, 'Packed up my things which I left in the care of a merchant here, to be sent on to Lexington; and having parted with regret, with my paroquet, to the gentleman of

the tavern'. Charles Waterton, Ord's English ally in his vendetta against Audubon, also published an extended and slightly different version of Wilson's diary entry which he claimed to have seen (see Chapter 11, p. 140).

There is reason to doubt the accuracy of both accounts of the meeting.[2] Audubon's recollection, written 21 years after the event, may well have been coloured with the objective of presenting himself in a favourable light – a tendency which recurs not infrequently in his writings. There is no doubt that he planned to 'present the fruits of his labours to the world' long before he met Bonaparte. It also seems most unlikely that Wilson should have rejected his offer of assistance, for he sought help with his task at every opportunity.

Wilson's version, as retailed by Ord, is equally suspect and there are other instances of Ord altering Wilson's writings.[3] Ord said that it was transcribed from Wilson's diary to which he fell heir. This diary was never seen after Ord's death and there is reason to believe that he may have edited it in his attempt to discredit Audubon. There is, for example, one clear inaccuracy in the above extract relating to Wilson's pet 'paroquet' (Poll). The Carolina parrot which he had captured during his long voyage down the Ohio River continued to accompany him after his visit to Louisville.

Wilson gives an account of his pet parrot in *American Ornithology*:

Anxious to try the effects of education on one of those which I procured at Big Bone Lick and which was but slightly wounded in the wing, I fixed up a place for it in the stern of my boat, and presented it with some cockle burs, which it freely fed on in less than an hour after being on board. The intermediate time eating and sleeping was occupied in gnawing the sticks that formed its place of confinement, in order to make a practicable breach; which it repeatedly effected. When I abandoned the river, and travelled by land, I wrapt it up closely in a silk handkerchief, tying it tightly around, and carried it in my pocket. When I stopped for refreshment, I unbound my prisoner, and gave it its allowance …. In recommitting it to 'durance vile,' we generally had a quarrel; during which it frequently paid me in kind for the wound

Above: Audubon's painting of the Carolina parrot, plate 26 from *The Birds of America*. (Courtesy of the National Museums of Scotland Library)

Above, right: The same bird by Wilson – the plate includes flycatchers.

I had inflicted, and for depriving it of liberty …. The path through the wilderness between Nashville and Natchez is in some places bad beyond description …. In some of the worse of these places, where I had … to fight my way through, the paroquet frequently escaped from my pocket obliging me to dismount and pursue it through the worse of the morass before I could regain it …. When at night I encamped in the woods I placed it on the baggage beside me where it usually sat with great composure dozing and gazing at the fire till morning. In this manner I carried it upwards of a thousand miles in my pocket where it was exposed all day to the jolting of the horse, but regularly liberated at meal times and in the evening, at which it always expressed great satisfaction …. In this short space she had learnt to know her name; to

answer, and come when called on; to climb up my clothes, sit on my shoulder, and eat from my mouth. I took her with me to sea determined to persevere with her education; but, destined to another fate poor Poll having one morning … wrought her way through the cage while I was asleep, instantly flew over-board and perished in the Gulf of Mexico.

Clearly this detailed account is inconsistent with the diary entry as related by Ord, yet it seems most unlikely that Ord would have falsified this entry for no purpose. The mystery remains unsolved. In a letter to his friend Lawson, he wrote, 'This place … afforded me a fund of amusement in shooting ducks and paroquets, of which last I skinned twelve and brought off two slightly wounded …'. [Perhaps he kept two pets?]

The Carolina parrot is one of the twelve species described by Wilson and Audubon which have since become extinct. In Audubon's day it

24

was still common. 'It is found much too plentiful in every State west of the Alleghanies, and in still greater profusion as you advance towards the Southern Districts.' They caused considerable damage to crops and, being easy targets, were shot in large numbers by farmers. 'I have seen several hundreds destroyed in this manner in the course of a few hours, and have procured a basketful of the birds at a few shots, in order to make choice of good specimens for drawing.' Later he observes without comment, 'Our parakeets are very rapidly diminishing in number …'.[4]

Ord attacked Audubon again at a meeting of the American Philosophical Society. The matter concerned an account of a painting of the small-headed flycatcher which Audubon stated in his *Ornithological Biography* had been copied by Wilson from a drawing of his own, and published in Wilson's *American Ornithology* without acknowledgement. Audubon wrote:

When Alexander Wilson visited me at Louisville, he found in my already large collection of drawings, a figure of the present species, which being at that time unknown to him he copied and afterwards published in his great work, but without acknowledging the privilege that had thus been granted to him. I have more than once regretted this, not by any means so much on my own account as for the sake of one to whom we are so deeply indebted for the elucidation of our ornithology.[5]

Ord averred that Wilson had discovered and painted the bird himself and had indeed been with him when he made the discovery. The truth of the matter will never be known, but it seems to have been blown out of all proportion by Ord – particularly as the bird in question has not been identified by subsequent ornithologists.

Audubon also commented in his article on the whooping crane:

Above, left: Wilson's painting of the red winged blackbird (red winged starling).

Above: Audubon's rendering of the same bird, plate 67 from *The Birds of America*. It is clearly copied from Wilson – why Audubon should have done this is puzzling, for he had no shortage of specimens. He wrote, 'I have myself shot hundreds in the course of an afternoon, killing from ten to fifteen at every discharge.' (Reproduced by kind permission of the President and Council of the Royal College of Physicians and Surgeons of Glasgow)

25

I had the gratification of taking Alexander Wilson to some ponds within a few miles of town, and of showing him many birds of this species, of which he had not previously seen any other than stuffed specimens. I told him that the white birds were the adults, and that the grey ones were the young. Wilson, in his article on the Whooping Crane, has alluded to this, but, as on other occasions, he has not informed his readers whence his information came.[6]

It was unwise and unseemly of Audubon to accuse Wilson of plagiarism, for Audubon was himself guilty of this to a much greater degree and his accusations simply stirred Ord to greater reaction. Ord's complaints of plagiarism by Audubon were well justified, although plagiarism of illustrations was not an offence until 1864 when painters were granted a copyright. Audubon, despite his initial refusal to subscribe to Wilson's

book, must subsequently have acquired a set, for his writings contain frequent and usually favourable reference to *American Ornithology*, and several of his plates contain obvious copies of Wilson's illustrations. Robert Havell, Audubon's engraver who not infrequently made alterations or additions to Audubon's paintings, is thought to have been responsible for copying at least one of Wilson's birds, the Mississippi kite.

Wilson died 14 years before the first volume of Audubon's paintings was published, unaware of the controversy that was to follow. Audubon seems in general to have admired Wilson's contributions and certainly makes much use of them in his writings, with the occasional snide remark. When, many years after his meeting with Wilson, Audubon received a favourable criticism of his paintings from Thomas Bewick (1753-1828),[†] he wrote: '… be assured I regard it with quite as much pleasure as a manuscript "Synopsis of the Birds of America," by Alexander Wilson, which

that celebrated individual gave to me at Louisville in Kentucky, more than twenty years ago.'[7]
In his account of Wilson's plover, Audubon noted:
'I love the name because of the respect I bear
towards him to whose memory the bird has been
dedicated. How pleasing … it would have been
to me, to have met with him on such an excursion
… to have listened to him as he would speak of
a thousand interesting facts connected with his
favourite science and my ever-pleasing pursuits
….'[8] Clearly no bitterness or animosity there.

The antipathy attributed to the two men was
fostered by others – notably by George Ord, who
seized every opportunity to discredit Audubon.
With the benefit of historical perspective it is
generally recognised that Wilson was the better
ornithologist, but Audubon the better artist. One
commentator wrote: 'When Wilson and Audubon
are compared as scientists and not as artists,
Wilson's greater exactness, his patient method
and his lucid and honest descriptions mark him
unquestionably as the better ornithologist.'[9]

John Wilson, using the pen name Christopher
North in *Blackwood's Magazine*, compared the
two men in 1831. He pointed out that Alexander
Wilson did not commence his scientific study
of ornithology until he was in his mid-thirties,
and only then did he attempt to learn the art of
painting. Audubon, on the other hand, had been
fascinated by birds from earliest childhood and
had developed his painting technique over a lifetime. Inevitably Alexander Wilson's paintings
suffered by comparison. 'Compare the birds there,
bright and beautiful as they are, and wonderfully
true, too, to nature, with the birds of Audubon,
and you feel at one glance the immeasurable and
mysterious difference between the living and the
dead.' Wilson's skill with the pen, however, had
been honed from childhood, and his literary skills
were much greater than those of Audubon, whose
education and dedication to his studies had been
sketchy to say the least. According to Christopher
North, 'Wilson, on the whole, is the better writer
of the two – indeed he is the best painter in words
of birds that the world has yet seen'. Audubon,
and many others since, have mined the rich vein
of Wilson's writings to enhance their own, often
without acknowledgement.

Audubon recognised Wilson's superiority
as a writer: 'Poor Wilson was only better off than
I on account of his superior talents over me at

Portrait of Charles
Lucien Bonaparte.
(Musée National du
Chateau de Malmaison)

driving the goose quill but … I could drive the
pencil, the brush, the Fiddle Bow … [better]
than he.'[10]

There is another curious link between the
two men.

Charles Lucien Bonaparte, Prince of
Musignano and a nephew of Napoleon, was a
keen ornithologist who lived for a time in the
United States in order to study the bird life of
that country. He was elected a member of the
Academy of Natural Sciences, to which body
he tried to introduce Audubon whom he had
befriended in 1824. Audubon was not then granted
membership because of the opposition of George
Ord and others. Ord, however, gave Bonaparte
encouragement to produce an updated version
of Wilson's *Ornithology*. He did this under the
title *American Ornithology; or, The Natural History
of Birds Inhabiting the United States Not Given
by Wilson*, adding nearly 100 birds to those
recorded by Wilson, bringing the total to 366.
Bonaparte was no artist and asked Audubon if
he could use some of his paintings to illustrate
his new edition. However, Lawson, also a friend
of Ord, refused to copy them, declaring that
they were 'ill drawn not true to nature, and
anatomically incorrect'.

It is interesting to speculate that, had
Bonaparte's offer been accepted, Audubon might
have been remembered only as one of the several

artists who contributed to the Wilson/Bonaparte publication. Despite this rejection, Bonaparte and Audubon remained good friends and corresponded regularly for a time. However, their friendly relations broke down after Bonaparte, in the preface to *A Geographical and Comparative List of the Birds of Europe and North America*, compared the works of John Gould and Audubon, writing: 'The merit of M Audubon's work yields only to the size of the book; while Mr. Gould's work on the *Birds of Europe*, though inferior in size to that of M Audubon – is the most beautiful work on Ornithology that has ever appeared in this or any other country.' This may have been a reaction to a reference to Bonaparte contained in the first volume of Audubon's *Ornithological Biography* to which he took offence, although none was intended. It is inevitable that the paintings of John Gould (1804–81)[†] should be compared with those of Audubon, as both men were engaged in similar tasks at the same period. Their association is discussed more fully in Chapter 13.

Notes

1   Audubon, J J: *Ornithological Biography,* vol. I, pp. 438-40.
2   Hunter, C: 'The influence of Alexander Wilson upon John James Audubon', in *The Scottish Naturalist* (1983), 101: 85-95.
3   Grosart, A B: *The Prose and Literary Prose of Alexander Wilson,* vol. I, p. xiviii.
4   Audubon, J J: op. cit., vol. I, pp.135-9. Audubon in his younger days revelled in the slaughter of birds.
5   Ibid, vol. V, p. 292.
6   Ibid, vol. III, p. 203.
7   Reminiscences of Thomas Bewick, *Ornithological Biography,* vol. III, p. 303.
8   Audubon, J J: op. cit., vol. III, pp. 73-4.
9   Allen, E G: 'The History of American Ornithology before Audubon', in *Transactions of the American Philosophical Society* (1851), series XLI: 387-591.
10 From a letter to Audubon's benefactor Edward Harris of 5 July 1835, cited in Herrick, F H: *Audubon the Naturalist,* p. 143.

The Journey to Edinburgh 4

AUDUBON described his travels to Edinburgh in detail in his journal of 1826.[1] Having made his farewells to Lucy and son John Woodhouse at St Francisville, he set sail from New Orleans on the *Delos* on 17 May 1826, which was bound for Liverpool with a cargo of cotton. The winds were light and the captain and crew relieved the monotony by catching dolphins, the flesh of which Audubon found quite acceptable. Porpoises and sharks were also taken and typically Audubon seized the chance of studying their stomach contents and physical characteristics. Many birds were seen – some of them new to Audubon, who shot and sketched them as opportunity offered. When becalmed he disported himself by swimming in the sea.

When at last the ship left coastal waters and entered the Atlantic, Audubon wrote: 'The purpose of this voyage is to visit not only England but all Europe, with the intention of publishing my work of the Birds of America. If not sadly disappointed, my return to these happy shores will be the brightest birthday I shall have enjoyed.' In the event his ambitions were amply fulfilled.

The *Delos* reached Liverpool on 20 July after a voyage of 65 days. Audubon was initially given a cool reception by his brother-in-law, Alexander Gordon, who headed a mercantile house in that city, but his morale recovered when he was warmly welcomed by Mr William Rathbone (1787-1868),[†] a Quaker and prominent Liverpool merchant and shipowner to whom Audubon had a letter of introduction given him by Vincent Nolte of New Orleans. Audubon paid many visits to the Rathbone family home, Green Bank, an elegant and gracious house in extensive grounds. It is now in possession of Liverpool University, to which the Rathbones made many benefactions.

Through the influence of the Rathbones, Audubon was introduced to many of the local gentry. Audubon was always ill at ease and 'painfully awkward' in high society, although generally he managed to conceal his discomfiture and was delighted by the reception which he received. Among those who offered him friendship and advice were William Roscoe (1756-1831), a distinguished historian and botanist; André Melly, a Swiss entomologist; and Thomas Stewart Traill (1781-1862),[†] a Scottish doctor with a wide scientific interest, then living in Liverpool.

Audubon was invited to display his paintings in the Liverpool Royal Institution, where they attracted many visitors and earned him a welcome £100 from entrance fees. His paintings were much admired by Lord Stanley, later the thirteenth Earl of Derby, who inspected the paintings for five hours and impressed Audubon by kneeling to examine them closely. Lord Stanley was a keen naturalist and one of the early subscribers to Audubon's *Birds of America*. Later he was to nominate Audubon for fellowship of the Royal Society of London. 'Honours which … Philadelphia had refused, Liverpool freely accorded.'[2]

By 6 August Audubon was able to write:

Green Bank today, much as it would have appeared in Audubon's time. (Photograph by Dr J T Joy)

Thomas Stewart Traill
by Alexander Moses.
(Scottish National
Portrait Gallery)

When I arrived in this city I felt dejected, yes miserably so. The uncertainty of being kindly received, of having my work approved, were all acting on both my physical and mental powers …. Now how different are my sensations! I am well received wherever I am known … and my poor heart is at last relieved the great anxiety that has for so many years agitated it, by [the feeling that] I have not worked altogether in vain ….[3]

This is a very typical Audubon outburst – his writings reveal marked swings of mood from deep depression to high elation, usually triggered by the response of the public to his paintings and the progress of their publication. In his elated moods he tended to see the world through rose-tinted spectacles. In a letter to Lucy dated 1 September 1826 he wrote:

I am most comfortably situated and my entry in England having been at once in the best Circles of Society will afford me a great length of continuation of favors — Victor would have profited by this voyage immensely; The young Gentlemen here have a superiority of education that bears no parallel with our young Countrymen — The Ladies are still more remarkable for their *plaines of manners* and superior acquirements. All those I have the pleasure of visiting possess the French, Italian & Spanish Languages, draw beautifully, are good musicians and as *fresh as roses*![4]

A visit to Manchester was less successful. Few visited the exhibition of his paintings there. Audubon overheard a conversation in which his exhibition was being discussed – 'Puh, it's all a hoax. Save your shillings for better use. I have seen them. Why the fellow ought to be drummed out of town.' He was further depressed by the poverty and drabness of the city and was upset by the condition of the many thousand cotton-mill workers in the city whom he described as 'poor miserable, abject wretches as ever worked the mines of Golconda'.

The redeeming feature of Manchester was the friendship of mill-owner Samuel Greg who invited Audubon to his home, Quarry Bank,[5] near the city. In a letter to Miss Hannah Rathbone Audubon wrote, 'I cannot bear Manchester. With the exception of two of the Misses Greg, I have not seen any ladies yet with whom I have been able to chat without either blushing, or trembling as awkwardly as ever.' Audubon always had an eye for a pretty face: 'I again looked at Miss Ellen [Greg] very much. I could not help it. She is so very attractive of looks and manners, and so polite, and so—God bless thee, my Lucy, good night.' One wonders what Lucy thought of this and many similar admiring accounts of the young ladies whom Audubon encountered on his travels. Ellen Greg was to marry André Melly, and her sister Elizabeth (whom Audubon also admired) eventually married William Rathbone.

To repay those who gave him hospitality Audubon had the agreeable habit of leaving small sketches. He is known to have given one of his 'visiting cards' to André Melly, and others to the much-admired Ellen Greg. (The turkey cock sketch shown on the opposite page is inscribed on the back with Ellen Greg's name.)

Another way of giving due recognition to those who befriended him was to name a bird after them. In all Audubon honoured 57 of his friends in this way and 20 birds still retain this identification. Several of his Liverpool friends were given this distinction including Traill, Roscoe, Rathbone and Lord Stanley. Of these only the willow flycatcher (*Empidonax traillii*) retains current usage.

At Dr Traill's house in Liverpool, Audubon met a London bookseller, Mr Bohn, who advised him that he should go to London, Paris, Brussels, or possibly Berlin to find the best engravers and colourists. He also advised that the engravings would only succeed if they were produced in a small format. Both Roscoe and Traill endorsed this advice. Audubon responded firmly: '*This I will not do*'. Audubon was determined that his birds be reproduced life-size, and indeed Mr Bohn later agreed. With the encouragement of Dr Traill Audubon also resolved at this time to write an account of his birds: 'I will proceed with firm resolution to attempt *being an author*. It is a terrible thing to me; far better am I fitted to study and delineate in the forest, than to arrange phrases with sensible grammarian skill.'[6]

Before proceeding to London and the continent in order to pursue his objectives, he decided to pay a brief visit to Edinburgh, for he 'longed to see the men and the scenes immortalised by the fervid strains of Burns, and the glowing eloquence of Scott and Wilson'.[7] On 23 October 1826 he left Manchester on the stagecoach for Scotland, armed with letters of introduction from Dr Traill. The journey took two days and cost five guineas, which Audubon thought excessive.

In a letter to his son John Woodhouse, now aged 14, he wrote:

> The coach carried four inside passengers and ten outside or rather on the top, besides a guard and a driver and all the luggage for the parties. I sometimes stayed in, and sometimes rode outside to have better views of the country .... Now and then I saw some fine English Pheasants that you would delight in killing; and some curious small Sheep with black head and feet ... and those pretty little ponies that you are so fond of. I wish I could send you one.[8]

He describes a curious incident which took place during the journey:

> At a little village where the horses were changed, it was discovered that a shocking smell existed on the top of the coach .... The guard spoke of it and told us that he could not keep his seat. I felt anxious to view the country, and got out to mount up and behind, but the smell was so insufferable and the appearance of the man near whom I had

seat myself so far from being pleasing that I immediately jumped down to take my inside seat. Judge of my dismay, Lucy, when I was asked if my trunk belonged to me, and if it did not contain a dead body intended for dissection at Edinburgh, I answered no, thou may be sure. The guard smiled as if quite sure my trunk contained such a thing, and told my companions that he would inform against me at Lancaster. I bore all this very well. I was innocent! I offered to open my trunk and would have certainly done so at Lancaster: but, whilst we were proceeding, the guard came to the door and made an apology. He said the smell had been removed, and that it was positively attached to the inside part of the man's breeches who was on the seat by him. This caused much laughter and many coarse jokes.[9]

There was a great demand for bodies for dissection by the several teachers of anatomy who taught in Edinburgh, the most popular of whom was Robert Knox (1793-1862),[†] who was to become a close friend and supporter of Audubon. Ireland provided many of the subjects for this illegal trade which flourished at the time. Only a year after Audubon's experience on the coach, William Hare and William Burke in Edinburgh commenced their activity of procuring corpses for the anatomy school run by Robert Knox. At first they obtained subjects who had died of natural causes, but later they found it less laborious to supply bodies by smothering

Audubon's 'visiting card' given to Ellen Greg. (Reproduced with the kind permission of Dr A W O Taylor)

'The Black Bull Inn' by William Turner. (City Art Centre: City of Edinburgh Museums and Galleries)

(burking) their victims after plying them with drink. In all they murdered at least 16 victims before they were caught. Their trial in 1828 caused great public interest. Hare turned King's Evidence and Burke was convicted and publicly hanged before massed crowds. Although Knox was found innocent of any involvement, his reputation suffered and this episode marks the decline of his fortunes. Audubon, who was in Edinburgh during this time, must have been aware of these stirring events but does not mention them in his writings.

At Hawick he was introduced to Scotch whisky for the first time. He found the taste agreeable, but it 'was too powerful for my weak head'. While travelling through the border country he commented on the contrast between the wealth of the Duke of Buccleuch who had an income of £200,000 per annum and his poor shepherds who survived on 200 pounds of oatmeal. 'Miserable contrast, man's moral and physical perdition—will it be endured long?'

The coach arrived in Edinburgh, 'the Splendid City', at 11pm on 25 October 1826 and stopped at the Black Bull Inn, 1 Katherine Street, the main mailcoach terminal.

There was no room available so Audubon was taken to the Star Hotel, 34 Princes Street, where he enjoyed a good supper and went late to bed thinking 'of the multitude of learned men that abound in this place that I dreaded the delivering my letters tomorrow. I wished that thou hadst known at this very moment that I was positively bidding thee good night in Edinburgh'.[10]

Notes

1   Ford, Alice: *The 1826 Journal of John James Audubon* (Abbeyville Press, New York, 1987).
2   Audubon, J J: *Ornithological Biography*, vol. I, p. xv.
3   *The 1826 Journal*, p. 123.
4   *Letters of John James Audubon 1826-1840*, pp. 5-6.
5   Quarry Bank Mill can be seen today much as it would have been in Audubon's time. It is now a textile museum and the estate a public park.
6   *The 1826 Journal*, p. 238.
7   *Ornithological Biography*, vol. I, p. xv.
8   *The 1826 Journal*, p. 312.
9   Ibid, p. 298.
10 Ibid, p. 302.

The First Visit: Audubon's Introduction to Edinburgh | 5

ALTHOUGH Audubon had intended to pay only a short visit to Edinburgh, he was immediately attracted to the city and decided to extend his stay. In making this decision he was following in the footsteps of many other Americans. Benjamin Franklin was honoured with the freedom of the city during his first visit to Edinburgh and met many of the great men who lived there during this period of intense intellectual activity which became known as the Enlightenment. After this visit he wrote:

I think the Time we spent there, was Six Weeks of the *densest* Happiness I have met with in any Part of my Life. And the agreeable and instructive Society we found there in such Plenty, has left so pleasing an Impression on my Memory, that did not strong Connections draw me elsewhere, I believe Scotland would be the Country I should chuse to spend the Remainder of my Days in.[1]

Stimulated by Franklin, a great number of American visitors followed him to Edinburgh. About 100 students came to the university in the years leading up to the American Revolution, including many medical students who were to become leading figures in their profession on their return. One of these, Benjamin Rush, wrote of his stay in Scotland, 'the happiest period of my life is now near over. My halcyon days have been spent in Edinburgh', and later, 'The two years I spent in Edinburgh I consider as the most important in their influence upon my character and conduct of any period of my life'.[2] Rush wrote in 1809 to his son who was then a student in Edinburgh:

However wishfully you may cast your eyes across the Atlantic and long for a seat at your father's fireside, be assured you will often lick your fingers in reviewing the days and hours you are now spending in the highly cultivated society of Edinburgh. Perhaps there is at present no spot upon the earth where religion, science, and literature combine more to produce moral and intellectual pleasures than in the metropolis of Scotland.[3]

In all, about 650 American medical students obtained MD degrees in Edinburgh between 1750 and 1850, and the first American medical school was founded in Philadelphia in 1765 by Edinburgh graduates including Benjamin Rush.

The friendship between America and Scotland inevitably suffered a temporary setback during the Revolution, but it was restored quickly thereafter. Two magazines published in Edinburgh had a profound impact on this relationship. The *Edinburgh Review*, founded in 1802, set a high standard. This Whig publication, conceived by the Reverend Sydney Smith (1771-1845)[†] and edited by Francis Jeffrey (1773-1850),[†] was an instant success and became the most influential magazine of its day both in Britain and America where it was widely read and reprinted. Jeffrey married an American, Charlotte Wilkes, and had visited that country and could write of it with first-hand knowledge and empathy. In 1808 he noted with reference to the Revolution:

The sanguine people of this country would do well, though the retrospect cannot be pleasing, sometimes to turn back their thoughts upon this unhappy contest, – to recollect, that measures, triumphantly voted wise and just and vigorous, proved only wasteful folly, – that a spirit of arrogant domination, and heedless indifference to the rights of others, lost the wing of an empire.[4]

The other influential magazine, *Blackwood's*, was launched in 1817 with John Wilson (who used the pen name Christopher North) as its main

George Street looking east, from Shepherd's *Modern Athens*. Audubon's lodgings were almost opposite St Andrew's Church, seen on the left. The tall monument to Henry Dundas (Viscount Melville), erected in 1821, still stands.

Charles Darwin (1809-82), who came to Edinburgh as a medical student with his brother Erasmus a few months before Audubon, also had a favourable first impression. In a letter to his father soon after his arrival he wrote: '... all the Scotchmen are so civil and attentive that it is enough to make an Englishman ashamed of himself .... We ... walked about the town; which we admire excessively ....' Nine hundred medical students enrolled at the university in the same year as Darwin. It was unchallenged as the leading medical school in Britain at that time, although many of the students abandoned their medical studies before completing the course. Another, like Darwin, who came to study medicine but changed course to become a natural historian was Edward Forbes (1815-54),[†] who was to achieve his ambition of becoming professor of natural history at the university. Writing of his student days in Edinburgh, he said:

contributor. *Blackwood's Magazine* was established in opposition to the *Edinburgh Review* with the purpose of presenting the Tory point of view. Like the *Review* it maintained a high literary standard and was widely read on both sides of the Atlantic, but *Blackwood's* also frequently commented on the American scene and reviewed American publications, including those of Alexander Wilson and Audubon (see pp. 27, 44–46 and 124).

Scottish writers were also popular in America. Many editions of Burns' poetry were published there, and the poems of Alan Ramsay and Robert Fergusson were likewise well known. Above all in popularity and influence were the Waverley novels of Walter Scott, with which Audubon was very familiar. Indeed one of his objectives in coming to Edinburgh was to meet this great man whom he held in such reverential regard.

Many other American visitors commented favourably on their reception in Edinburgh. A year before Audubon arrived, Nathaniel Carter, a New York editor, wrote:

> The capital of the North was perhaps never more flourishing nor more prominent in the great republic of letters, than at the present moment .... A literary spirit is predominant in the metropolis, and constitutes the controlling principle in its associations. Every body reads, and a great many write. It is fashionable for both sexes to be numbered among the *literati*, and it would be extremely difficult for a person, who has not some pretensions of the kind, to find a passport to good society ....[5]

> If any spot on earth is peculiarly adapted for the study of natural history it is this .... Everywhere about us are abundant and admirable illustrations of zoology, botany and geology .... It is a great gain to a university to be placed like this, amid scenes of unrivalled beauty. The youth whose hours of relaxation are spent in these magnificent prospects ... carries with him in after-life the memory of their beauty and grandeur .... It is not to be wondered at that this university has been a hotbed of naturalists, and that their philosophy has been one catholic in essence and far-extending in its range.

It is perhaps not surprising that Audubon was persuaded to linger. Let his journal continue the narrative:

George Street Edinburgh　　　　　　Oct 26th
　　　　　　　　　　　　　　　　Thursday 1826

My companions, who knew all about Edinburgh, offered to accompany me in search of decent lodgings, and we proceeded, soon turning and entering the second door in George Street, (perhaps the most beautiful street here)[6] and in a moment made a bargain with Mrs. Dickie for a fine bedroom and a fine, well furnished setting-room. I am to pay her one guinea per week. I considered it very low. The situation is fine. I can see from where I now am writing the Frith [Firth of Forth] and the steamboats plying about. I had my baggage brought here by a man with a tremendous beard who imposed on me most impudently by bringing a brass shilling which he said he would swear I had given him. I gave him another, threw the counterfeit in the fire, and promised myself to pay some attention hereafter what kind of money I received or gave away.[7]

The 'setting-room' was furnished with a black hair sofa, armchairs, stuffed pheasants on the buffet, cherubs on the mantlepiece, a painted landscape and a mirror. On looking in the mirror Audubon was struck by his resemblance to his father, and was overcome by homesickness.

The thought of my mother flew about me, my sister was also present, my younger days, those I have enjoyed with thee and those I have spent, miserable, from thee .... but my Lucy, such reflexions will not do. I must close my book, think of tomorrow ... that always, as we reach it, evaporates and becomes mere yesterday ....[8]

As we know, Audubon was subject to swings of mood and this depressing entry in his journal may have been triggered by his initial lack of success in contacting people to whom he had letters of introduction. 'I walked to Professor Jameson's in the Circus; not at home. James Hall [1761-1832],[†] advocate ... absent in the country. Dr Charles Henry of the Royal Infirmary was sought after in vain. Dr Thompson [1765-1846][†] was out also and Professor Duncan could not be seen until 5 o'clock.' When he did meet Professor Jameson (1774-1854), regius professor of natural history, he was met with a cool reception. This may have been because Jameson was engaged at the time in producing an Edinburgh edition of Wilson and Bonaparte's *American Ornithology* and, as Ord had done before, no doubt looked upon Audubon as a potential rival. 'Perhaps I met him at a bad moment. I will draw no further conclusions until I know more ... of him.' Jameson depressed Audubon further by telling him Sir Walter Scott had become a recluse and that he had little hope of meeting him. 'Not see Walter Scott, thought I – by Washington I shall, if I have to crawl on

George Street looking west towards St George's Church, from Shepherd's *Modern Athens*.

Below: Silhouette of Robert Knox by Augustin Edouart. (Scottish National Portrait Gallery)

all fours for a mile.' Jameson was to become an important figure in the lives of both Audubon and others who figure in this book and is considered more fully in Chapter 6.

Dr Robert Knox, the anatomist, gave him a warmer welcome. He greeted him in a gown and with bloody fingers, and having read Dr Traill's letter of introduction wished him well, promised to do all in his power to assist him, and arranged to see Audubon's drawings the following day.

Although his initial reception may not have been to his liking, the city itself pleased Audubon greatly.

I walked a good deal and admired this city very much, the great breadth of the streets, their good pavement and footways, the beautiful uniformity of the buildings, their natural grey coloring and wonderful cleanliness of the [whole] was felt perhaps more powerfully, coming direct from dirty Manchester. But the picturesque *tout ensemble* here is wonderful. A high castle here, another there, a bridge looking at a second city below, here a rugged mountain and there beautiful public grounds, monuments, the sea, the landscape around, all wonderfully managed .... After a good walk I returned more at ease ....[9]

Oct 27th 1826 I visited the market this morning, but to go to it I first crossed from the new town into the beginning of the old, over the north bridge, went down many flights of winding steps, at last reaching

Above: View of the North Bridge, Edinburgh, from Shepherd's *Modern Athens*.

Above, right: Example of Audubon's 'lower class' of Edinburgh citizenry: 'Very fou' by Walter Geikie.

Right: Patrick Neill, from Crombie's *Modern Athenians.*

the desired spot. I was then positively under the bridge that no doubt was built to save the trouble of descending and mounting from one side of Edinburgh to another …. The vegetable markets are well arranged and look well, as well as the fruits and meats, but the low situation and narrow kind of booths in which the whole is exhibited is not agreeable ….[10]

While the scenery was pleasing, the lower social classes were not so agreeable:

I was struck with the relative appearance of the woman of the lower class with our Indian squaws of the West. Their walk is precisely the same, and their mode of carrying burthens also. They have a leather strap passed over and poised on the forehead attached to large baskets without covers, and waddle through the streets with toes inward, just as the Shawanees for instance. Their complexions, if fair, is beyond rosy, partaking indeed of purple, cold and disagreeable …. Many of the men wear long whiskers and beards, are extremely uncouth of manners, and still more so of language.[11]

The following day Audubon tried once more to make contact with those to whom he had letters of introduction, but again with limited success. He did, however, meet Patrick Neill (1776-1851), who was to give him great encouragement and support.

Neill was a printer and a keen naturalist. His company printed the *Encyclopaedia*

Britannica, to which he also contributed the entry on gardening. Such was his personality that his business premises in Fishmarket Close was a meeting place for scientists and men of learning. Dr Andrew Duncan Sr (1744-1828)[†]

said of him that 'his superior knowledge in every branch of natural history is universally admitted by all who have science enough to appreciate that knowledge'. Henry Cockburn (1779-1854)† said that he was 'a useful citizen, a most intelligent florist, and one of the few defenders of our architectural relics'. Neill kept a menagerie and an exotic garden at his home at Canonmills which overlooked the loch created there by the mill dam – a feature which has long disappeared. The proximity to the loch was necessary to provide water for the daily watering of his 2000 pot plants.

Audubon visited Neill's home on 3 November 1826. 'Sweet spot, quite out of town, nice garden, house, with exotics, and house walls peopled by thousands of sparrows secured in the luxuriant masses of ivy ....' Among the tame birds were a kittiwake, a cormorant, a gannet, bantams and pigeons, and a greater black-backed gull which returned annually for 17 years and responded to Neill's call. (Audubon gives a colourful account of this 'scorie' in *Ornithological Biography*.) Three years earlier, Thomas Bewick had also been fascinated by 'seeing the tamed birds and other curiosities which embellished his little paradise. His uncommon kindness will ever remain impressed upon our memories.'[12]

Neill will be met again in this narrative as secretary of the Wernerian Society. This many-talented man was also an archaeologist, a founder member of the Caledonian Horticultural Society, and its secretary for 40 years. The present Royal Botanical Garden was developed alongside the society's Experimental Garden.

Neill is also remembered as the individual responsible for the creation of the East Princes Street Gardens on the site of the Nor' Loch lying at the foot of the castle rock, which had been drained in 1820. Between 1829 and 1931 he organised and supervised the planting of many thousand trees and shrubs which transformed the polluted foetid marsh into one of Edinburgh's most attractive features, remaining largely unspoiled to this day. Such was Neill's persuasive power that donors contributed their plants freely and the cost to the town council of the entire planting was less than £5.[13]

Audubon continued that day to explore Edinburgh and its environs. He walked to Trinity and looked at the naked and hilly shores of Fife, seven miles across the Forth:

During my walk I frequently turned round to view the beautiful city back of me, rising gradually [like an] amphitheatre most sublimely and backed by mountainous clouds that improved the whole really superbly. The wind was high .... The vessels pitched at anchor. All was Grand! ... I saw a very pretty, iron, suspended jetty with three arches, at the extremity of which steam vessels and others land their passengers and freight ....

Leith was

... a large village ... mostly connected with Hamburg and other sea ports of Holland. Much business was going on. I saw there a great number of herring boats and the nets for capturing the fishes, also some curious drags for oysters, clams, and other shell fish. The docks are small and contained mostly Dutch vessels of small size.[14]

Above, top: Canonmills Loch, from Ewbank's *Picturesque Views of Edinburgh*.

Above: 'The Nor' Loch and Edinburgh Castle' by Alexander Nasmyth (1758-1840). (National Gallery of Scotland)

That evening he went to a performance of Scott's play 'Rob Roy' at the Theatre Royal. The theatre was 'very small but well lighted .... Ladies of the second class go to the pit, the superior class to the boxes, and those of neither, unfit to be classified, way above.'[15]

'Rob Roy' was

> … represented as if positively in the Highlands. The characters were good and natural, the scenery perfectly adapted, the dress, the manners and language quite true. I may safely say that I saw as good [a] picture of the great outlaw, of his Ellen, and of his unrelenting Dougal as ever could be given. I would, were it possible, always see 'Rob Roy' in Edinburgh, 'Le Tartuffe' in Paris and the 'She stoops to Conquer' in London.[16]

Audubon liked Miss Stephens (Ellen) 'pretty well; her voice is not sweet but much affected …. I left her and the house at half past 10, extremely pleased with "Rob Roy" his Ellen, his Dougal, the magistrate and his Matte'. 'Rob Roy' was a perennial favourite guaranteed to draw full houses. Audubon was very fond of the theatre: 'I think it the best of all ways to spend an evening for *délassement*. I often find myself when there laughing or crying like a child.' During his time in Edinburgh he saw many performances, including the 'Merchant of Venice', the 'School of Reform', the 'Beggar's Opera', the 'Comedy of Errors' and the 'Lord of the Manor'.

The next day Audubon visited Holyrood Palace. He saw the apartments where the then King of France (Louis XVIII) resided during his exile; and the fine rooms George IV had used for a reception four years earlier when he visited Edinburgh. Afterwards he climbed Arthur's Seat, the hill overlooking Holyrood Palace, which gave him 'a splendid view of the whole city, country, and sea around for miles. The more I look on Edinburgh the better I like it.'

Audubon's life at this time seems to have been one of feverish activity. As well as sightseeing and recording all his movements and meetings in his journal, he maintained a prolific correspondence and made copies of his letters. Four days after his arrival he was still undecided about his future. Audubon was still considering a move to London, or to one of the European capitals. Although impressed by Edinburgh and wishing that his sons could have been educated there, he had qualifications about Scotland in general (although at that time he had seen little of the country). In a letter dated 29 October 1826 to his 17 year-old son Victor Gifford, he wrote:

> Scotland generally is a barren, poor-looking tract. The mountains are merely covered with earth, and the shepherds the most abject beings I ever saw. None but the rich here seem to enjoy life, and was it not my interest to remain some weeks to form a close acquaintance with all the great men of this portion of the world, I would leave its rigid climate and poverty behind me tomorrow.

He went on to give Victor fatherly advice to see how much could be done if time was not to be squandered. 'Talents will lay dormant in man if he does not, by exercise, cultivate them.' He himself followed this precept, maintaining that he required only four hours sleep a night.

By this time, only four days after his arrival, people began to flock to his lodgings to see his paintings. They included Andrew Duncan Jr (1773-1832),[†] professor of medical jurisprudence, 'a truly kind friend'. Professor Duncan was the son of the more famous Andrew Duncan Sr. The two Duncans were leaders of the medical profession in Edinburgh at that time. Dr Knox also called, and pronounced Audubon's drawings 'the finest in the world'. He promised to introduce him to the Wernerian Society.

On 30 October Audubon was overcome by depression. No one had come that morning to visit his paintings. He decided to visit Patrick Neill to express his disappointment with the lack of response to his letters of introduction. He was considering departing for London. The kindly Neill dissuaded him and took him to meet William Home Lizars, a painter and engraver. Lizars came at once to see Audubon's paintings, sharing the same umbrella and talking the while of the talents of the ornithologist Prideaux John Selby (1788-1867),[†] whose *Illustrations of British Ornithology* he was currently engaged in engraving.

When they arrived, Audubon unbuckled the straps of his portfolio, 'and putting a chair for him to set, without uttering a word, I turned up a drawing! Now Lucy, poor Mr Selby was the sufferer by that movement. Mr Lizars, quite surprised, exclaimed, "My God, I never saw anything like this before!"' This endorsement by Lizars was to prove one of the landmarks in Audubon's life, perhaps of similar significance to his meeting with Alexander Wilson.

Lizars learned his trade as an engraver from his father who died when his son was 22, leaving him with the responsibility of running the family business. In addition to his skill as an engraver, he was a considerable artist in his own right, having been a fellow student of the Scottish painter David Wilkie. Two of his paintings – the 'Scotch Wedding' and 'Reading the Will' –

Above, top: Holyrood Palace from Calton Hill, from Ewbank's *Picturesque Views of Edinburgh*.

Above: View of Edinburgh from Salisbury Crags, engraved by Robert Havell Jr in 1828 from a painting by E Crawford. (Courtesy of the Edinburgh City Library) This engraving, and also the view of Edinburgh on p. 90, was published by 'Wm. Fletcher' – probably the William Fletcher who brought an action against Audubon for an unpaid debt (see Chapter 12).

were exhibited at the Royal Academy in London and are now in the National Gallery of Scotland.

By the time of Audubon's visit, Lizars was a prominent figure in Edinburgh society and able to open many doors to him, as well as offering much hospitality and friendship. Audubon became almost a daily visitor to the Lizars' home in St James Square, adjacent to his lodgings. He had an admiration for Lizars' wife Henrietta, who was 'very affable, and has fine large eyes well colored with burnt amber, or perhaps Vandyke brown …. She is the first lady to whose house I have yet been, and received kindly, I will hereafter, call her Lady No. 1.'

Lizars at this time was busily engaged in engraving not only Selby's *Illustrations of British Ornithology* but also Sir William Jardine and Selby's *Illustrations of Ornithology*. However, Audubon was not alone in thinking that his paintings were superior to those of Selby. The *Edinburgh Evening Courant* of 6 November 1826 reported on Audubon's paintings:

Every bird has its own character, and every picture tells its own story, and is full of life and interest. It is invidious to make comparisons, yet there is no conceding or disguising the fact, that before the works of this artist, the splendid illustrations of ornithology by Mr Selby must hide their diminished heads and sink into comparative insignificance.

Lizars' endorsement was the turning point which persuaded Audubon to remain in Edinburgh. He acknowledged that 'I owe the vast attentions bestowed on me since' to Lizars' influence. Lizars induced the reluctant Professor Jameson to come and see Audubon's paintings on 31 October. 'He was kind to me, very kind, and yet I do not understand the man clearly. He has a look quite above my reach …. I am to breakfast with him tomorrow.' Other visitors that day were the sons of Dr Thomson, a neighbour in George Street, and Dr Henry and Patrick Syme who 'entertained me very much' at his home in 63 Great King Street. Patrick Syme (1774–1845) was the official artist to the Wernerian Society and author of *A Treatise on British Song-Birds*. He was the uncle of John Syme (1795–1861), an associate of Henry Raeburn (1756–1823) who painted the portrait of Audubon reproduced in the Introduction of this book. Audubon called later that evening on Lizars. 'He showed me some of his work, and judge how abashed I felt when I discovered him to be a most wonderful artist.'

The following day the breakfast with Professor Jameson took place.

A most splendid house, splendid everything, a good breakfast to boot. The professor wears his hair [in] three distinct, different courses, when he sits fronting the south, for instance, those on the upper forehead are bent westwardly, towards the east, those that cover both ears are inclined: and the very short sheared portion behind mounts directly upward … like the … quills of the 'fretful porcupine'. He accosted me most friendly, chatted with an uncommon degree of cordiality, and promised me his powerful assistance so forcibly, convincingly, that I am quite sure I can depend upon him. I left him and his sister at 10, as we both have a good deal to do besides drink hot, well creamed coffee.[17]

Later that morning, Jameson visited Audubon again to see the paintings, together with some companions. That evening Audubon visited Lizars once more and was presented with a copy of *Picturesque Views of Edinburgh*, engraved by Lizars from paintings by John Ewbank.[18] Lizars inscribed it 'To John J Audubon as a very imperfect expression of the regard entertained for his abilities as an artist, and for his worth as a friend by Will H. Lizars, Engraver of the Views of Edinburgh'. Audubon later sent the book to Lucy.

On 3 November, among the many who visited his paintings was James Wilson (1795-1856), 'a naturalist of pretensions, an agreeable man who invited me to dine at his cottage next week'. James Wilson and his brother John (Christopher North) became great admirers of Audubon and were to offer him much hospitality and friendship during his time in Edinburgh. The two brothers had been born in Paisley. They were no relation of Alexander Wilson who was also from Paisley but shared with him a love of poetry. Both brothers were friends of William Wordsworth whose home at Rydal Mount in the Lake District was close to their country estate of Elleray. James knew by heart many of the works of Wordsworth, Milton and Byron. Their father, a wealthy banker and manufacturer of cloth, died when they were still young. The family then moved to Edinburgh to live at 53 Queen Street.

James Wilson was described by Lockhart as being 'a thin, pale slender, contemplative-looking person, with hair of rather a dark colour, and extremely short-sighted. In his manners ... he is as different as possible from his brother; his voice is low, and his whole demeanour as still as can be imagined. In conversation he attempts no kind of display but seems to possess a very peculiar vein of dry humour, which renders him extremely diverting.'

He was educated at the High School and started a legal training but did not persevere. Being of independent means he preferred to pursue his life-long interest in natural history, particularly entomology and ornithology. Through his interest in entomology he became a friend of André Melly, Audubon's Liverpool acquaintance, from whom James received 'a box of beetles of the most *recherché* character ... and therefore great acquisitions to my collection. His own is the finest and most orderly I have ever seen.'

Although largely self-taught, James Wilson's profound knowledge of natural history was acknowledged. He was elected to the Wernerian Society in 1812 at the age of 17 and was its librarian throughout its existence. He became a Fellow of the Royal Society of Edinburgh on the same day as his friends Selby and Audubon, and eventually became its general secretary, editor of its *Transactions* and curator of its museum.

In 1816 James Wilson had been commissioned by Edinburgh University to travel to Paris to arrange the purchase, for the University Museum, of the Dufresne Collection of ornithological specimens (see p. 75). He was invited to undertake

Royal Circus, where Jameson lived at number 21, from Ewbank's *Picturesque Views of Edinburgh*.

James Wilson (artist unknown), from *Memoir of James Wilson of Woodville* by James Hamilton.

Far right: Page from the list of Fellows of the Royal Society of Edinburgh, showing the signatures of Selby, James Wilson and Audubon. (Reproduced by permission of the Royal Society of Edinburgh from the first roll book of the society.)

Below, right: Audubon's fellowship diploma from the Royal Society of Edinburgh, reproduced from *Audubon and his Journals*, volume two.

the editorship of the natural history section of the seventh edition of the *Encyclopaedia Britannica* and contributed the major part – about 900 pages – himself. He also published *Illustrations of Zoology*, contributing many of the paintings that show the remarkable artistic ability which many natural historians of that period seem to have possessed. His ornithological paintings in particular show the influence of his '… intelligent friend Mr Audubon of Louisiana, whose magnificent collection of ornithological drawings has lately excited such general interest in Edinburgh'.

In 1824 James married and took up residence in Woodville cottage in Morningside, then in the outskirts of Edinburgh, and this house remained his home for the rest of his life.

It was to this house that Audubon was invited. It remains today much as it was then, but alas the beautiful garden 'of two acres … in respectable proportions, orchard and lawn, flower-garden and shrubbery; and snugly ensconsed amidst the groves of Morningside' has recently suffered the fate of being 'developed' into a dense housing complex. James loved wildlife and acquired many tame pets which enjoyed free range of his house and garden, including a tame coati mundi, a robin, a chaffinch that lived for 15 years, a tit, a mule bird, pigeons, jackdaws, parakeets, hedgehogs, ichneumons, dogs and rabbits, and many others, all living in surprising harmony. Perhaps his most curious pet was a glowworm that he carried around with him for many months. On one occasion, finding a snake while on a walk, he collected it into his hat, which he then restored to his head while he walked home. 'It did not hotch so much as you might have expected, but lay very resigned and peaceable.' Unlike many of his contemporaries James was much more inclined to observe nature than to kill it for closer inspection, but this policy of conservation did not extend to trout; he was a passionate angler and regarded catching only 26 trout as a poor day's fishing.

On a tour of northern Scotland in the company of his friends Sir William Jardine and Prideaux John Selby (who brought his butler with him), James found the nest of a black-throated diver on an island on Loch Craggie. He went to the other side of the loch so 'that their wild though sweet home might not be disturbed'. Alas, he told his companions of his discovery and the following day, 'Sir William and Selby each armed with their fowling pieces, and much excited by my account of the divers and their woolly young ones', set out and succeeded in shooting the adults and one young, much to

James' grief when he saw 'the gorgeous creatures which I had so lately seen so full of life and vigour, extended cold and stiff upon the shore'. His sadness was mitigated by 'killing fifteen very fine trouts, many of them over two pounds weight'.[19]

James Wilson was offered the chair of natural history in 1854 after the premature death of Edward Forbes, who had succeeded Professor Jameson: he declined. 'My fittest as well as most familiar place is by the fireside and there I shall remain.' He died two years later in 1856.

John Wilson (1785-1854) was ten years older than James. He read law at Oxford, where he was 'the first boxer, leaper and runner among the students', and was called to the Scottish Bar although he never practiced as an advocate. He is chiefly known for his association with *Blackwood's Magazine*, to which he was the main contributor from 1817 until his death, writing under the pseudonym of Christopher North. His contributions were described as 'grave and gay, satiric and serious, mad and wise, nonsensical and profound, fierce and congenial which were destined to irradiate or torment its pages for fully a quarter of a century'.

Audubon described a visit to the home of John Wilson, on whom he had called to seek assistance with putting his article on turkeys into 'good English':

… taking my hat, slippers – undressed as I was – I pushed to his residence …. I ordered the man waiting to tell his master that Mr. Audubon from

Illustrations from Wilson's *Illustrations of Zoology* (National Library of Scotland): (a) 'The Jasius Butterfly', drawn by Wilson and lithographed by G Greaves; (b) 'The Quezal or Golden Trojon', drawn by Wilson and engraved by W H Lizars; (c) 'Jameson's Gull', drawn by Wilson and engraved by W H Lizars. It was most unusual for bird painters of that era to depict birds as dead – the very antithesis of Audubon's style of lively representation. Only once did Audubon paint a dead bird – the Eskimo curlew. Wilson named this hitherto undescribed gull from New Holland in honour of Professor Jameson. (All courtesy of the Trustees of the National Library of Scotland)

Below, left: Woodville cottage at the time of Audubon's visit, from *Memoirs of James Wilson of Woodville* by James Hamilton.

43

America wished to speak to him. In a moment this person returned and conducted me in a room where I wished that all that ever was written in it was my own. I did not [wait] long before a sweet child … begged that I should go upstairs …. Could I have gone upstairs? Could I have intruded, undressed and in slippers, into the heart of such a family? Not I. I shrunk, I am sure, very considerably, from my usual size and apologized very awkwardly. I had scarce done speaking … when the Professor came in with freedom and kindness [in his] hand, life in his eye, and benevolence at heart.[20]

John Wilson greatly admired Audubon's work and wrote glowing appreciations in *Blackwood's*. He was well qualified to do so, for like his brother

John Wilson, from Crombie's *Modern Athenians*.

he was a keen natural historian. Wilson was a celebrated host and companion and 'made others happy by being so intensely happy himself, when his brighter moods were on him'. Among his many friends were Sir Walter Scott and the poets William Wordsworth, Robert Southey, Samuel Taylor Coleridge and Thomas de Quincey. (John was himself a considerable poet.) Audubon and his family were frequent visitors to the Wilson home in Gloucester Place, where Audubon in particular must have felt at ease, for John, like Audubon, took pride in his crowning glory of fair hair which he grew to an unfashionable length: 'His face was magnificent, his hair long and flowing fell about his massive features like a lion's mane to which, indeed it was often compared. His dress was slovenly.'[21]

John Wilson was elected to the chair of moral philosophy in Edinburgh University in 1820, largely on the recommendation of Walter Scott. He filled the chair with distinction despite an apparent lack of appropriate academic qualifications. After Walter Scott's death in 1832, John became the dominant literary figure in Scotland. Wilson died in 1854, two weeks before the death of Robert Jameson. His statue, by John Steell, stands in the Princes Street Gardens adjacent to the Scott Memorial.

John (Christopher North) wrote of Audubon in *Blackwood's Magazine*:

He is the greatest artist in his own walk that ever lived, and cannot fail to reap the reward of his genius and perserverence and adventurous zeal in his own beautiful branch of natural history both in fame and fortune. The Man himself whom I have had the pleasure of frequently meeting – is just what you would expect from his works – full of fine enthusiasm and intelligence – most interesting in looks and manners – a perfect gentleman and esteemed by all who know him for the simplicity and frankness of his nature.[22]

Audubon's 'interesting looks and manners' were indeed one of the great assets of which he was acutely aware. He was tall and handsome with flowing hair anointed with bear grease, and had piercing eyes which commanded attention. He wore the clothes and adopted the persona of an American woodsman, which captured the imagination of the Edinburgh citizens. As his fame spread, visitors increasingly called upon him.

> Every day I exhibited my drawings to those
> who came to see them. I had many noblemen,
> among whom I especially liked Sir Patrick
> Walker and his lady; but I welcomed all ladies,
> gentlemen, artists, and, I dare say critics.[23]

One of his visitors was the actress Miss Stephens
whom he had admired in 'Rob Roy'. Much as he
welcomed these attentions he did find that they
interfered with his work, for he had started painting
again his favourite subjects – the wild turkeys.

During the next fortnight Audubon again
became very depressed, chiefly because he had not
had a letter from Lucy, and he uncharacteristically
failed to maintain his journal during what must
have been a very eventful period. Two important
incidents occurred which should have raised his
spirits: first the committee of the Royal Institution
offered him without charge a room in which to
exhibit his paintings; and second Lizars agreed
to undertake their engraving.

The Royal Institution at the foot of the Mound,
a fine building designed by the architect William
Henry Playfair (1789-1857),[†] had been completed
just the previous year and Audubon's exhibition
was the third to be shown in its halls. It housed
three organisations: the Royal Society of Edinburgh, the Society of Antiquaries, and the Royal
Institution for the Encouragement of the Fine
Arts in Scotland.

Audubon's exhibition ran from 14 November
to 23 December 1826 and was a great success.
Entrance fees produced £152, and catalogue
sales £20.

> My drawings were put up in the splendid
> Room — all the Newspapers took notice of
> them in a very handsome manner and having
> continued to do so constantly the rooms have
> been well attended when the weather has in
> the least permitted it — Last Saturday I took
> in £15. It will continue open to the last of
> Christmas week ....'[24]

Meanwhile, Lizars commenced the engravings
with such industry that within a month he had
produced five engravings – a truly remarkable
achievement. Audubon insisted that each plate
should be of double elephant folio – 29½ by 39½
inches (75 by 100cm) – so that he could achieve

his ambition of reproducing all birds life-sized.
This represented a considerable challenge to the
engraver. Each painting had to be reproduced on
a large and expensive polished copper sheet using
a sharpened steel pen (known as a burin), supple-
mented with aquatinting (a type of tonal etching).
Ink was then worked into the grooves cut in the
plate and the outline transferred to paper in a
large press, producing a reversed image of the
original. A team of colourists then copied the
details of the artist's painting onto the engraved
print – altogether a time-consuming and expensive process, and one which could result in slight
variation depending on the skill and experience
of the individual colourist (a source of recurrent
irritation to Audubon). Lizars and Robert Havell,
who succeeded him as Audubon's engraver, were
the leading exponents of this technique at the
time, and Audubon was indeed fortunate to obtain
the help of such talented men.

John Wilson, writing in *Blackwood's Magazine*,
described the exhibition:

> Soon after his arrival in Edinburgh where
> he soon found many friends, Audubon
> opened his Exhibition.
>
> Four hundred drawings of about two
> thousand birds, covered the walls of the
> Institution-Hall, in the Royal Society
> Buildings, and the effect was like magic.
> The spectator imagined himself in the
> forest – all were of the size of life, from
> the wren and the humming-bird to the
> wild turkey and the bird of Washington
> [the bald eagle] .... The colours were all
> of life too – bright as when borne in
> beaming beauty through the woods ....

'The Building of the
Royal Institution' by
Nasmyth. (National
Gallery of Scotland)
The view is of Princes
Street, looking towards
the North Bridge linking
the Old Town to the
New Town. On the
right is the construction
work of the Royal
Institution in 1824.

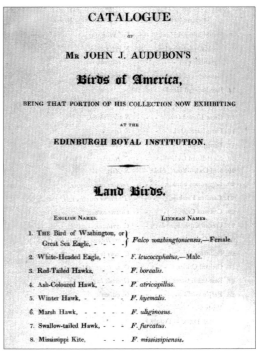

CATALOGUE
OF
MR JOHN J. AUDUBON'S
Birds of America,
BEING THAT PORTION OF HIS COLLECTION NOW EXHIBITING
AT THE
EDINBURGH ROYAL INSTITUTION.

Land Birds.

ENGLISH NAMES.	LINNÆAN NAMES.
1. THE Bird of Washington, or Great Sea Eagle, - - - -	} Falco washingtoniensis,—Female.
2. White-Headed Eagle, - - -	F. leucocephalus,—Male.
3. Red-Tailed Hawks, - - -	F. borealis.
4. Ash-Coloured Hawk, - - -	F. atricapillus.
5. Winter Hawk, - - - - -	F. hyemalis.
6. Marsh Hawk, - - - - -	F. uliginosus.
7. Swallow-tailed Hawk, - - -	F. furcatus.
8. Mississippi Kite, - - -	F. mississipiensis.

The Royal Institution, from Shepherd's *Modern Athens*. The building exists today with some additions, including Steell's statue of Queen Victoria over the portico. It was until recently the Royal Scottish Academy but is now undergoing incorporation with the National Gallery of Scotland.

Above, right: Catalogue of Audubon's exhibition in the Royal Institution. (Courtesy of the Royal Scottish Academy)

'Twas a wild and poetical vision of the heart of the New World, inhabited as yet almost wholly by the lovely or noble creatures that 'own not man's dominion.'

That all this wonderful creation should have been the unassisted work of one man – in his own country almost unknown, and by his own country wholly unbefriended, was a thought that awoke towards the 'American woodsman' feelings of more than admiration, of the deepest personal interest; and the hearts of all warmed towards Audubon, who were capable of conceiving the difficulties, and dangers, and sacrifices, that must have been encountered, endured, and overcome, before genius had thus embodied these the glory of its innumerable triumphs.

John Wilson was well qualified to comment on Audubon. His friend de Quincey wrote, 'Perhaps you already know from your countryman Audubon that the Professor is himself a naturalist, and of original merit; in fact, worth a score of such meagre bookish naturalists as are formed in museums and by second hand acts of memory; having (like Audubon) built much of his knowledge upon personal observation.'[25] Audubon was delighted with this review in *Blackwood's*. 'The editor John Wilson … is a clever good fellow, and I wrote to thank him.'[26]

The *Edinburgh Evening Courant* of Monday, 4 December gave this account:

Mr Audubon's illustrations of American Ornithology – this very interesting collection of drawings, the fruits of the author's constant exertions of the last 25 years, most deservedly, continues to attract the admiration of the gay and learned of this city …. Mr Audubon's quick perception of the most expressive attitudes for his subjects, so as to display their varied and lovely plumage to the best advantage – his choice of the situations in which they are represented – together with the elegance and beauty of the accompaniments with which many of them are adorned, evince on the part of the artist the finest feeling and taste, and the most accurate observation. His life (which has been an eventful one) has indeed been profitably occupied for the world at large; for who has enthusiasm enough again to explore the woods and wilds of America with the indefatigable zeal of our author? or who if he had the nerve for such an undertaking, is possessed of his keen discriminating eye? And his ardour is as great as ever, his oil painting of the wild turkey of America, now in the Royal Institution is worthy of a place in any collection. A circumstance of no small astonishment to us is that a

The recently discovered painting by Audubon of the 'Turkey Cock, Hen and Young' which he presented to the Royal Institution (see also illustration on p.161). (Courtesy of the Royal Scottish Academy)

work of so much labour, spirit and beauty, could have been executed in the incredible short period of ten days ….

The Scotsman newspaper (4 November 1826) was equally enthusiastic: '… the specimens exhibited by Mr Audubon's pencil are all beyond praise …. Hondekoeter … may not be placed in the rank of this artist.'

In gratitude for the privilege of displaying his paintings, Audubon gave the Royal Institution the copy of his painting of the turkey family referred to above, for which he had been offered £100 by a dealer – a princely sum which he could have well used. It was recently discovered in the attics of the Royal Scottish Academy which later occupied the entire building.[27]

A curious event occurred at the exhibition – the painting of the black poll warbler was stolen. In his journal of 8 December 1826, Audubon gave this rather garbled account:

> … a drawing of mine was *gently purloined* last evening from the rooms of the Royal Institution by someone teasing nettle, who had certainly strong propensities for drawing. So runs the fact, perhaps a few minutes before the closing of the doors, A Somebody in a large cloak paid his shilling, entered the hall, and made his rounds watchmanlike, with great caution, took a drawing from the walls, rolled it up carefully, and walked off …. I issued a warrant against a young man, deaf and dumb, of the name of Ingles who was unfortunately strongly suspected. Mr Lizars and I had called on a friend of this youth who told us that he would sift the business ….

Later that day when returning home, Audubon found the rolled-up painting on his doorstep.

> The thief, whoever he may be, God grant him pardon, had been terror struck and … had taken this method of returning the drawing before detection. I was in time to stop the warrant and the affair was silenced. The wonder of all this is that the lad suspected is the son of Sir Henry Raeburn, a distinguished family.[28]

Biographers of Audubon have assumed from this account that the lad 'Ingles' was an illegitimate son of Raeburn's, but he was in fact his legitimate step-grandson.

Raeburn submitted the delightful picture of his step-grandson as his diploma entry for fellowship of the Royal Academy of London.

It is a most curious coincidence that this portrait was displayed in 1997 on the very walls from which the subject of the painting stole Audubon's painting in 1826.[29]

Captain Basil Hall (1788-1844),[†] a friend of the Raeburn family, had mediated with Audubon on behalf of the young Inglis, and to thank Audubon for taking no further action in the matter presented him with copies of his own publications. He was a retired Royal Naval captain who had published accounts of his travels in the Pacific Ocean which had been highly acclaimed. He was later to write a book on a visit to North America. Captain Hall was a pillar of Edinburgh society and was able to be of great assistance to Audubon.

Above: The stolen picture, the 'Black Poll Warbler', plate 133 from *The Birds of America*. (Reproduced by kind permission of the President and Council of the Royal College of Physicians and Surgeons of Glasgow)

Above, right: The thief! 'Henry Raeburn Inglis' by his step-grandfather Henry Raeburn. (Royal Academy of Arts, London)

Notes

1 Cited in Hook, A: *Scotland and America 1750-1835*, p. 20.
2 Ibid, p. 25.
3 Ibid, p. 176.
4 *Edinburgh Review* (1808/9), XII: 153.
5 Hook, A: op. cit., pp. 176-7.
6 George Street was indeed one of the most beautiful streets in Edinburgh. It was the main axis of James Craig's plan for the New Town of Edinburgh which commenced development in 1767. During Audubon's time it housed a mixture of business and domestic premises. Many of the properties remain today as they would have appeared in his day. Among the notable buildings nearby was the old College of Physicians at number 14, not far from Mrs Dickie's lodging house at number 2 (which has since been replaced by a modern office building). St Andrew's Church was almost opposite, and the Assembly Rooms not far away. Many professional men lived there including the surgeons Robert Liston, John Thomson, an 'M Hossack, chiropodist to his Majesty', 'J Maples, cupper to his Majesty', and many lawyers, advocates, bankers and teachers. The business premises ranged from insurance offices and *Blackwood's Magazine* to less prestigious

shops occupied by perfumiers, peruke makers, dyers, calico glaziers, straw hat makers, silk mercers, spine machine and truss makers, booksellers, cheesemongers, painters and ivory turners.

7   *The 1826 Journal of John James Audubon*, pp. 303-4.

8   Ibid, p. 306.

9   Ibid, pp. 305-6.

10   Ibid, p. 306.

11   Ibid, p. 307.

12   *A Memoir of Thomas Bewick written by himself*, p. 183 (The Cresset Press: London, 1961).

13   Byrom, C (personal communication).

14   *The 1826 Journal of John James Audubon*, pp. 308-9.

15   A visit to the theatre in Audubon's time was not without its hazards. A notice in the *Edinburgh Evening Courant* of 2 December 1826 reported that 'several ladies and gentlemen in the pit of the Theatre Royal have lately been considerably annoyed and their clothes much injured by the filth and dirt cast upon them by some persons occupying … the one shilling gallery. The Manager takes this method of expressing his regret that … the ill conduct by a few mischievous boys be converted into an annoyance to the other parts of the Theatre and respectfully solicits the assistance of the very many respectable persons sitting in that part of the gallery in putting a stop to this nuisance, by pointing out to the Officers of the Police any individual disgracing himself by so dirty a practice.'

16   *The 1826 Journal of John James Audubon*, p. 310.

17   Ibid, p. 329.

18   John Ewbank (1799-1847) started his career as a house painter but graduated from that to marine and landscape painting, having had lessons from Alexander Nasmyth. For a time he was very successful and his paintings were in demand, but he became an alcoholic and sank into obscurity and an early death. His *Picturesque Views of Edinburgh*, engraved and published by Lizars, was his main legacy. His wife and daughter were left destitute and were sentenced to three months' hard labour for the theft of three sheets of paper.

19   This and the previous quotations relating to James Wilson are taken from *Memoirs of the Life of James Wilson of Woodville* by James Hamilton (London, 1859).

20   *The 1826 Journal of John James Audubon*, pp. 342-3.

21   This and the previous quotations relating to John Wilson are taken from his obituary in *Gentleman's Magazine* (1854), New Series 41: 656-7.

22   *Blackwood's Magazine* (1827), 21: 105.

23   *Audubon and His Journals*, vol. I, p. 159.

24   *Letters of John James Audubon, 1826-1840*, p. 7.

25   From Masson, David (ed.): *The collected writings of Thomas de Quincey*, vol. V, p. 260 (Adam & Charles Black: Edinburgh, 1890). De Quincey lived as a guest in the house of John Wilson from 1828-30 and would no doubt have met Audubon during his frequent visits to this hospitable home.

26   Audubon, L: *The Life of John James Audubon the Naturalist*, p. 207.

27   The Scottish Academy of Painting, Sculpture and Architecture (SA) was founded in 1826, the same year in which the Royal Institution was established with similar aims, and at first there was considerable rivalry between the two organisations. In 1829 the lawyer Henry Cockburn (later Lord Cockburn), with great tact and diplomacy, brokered a union of the two bodies and in 1835 the SA became a tenant of the Royal Institution. It became the Royal Scottish Academy (RSA) in 1838 and gradually displaced the other tenants, so that by 1910 it became the sole occupant of the building. It is of interest that the first four Honorary Members of the SA, elected in 1827, consisted of Audubon and three of his friends – Thomas Sully, Sir William Jardine, and Prideaux John Selby. The RSA building is currently (2003) being linked to, and becoming part of, the National Gallery of Scotland.

28   *The 1826 Journal of John James Audubon*, p. 377.

29   Thomson, D: *The Art of Sir Henry Raeburn 1756-1823*, p. 176. This book accompanied an exhibition of paintings of Henry Raeburn held in the Royal Scottish Academy in 1997.

6 | Social Distractions

AUDUBON became increasingly involved in Edinburgh's social scene. The city's matrons vied with each other to have the now celebrated woodsman as their guest. Much as Audubon liked this attention, his *mauvais honte* continued to make him feel awkward in society. After a rather embarrassing dinner at the home of Professor Robert Graham (1786-1845),[†] a botanist who is remembered chiefly for establishing the Royal Botanic Garden in its present site, Audubon wrote in his journal on 20 November 1826:

> The sumptuous dinners of this country are quite too much for me. This is not [as] with friend Bourgeat on the Flat Lake, roasting the orange-fleshed Ibis and a few Sun Perch; neither is it on the heated banks of Thompson Creek on the fourth of July, where the roasted eggs of the large Soft-shelled Turtle are quickly swallowed. Neither was it [as] when, with my Lucy at Henderson at good Dr Rankins, I listened to the howlings of the wolves while eating well roasted and jellied venison in full security.[1]

The dinners were not always sumptuous. At a meal with Mr Ritchie (editor of *The Scotsman*) – a 'well meaning man' with a 'well-doing wife' – Audubon discovered that some of the ingredients were raw.

Another invitation was to the home of Professor Alexander Monro Tertius (1773-1859)[†] at Craiglockhart on the outskirts of the city. Audubon hired a coach for twelve shillings and then had to pay another shilling toll charge – 'A dear dinner this.' However, he found Professor Monro more agreeable than he anticipated and appreciated the flirtations of his daughter Maria. As ever Audubon enjoyed female companionship: 'I have formed the acquaintance of a few extremely agreeable ladies, where I go to relax at evening from the labours of the day.'

On 26 November his journal again records his deep depression:

> I had thought a thousand times of thee, and my chagrin was greater than usual. I could not well understand why no tidings from thee reached me. Oh how much I thought of the dear wife, the dear girl, the dear woods, all in America. I walked in thought by thy lovely figure, kissed thee, pressed thee to my bosom, heard, I thought, thy sweet voice. But good God, when I positively looked around me and found myself in Edinburgh, alone, quite alone – without one soul to whom I could open my heart – my head became dizzy and I must have fallen to the floor, for when my senses came again to me I was stretched on the carpet and wet with perspiration ....[2]

Fortunately Lizars called and invited him to dinner, which lifted his spirits.

The following day Audubon was invited to a meeting of the Phrenology Society at the home of George Combe (1788-1858).[†] Phrenologists believed that it was possible to assess one's character and abilities from the configuration of the skull, and the cult enjoyed a great following in the early nineteenth century. Combe was one of its principal disciples and the society founded by him in 1820 flourished under his influence. At this meeting the skulls of Audubon and Charles N Weiss, a visiting German flautist, were examined by one of the members, who pronounced of Audubon that 'there cannot exist a moment of doubt that this gentleman is a great painter, compositor, colorist, and I would add a very amiable man ...'. By this time Audubon's fame in Edinburgh was so widely known and reported in the press, that this analysis could hardly be regarded as a critical test of phrenology.

On 20 December he was invited back for a more thorough study of his skull:

Phrenology was the order of this morning. I reached Brown Square at 9, and breakfasted most heartily on mutton, ham and good coffee with George Combe. The cloth was left and we proceeded upstairs into his sancto sanctorum. A beautiful silver box containing the instruments for measuring was opened .... I was seated facing the light. Dr Combe acted as secretary; and George Combe, thrusting his fingers about my hair, began to search for miraculous bumps! My skull was measured accurately as I measure the bill or legs of a new individual, and all was duly noted by the scribe. Then with most exquisite sense of touch each protuberance was found, as numbered by phrenologists, and also put down according to their respective sizes. I was astounded when they both said that I must be a strong and constant lover and affectionate father, that I had great veneration for high, talented men, that I would have made a brave general, that music was not to be compared with painting in me, that I was extraordinarily generous, etc. Now I know all these to be facts, and how they discovered them to be so is quite a puzzle to me.[3]

Audubon's puzzlement was rather naïve, for he had dined on several occasions with Combe, who must by then have known most of his characteristics.

The phrenologists seized every opportunity of obtaining face masks of distinguished individuals and Audubon consented to have one made:

January 14 1927 .... After receiving many callers I went to Mr O'Neill's to have a cast taken of my head. My coat and neckcloth were taken off, my shirt collar turned down, I was told to close my eyes; Mr. O'Neill took a large brush and oiled my whole face, the almost liquid plaster of Paris was poured over it, as I sat uprightly till the whole was covered; my nostrils only were exempt. In a few moments the plaster had acquired the needful consistency, when it was taken off by pulling it down gently. The whole operation lasted hardly five minutes; the only inconvenience felt was the weight of the material pulling downward over my sinews and flesh. On my return from the Antiquarian Society that evening, I found *my face* on the table, an excellent cast.[4]

Later, Combe wrote:

Mr Audubon, we are happy to say, is still residing among us, and any of our fellow-citizens may have an opportunity of verifying or disproving our assertion, that in his head the organs of Form, Size, Weight, Colouring, Locality and Lower Individuality (forming what is called the superciliary ridge, and comprising the principal observing powers most necessary to a painter) are all developed in a more than ordinary degree .... this description will be better understood by inspecting a mask of the face from nature, now in the Phrenology Society collection.[5]

George Combe, from Crombie's *Modern Athenians.*

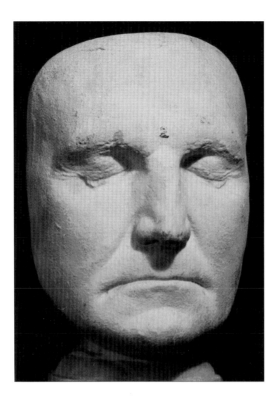

Mr Weiss, the flautist, needless to say had a well-developed organ of Tune!

Although phrenology had a strong following thanks to the influence of Combe, it was not without its critics; indeed it generated a debate quite as intense as the Huttonian/Wernerian controversy, of which more later. Henry Cockburn wrote in his journal:

> This George Combe, the patron and expounder of Edinburgh phrenology, is a calm, excellent man, with a clear natural style of didactic speaking and very benevolent objects. Some wise people call him a quack, of which his phrenological pretensions are their proof; but I am satisfied that he really believes in that folly, as many other honest men do. Some allowance must surely be made of the attractions which any creed has to a person whose adventure in it has ended in him finding himself its apostle.[6]

Sir Walter Scott referred to phrenologists as 'turnipheads' and Francis Jeffrey wrote a scathing article against Combe's *System of Phrenology* in the *Edinburgh Review*, copied by the *Edinburgh Evening Courant* of 8 November 1826. An extract from the lengthy article reads:

This folly should have been consigned to the great limbo of vanity ... but it seems that we had underrated the taste for the marvellous which still prevails in the world: for the science, still flourishes in certain circles – and most of all, it would appear in this intellectual city where there is not only a regular lecture on the subject but a quarterly journal devoted exclusively to its discussion; and where, besides several smaller elementary works, this erudite and massive system of 566 very close printed pages, has come to a second edition in the course of the present year .... It is not popular in London, Paris, Vienna or Weimar .... Our Northern race has not hitherto been supposed to sin on the side of overcredulity, we are really something at a loss, and to say the truth, less proud than surprised, to find that Edinburgh should be the great nursing mother of this brood of Germany. The phenomenon we think can only be solved by the circumstances of a person of Mr Combe's sense and energy having been led, by some extraordinary accident, first to conceive a partiality for it – and then, induced with the natural ambition of a man of talent, to make a point of honour to justify his partiality. We cannot but wish that it had been directed to a worthier object.

Combe wrote a lengthy 82-page defence in his *Phrenology Journal* but Jeffrey proved to have the sounder judgement, for phrenology went out of fashion following Combe's death. When the society disbanded its collection of about 1000 face masks and skulls passed in 1879 to the custody of the anatomy department of Edinburgh University. The collection includes life and death masks of many of the famous and infamous personalities of the period. A curious juxtaposition is the mask of Audubon together with that of the poet John Keats, prepared by his friend the artist Benjamin Robert Hayden in 1816. Keats, it will be remembered (see Chapter 1, p. 4), had written about Audubon, 'I shall not like the sight of him – I shall endeavour to avoid seeing him'. It is a strange coincidence that their masks should end up within sight of each other.

During this period Audubon had his portrait painted by John Syme at his home in 32 Abercrombie Place (see p. x). Audubon did not enjoy the experience. 'At 12 [o'clock] I went to *stand up* for my picture, and sick enough of it I became by 2.' Three days later the portrait was finished. 'I cannot say that I thought it a very good resemblance, but it was a fine picture and the public is the best judge ….' It was displayed at the first exhibition of the Scottish Academy (later the Royal Scottish Academy) with general approval. Syme offered the portrait to Sir William Jardine, who would have liked the painting but said that he could not afford it. (Jardine was perennially short of funds.) It eventually came into the possession of James Wilson, who greatly admired Audubon and hung the painting on the wall of his study at Woodville cottage. The painting is now in the White House collection, having been purchased from a descendant of Wilson. On 16 January 1827 Audubon solicited John Syme's support in his successful application for honorary membership of the Scottish Academy.

On 30 November Audubon was invited to a dinner of the Society of Antiquarians. The society had been founded in 1780 'for the purpose of promoting the investigation of the history of Scotland and its antiquities'. In Audubon's day it was housed in the Royal Institution with the Royal Society of Edinburgh. The dinner at the Waterloo Hotel was

> … a sumptuous dinner indeed. It at first consisted entirely of Scotch messes of old fashion, such as marrow bones, codfish heads stuffed with oatmeal and garlic, black puddings, sheep's heads, tracheas of the same, and I do not know what all. Then a second dinner was served, quite a l'anglaise ….

After the meal many toasts were drunk, including one to Audubon – much to his embarrassment:

> I thought I would faint … I had seen each toasted individual rise and deliver a speech. That being the case could I remain speechless like a fool? No, I summoned resolution and for the first time in my life addressed a large assembly thus: 'Gentlemen, my powers of voice are as humble as those of the Birds now hanging on the wall of the Institution. I am truly obliged for your favor. Permit me to say, may God bless you all and may this Society prosper.' I felt my hands and they

John Syme, self portrait. (Scottish National Portrait Gallery)

were positively covered with perspiration. I felt it running down along my legs.[7]

Once again Lizars, who was sitting next to him, came to the rescue with encouragement and a drink.

Audubon refers frequently to his social unease in high society. On another occasion he was reading his manuscript on the carrion crow to Dr David Brewster (1781-1868).[†] Having blown his nose and put his neck in a good attitude to suffer his lungs to operate freely, he

> … began reading …. About mid-way my respiration became encumbered. While I rested a moment to breathe, the doctor took this opportunity to say that it was 'very good and interesting.' I soon resumed and went through, thank God!
>
> He who all his life has been … brought up in the Green Room of Convent Garden Theater, for instance … knows nothing about the feelings that agitate me on such an occasion …. A man who has never looked into an English grammar and very seldom, into a French or a Spanish one, a man who has always felt awkward and very shy in the presence of a stranger … seated opposite Dr Brewster, reading one of my puny efforts at describing habits of birds … was so ridiculously absurd

Sir David Brewster by William Bewick. (Scottish National Portrait Gallery)

It was determined by Dr Knox to propose me as an honorary member of the Wernerian Society …. At half past 1, after having been dubbed a great philosopher and an extra-ordinary man, my health drank … I retired with Dr Knox …. As we walked together the doctor spoke by no means very favourably of reserved Mr. Jameson.

Audubon accepted an invitation from Dr Knox to attend his lecture the following day.

… on entering the room where probably 150 students were already assembled, a beating of feet and clapping of hands took place that quite shocked me …. Each person who entered the room was saluted as we had been …. The Doctor came and all was hushed as if silence had been the principal study of all present.[9]

He was interested in the lecture, but it may not have been one of Dr Knox's best as his head ached confoundedly after the previous night's indulgence. He then went to see Dr Knox's anatomy museum but found the sights disagreeable: 'I was glad to leave this charnel and breathe again the salubrious atmosphere of fair Edina.'

… in my estimation …. A cold sweat ran over my body much worse than when I dined with the Antiquarians.

In his journal he described a dinner with Henry Witham[8] at 24 Great King Street, where Robert Knox, the anatomist, was also a guest.

Audubon's hectic schedule continued with more dinners, visits to the theatre and concerts. He went to one concert in the Assembly Rooms close by his lodgings to hear his phrenology companion, the flautist Weiss, perform. *The Scotsman* reported:

We dined, we drank coffee, we supped at 11. At 12 the ladies bid us good night. I wished and longed to retire, but it was impossible …. We all talked much, for I believe the good wine of Mr. Witham had a most direct effect.

The Assembly Rooms in George Street, adjacent to Audubon's lodgings, from Shepherd's *Modern Athens.*

Those of the public who attended the concert, which was given last night in the Assembly Rooms, will allow that … for purity sweetness and we should like to say elasticity of tone, we are not aware that he has any equal. We liked his manner of giving our simple melodies – 'Auld Robin Gray' and 'The Bluebells of Scotland' – and in executing the variations he displayed very great skill as well as taste. We liked his concert piece better, however, than his Fantazia; this performance throughout being more characterised, as we conceive, by delicacy, lightness, and skill, than fancy: but on seeing more of him we may be induced to change our opinion. Miss Eliza Paton's 'Lo! Hear the Gentle Lark', with Mr Weiss's flute accompaniment delighted the audience ….

When not so engaged, Audubon continued to paint in oils his favourite subjects, the wild turkeys, and 'The Otter in the Trap', as well as 'Black Cocks Sunning Themselves', 'Pheasants Surprised by a Fox', 'Two Cats Fighting over a Dead Squirrel', and 'Wood Pigeons'. The last three paintings were exhibited at the Scottish Academy exhibition of 1827. Some he sold, others he gave as gifts; the 'Wood Pigeons', which he gave to Mrs Lizars, is now in the collection of the National Gallery of Scotland. His productivity during this period was remarkable considering the social pressures to which he was subjected.

At this time Audubon also commenced the labour of seeking purchasers for his *Birds of America*, for he had no financial resources and could not proceed with his ambitious plans unless funding was ensured. The work was to be published in a series of fascicles of five plates, each costing two guineas. Eventually 87 parts consisting of 435 plates were produced, costing in all 170 guineas (£187) or $1000. Inevitably a work of this size and cost could only be purchased by the very wealthy or by institutions. During the next decade Audubon devoted a great deal of time and effort to obtaining subscribers and persuading them to maintain their subscriptions. The day 7 December 1826 was a red letter one, for Professor Jameson placed an order on behalf of the University of Edinburgh – which became one of the first subscribers. Audubon was overjoyed. 'The University of Edinburgh having subscribed I look to the rest of them, 11 in number to follow.'[10]

Alas, in 1992 Edinburgh University sold its set of *The Birds of America* at auction in New York for $4.1 million. This was a tragic loss, being the only complete set in the city where Audubon's ambitions were first realised. The only remaining engravings in Edinburgh are a set of 29 of the first 30 plates and 15 loose plates in the National Museums of Scotland (see Appendix 3).

Despite maintaining a prolific correspondence with his friends in Liverpool, Manchester and America, and with his sons, Audubon's first letter to Lucy from Edinburgh is dated 10 December 1826. Perhaps this apparent neglect was due to the fact that he was keeping his daily journal, which was intended for Lucy and may have made him feel that he was communicating with her. It is due to the existence of this journal and the surviving copies of many of his letters that so much is known about Audubon's first visit to Edinburgh. The journal contains many references to his distress at not hearing from his wife. In his first long letter to Lucy he details the main events since his arrival in Edinburgh.[11] In general it is enthusiastic:

Audubon's painting 'Wood Pigeons' (see also illustration on p. 160). (National Gallery of Scotland)

Audubon's 'Turkey Cock', plate I from *The Birds of America*. It was the first of Audubon's paintings to be engraved by W H Lizars. (Reproduced by kind permission of the President and Council of the Royal College of Physicians and Surgeons of Glasgow)

My situation in Edinburgh borders almost on the miraculous. Without education [and with] scarce one of those qualities necessary to render a man able to pass thro the throng of the learned here, I am positively looked on by all the Professors & many of the principal persons here as a very extraordinary man …. What different times I see here, courted as I am, from those I spent at the 'Beech Woods,'[12] where certain people scarcely thought fit to look upon me.

He goes on to describe the success of his exhibition and his reaction to the first engravings:

It is now a month since my work has been begun by Mr W. H. Lizars of this city – it is to come out in numbers of 5 prints all the size of life and in the same size paper of my largest drawings that is called double eliphant – they will be brought up & finished in such superb style as to eclipse all of the kind in existence. The price of each number is two guineas and all individuals have the privilege of subscribing for the whole or any portion of it. Two of the plates were finished last week – some of the engravings colored are now put up in my Exhibition Rooms and are truly beautiful …. I shall send thee the very first and I think it will please thee – it consists of the Turkey Male – the Cuckoos in the Papaws and three small drawings … the little drawings in the centre of those beautiful large sheets have a fine effect and an air of richness and wealth that help insure success in this country. I cannot yet say that I will ultimately succeed but at present all bears a better prospect than I ever expected to see. I think this under the eyes of the most discerning people in the world. I mean Edinburgh. If it takes here, it cannot fail anywhere.

The Scotsman reported that Lizars' engravings were so exquisitely coloured that it required close examination to discover that they were not the original paintings. Audubon mentions the favourable reviews of his exhibition that had appeared in Jameson's *New Philosophical Journal*, Brewster's *Edinburgh Journal of Science* and in *Blackwood's Magazine*: '… these three journals print upwards of 30,000 copies so that my name will spread quickly enough.' He pleads with Lucy

to bring the children and join him. He wanted Victor to help him with the business side of the publication and felt that John could get a better education in Edinburgh. 'Cannot we move together and feel and enjoy the natural need of each other?'

Edinburgh had its disadvantages, however:

The difference of manners here from those of America are astonishing. The great round of company I am thrown in has become fatiguing to me in the extreme, and does not agree with my early habits. I go to dine out at 6, 7, or 8 o'clock in the evening, and it is 1 or 2 in the morning when the party breaks up. Then painting all day, until, with my correspondence that increases daily, my head is like a hornet's nest, and my body wearied beyond calculation. Yet it has to be done. I cannot refuse a single invitation. Edinburgh must be the handsomest city in the world – thou wouldst like it, of all things, I think, for a place of residence.

The following day he received the long-awaited letters from Lucy. 'How I read them! Perhaps never in my life were letters so well welcome, and they were such sweet letters ….'

December the 16th was an important and busy day for Audubon. His journal details that it rained hard all day. First, he visited Mr John Stokoe (1775-1852)[†] at 42 Lothian Street in order to obtain the London address of Charles Bonaparte. He found Stokoe still abed and left him to snore further. The rest of the morning was spent writing difficult letters to Charles Bonaparte and William Rathbone, both of whom had offended Audubon for different reasons. He bought a pigeon and killed it in preparation for his demonstration to the Wernerian Society in the afternoon. On his way there he received a summons to meet Lady Morton at his exhibition at the Royal Institution. She spoke to him in excellent French, praised his paintings and extended an invitation to visit her home.

He had been invited to the Wernerian Society (see Chapter 9) to demonstrate his technique of fixing birds in life-like postures 'by means of wires'. 'We enter the room of the *Wernerian Society of Edinburgh!* What a name it has in America!' He unrolled his drawing of the buzzard for the members to inspect and his friend Patrick Neill, the secretary, read out his essay on the buzzard as non-members were not allowed to read papers.

> I then shewed them my manner of putting up my specimens for drawing birds. This they thought inconceivably ingenious. Professor Jameson [the president] then rose and offered me as an Honorary Member .... Everyone clapped hand and stamped the floor [as a] mark of approbation. Then the professor desired that the usual law of suffering the election to be tried for months should be infringed upon and that I be elected at the next meeting.[13]

In his 'Account of the Method of Drawing Birds'[14] Audubon writes, 'My drawings have all been made after individuals fresh killed ... and put up ... by means of wires ... in the precise attitude represented ... that I hope will always correspond with *nature* ... I have never drawn from a stuffed specimen'. Later he had to abandon this ideal and at least 66 of his subsequent paintings were done in Britain from bird skins or stuffed specimens obtained from the museums of Edinburgh University and the Zoological Society of London, and from his friends including Lord Stanley and the polar explorer James Clark Ross (nephew of the explorer John Ross who contributed many specimens to the University Museum). Many of these paintings, done out of context from specimens that he had never seen in life, lack the vitality and colourful backgrounds which are such an attractive feature of his earlier work.

That evening Audubon went to a formal dinner at 16 Hope Street, the home of Lady Hunter, mother-in-law of Captain Basil Hall. Many of Edinburgh's titled people were there. The nobility was 'so uncommonly kind, affable and truly well bred' that Audubon did not feel as uncomfortable as usual. He left long after midnight together with his friend and fellow guest William Greg, son of the mill-owner Samuel Greg of Quarry Bank, with whom Audubon had stayed while visiting Manchester. Young Greg was then a student at Edinburgh University and frequently visited Audubon, on one occasion borrowing money from him.

On returning to his lodgings after this late dinner, Audubon persuaded Mrs Dickie's son to help him kill two cats which he had been given by Daniel Lizars (brother of William). The cats were then put up in fighting attitudes ready for painting the following morning. It is extraordinary that after such a full day he still found time to record its events in a lengthy entry in his journal. The painting of 'Two Cats Fighting over a Dead Squirrel' was given to Mrs Dickie and sold at auction in 1832 for £4 with the rest of her effects, the Dickies having fallen into hard times as a result of 'dissipation'.[15]

All these attentions appealed to Audubon's considerable vanity. He discarded the trappings of the woodsman which had caused such a stir on his first arrival in Edinburgh. 'I have come to fine dressing again – silk stockings and pumps; shave every morning; and sometimes dress twice a day. My hairs are now as beautifully long and curly as ever, and, I assure thee, do as much for me as my talent for painting.'

He must have been pleased by Christopher North's later description of him in *Blackwood's*:[16]

> When some five years ago, we first set eyes on him in a party of literati ... he was such an American woodsman as took the shine out of us modern Athenians. Though dressed, of course, somewhat after the fashion of ourselves, his long raven locks hung curling over his shoulders, yet unshorn from the wilderness. They were shaded across his open forehead with a simple elegance, such as ... when practising 'every man his own perruquier,' in some liquid mirror in the forest-glade, employing, perhaps, for a comb, the claw of the Bald Eagle .... His whole demeanour was coloured to our thought by a character of conscious freedom and dignity, which he had habitually required in his long and lonely wanderings among the woods ... the entire appearance of the man was most appropriate to what had for so many years been his calling.

On 19 December, while walking to Barry's Hotel in Princes Street to meet Sir William Jardine and Prideaux John Selby, his emotions were aroused by the grandeur of the scene. 'The horizon was all like burnished gold. The walls of the castle white in the light, and almost black in the shade ... had a surprising effect on my feelings ... and [I] was launched in deepest reflections', when he encountered 'a child, bare-footed, ragged, and apparently on the eve of star-vation …. I gave him a shilling, the poor child, complained so of want that, [had] I dared I would have taken it to Sir William and made it break-fast at the hotel.' Instead he took the child back to his lodgings and gave him all his spare linen and five more shillings. 'I gave it my blessings, and I felt – oh, my Lucy, I felt such pleasure – I felt as if God smiled on me!'[17]

He then breakfasted with Jardine and Selby and took them back to his rooms, where he gave them a lesson and demonstration of his painting methods. Selby gave Audubon three pheasants which he used as models for a painting of 'Pheasants Attacked by a Fox' – he took great pleasure in depicting nature tooth and claw. Jardine and Selby came for further lessons and Audubon found in the two men kindred spirits.

Audubon wrote to Lucy on 21 December 1826:

About a fortnight since Sir Wm Jardine came to spend a few days here purposely to see me — he was most constantly with me — he and Mr Selby are engaged in a general Ornitho-logical Work and as I find I am a useful man that way it is most likely that I shall be con-nected with them with a good share of credit and a good deal of cash — they both will be in a few days when this matter will be discussed over at length and probably arranged.

Whether any cash was paid is not known, but close friendships developed. Audubon found Selby 'one of these rare characters that come on the earth only at very distant periods, to prove to mankind how good some of our species may still be found'. He received warm invitations to the homes of both men.

On 23 December his exhibition closed, having been open for 39 days. The entrance money, at a shilling a visit, produced £152.18.0 and from cat-alogue sales he received another £20.12.6.

On 27 December Audubon was invited to stay with the Earl and Countess of Morton.[18] The earl sent his coach which was large; the soft seats lined with purple morocco. He found the motion like a ship gliding on an even sea during the eight miles to their stately home at Dalmahoy. 'I was led though this hall and upstairs, my name was given, and I entered the drawing-room of the Earl of Morton! The Countess ran to me, then

Portrait of John Anderson, falconer. (Scottish National Portrait Gallery)

returned to her Lord and presented him to me, my Lucy. Yes, him to me!' Audubon had expected to meet a grand figure and was surprised to see 'a small slender man, tottering on his feet, weaker than a new hatched Partridge, welcoming me to his hall with tears almost trickling from his eyes'. Morton attempted to speak but found it difficult. The aged seventeenth earl, who was in failing health, died the following year.

Audubon was most impressed by the luxury of all he saw. Paintings by Rembrandt, Claude Lorrain, Van Dyke and Titian adorned the walls. His bedroom had a lighted fire. He found his clothes unpacked and his night apparel warming. The bed was large enough for four of his size; and there was a sofa at the foot and large arm-chairs on each side of the fire. Leading off his room was a neat little closet. 'It was a bathing room. Large porcelain tables, jars of water, dry-ing linens, and all else wanted, lay about …. Beau-tifully contrived. I saw but touched nothing. I was clean enough.' At dinner the waiters were powdered and dressed in rich red clothes, except one who was dressed in black and who gave plates with a neat napkin without touching them. The meal ended and the ladies departed with the earl, who was wheeled off leaving the male guests to talk and drink wine. At 10pm they rejoined the countess and looked at old signatures of kings, and ancient coins. After midnight the men were again left to their madeira and cakes. 'What a life – oh my Lucy I could not stand this! I prefer my primitive woods after all.'

The following day he explored the grounds and met the 'Great Falconer' John Anderson, who displayed the 'falcons ready for the chase perched on his gloved hand, with bells, – and hood and crest flowing'.

Audubon gave the countess a drawing lesson. She promised a subscription for his engravings (but did not maintain her payments for the complete set). He returned home that afternoon in the coach.

On New Year's Eve he went to dinner again with Captain Hall. Among the guests were Francis Jeffrey, editor of the *Edinburgh Review*, and his

wife. Audubon had been displeased with Jeffrey, who had not responded to a letter of introduction, nor to a note from Audubon and an invitation to attend his exhibition. Meeting him in person did not improve Audubon's impression:

> His looks were shrewd, but I thought much cunning resides over the eyes cast about. And the man talked so abundantly that I did not like him at all …. His American wife was dressy and had a twitch of a nervous nature that, joined to her uncommon share of *plainness* … rendered her not extremely interesting …. Thou must know that this gentleman has used me rather cavalierly.[19]

Francis Jeffrey, from Crombie's *Modern Athenians*.

This poor opinion of Jeffrey was shared by the family of John Wilson. Mrs Wilson described him as a 'horrid little man'.

Jeffrey was of small stature: his friend Sydney Smith said of him that 'he hasn't enough body to cover his mind decently with; his intellect is indecently exposed'. Lockhart likened him to Napoleon, both having '*mens magna in corpore parvo*' ('a large brain in a small body'). He described Jeffrey's speech as 'a mixture of provincial English, with undignified Scotch, altogether snappish and offensive … but the flow of eloquence is so overpoweringly rapid, so unweariedly energetic … that continual effort … is required, in order to make the understanding …'.

Audubon left the dinner early and walked home briskly.

> This was the eve of a new year, and in Edinburgh it is rather a dangerous thing to be late in the streets, for vagabonds are want to commit many errors at this time. Murders and other sinful acts take place. To prevent these, the watch is doubled ….

His caution was justified. Only 15 years earlier, Edinburgh had been disgraced by the Hogmanay riots:

> After eleven o'clock at night the principal streets were taken possession of by bands of rough young men and boys from the lower part of the town. Armed with bludgeons they assaulted and for a time overcame the police. They also knocked

down and robbed of their money, watches and hats, respectable inhabitants.[20]

Two people died in the riots and three youths, all under 18, were arrested and found guilty of murder. A great concourse of people came to witness their execution in the High Street. Audubon was spared such excitement and saw the New Year in with a glass of toddy in the company of Mrs Dickie and a fellow lodger.

Having completed his 1826 journal Audubon sent it off to Lucy, for whom it had been intended. He had kept journals for many years but the majority were burnt in the warehouse fire of 1845 in which many of his engraved copper plates were also destroyed. Only three journals survive intact, for the years 1820, 1826 and 1840. Many of the quotations in this chapter have been taken from *The 1826 Journal of John James Audubon*, transcribed and annotated by Alice Ford (1987), which is a complete and accurate reproduction of Audubon's text. Lacking his subsequent journals, the details of Audubon's remaining visits to Edinburgh are inevitably more sketchy and incomplete, although Lucy Audubon's *Life of John James Audubon* (1868), granddaughter Maria R Audubon's *Audubon and his Journals* (1897), and Robert Buchanan's *Life and Adventures of John James Audubon* (1868) give abridged and sanitised versions of some of his missing journals which, together with his voluminous surviving correspondence, fill some of the gaps.

The start of 1827 found Audubon completing 'Pheasants Attacked by a Fox', the largest painting he had ever undertaken, but with difficulty due to poor lighting. 'Sometimes I like the picture, then a heat rises to my face and I think it a miserable daub.' Visitors continued to call regularly to see his paintings. He paid another overnight visit to the Mortons at Dalmahoy, delivered a lecture on alligators to the Wernerian Society, and visited the theatre, which he enjoyed. At another visit to the Phrenology Society, 'the deepest philosophers in this city of learning were there, and George Combe read an essay on the mental powers of man, as illustrated by phrenological researches, that astounded me … and will remain in my mind all my life'.

At this time Sir William Jardine invited Audubon to stay at Jardine Hall in Dumfriesshire.

Sketch of Sir William Jardine by his brother-in-law William Home Lizars. (Scottish National Portrait Gallery)

He replied:

> I most sincerely hope that you neither will be offended or much disappointed at my not having answered your letter sooner … but you must know that an Oil painting when begun is with me like the red hot Iron of the Smith lying on the Anvil, if it is not wrought while hot and at once, the spirit of the moment is Lost as well as the time and frequently both the Iron and the Painting are put aside and sometimes forever. My pheasants are now all dismay and one poor one positively in the Hungry Jaws of a Cunning Fox, the whole will be finished by tomorrow week … after that I assure you I will be your obedient servant and will spend a full week with you of enjoyment & relaxation ….

In the event, Audubon never found the opportunity to visit Jardine Hall, despite further invitations. January the 22nd was a great day:

> I was painting diligently when Captain Hall came in, and said: 'put on your coat, and come with me to Sir Walter Scott; he wishes to see you *now* ….' In a moment I was ready, for I really believe my coat and hat came to me instead of my going to them. My heart trembled; I longed for the meeting, yet wished it over. Had not his wondrous pen penetrated

my soul with the consciousness that here was a genius from God's hand? I felt over-whelmed at the thought of meeting Sir Walter, the Great Unknown. We reached the house[21] .... Captain Hall said: 'Sir Walter, I have brought Mr Audubon' Sir Walter ... pressed my hand warmly and said he was 'glad to have the honor of meeting me.' His long, loose, silvery locks struck me .... I could not forbear looking at him, my eyes feasted on his counte-nance. I watched his movements as I would those of a celestial being; his long, heavy, white eyebrows struck me forcibly .... He was wrapped in a quilted morning-gown of light purple silk; he had been at work writing on the 'Life of Napoleon'.[22]

Scott's daughter was brought in and there was much conversation. 'I talked little, but believe me, I listened and observed ....'

Scott recorded the visit in his journal:

Jan 22, 1827. A visit from Basil Hall with Mr Audubon the ornithologist, who has followed that pursuit by many a long wandering in the American forests. He is an American by nat-uralization, a Frenchman by birth, but less of a Frenchman than I have ever seen, – no dash, no glimmer or shine about him, but great simplicity of manners and behaviour; slight in person and plainly dressed; wears long hair which time has not yet tinged; his countenance acute, handsome and interesting, but still simplicity is the predominant charac-teristic.[23]

Thus was achieved one of Audubon's great ambitions and one of his reasons for coming to Edinburgh. He had been disappointed by his previous efforts to meet the great man but there were good reasons for Scott's remoteness and in-accessibility. His wife had just died and he was writing feverishly to try to pay off business debts. During 1826/7 Scott published his nine-volume *Life of Napoleon*, and was working on *The Fair Maid of Perth* and his *History of Scotland*, among a number of lesser works. His productivity was prodigious.

Scott had not visited Audubon's exhibition but had enjoyed a private viewing two days after their first meeting. In his journal of 24 January Scott noted:

Visit from Mr Audubon, who brings some of his birds. The drawings are of the first order – attitudes of the birds of the most animated character, and the situations appropriate .... This sojourner in the desert has been in the woods for months together. He preferred associating with the Indians to the company of the Back Settlers, very justly, I daresay, for a civilized man of the lower order – that is, the dregs of civilization – when thrust back on the savage state become worse than a savage ....

Audubon must have been embellishing his woodsman's image again!

Audubon was to meet Scott again at an exhi-bition at the Royal Institution for the Encourage-ment of Fine Arts, where Audubon was showing his latest painting of 'Black Cocks'. At this exhibition the two men chatted and Scott pointed out Edwin Landseer's[24] picture of the dying stag, saying, 'many such scenes, Mr Audubon, have I witnessed in my younger days'. Audubon was not impressed with the painting:

I saw much in it of the style of those men who know how to handle a brush and carry a good effect; but Nature was not there, although a Stag, three dogs, and a Highlander were intro-duced on the canves. The Stag had his tongue out and mouth shut! The principal dog, a greyhound, held the Deer by one ear just as if a loving friend; the young hunter has laced the Deer by one horn very prettily, and in the attitude of a ballet-dancer was about to cast the noose over the head of the animal.[25]

Two years later Audubon was to meet Landseer by chance during a visit to Paris and spent some time in his company. In 1833 he was more favourably impressed by Landseer's etchings of quadrupeds: 'The style is beautiful.'

Audubon tended to be critical of other painters who impinged on his territory. While in Edinburgh he saw a painting by the great Dutch painter of birds and animals, Melchior D'Hondecoeter (1636-95). 'It was destitute of *life*, the animals seemed to me to be drawn from poorly stuffed specimens, but the coloring, the finish, the manner, the effect, was most beautiful .... Would that I could *paint* like Hondekeoter!' In fact, D'Hondecoeter's vivid portrayal of birds in action anticipated Audubon's style.

On 5 February 1827 Audubon was invited by Dr Brewster to exhibit his plates at the Royal Society of Edinburgh.

Captain Hall came and took my hand and led me to a seat immediately opposite to Sir Walter Scott, the President, where I had a perfect view of this great man, and studied nature from nature's noblest work …. Sir Walter came and shook hands with me, asked how the cold weather of Edinburgh agreed with me, and so attracted the attention of many members to me, as if I had been a distinguished stranger.[26]

Charles Darwin was taken by the geologist Leonard Horner (1785-1864) as a guest to a meeting of the Royal Society at about the same time, and experienced similar emotions to Audubon. Scott, the president, was in the chair:

I looked at him and at the whole scene with some awe and reverence, and I think it was owing to this visit in my youth … that I felt the honour of being elected a few years ago an honorary member … more than any other similar honour.[27]

Dr Brewster introduced Audubon to the camera lucida, which he was to use to great advantage when producing his octavo-sized edition of *The Birds of America* many years later. [The camera lucida was a recently discovered optical device utilising a four-sided prism which enabled the operator to view a scene or picture and draw the outline onto a different scale.]

On 23 February 1827 Audubon felt the need for exercise and, with a companion, 'proceeded towards the village of Portobello, distant three miles, the weather delightful, the shore dotted with gentlemen on horseback galloping over the sand …. The sea calm and smooth, had many fishing-boats. The village is a summer resort, built handsomely of white stone ….' From there they proceeded across country to Duddingston to see the skaters, but there were none, the ice being too thin.

They then climbed Arthur's Seat and returned to Audubon's lodgings via the Old Town and the North Bridge. 'I was quite tired, and yet I had not walked more than ten miles. I thought this strange, and wondered if it could

be the same body that travelled over 165 miles in four days without a shade of fatigue.'

The following day Audubon read his paper on rattlesnakes to the Wernerian Society. This paper was to cause such a furore that a full account of it and the reaction to it is given in Chapter 11.

At this time Captain Hall and his wife Margaret, who had opened so many doors for Audubon, left for a 14-month tour of America with their 15 month-old daughter. Audubon had given them a great deal of information and helped them to plan their journey. Both Hall and Margaret left extensive accounts of their travels, during which they visited Henderson: '… a village in Kentucky, where our friend Audubon built Steam Mills. The Mills still stood but are no longer used …. It was a bad speculation, as I should suppose anything he undertook in the way of business would probably prove.'[28] They visited relatives of Audubon's wife Lucy, including her sister Eliza and brother-in-law Nicholas Berthoud who lived at Shippingport on the Ohio River. The Halls had been accustomed to an elegant lifestyle: Margaret had spent her childhood in the glittering society of the diplomatic corps in Spain where her father was British Consul-General, and she in particular found it difficult to adapt to the culture of pioneering America – particularly the eating habits:

We dined … at Mr Berthoud's at the very inconvenient hour of two which cuts up the

Engraving of Landseer's painting 'Taking the Buck' by C Thomas (1875). The original painting was the one criticised by Audubon. It was sold at auction in 1930 but its present whereabouts is unknown. (The Royal Collection © 2003, Her Majesty Queen Elizabeth II)

day entirely. Only imagine having to begin to dress for dinner at one o'clock, for we had two miles to go to Mr Berthoud's .... The annoyance of beginning the engagements of Society at so early an hour is by no means counterbalanced by the subsequent early period of returning home from dinner. I, at least, for one feel so completely tired by the result of dressing, driving, talking and making company during the hottest part of the day that when I get home at seven o'clock I am fit for nothing but going to bed. I wish the people would grow a little more civilised ....[28]

Hall, a more seasoned traveller, was more objective in his assessment and illustrated his account with drawings done with the camera lucida technique (see p. 18).

Audubon was again in one of his moods of deep depression. 'The wind blows a doleful tune and I feel utterly alone.' Uncharacteristically he lost his enthusiasm for work. His spirits were lifted, however, by meeting Joseph Bartholomew Kidd (1808-89),[†] a 'promising young artist in landscape, only nineteen .... I was charmed with his talents, and thought what a difference it would have made in my life if I had begun painting in oil at his age and with his ability .... I invited him to come to my rooms daily, and to eat and drink with me, and give me the pleasure of his

company and the advantage of his taste in painting.'[29] And so began a long association which was to prove not entirely harmonious.

Audubon invited Kidd to return to America with him in 1829, but Kidd declined. Audubon was aware that he had limited ability for landscape painting, which he regretted, for he recognised 'that as time flies Nature loses its primitiveness, and that pictures drawn in ten, or twenty, or more years, will no longer illustrate our delightful America pure from the hands of its Creator'.[30] This was a theme which preoccupied Audubon. 'Hundreds of times have I said quite aloud, "Oh Walter Scott, where art thou? Wilt thou not come to my country? Wrestle with mankind and stop their increasing ravages on Nature, and describe her now for the sake of future ages .... Without thee, Walter Scott, she must die, unknown to the world."'[31] In fact, Audubon's extravagant regard for Scott, uncharacteristically, belittled his own contributions. Through his paintings and writings he has left a lasting vivid depiction of the America of his day.

In a letter of 1 March 1827 Audubon recorded that he had visited Holyrood Palace with Scott and saw 'the little room where the murder was committed – it is verry curious.[32]'

Audubon was not a regular churchgoer: 'In my mind church attendance has been confounded with such rascally conduct otherwise that I cannot think of it without sadness.'[33] On 4 March, however, he overcame his scruples in order to hear the celebrated preacher Sydney Smith. Edinburgh was in the midst of a severe snowstorm, all roads were blocked and the drifts reached as high as the top of the stagecoaches. *The Scotsman* reported that the churches were comparatively deserted, and few people were visible out of doors – indeed the avalanches falling from the roofs rendered it perilous to venture abroad. It was the worst weather Audubon had seen for 20 years, and he decided to be conveyed for the first time in his life by sedan chair through the snow, which lay six feet deep in places: '... never will I again enter one of these machines, with their quick, short, up-and-down swinging motion, resembling the sensations felt during the great earthquake in Kentucky.' He found the sermon inspiring:

Oh! what a soul there must be in the body of that great man .... He made me smile, and he make me think deeply. He pleased me at times by painting my foibles with due care, and again I felt the color come to my cheeks as he portrayed my sins. I left the church full of veneration not only towards God, but towards the wonderful man who so beautifully illustrates his noblest handiwork.[34]

Later Audubon met Sydney Smith and his daughters socially, and he received a letter from him written in such a large hand 'that he would destroy more paper in day than Franklin in week'. The hectic rounds continued, sometimes agreeable and sometimes unwelcome. Audubon wrote to Lucy: 'I am engaged daily to some party or other, to dine, or to sup or to a dance or a Concert, this is a most gay City I assure Thee.' Sometimes the hospitality was overwhelming; dinner at Sir James Riddell's was particularly unpleasant:

> The *ton* here surpassed that at the Earl of Morton's; *five gentlemen* waited on us while at table, and two of these put my cloak about my shoulders, notwithstanding all I could say to the contrary …. Oh! my America, how dearly I love thy plain, simple manners.[35]

From his journals and letters it is possible to identify many of the buildings and houses which Audubon visited in and around Edinburgh. Many of these remain to this day virtually unchanged since Audubon's time. Some of these are listed in Appendix 4.

On 17 March Audubon walked to the village of Roslin, eight miles south of Edinburgh. The Gothic chapel[36] was ' … a superb relic; each stone is beautifully carved, and each differs from all the others. The ten pillars and five arches are covered with the finest fret-work, and all round are seen the pedestals that once supported the images that Knox's party were wont to destroy without thought or reason.' [This is a reference to John Knox, the militant Protestant reformer of the sixteenth century; not to be confused with Dr Robert Knox, the anatomist.] Audubon then visited the adjacent ruined Roslin Castle before walking briskly back to Edinburgh at 'six miles an hour'.

On 19 March Audubon made a great sacrifice on the advice of Captain Hall and the Countess of Morton, who told him that he should have his

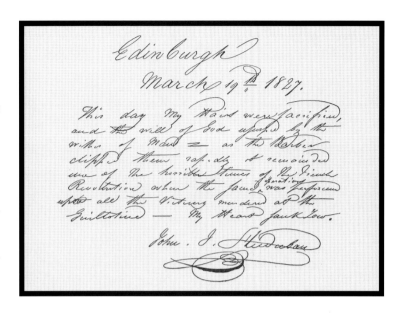

Audubon's journal entry mourning the loss of his crowning glory.

unfashionable long hair, in which he took such pride, shorn before he travelled to London. In his journal, surrounded by a black margin, he wrote:

> This day my hair was sacrificed, and the will of God usurped by the wishes of man. As the barber clipped my locks rapidly, it reminded me of the horrible times of the French Revolution when the same operation was performed upon all the victims murdered at the guillotine; my heart sank low.[37]

On 21 March Audubon visited one of his subscribers:

> Called on Miss D—, the fair American. To my surprise I saw the prints she had received the evening before quite abused and tumbled. This, however, was not my concern, and I regretted it only on her account, that so little care should be taken of a book that in fifty years will be sold at immense prices because of its rarity.[38]

It is interesting that Audubon appreciated at that early stage the potential value of his work. In 2000 a set was sold for $8.8 million (£5.04 million), a world record for any publication.

Before leaving Edinburgh Audubon visited the castle:

> We passed a place called the 'Mound',[39] a thrown up mass of earth connecting now the

Roslin Castle, from Swarbrick's *Sketches in Scotland*.

Right: Interior of Roslin Chapel showing the 'Apprentice Pillar', from Swarbrick's *Sketches in Scotland*.

New with the Old city of Edinburgh. We soon reached the gates … and I perceived … that I was looked upon as an officer from the continent. Strange! three days ago I was taken for a priest, quick transition caused only by the clipping of my locks. We ascended … until we reached the parapets …. The ocean was rugged with agitated waves as far as the eye could reach eastwardly; not a vessel dared spread its sails, so furious was the gale.

My eyes followed the line of the horizon and stopped at a couple of small elevations, that I knew to be the home of the Countess of Morton; then I turned to the immense city below, where men looked like tiny dwarfs, and horses smaller than sheep.

They then went to see the royal regalia of Scotland:

We each wrote our names, paid our shilling, and the … padlock was opened by a red-faced bulky personage dressed in fanciful scarlet cloth …. A high railing of iron surrounded a table … on which lay an immense sword … two sceptres … and above all the crown of Scotland. All the due explanations were cried out by our conductor, on whose face the reflection of all the red articles was so powerfully displayed … that it looked like a large tomato ….[40]

His last letter to Lucy from Edinburgh was on 24 March 1827:[41]

My Beloved friend

I have little to say that has happened since my last of the 11th Instant, I was in hopes daily to hear from thee. Nothing has yet arrived of thy shipping and I should not wonder if they never do. For upwards of a month we have had nothing else but tremendous storms constantly: a great number of shipwrecks are noticed in the different papers, many lives have been lost both at Sea and on Land in the snows that have been so deep as to put a stop to all communication south of Scotland.

I intended leaving this more than ten days ago but found it impossible. I will however do so now shortly. A few days since I received a most valuable letter of introduction to the Secretary of the King for the home department Mr Peel, from Lord Meadowbank, the Lord Advocate of Scotland. This letter was given me at the particular request of the Countess of Morton, a most amiable charming Lady; it would have come direct from her husband the Earl of M. but his low state of health prevents his writing …. I have great number of letters for London and some hopes to succeed there in augmenting my list of

Subscribers sufficiently to enable me to write to thee, Lucy my Love come to me. Oh my dear Wife how I pray God and hope that this may soon come! …

I will leave Edinburgh with regret, my time has been pleasantly and usefully spent here I think altho I will leave it really no richer of Cash then I have entered it, so enormous are the expenses of the fashionable City where I really believe that as well as in America every person live perhaps rather above their income ….

My prospectus will show thee the different Societies of which I am now a Fellow or a Member. [The Royal Society of Edinburgh, Wernerian Society and the Scottish Academy] I do not lose the hope of being presented to the King of England shortly after I have formed the personal acquaintance of Mr Peel, Sir Thomas Lawrence, Mr Gallatin and others – Capn Hall whose works I also send thee has been unremittingly kind to me and has given me 20 letters all valuable introductions …. I am engaged daily to some party or other, to dine, or to sup or to a dance or a Concert. this is a most gay City I assure thee …. I do not think I will write again from this place. Yesterday I saw the Crown and sceptre of Queen Mary – 430 years old.[42]

Audubon had written to Sir Walter Scott shortly before his departure from Edinburgh: 'I feel an ardent desire to be honoured by being the bearer of a few lines from you own hand to whoever you may please to introduce me.' Scott declined with typical courtesy:

Dear Mr Audubon,

I am sure you will find many persons better qualified than myself to give you a passport to foreign countries, since circumstances have prevented our oftener meeting, and my ignorance does not permit me to say anything on the branches of natural history of which you are so well possessed. But I can easily and truly say, that what I have had the pleasure of seeing, touching your talents and manners, corresponds with all I have heard in your favour; and that I am a sincere believer in the extent of your scientific attainments, though I have not the knowledge necessary

to form an accurate judgement of the subject. I sincerely wish much your travels may prove agreeable.[43]

Audubon departed from Edinburgh for London on 5 April 1827, having left many of his effects with Mrs Dickie as he planned to return. The account of this return visit is given in Chapter 10, but before continuing with the story of Audubon in Edinburgh, let us digress to consider in more detail Professor Jameson and his assistant William MacGillivray, who were to play important roles in furthering Audubon's publications and helping to establish his reputation as an ornithologist.

Above, top: Edinburgh Castle, from Shepherd's *Modern Athens*.

Above: The regalia of Scotland, from Grant's *Old and New Edinburgh*.

Notes

1   *The 1826 Journal of John James Audubon*, p. 344. The 'friend' was Augustin Bourgeat, who assisted Audubon in obtaining specimens.

2   Ibid, p. 353.

3   Ibid, p. 403.

4   Audubon, M R: *Audubon and his Journals*, vol. I, p. 205. Harvard University Museum of Comparative Zoology possesses another life mask of Audubon which at one time was in the possession of Robert Havell.

5   Combe, G: *Phrenology Journal* (1827), 13: 295-302.

6   *Journal of Henry Cockburn*, vol. I, p. 74.

7   *The 1826 Journal*, pp. 364-5.

8   Henry Witham (1779-1844) was born Henry Thomas Silvertop, but adopted his wife's surname. He was a member of the Wernerian Society and was one of the four Edinburgh subscribers to *The Birds of America* who completed their sets. His folio was sold by a descendant in 1951 for £7000. Witham was elected a Fellow of the Royal Society of Edinburgh on the same day as Audubon and later proposed William MacGillivray for fellowship in 1834. When Witham in his mature years 'grew too fat for fox-hunting', he became interested in geology. MacGillivray had helped him with his publication *Observations on Fossil Vegetables* (1831) by writing the descriptions and drawing the microscopic sections.

9   *The 1826 Journal*, p. 371.

10   Ibid, p. 382.

11   Ibid, pp. 380-6.

12   This refers to an incident which occurred during 1823. Lucy had obtained a position as a teacher in a plantation called Beech Woods belonging to a widow, Jane Percy, near St Francisville, Louisiana. There she remained for five years, earning sufficient money to support herself and her husband while he was occupied in his ornithological pursuits. From time to time Audubon joined Lucy at Beech Woods but fell out with Mrs Percy over paintings which he did of her daughters which were rejected by Mrs Percy. He reacted in a manner which led to his being banned from the plantation. Three days later he returned at night, but was found by Mrs Percy in bed with Lucy and once more ejected. Lucy was still living at Beech Woods when he wrote this letter.

13   *The 1826 Journal*, p. 396.

14   *Edinburgh Journal of Science*, (1828), 8: 48-54.

15   Letter from J B Kidd to Audubon, 22 Nov 1832, cited in *The 1826 Journal*, p. 398.

16   *Blackwood's Magazine* (1830), 30: 1-16.

17   *The 1826 Journal*, pp. 400-1.

18   Ibid, pp. 417-24.

19   Ibid, pp. 425-6.

20   Gilbert, W M: *Edinburgh in the nineteenth century*, pp. 54-5 (1901).

21   Scott was then living in rented accommodation in 3 Walker Street. His beloved town house at 39 Castle Street, which had been his home for 25 years, had been sold in 1826 to help pay his debts.

22   Audubon, M R: *Audubon and his Journals*, vol. I, pp. 206-7.

23   *Journal of Sir Walter Scott*, entry for 24 January 1827, pp. 308-9.

24   Sir Edwin Henry Landseer (1802-73) was celebrated for his animal paintings, often depicting his subjects in aggressive attitudes, much as Audubon liked to do. His painting 'Taking the Buck', which Audubon saw, was painted in 1825 and was his first of many Highland scenes. It was originally exhibited at the Royal Academy in the same year. An anonymous reviewer in the *Examiner* described it as ' … that rarest of all graphic works, an approximation to perfection'. Subsequent commentators, however, agreed with Audubon that it was not very good.

25   *Audubon and his Journals*, vol. I, pp. 210-11.

26   Ibid, pp. 209-10.

27   *The Life and Letters of Charles Darwin*, vol. I, p. 40.

28   Pope-Hennessey, U (ed.): *The Aristocratic Journey*, pp. 265 and 269-70.

29   Buchanan, R: *The Life and Adventures of John James Audubon*, p. 120.

30   *Edinburgh Journal of Science* (1828), 8: 54.

31   *The 1826 Journal*, pp. 388-9.

32   This refers to the murder of David Riccio, secretary to Mary, Queen of Scots, by her jealous husband Lord Darnley in 1566.

33   Buchanan, R: op. cit., p. 95.

34   Audubon, M R: op. cit., p. 215. Audubon was not the only one to be moved by Sydney Smith's preaching. Henry Cockburn, in his *Journal*, vol. II, pp. 244-5, wrote: ' … I doubt if there were a dozen dry eyes or unpalpitating hearts in the church; and every sentiment, and many of the expressions, and the whole scope and pathos of the discourse, are still fresh upon my mind at the distance of many years.'

35   Ibid, p. 218.

36   Roslin Castle and Roslin Chapel were built in the fifteenth century by the St Clair family. The stone carving in the chapel is exceptionally fine. Legend has it that the exquisitely carved pillar shown on the left in the illustration on p. 66

was done by an apprentice during his master's absence. On his return the master is said to have been so jealous of the superior craftmanship of his apprentice that he murdered him in a fit of rage. Roslin Chapel is a jewel of Gothic architecture much admired by the writers Robert Burns, William Wordsworth and Walter Scott, and painted by many artists including William Delacour, Samuel Bough, John Ruskin, Alexander Nasmyth, David Roberts and Louis Daguerre. It remains today a popular tourist attraction.

37   Audubon, M R: op. cit., p. 221.

38   Ibid, p. 222. 'Miss D—' was Harriet Douglas of New York, Audubon's first American subscriber, who was visiting Edinburgh with her brothers to wind up an uncle's estate. She had met Audubon at a party given by Professor Jameson.

39   The 'Earthen Mound' was created over a period of 50 years from the soil removed from the foundations and basements of the New Town houses. Two million cartloads of soil went into its construction. It made a convenient gradient between the Old Town and the New. The Royal Institution had just been built at the foot of the Mound when Audubon arrived in Edinburgh. Later the National Gallery of Scotland was built behind it.

40   Audubon, M R: op. cit., p. 224.

41   *Letters of J J Audubon 1826-1840*, pp. 17-19.

42   The regalia of Scottish royalty had disappeared after the Act of Union in 1707 and were thought to have been seized by the English. In 1817, however, they were discovered in a room in the castle in which they had been locked by royal decree a century earlier. They have since been displayed to public view.

43   Buchanan, R: op. cit., p. 123.

7 | Robert Jameson and the Edinburgh University Museum

Bust of Robert Jameson by Sir John Steell, now in Edinburgh University Upper Library. The bust was paid for by the members of the Wernerian Society, 'which he had laboured so devotedly and successfully to render worthy of the University and of the Metropolis of Scotland'.

Below: A drawing by Charles Bell, from his *Anatomy of Expression*.

THE name of Robert Jameson (1774-1854), doyen of natural history in Edinburgh, keeps recurring in the story of Audubon in Edinburgh. He was born in Leith, the son of a prosperous soap manufacturer, and went on to attend the High School, but showed no particular love of letters there and was a frequent truant. An interest in natural history and exploration was aroused in his early teens by reading an account of Captain Cook's voyages, *Robinson Crusoe*, and *A Description of Three Hundred Animals* by Thomas Boreman,[1] which he later said inspired him to become a professor of natural history.

However, Jameson entered the University of Edinburgh at the age of 14 still undecided about his future. He first studied classics but soon changed to medicine, while John Walker (1734-1804),[†] the professor of natural history, reinforced Jameson's interest in this subject.

Jameson briefly practised as an assistant to Dr Cheyne of Leith and is said to have been popular with the elderly female patients. He decided, however, that the benefits of therapy were largely psychological and abandoned medicine in favour of natural history.

Jameson's next few years were spent in a manner which anticipated William MacGillivray's activities of 20 years later. He made a visit to the British Museum in London and travelled extensively throughout Scotland, making a particular study of geology (then considered a part of natural history). In the course of these travels he walked long distances, often in the company of Charles Bell (1774-1842),[†] a fellow medical student. Bell went on to become a distinguished professor of surgery and an excellent artist; while Jameson published several articles and a major book based on these travels, which established his reputation as a mineralogist.

In 1800 Jameson went to Freiberg in Saxony to study under Abraham Gottlob Werner (1750-1817), a highly regarded professor of mineralogy.

Far left: James Hutton, from John Kay *A Series of Original Portraits* (1837). The rock face shows the silhouette of three of his critics.

Left: Cartoon of Robert Jameson by Edward Forbes, from *The University Maga* volume XI, 1836. The legend reads: 'The weather-beaten but intellectual countenance of our worthy Professor of natural History, at present one of the chief lights and attractions of our University; celebrated as the first minerologist of Europe ....'

He spent two years under Werner's tutelage and was required, as were all of Werner's pupils, to gain practical experience by working in the mines. Werner, who believed in the biblical chronology of the development of the Earth, was an inspiring teacher with firm beliefs in the mechanism of rock formation, which he held to be largely the result of aquatic influences. This contradicted the theory of the Scottish geologist James Hutton (1726-97),[†] who believed in a constantly changing and continuing development of the world and considered rock formation to be principally determined by thermal forces. Hutton incurred the wrath of the established Church for his evolutionary theory, just as Darwin did at a later date.

Jameson returned to Edinburgh in 1802 totally committed to Werner's views. He discounted Hutton's theories because he thought they 'would give an age to the world quite inconsistent with the Hebrew chronology .... I am fully persuaded that any chain of reasoning that does not coincide with that chronology is false.'[2]

The conflicting theories of Hutton and Werner were the subject of a prolonged and heated debate: the Plutonists versus the Neptunists.[3] Jameson published a three-volume *System of Mineralogy* in 1804, in which he endorsed Werner's theories with such conviction that a reviewer in the *Edinburgh Review* wrote, 'no

devotee ever more zealously maintained the infallibility of the Pope, than Mr Jameson has done that of his master'. Jameson founded the Wernerian Natural History Society in honour of his mentor in 1808 and it was held in a high esteem (see Chapter 9).

Towards the end of his life, however, Jameson recanted and acknowledged the greater validity of Hutton's views at a meeting of the Royal Society of Edinburgh, 'with perfect candour and the love of truth'. This must have been a difficult admission for one who had spent almost his entire working life opposing Huttonian views. Werner is now almost forgotten now, whereas Hutton is recognised as one of the founding fathers of the science of geology.

In 1804 Jameson succeeded John Walker as regius professor of natural history at Edinburgh University, at a salary of £70 per annum. He was to occupy the chair for 50 years.

Jameson was a domineering figure who exerted considerable influence without being universally popular. Audubon, when he was finally granted audience with the great man, noted:

The professor's appearance is remarkable and the oddities of his hair are worthy of notice. It seems to stand up all over his head and points in various directions so that it looks strange and uncouth. Around a rough

Above: Cartoon of Alexander Monro III by Edward Forbes , from *The University Maga* volume VI, 1835. The legend reads: 'Behold … our good friend, ANATOMY, enjoying himself over a basin of Mock Turtle at Old Broadbrim's. See the epicureanism of his countenance, clouded only by the melancholy thought, that his breeches' pockets must be unbuttoned, to pay for the soup!'

Right: Alexander Monro III, from Crombie's *Modern Athenians*.

exterior he owns a generous heart, but which is not at first discernible.[4]

Charles Darwin, a medical student in Edinburgh for two years from 1825, attended Jameson's lectures on geology and zoology but found them '… incredibly dull. The whole effect they produced on me was the determination never to read a book on Geology or in any way to study this science.'[5] It is interesting, however, that one of the lectures was entitled 'On the origin of species of animals'.

Darwin's criticisms were not restricted to Jameson. In a letter to his sister Caroline, dated 6 January 1826, he refers to 'a long stupid lecture from Duncan [Andrew Duncan Jr][6] on materia medica …. Dr Duncan is so very learned that his wisdom has left no room for his sense'. Darwin wrote that his lecture 'cannot be translated into any word expressive enough of its stupidity'.

He also attended lectures given by Andrew Duncan Sr: '… what an extraordinary old man he is, now being past 80 and continuing to lecture.' Duncan Sr invited the young Charles to dinners, which he found dull occasions. (Duncan Sr had befriended Darwin's uncle, also Charles Darwin, when a medical student in Edinburgh in 1775-8.[7]) As for Alexander Monro tertius on anatomy, Darwin wrote: 'I dislike him and his lectures so much that I cannot speak with decency about them. He is so dirty in person and actions.'[8]

On the other hand, Darwin liked John Lizars, 'a charming lecturer' whose extra-mural talks on anatomy he much preferred to those of Monro. He also liked Dr Thomas Hope and his lectures very much. Hope, professor of chemistry, was exceedingly popular – more than 500 students attended his lecture/demonstrations during Darwin's time.

John Lizars, a surgeon, was the brother of William Home Lizars, and shared with his brother a fine artistic talent. Together they published the *System of Anatomical Plates of the Human Body*, which raised anatomical drawing to an art form. Darwin also found a kindred spirit in William MacGillivray (see Chapter 8, p. 93).

An American visitor described Jameson as 'a stiff, ungainly, forbidding looking man, who gave us the most desperately dull, doleful lecture I ever heard'. Others were not so critical. Sir Robert Christison (1797-1882)[†] wrote that Jameson's lectures '… were numerously attended in spite of a dry manner … the popularity of his subject, his earnestness as a lecturer, his enthusiasm as an investigator, and the great museum he had collected for illustrating his teaching were together the causes of his success'.

George Wilson, author of the *Memoir of Edward Forbes* and, as regius professor of technology at Edinburgh University, a colleague of Jameson, wrote:

Jameson was a remarkable man. Grave, taciturn, and reserved in manner, devoted especially to Mineralogy, the narrowest in some respects of all the departments of the science he professed, he seemed much better fitted for the secluded life of a student than for the duties of a University chair. Nevertheless, there was in him a deep, quiet enthusiasm for his favourite science, which his ungeniality of nature could not prevent being contagious, and he became, what many of his brilliant colleagues failed to become, the founder of a School. The spectacle of his perseverance, earnestness, and life-long devotion to his work, overcame the effect of his taciturnity and reserve …. They formed only a tough rind to the man, like that of the pomegranate, which when pierced yields a pleasant juice, fragrant and sweet, though not without acidulous sharpness. Intercourse with him, accordingly, soon dispelled the notion that he was a man wrapped up in himself, happy only when fingering or scratching minerals. Side by side with some of the narrowest opinions, which he held and defended most obstinately, was a wide and intelligent sympathy with the progress of every department of physical science.[9]

Jameson's successor and former pupil, Edward Forbes, said in his inaugural address:

Who that in time past was his pupil … can ever forget his enthusiastic zeal, his affection for all … who manifested sincere interest in his favourite studies? When … their fates scattered them far and wide over the world … none who remained constant to the beautiful studies of his pupilhood was ever forgotten by the kind and wise philosopher …. The value of professorial worth should chiefly be estimated by the number and excellence

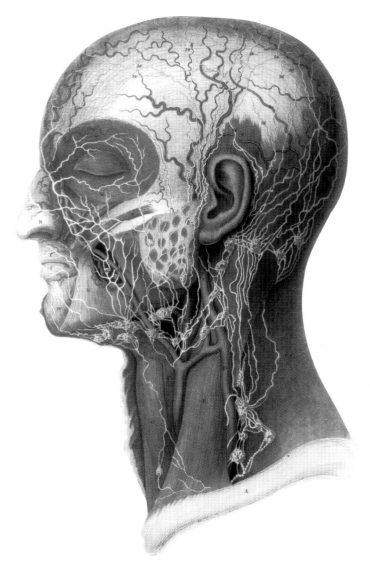

of disciples. A large share of the best naturalists of the day received their first instruction … from Professor Jameson …. The greatest praise of a great Professor is that which proclaims he has founded a School.[10]

Charles Darwin, writing to J D Hooker, remained unimpressed by Forbes eulogy: 'I wish … he would not praise so much that old brown dry stick Jameson.' Clearly Jameson generated very conflicting opinions, but despite the dullness of his lectures he seems to have had the ability to inspire others. His influence is apparent in the long list of his distinguished pupils – more than 40 of whom became successful physicians, explorers and scientists.

The Edinburgh University natural history museum, which was to become important in the lives of Audubon and MacGillivray, was certainly

Anatomical drawing of the lymphatic vessels of the head and neck, from *A System of Anatomical Plates of the Human Body* by John and William Lizars.

73

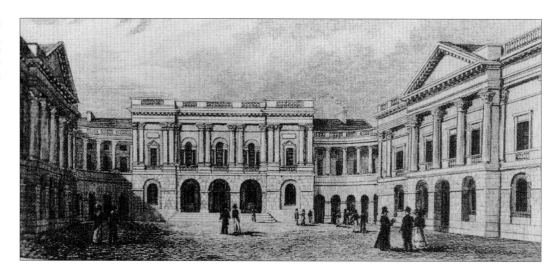

one of Jameson's greatest achievements. When he took office he found it in a state of great neglect and poorly housed. The existing museum had had a chequered history. Most collections up to that time were in private ownership and there were few public collections. The university had received two valuable bequests in the late seventeenth century, from Sir Andrew Balfour (1630-1694) and Sir Robert Sibbald (1641-1722), the founders of the Royal College of Physicians of Edinburgh and a Physick Garden. However, these specimens gradually disappeared or decayed except for the os penis of a whale (*Balaenoptera sibbaldi*) which is still preserved in the Royal Museum (now part of the National Museums of Scotland).

In the 1760s Principal Robertson, principal of the university from 1762–93, made efforts to re-establish a proper museum in association with a new chair of natural history. Jameson's predecessor John Walker had done his best, but lack of suitable accommodation and Walker's declining health in his latter years resulted once more in failure. When Jameson took over in 1804

> … the museum was so inconsiderable, that the whole of the articles were contained in a few cases. The specimens were of birds, serpents, minerals, and dresses and weapons of savage nations. The birds were in so decayed a state, that I was forced very soon to throw them out, and thus the original collection was reduced to a few glasses of serpents, a small collection of minerals, and the arms and dresses already mentioned.[11] Techniques of preservation of animal and plant specimens at that time were poorly developed, and despite

his best efforts and intentions Jameson encountered much difficulty in keeping his collection in good condition.

The rebuilding of the university was then under active consideration. The foundation stone of a new building had been laid in 1789, but the ambitious plan of Robert Adam proved too expensive and it had been abandoned. With the ending of the Napoleonic Wars, however, the interest in rebuilding was revived. William Henry Playfair won the competition for a revised plan and building was recommenced in 1817. Jameson insisted that the creation of a new museum should take priority over the other 'great public portions of the college', and such was his influence that this did indeed come about. The museum occupied two floors of the western side of the quadrangle of the new building (now the Old College of Edinburgh University) and was completed and furnished to a high specification, including a central heating system, by 1820.

Jameson worked tirelessly to accumulate specimens for his museum. A government grant of £100 towards it proved inadequate and Jameson used some of his own money to fund the collection. He did not even claim the honorarium of £50 to which he was entitled as regius keeper.

In 1819 two large collections of specimens were offered for sale to the university. William Bullock (1795-1840), a wealthy private collector, had spent £55,000 on his collection which was housed in London. It was offered to Jameson for £9000, which he was unable to raise, and so eventually the collection was broken up and sold at auction. Jameson authorised two of his ex-pupils to buy on his behalf, and £283 was spent on a number of specimens, including a baby African elephant which can still be seen in the Royal Museum[12] (see also Chapter 8, note 33).

The other collection offered to Jameson was was that of Louis Dufresne (1752-1832). Dufresne was employed as *aide-naturaliste* in the Musée Royale d'Histoire in Paris. He was a skilled taxidermist and head of the zoology laboratories. In 1785 he went as naturalist on La Perouse's expedition to the Pacific, Alaska and China. It is not known why he decided to offer his collection to Edinburgh, for he had received offers from the emperors of Russia and Austria. However, there were two families of Dufresne in Edinburgh at that time (possibly relations), and he knew that Edinburgh was building a fine new museum where his collection would be seen to advantage.

James Wilson of Woodville, a friend of Dufresne, was sent by the university to examine his collection. On his advice the Senatus authorised £3000 for the collection. Dufresne and his family personally carried out the packing and shipment to Le Havre. There was endless discussion about how it should be shipped, but eventually the Lord Provost persuaded the First Lord of the Admiralty to allow a naval vessel to be diverted to Le Havre. The vessel, the *Prince Ernest Augustus*, was so small that to accommodate the collection the crew were forced to sleep on deck and to store cables and sails there too, instead of in the usual lockers. When the ship arrived at Leith docks Jameson, assisted by James Wilson, personally supervised the unpacking. Of the original collection of 1640 birds, 12,000 insects, 4000 shells and 800 eggs and more, some items can still be identified in the collection of the Royal Museum, including rarities such as the Mauritius blue pigeon which became extinct in 1830, and an egg of the great auk, which became extinct in the 1840s.[13] Ornithological specimens from this collection were used by Audubon in his paintings.

Although the museum was intended primarily for teaching purposes, visitors were allowed on payment of an entry fee of two shillings and six-pence, which produced a useful source of income. In 1822, during the two-week visit of King George IV to Edinburgh, nearly 1000 visitors were recorded, including several members of his majesty's household, and during the open day to celebrate Queen Victoria's coronation in 1837 there were more than 20,000 visitors (see Chapter 14, p.172).

George Wilson, writing in the 1850s, noted:[14]

… the greatest proof of the broad view which Jameson took of the territory rightfully belonging to Natural History, is to be found in the Museum he collected at Edinburgh, where it remains a memorial of him …. I had known the Museum from boyhood, and would have been glad to have known so delightful a place a great deal better, but the charge of a shilling, which was then exacted for admission, was often beyond the holiday resources of a schoolboy's pocket …. The larger vertebrates, and especially the mammals, were well represented by stuffed specimens. Of stuffed birds there was a large and very fine collection; and in mineralogy, as might have been expected from the tastes of the Professor, the Museum was peculiarly rich. Of shells, there was a goodly show, and of insects there was understood to be a large collection, which was not usually displayed, as light is highly destructive to the specimens. Fishes and reptiles were represented, to some considerable extent …. and there was a highly interesting, though not very numerous assemblage, of the skulls of different nations, which, however, was not open to general inspection. Besides the objects enumerated, there was the usual array of miscellaneous varieties, – the tattooed head of a New Zealand chief, an Esquimaux canoe, a narwhal's horn, a brain coral, and much else … a large number of specimens … were unavoidably shut up in storerooms and cellars, from want of space to display them. The Museum, however, could not but be considered as tolerably ample in its dimensions.

The Custom House, Leith, from Shepherd's *Modern Athens*. Jameson and his assistant MacGillivray paid many visits to this building to collect imported specimens.

The lower hall was almost entirely occupied by large stuffed quadrupeds and other mammals. The upper hall was devoted to mineralogy, and in part to birds, to which also the greater part of the galleries was consigned ….

With all its defects it was a highly instructive Museum, and Jameson made excellent use of it in illustrating his lectures. It was too much, however, regarded by the Professor as an appendage to the lecture room. He resisted to the last throwing it open to the public and those who paid a fee for admission into its halls, did not find them so occupied, arranged and placarded as to make the Museum what if possible every museum should be, a self-interpreting, illustrated series of treatises on the various groups of objects it contains ….

In 1807 Jameson obtained Treasury permission to circulate Crown officers in all foreign dependencies of the British Empire, encouraging them to send suitable material, and they responded enthusiastically. It was a time of rapid expansion and numerous voyages of exploration were initiated by the Admiralty to

> … chart unknown seas, partly to survey little known shores, and partly to chart the plants and animals of distant seas and strange lands. And the University of Edinburgh was predominant in supplying from its former students in the Medical Faculty – pupils of Professor Jameson – the naturalists selected for these Government Expeditions.[15]

Jameson, himself a frustrated explorer, encouraged his ex-students to take part in these journeys and was rewarded with contributions from the expeditions of John Ross, James Clark Ross, W E Parry, Lord Byron, John Franklin, John Rae, Meredith Gairdner, John Richardson and Captain Fitzroy of the *Beagle*. William Scoresby (1789-1857)[†] had a particular admiration for Jameson and named a bay in Jan Mayen island after his mentor; and an area of West Greenland 'received the name of Jameson's Land in token of friendship to Professor Jameson the highly respected President of the Wernerian Society'. (Scoresby named geographical features of the Arctic region in honour of those whom

he admired, including many of the personae of this book such as Patrick Neill, Walter Scott, William Swainson, David Brewster and Thomas Stewart Traill.) Audubon used some of the contributions to the Edinburgh University Museum as subjects for paintings in his *Birds of America*.

Jameson successfully petitioned the Lords of the Treasury to allow goods from these voyages to be imported at Leith docks without payment of customs duty. There was an understanding that 'of those articles of Natural History brought home by expeditions fitted out at the public expense … one part of each collection is deposited in the British Museum, another part is sent down to the King's Museum in the University [of Edinburgh] '.

Among the items donated were the skins and skeletons of birds and animals, insects, geological specimens, fossils, artefacts such as weapons, clothing, coins, medals, models, manuscripts and archaeological finds, all meticulously documented by Jameson's assistant, William MacGillivray. All contributions were welcomed, except for the offer of an elephant and a live alligator! Typical offerings during 1821/2 included a Zeus Luna (kingfish) from the Earl of Wemyss, boxes of birds from New Holland donated by Lady Scott, basaltic columns from Staffa, assagays [*sic*] from Africa, the tusk of a mammoth, fragments of a Theban sepulchre, an ornithorynchus (duck-billed platypus) from New South Wales donated by Governor Sir Thomas Brisbane (1773-1860),[†] and furs from the North West Company from the Earl of Dalhousie. Other donors included Sir Stamford Raffles, the Marquis of Hastings, Viscount Melville, Lord Hume, Earl St Vincent, and many others of lesser fame. James Wilson was particularly generous in his donations of entomological specimens.

Occasionally live creatures were accepted, including a Persian sheep, a swan donated by Sir Walter Scott, and a rattlesnake which did not live long. William Scoresby sent a polar bear, which Jameson kept in a 'commodious den' in the university. A puma, a young female, was the gift of William John Napier, ninth Lord Napier and captain of the *Diamond* frigate, who brought it from South America with other animals. The puma had become quite tame and was reported to play well with dogs and monkeys, although it was less tolerant of goats and fowls while aboard ship. It was delivered to the museum on 8 January 1827. MacGillivray sought the advice of the keeper of a menagerie based at the Mound (see p. 78) regarding its care.

The puma appears to have been allowed considerable freedom in the museum and became quite a pet. Eventually, however, its playfulness appears to have become a nuisance. There is a suggestion in the Museum Day Book that James Wilson of Woodville was asked to assume responsibility for its care, but whether he did is not confirmed. Wilson kept many pets in his home and garden, including birds which were allowed free range of his study, so it is unlikely that he would have accepted the puma, which had retained its hunting instinct as far as birds were concerned. Wilson does, however, describe the puma in detail in his *Illustrations of Zoology*. He notes that it had 'extreme gentleness of disposition, manifesting all the elegant playfulness of the cat, without any of its alleged treachery. It rejoices greatly in the society of those to whose company it is accustomed, lies down upon its back between their feet and plays with the skirts of their garments …. When let loose, it exhibits the most extraordinary of feats of activity, springing about in a large lumber room ….'

On 27 June 1827 the puma was delivered to a private menagerie of Mr Pringle at the Haining near Selkirk, and its ultimate fate is not known.[16] No further live specimens were accepted after the puma, Jameson having recognised that the museum lacked suitable accommodation.

Another valuable source of specimens was the Royal Society of Edinburgh. The First Charter of the society had ordained that all natural history specimens submitted should be transferred to the University Museum. This arrangement was due in part to the society's lack of suitable accommodation at that time, but also to the influence of John Walker, Jameson's predecessor, who was a founder member of the society and who saw this as an opportunity for augmenting the museum. This arrangement continued into the Jameson era, until cancelled by the society's Second Charter in 1811.

It was as a result of this agreement that the University Museum fell heir to Hutton's collection of geological specimens, which had been donated after Hutton's death to the Royal Society. Jameson, the champion of Werner, abused his position as curator by refusing scientists access

Above, top: The Edinburgh University puma, from James Wilson's *Illustrations of Zoology*. Drawn and engraved by W H Lizars. (Courtesy of the Trustees of the National Library of Scotland)

Above: Lizars' engraving of the museum, showing the puma appearing under the display table and elsewhere. This plate was used by Jameson as his letter heading. (Edinburgh University Library, Special Collections, GEN 1996/2/14)

The menagerie at the Mound, depicted by Charles Halkerston. (City Art Centre: City of Edinburgh Museums and Galleries)

was denied access and complained at length to the commissioners about it,[18] as did Henry Hulme Cheek, an active member of the Plinian Society and erstwhile student of Jameson. Cheek also complained about the high entry charge which exceeded that of any other museum in the country.[19] He appears to have had an enormous chip on his shoulder regarding anything to do with Jameson, for he also publicly attacked the latter's running of the Wernerian Society (see Chapter 9, pp. 116–18).

Two shillings and sixpence at that time was the equivalent of several pounds today, and this fee was clearly a major factor in limiting access, particularly to students. Jameson, however, would not yield in his insistence that it should be paid. Only his own students and a few favoured friends were allowed free access. Even his friend and fellow editor David Brewster had to pay entrance money, although he maintained to the commission that in his opinion it should be open free of charge to individuals pursuing scientific research. Brewster, as representative of the Royal Society, was asked if he knew anything of Hutton's collection. He replied: 'I do. I believe that I am one of the curators of the collection, but I have never had access to it …. They have a great value as being the collection of Dr Hutton, and as illustrative of his curious speculations respecting the Theory of the Earth.'

Jameson's attitude to entry fees is understandable, in view of the fact that the running costs of the museum were £700 a year and his grant for this purpose was only £100. The entrance money brought in a further £500 and made a significant contribution to the total costs.

The commission reported with regard to the museum:

to this collection. At the height of the Huttonian/ Wernerian debate, a Royal Commission was appointed for 'enquiring into the state of the Universities and Colleges of Scotland'. They received complaints, notably from the Royal Society of Edinburgh, regarding Jameson's jealous guardianship. A petition to the commission, signed by the president of the Royal Society, Sir Walter Scott, commented that

> … the Keeper of the Museum, actuated by what motive your petitioners are unable to say, as he has not himself expressed it, thought proper to refuse to the members of the Royal Society admission to their own collection; and after fruitless … and unsatisfactory correspondence upon the subject, that refusal has been persisted in.

The commission repeatedly questioned Jameson regarding his management of the museum, and in particular his opinion that the contents were largely his own private possession, a position which he arrogantly maintained against all reasonable argument. The commissioners further discovered that Hutton's collection had never even been opened by Jameson: 'It was shown to the Commissioners in boxes.' Clearly Jameson treated the museum as if it had been created for his own purposes.[17] He was quite arbitrary in permitting or refusing access to the museum for the purpose of using specimens for illustration. MacGillivray, Selby, Jardine and Audubon, for example, were allowed free access (although both Audubon and MacGillivray later had this permission withdrawn). However, Captain Thomas Brown

> It is impossible to conclude this short detail … without particularly adverting to the ardent zeal, the unvaried efforts, the profound science, and the taste of Professor Jameson, whose name will be transmitted with this magnificent collection, and who will ever be regarded as one of the most successful cultivators and illustrious benefactors of the Science of Natural History.

It then proceeded to criticise and castigate Jameson over such matters as the entry charge for students, for 'granting or refusing permission to draw specimens according to the individual and the opinion and discretion of the Keeper', and for not regarding the museum as belonging to the university. It concluded that 'the whole arrangement is brought too much under the control of one individual, who acts according to his own opinion and discretion. In the present case, his private interests interfere with the management of a great public institution.' The commission ordained that all articles deposited in the museum should become property of the museum and that no professor should be allowed to reclaim any articles deposited there. The Senatus Academicus was directed to frame regulations for the admission of scientific individuals.

In the event, little changed. The entry fee was reduced to one shilling but this was the only concession – Jameson continued to run the museum in his own way. Hutton's priceless geological collection, upon which he had based his seminal *Theory of the Earth*, was still extant in part in 1835 but subsequently disappeared, probably as a result of neglect. Historically this must be regarded as the most valuable possession ever held by the museum, and its loss reflects badly on its curator.

Curiously, at the same time as complaints were being made regarding Jameson's custody of the museum, similar complaints were being directed at the British Museum in London. An ornithologist, Edward Blyth, complained to the trustees regarding the 'cool and ungracious, most repugnant, little less than harsh, demeanour, which I (in common with many others) ordinarily experience on the part of Mr George Gray'. John Children (1777-1852),[†] keeper of the zoological department, rallied to the defence of his assistant Gray, who was responsible for the ornithology section, and obtained letters of support from Darwin, Gould, William Yarrell (1784-1850)[†] and Audubon. The trustees rejected the complaint.[20]

The Edinburgh University Museum plays a prominent role in our narrative as it was used by Audubon and William MacGillivray as a source of specimens for their publications and paintings. Audubon wrote, 'I gladly embrace the opportunity offered of presenting my best thanks to Professor Jameson, for the kindness and liberality with which he has allowed me the free use of the splendid collection of birds in the museum of the University of Edinburgh.'[21]

Audubon first visited the museum on 9 December 1826. He was allowed access without payment of the usual entry fee, but later his permission to borrow specimens was withdrawn because he returned two specimens 'covered with dust, stands so much soiled that it was necessary to repair them'.[22] Audubon contributed three 'splendid' snakes and specimens of male and female wild turkeys and a collection of other birds in 1834/5.

William MacGillivray, who was appointed as Professor Jameson's assistant in 1822, was chiefly responsible for the day-to-day running of the museum during his eight-year term of office. (His activities during this period are considered in Chapter 8.) Following MacGillivray's diligent conduct, Jameson's nephew Laurence Jameson was appointed as the assistant. Despite considerable affection and respect for his uncle, however, he does not seem to have been so assiduous in his duties, for the museum appears to have gone into a decline – perhaps it simply grew too large for its resources. Some years before his death, Robert Jameson is recorded as saying:

> I am afraid my collections are not in such a condition as I would like to have them and I should like to leave them all in a tolerable condition before I leave this Earth. I have not been able to realise what I wanted from want of funds …. It pains me to say that my catalogue will be left in a very imperfect state.[23]

He became dissatisfied with the work of his taxidermists, or 'stuffers', and threatened that if his birds 'did not last … in good condition for several years, their employment would be discontinued and damages laid against them'.

Laurence wrote that towards the end of his uncle's life, 'museum control he resigned privately into my own hands on his last museum visit. He put into my hands the key of his private museum drawers in which he contained the keys that gave access to the whole Museum Collections. Ever after that he looked up to me in the protection and safety of the Collections.'[24]

By the end of Jameson's life the museum possessed over 74,000 specimens of zoological, geological and fossil interest, second only in size to the British Museum. The writer of his obituary noted that 'The access of visitors to this vast collection has been hitherto restricted with an excess of care. Since it is determined

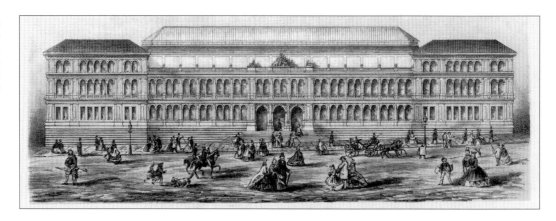

to found a National Museum … it will probably become more available to the public.'[25]

The Royal Museum can be said to have grown out of the Edinburgh University Museum. Jameson had long held an ambition that a building be raised on the site to the west of the Old Quadrangle to provide adequate accommodation for his overcrowded museum. In 1852 the university Senate offered the collection to found a national museum, on the condition that the principal keeper should be the regius professor of the university. Protracted negotiations took place between the university, the city and the government, but eventually funds were raised and the building was built in stages between 1861 and 1885, taking its inspiration from the Crystal Palace of the Great Exhibition of 1851. In 1865 the University Museum was transferred to the first phase of the newly built National Museum of Science and Art, now the Royal Museum. Other collections were added, including those of the Highland and Agricultural Society and the Royal Society of Edinburgh.[26]

The new building was connected to the old University Museum by a bridge, which still exists, to allow the students access. Gradually, however, any residual control which the university had over the museum was eroded, despite a resolute rearguard action by the university Senate. The linking bridge was locked in 1871 after an incident in which the students discovered that refreshments for a museum *conversatzione* were being stored there, and proceeded to consume the lot! In 1873 a Commission of Enquiry recommended that the university should cease to have any part in the running of the museum.[27] The rooms in the Old Quadrangle previously occupied by the museum have now become the Talbot Rice Art Gallery and the Senate Hall.

Jameson was also responsible, together with David Brewster, for founding and editing the *Edinburgh Philosophical Journal* – a journal devoted to natural history which was begun in 1819. In 1824, after a disagreement with his co-founder Brewster, possibly over the matter of access to the museum, Jameson created the *Edinburgh New Philosophical Journal* of which he was the sole custodian, while Brewster started the *Edinburgh Journal of Science*.

Jameson never married. He maintained a ménage with four unmarried sisters, one widowed sister, a blind brother and five orphans of his brother Laurence. His homes, for he owned several, were centres of much hospitality and were renowned for their parties, dances and concerts. Favoured students highly prized an invitation to such functions. Clearly his rather forbidding exterior concealed a warmth and generosity not apparent to the casual acquaintance.

William Scoresby, the Arctic explorer, described a dinner with Jameson when he was one of his students:

… extreme diffidence rendered my introduction into a party consisting of scientific men of eminence, with accomplished and intelligent women, at first inconceivably painful. I felt such a degrading sense of my own inferiority, that I could not summon vanity enough to imagine that I could be the object of any attention. The free and encouraging manners of the professor and his friends, however, and the frankness of the ladies, soon dissipated every painful feeling, and enabled me at length to enjoy the uncommon treat that such a party presented. To my great surprise the civilities of the kind professor and his family did not terminate here. I was

Left: William Scoresby, copied from *William Scoresby Arctic Scientist* by T & C Stamp.

Right: Calotype of Edward Forbes taken in 1844 by Hill and Adamson. (Scottish National Portrait Gallery)

repeatedly invited to dine with him, and invariably met that kind of refined and intelligent society for which Edinburgh is so eminent and from which I derived incalculable advantages.[28]

Later he wrote:

My friendship with Professor Jameson was fully confirmed before I left Edinburgh. While his amiable, friendly manner and his great intelligence, won my highest esteem, his disinterested hospitality, and his anxiety to bring me forward and to encourage me to persevere in scientific pursuits, excited my lively gratitude.[29]

Thomas Bewick also enjoyed Jameson's hospitality during his visit to Edinburgh in 1823.

We were often at the table of the former [Jameson] surrounded by men of learning and science who visited him, on which occasions the amiable manners and affability of his sisters, the Misses Jameson, made every place appear like a home.[30]

Jessie M Sweet, who made a study of Jameson, concluded that

Far from being a boring old curmudgeon as was often thought both then and recently,

Jameson's help and influence was to shape the life of many a young man who bothered to take a real interest in his studies.

Fifteen days before his death on 19 April 1854 Jameson heard the welcome news that the plans for a national museum had been approved. This had long been his wish and must have given him great satisfaction, marking a satisfactory conclusion to his long professorship.

Jameson's standing in the community may be gauged by his funeral procession, which included representatives of the students, Royal Scottish Society of Arts, Royal Scottish Academy, Royal Physical Society, Wernerian Society, Royal Society, Royal College of Surgeons, Royal College of Physicians, Senatus Academicus, the Lord Provost, magistrates, the council, chief mourners and private friends. After his death his extensive library was sold at auction. It is interesting that no books by MacGillivray or Audubon were among them. He certainly at one time had Audubon's books, for the copy of *Ornithological Biography* in the Mitchell Library in Glasgow is inscribed to Professor Jameson 'from his sincere friend J J Audubon, November 1838'.

Jameson was succeeded by one of his old pupils, Edward Forbes. Forbes died tragically six months after his appointment, denying Edinburgh the opportunity of becoming a leading centre of oceanography, which was his major interest.

Notes

1   *A Description of Three Hundred Animals* by Thomas Boreman was first published in 1730 as a child's introduction to natural history. It ran to many editions with a succession of editors, not always named. The last edition was published in 1833. The edition which excited Jameson was probably that of 1787, published in Leith when he was aged 13. James Wilson of Woodville and Thomas Bewick were also influenced by this book. In his autobiography *A Memoir of Thomas Bewick written by Himself*, Bewick wrote: 'Having, from the time that I was a schoolboy, been displeased with most of the figures in children's books and particularly with those of the *Three Hundred Animals*, the figures in which, even at that time, I thought I could depicture much better; and having afterwards very often turned the matter over in my mind, of making improvements in that publication – I at last came to the determination of making the attempt …. In this, my only reward besides was the great pleasure I felt in imitating nature …. I minded little about any self-interested considerations.' He goes on to describe the various sources of his illustrations. This inspired Bewick to write and illustrate his own classic *General History of Quadrupeds*, first published in 1790, which shares many of the illustrations with the later editions of *Three Hundred Animals*.

2   Jameson, R: *Mineralogical Travels* (1813), vol. I, p. 138.

3   Chitnis, A C: 'The University of Edinburgh's Natural History Museum and the Huttonian-Wernerian Debate', in *Annals of Science* (1970), 26: 85-94.

4   *The 1826 Journal of John James Audubon*, p. 329. Jameson's predecessor, the Reverend John Walker, was also noted for his remarkable coiffure. He is said to have spent two hours each day at the hands of his hairdresser.

5   Darwin, Francis (ed.): *The Life and Letters of Charles Darwin* (1887).

6   Andrew Duncan Jr, see Biographical Profiles (see p. 205).

7   The Darwins in general did not share Charles Darwin's jaundiced view of Edinburgh. Seven men from the family studied medicine in Edinburgh between 1754 and 1840, the first being Charles' grandfather Erasmus Darwin (1731-1802). His uncle, also Charles, had 'sighed to be removed [from Oxford] to the robuster exercise of the medical school of Edinburgh', where he studied from 1775-8. He was awarded a gold medal for his work on pus and mucus but died in Edinburgh at the age of 20 from an infection acquired during the course of a dissection. Professor Andrew Duncan Sr, who had befriended the young Darwin, arranged for his body to buried in his own family vault.

8   Alexander Monro Tertius, see Biographical Profiles (see p. 205).

9   Wilson, G and Geikie, A: *Memoir of Edward Forbes* (1861), pp. 108-9.

10   Ibid, p. 554.

11   *Evidence, Oral and Documentary, taken and received by the Commissioners ….*, vol. I, University of Edinburgh, London (1837). Despite Jameson's dismissal of Walker's collection, some specimens from Walker's time have survived and can still be identified in the Royal Museum.

12   Sweet, J M: 'William Bullock's Collection and the University of Edinburgh 1819', in *Annals of Science* (1970), 26: 23-32.

13   Sweet, J M: 'The Collection of Louis Dufresne (1752-1832)' in *Annals of Science* (1976), 26: 33-71.

14   *Memoir of Edward Forbes*, pp. 109-111.

15   Ritchie, J A: 'The Edinburgh Explorers', in *University of Edinburgh Journal* (1943), 12: 155-9.

16   Sweet, J M: 'The University Puma', in *University of Edinburgh Journal* (1976), 27: 218-221. In a letter to Sir William Jardine, Jameson describes an ocelot 'which we had in a domestic state in the College. I can only say that it was in general not more troublesome than a <u>mischievous</u> domestic cat ….', EUL MS Dk 20/152. Jameson, writing this letter about six years after the departure of the puma, probably confused an ocelot with the puma, both being New World felines.

17   Jones, J: 'The Geological Collection of James Hutton', in *Annals of Science* (1984), 41: 223-4.

18   *Evidence, Oral and Documentary ….*, op. cit., vol I, pp. 492-5.

19   Ibid, p. 629.

20   Brandon-Jones, C: 'Charles Darwin and the Repugnant Curators', in *Annals of Science* (1996), 53: 501-10.

21   *Ornithological Biography*, vol. II, p. xxiv.

22   Entry in the Edinburgh University Museum Annual Report Book, 26 December 1835.

23   Jameson, L: 'Biographical Memoir of the late Professor Jameson', in *Edinburgh New Philosophical Journal* (1854), 57: 1-49.

24   Jameson, L: *Life of Robert Jameson*. Unpublished manuscript in Edinburgh University Library (EUL) Special Collections (DC 2.73).

25   Anon. Robert Jameson's Obituary in *Gentleman's Magazine* (1854), New Series 41: 656-7.

26   Waterston, C D gives a detailed account of the lengthy negotiations which led to the founding of the National Museums of Scotland in his book *Collections in Context*, Chapter 4.

27   Swinney, G N: 'A natural history collection in transition', in *Journal of the History of Collections* (1999), 11: 51-70

28   Stamp, T and Stamp, C: *William Scoresby Arctic Scientist*, p. 36.

29   Sweet, J M: 'Robert Jameson and the Explorers' in *Annals of Science* (1979), 31: 21-47.

30   Bewick, T: *A Memoir of Thomas Bewick written by himself*, p. 182.

William MacGillivray's
Early Life

AUDUBON'S friend and collaborator in Edinburgh was William MacGillivray (1796-1852). Although the account of the association of the two men appears in later chapters, MacGillivray's name will keep recurring so it is appropriate to introduce him here. Audubon and MacGillivray had much in common. Both were illegitimate, both had a consuming love of nature, and both endured long periods of poverty and periods of deep depression. However, in other respects their lives differed. MacGillivray had been earnest, serious and diligent in his early studies while Audubon had led a hedonistic carefree youth, avoiding formal education as far as possible. Each was the product of the society in which he lived: MacGillivray was the typical Highland Scot, frugal, conscientious and imbued with the Calvinistic teaching – praise God and work hard; while Audubon embodied the colourful but disorganised lifestyle of Revolutionary France.

Both men kept journals for long periods, only fragments of which survive. MacGillivray's were lost in a fire at his son's home in Australia, except for fragments covering periods from 1817-19.

Audubon's were also destroyed by fire, except for the journals of 1826, 1840 and 1843. The extant writings of both men reveal wonderful talents for describing scenes and places.

Perhaps the differences between them are also best revealed in their writings. MacGillivray, in the preface to his *Descriptions of the Rapacious Birds of Great Britain*, wrote: 'The love of money and the love of fame, the two great stimuli to exertion, have not been among the exciting causes of this attempt to describe the Rapacious Birds of my native land. The latter, as a principle of action, I have always considered contemptible ....' Audubon, after seeing the first engravings by Lizars, wrote in his journal: 'Perhaps even yet fame may be mine and enable me to provide all that is needful for my Lucy and my children.'

Audubon revelled in the adulation which was heaped upon him during his later life, while MacGillivray avoided the limelight, although not indifferent to the opinion of others. 'He who professed the greatest contempt for public opinion is always the most anxious for general applause.'[1]

Audubon, with his striking appearance – tall and handsome with flowing hair and piercing eyes – was an extrovert personality who readily made friends and attracted attention wherever he went. He described himself as being 'five foot ten inches, erect, and with muscles of steel'. MacGillivray on the other hand was described as being

> ... under medium height, spare in form, shy and reserved in manner, he walked swiftly along the street, generally alone, with his head inclined downwards and his eyes bent towards the ground, wrapt in his own thoughts. Celt of the Celts, he was singularly courteous and polite, with fine quiet dignity, but when offended he could use sharp words which left their sting. He made few friends, but once made he clung to them with tenacity.[2]

Left: Woodcut of William MacGillivray, from a self portrait reproduced in J A H Brown's *Vertebrate Fauna of the Outer Hebrides* (1881).

Elliott Coues, a later American ornithologist, wrote:

MacGillivray appears to have been of an irritable, highly sensitised temperament, fired with enthusiasm and ambition, yet contending, for some time at least, with poverty, ill-health, and a perhaps not well-founded, though not therefore the less acutely felt, sense of neglect; thus ceaselessly nerved to accomplish, yet as continually haunted with the dread of failure .... He was a lover of nature, an original thinker, a hard student, and finally an ornithologist of large practical experience, who wrote down what he knew or believed to be true with great regard for accuracy of statement, and in a very agreeable manner.[3]

The 'MacGillivray Warbler', plate 399 from *The Birds of America* (the MacGillivray warblers are facing to the right). Audubon never saw a living MacGillivray warbler; his paintings were made from specimens provided by Dr Townsend from the Columbia River (see Chapter 14, note 1). The other birds shown are the black-throated green warbler and the Blackburnian warbler. (© The Natural History Museum, London)

Another writer, who had more intimate contact with MacGillivray, wrote in the *North British Review* (volume XIX, p. 9, 1853) that he was

... a person of strong feelings and warm affection and remarkable for his love of truth. He was somewhat restrained in the society of strangers, and possessed a less enlarged circle of personal friends than might have fallen to his lot, had not a peculiar and not infrequent combination of pride and prejudice not only prevented his seeking the society of others but even induced the groundless fancy that he was intentionally disregarded by them .... Although there was a great deal of quietude, even of reserve or shyness, in his general bearing there is no doubt that he was a person of great determination of character, and much more likely in a fray to offer the clenched fist than the cheek to the smiter. But he was mild and gentle in manner to those whom he esteemed ....

In a lengthy poem that MacGillivray wrote in memory of his beloved medical tutor Dr Barclay, who died at the age of 27, he included this sad and revealing line: 'Friend of the friendless, he was all to me.' Perhaps his rather introverted and withdrawn personality could be attributed to absence of parental love and influence from earliest childhood.

Despite the differences in their personalities, Audubon and MacGillivray developed a fruitful working relationship and mutual respect. MacGillivray came to regard 'the warm-hearted and generous Audubon' as his 'familiar and beloved friend' and gave one of his sons the christian name of Audubon. He dedicated his *Rapacious Birds of Great Britain* to 'John James Audubon in admiration of his talents as an ornithologist, and in gratitude for many acts of friendship'. Audubon wrote to his friend John Bachman, 'I am quite proud of such a Compliment from one of so much talent and Intrinsic Worth'.

MacGillivray describes his regard for Audubon in *A History of British Birds*:

I have the pleasure of being familiar with an ornithologist who has spent thirty years in study, who has ransacked the steaming swamps of Louisiana, traversed the tangled and trackless woods of the Missouri, ascended the flowery heights of the Alleghanies, and clambered among the desolate crags of cold and misty Labrador; who has observed, and shot and drawn, and described the birds of half a continent. Well, what then? Has this man the grave and solemn croak of that carrion-crow, or the pertness and impudence of the pilfering jackdaw. No, I have seen him chasing tom-tits with all the glee of a truant school boy, and have heard him communicate his knowledge with the fervour and feeling of a warm-hearted soul, as he is.[4]

Audubon in his turn developed a deep regard for MacGillivray, and gave his name to the MacGillivray warbler: 'I cannot do better than dedicate this pretty little bird to my excellent friend William MacGillivray, Esq., I feel much pleasure in introducing it to the notice of the ornithological world, under a name which I trust will endure as long as the species itself.'[5] He also designated another bird as the MacGillivray finch, but this has subsequently been thought to be the seaside sparrow or finch which Audubon also recognised. He relates, 'Having one day shot a number of these birds, merely for the sake of practice, I had them made into a pie, which, how-ever, could not be eaten, on account of its fishy savour'.

MacGillivray's parentage is even more obscure than Audubon's. He was born on 25 Janury 1796. His first biographer[6] (MacGillivray 1910) states that his father was an army surgeon in the Cameron Highlanders who was killed in the Battle of Corunna in 1809. A recent biography[7] (Ralph 1993) records that his mother was Anne Wishart, of whom nothing is known. His father, also William MacGillivray (hereafter designated William Sr to avoid confusion), who came from farming stock in Inverness-shire, was a student of medicine at King's College in Old Aberdeen between 1793 and 1797, but did not complete his studies. The Historical Records of the Cameron Highlanders record that a William MacGillivray joined that regiment as an assistant surgeon in 1804 and was transferred as surgeon to the 60th Foot in August 1809, seven months after the Battle of Corunna. He died on 11 October 1809, possibly of 'Guadiana fever', from which the British troops suffered severely during the latter half of 1809.

After joining the army, William Sr married Euphemia MacNeill of Newton in North Uist and had a son, Donald. MacGillivray makes scant reference to his parents in his writings, but kept in touch with his half-brother, who lived with him when he was a medical student in Edinburgh. Donald subsequently practiced medicine and farmed in South Uist and on the island of Eoligarry. He also was a keen ornithologist.[8]

At the age of three MacGillivray was taken to Harris in the Outer Hebrides, where he was brought up by his uncle Roderick MacGillivray,[9] who farmed at Northton in the south of the island. William Sr had a major financial interest in the farm and may indeed have been its owner. Young MacGillivray attended the local school

The beautiful setting of the farm at Northton in Harris overlooking the sands of Luskintyre where MacGillivray spent his childhood and acquired his love of nature. Only remnants of the original steading remain.

at the village of Obbo, where he acquired sufficient learning to enter Aberdeen University at
the age of twelve to study for a Master of Arts
degree. His studies were not confined to his
academic subjects, however, for even then he
had an interest in natural history:

> The solitudes of Nature were my school,
> And in the moaning voice of streams and
>   winds,
> Without the aid of dull scholastic rule,

I felt the tone which in the lone heart finds
    its echo.

Later he wrote, 'Let Latin and Greek have their
due share, but let not the incubus of classic lore
be permitted to smother the mind, that, if unre-
strained would inhale with delight the pure air
of heaven'.[10]

While a student at Aberdeen University,
MacGillivray regularly walked to and from the
sea-crossing to his home in Harris, a distance

Golden eagle by
MacGillivray.
(© The Natural History
Museum, London)

of 180 miles – no mean undertaking for a young teenager laden with books and personal effects. He seemed to relish hardship: 'There is little pleasure in passing through life dry shod and ever comfortable.'[11] During his holidays he occupied himself by teaching in his local school and observing the behaviour of the local wildlife.

In this period he developed his skill with a gun, which was an essential accomplishment for the ornithologist in those days.

I had just commenced the use of the gun, under the guidance of my uncle, and had only as yet fired five shots; with the first of which I had riddled a table, with the second demolished a rock-pigeon, killed two with the third, and with the rest had done nothing to my credit as a marksman. The sixth was destined for a higher deed. Not finding any flesh or fish, recent or putrid, about the place, I laid hold of a white hen, to the legs of which I fastened a bit of twine and a wooden peg, filled one of my jacket-pockets with barley-grain, the other with old newspapers; and, taking the hen under my arm, and my gun on my shoulder, proceeded to the farther brow of the hill. There I fastened the bird to the turf by means of the peg, left her the barley, put a double charge of buck-shot into the gun, and shut myself up in the pit. Before I had been there an hour, the rain had made its way through the roof, the newspapers had ceased to amuse, and I had fallen into a sort of slumber, from which I was startled by a shrill scream. My first motion was to peep through the hole, when I beheld an eagle perched on the back of the hen, which crouched close to the ground in terror; my second was to raise to my shoulder the but of my gun, of which the muzzle lay in the aperture of the hut; and, at the moment when the eagle was in the act of raising his head, as if to inflict a blow upon the unresisting victim, I fired, and received a severe contusion on the cheek, the gun having been overcharged. Impatient to know the result, I raised the roof on my back, forced myself through it, and, running up to the place, found the eagle quite dead; the whole shot having entered its side …. I threw the eagle upon my back, brought a leg on each side of my neck tied the feet before, put the hen, which had been but slightly injured by the grasp of the tyrant, under

one arm, the gun under another, and thus accoutered, soon made my appearance on the brow of the hill. As I descended, the people came out to see what I had got; some thinking it a bunch of heather put up with the view of deceiving them, others alleging that *Uilleam beg* [little William] had actually shot an eagle … my uncle was as proud as myself, for I had proved a hopeful scholar, and saved him, perhaps, half a score of lambkins.[12]

This pride and pleasure in his skill at shooting birds was a characteristic which he shared with Audubon, and indeed with most ornithologists of that period. It was generally regarded as a respectable way of obtaining specimens for scientific study. MacGillivray despised the slaughter of driven grouse, calling it 'a pitiful and barbarous sport' of those who did not even have the labour of loading their own gun or carrying home the produce of their idle industry; but he relished shooting for the pot or for study.

The pleasure experienced by the young sportsman, who … returns from a long day's excursion, with two or three braces of ptarmigan, and as many plovers, is scarcely attainable by the … wholesale slaughterer. Indeed, it is neither the quantity nor the quality of the game that affords pleasure; for I have been as much delighted with obtaining half-a-dozen thrushes, two or three water-ouzels, or a few wagtails, as an entire burden of large birds ….[13]

He does, however, record with pride elsewhere that he had killed 23 pigeons with three shots! Then, in the same chapter, he describes his fondness for his tame rock dove, which he says 'whenever I escaped from the detested pages of Virgil and Horace … was sure to fly to me'.

At the age of 18 MacGillivray commenced the study of medicine, and was apprenticed, as was the custom of the time, to a George Barclay MD. The medical course involved the study of botany and zoology, and he became so absorbed in these sciences that after five years he abandoned his medical studies and devoted the next few years to the study of natural history.

To this end MacGillivray carried out extensive travels throughout Scotland, sometimes in the company of a like-minded companion,

William Craigie.[14] He does not relate how he supported himself on these journeys, but his material wants appear to have been few. He described a typical night on his travels, when he was journeying to find the source of the River Dee, where he had arranged to meet his friend Craigie.

It was sunset when I got to the top of the first hill, whence I struck directly east, judging by the place where the sun disappeared behind the rugged and desolate mountains. After traversing a mile of boggy heath, I found myself put out of my course by a long, deep, rocky valley or ravine which I was obliged to double, and before I had accomplished this night fell. I travelled on, however, about two miles farther, and coming upon another but smaller valley, in which I was apprehensive of breaking my neck if I should venture through it, I sat down by a rock, weary, and covered with perspiration. Rest is pleasant, even in such a place as this; and when I had experienced a little of its sweets, I resolved to take up my abode there for the night. So, thrusting my stick into the peat between me and the ravine below, I extended myself on the ground and presently fell into a reverie, reviewed my life, gave vent to the sorrow of my soul in a thou-sand reflections on the folly of my conduct, and ended with resolving to amend! Around me were the black masses of the granite hills rising to heaven like the giant barriers of an enchanted land; above the cloudless sky, spangled with stars; beneath a cold bed of wet turf; within, a human spirit tortured with wild imaginings and the pangs of a sprained foot. In such a place, at such a time and in such a mood, what are the vanities of the world, the pomp of power, the pride of renown, and even the pleasures of bird-nesting! Having in a short time become keenly sensible that a great portion of vital heat had oozed out of me, I looked out for a warmer situation; but, alas, with little success; for although I pulled some stunted heather and white moss, with which I covered my feet and laid me down by another crag that afforded more shelter I could not sleep. After a while, having experienced a fit of shivering, I got up to gather more heath, with which I formed a sort of bed and lay down again. But even heath was not to be obtained in sufficient quantity, so that for a covering I was obliged to bury myself in moss and turf, with the soil adhering. At long, long length the sky began to brighten in what I supposed to be the north-east, and I was anxiously looking for the approach of morn, when gradually the pale unwelcome moon rose over a distant hill .... However, morning actually came at last, and I started up to renew my journey.

The sight of a moor-cock 'was a good omen; the night and dullness had fled, and I limped along as cheerily as I could. My half-frozen blood soon regained its proper temperature.'

MacGillivray reached the source of the Dee without encountering his friend and decided to follow the stream:

For seven long miles I trudged along, faint enough, as you may suppose having obtained no refreshment for eighteen hours, except-ing two mouthfuls of cold water .... At one o'clock I came to a hut, tenanted by a person named MacHardy, who ... treated me to a glass of whisky and some bread and milk .... A mile and a half farther down I came upon a wood, the first that I had seen since I left Blair. The silver Dee now rolled pleasantly along the wooded valley, and in the evening I reached Castleton of Braemar, where, while seated in the inn ... reading *Zimmerman on Solitude*, which, to my great joy, I had found there and sipping my tea, I heard a rap at the door .... It was my best friend, with whom I spent a happy evening.[15]

He records the 'accoutrements' that he took with him on one of his journeys, which included changes of clothing and shoes, the first and third volumes of *Systema Naturae*, Sir Charles Smith's *Flora Britannica*, Campbell's *Pleasures of Hope*, drawing paper, pencils, paints, crayons, ink and pens, one pound of gunpowder, a powder-horn and fowling piece, handline and hooks, and a quarter-pound of snuff. Other items included a compass, knife, soap, razors, silk thread, wax, buttons, a sharpening stone, needles, lancets, opium, and a flute. He listed his objectives as improvement in knowledge of natural history, particularly in ornithology, ichthyology, botany and mineralogy; inurement to hardship; the habit of early rising; dexterity in the use of the gun; drawings in zoology and botany; some patience, resolution and inflexibility. He notes: 'If I had lived in the days of chivalry, I had certainly been another Quixote'.

Audubon in his travels would probably have taken much the same, except for the books, but his objectives, certainly in his younger days, would have been less earnest. Both men were alike, however, in their enjoyment of travel for long distances in wild places with little regard for creature comforts – and both undoubtedly became 'inured to hardship'. MacGillivray's lancets may well have been for use in treating those whom he encountered on his travels, for he made use of what medical knowledge he had acquired in his brief apprenticeship. He describes one narrow escape from drowning when he was being rowed six miles to an island to see a patient.[16]

In 1819, at the age of 23, MacGillivray decided to travel from Aberdeen to London in order to see the British Museum. His journal of the journey is in the library of Aberdeen University. Typically, he planned to travel on foot so that he could 'extend his knowledge of natural history'. To this end, instead of taking the most direct route which most people would have chosen for such an epic journey, he deviated to traverse Scotland, taking in Braemar, Ben Macdhui, Fort William and Ben Nevis before proceeding south via Glasgow. He travelled light, carrying only 'a penknife, a small ink piece with pens, a small itinerary of Scotland, a glass for drinking by the way, and a towel. To my dress I have added a greatcoat and a pair of old gloves.' His budget was £10 and to make this frugal sum last he frequently slept in the open. He regretted one night which he spent in a bed: 'I am almost covered by tumours and vesications produced by the bites of bugs .... How gladly I would have exchanged my bed last night for the couch of grass on the side of Cairngorm.'

Glasgow impressed him with its gas lighting in streets and houses. At Alloway he visited the cottage in which Burns was born, then used as a public house.

> I entered it and got half a mutchkin of the favourite potation of the unfortunate bard. I knelt down upon the floor with my hat off. 'Immortal Burns' said I aloud, 'here on my knees I do homage to thy genius,' and poured

the liquor on the floor .... Big drops trickling down my cheeks.

Interior of birthplace of Burns, from Beattie's *Scotland Illustrated.*

Clearly beneath his austere exterior there was a romantic heart.

By the time he reached the English Border he had already travelled 500 miles in 30 days, and had spent half his money. He economised by restricting his meals to two a day. Breakfast sometimes consisted largely of bread washed down with whisky or water – such a meal cost him two pence.

MacGillivray was shocked by the lack of religious observance by the English on the Sabbath: shops open, boys flying kites, and other such wicked activities. He wrote, 'I like to see the Sabbath kept, even with puritanical strictness.' By this stage of his travels his clothing was so ragged and plastered with mire that he had great difficulty in obtaining lodging, and at times was overcome with depression resulting from fatigue and hunger. His love of travel and the opportunity to observe nature and mankind was tested to the limit. He arrived in London penniless and exhausted on 20 October, having walked 830 miles in 43 days.

At the British Museum MacGillivray spent most of his time studying the collection of British birds, which reinforced his opinion that the Linnaean system of classification of species was imperfect: '... possibly I may become some day the author of a new system.' He returned to Aberdeen by the steamboat *Escort* after a week in London, during which time he visited St Paul's Cathedral, Westminster Abbey and the Tower.

For several years MacGillivray had courted Marion M'Caskill, the younger sister of his uncle's wife, and on 20 September 1820 they were married. Previously he had shown little interest in money. He had made small sums from teaching and dissecting in the anatomy class, but had had no regular employment. Marriage necessitated that MacGillivray should obtain regular income and he decided to seek his fortune in Edinburgh. He had visited the city when he attended Jameson's lectures in the winter of 1819/20 and, like Alexander Wilson and Audubon, had fallen under the spell of its attractions.

Few landscapes in Britain combine more of the elements of natural and artificial beauty and grandeur than that which now presents itself to our view. From this craggy eminence on the Fifeshire coast, one sweep of the eye discovers the wide entrance of the Frith [Firth] of Forth, with the Bass and North Berwick Law, two mounds of plutonic rock that have emerged from the primal abyss, the gently rising grounds of East Lothian, blending into the dim ridge of the Lammermuir, which runs into the Peeble-shire hills, the Pentlands clad in their wintry garb of pure white, the nearer prominences of Salisbury Craigs, and Arthur's Seat, the beautiful expanse of waters, with its islands and undulated shores. Right opposite is the capital of old Scotland. How beautifully, ridge beyond ridge, rises the noble city, from the sea-shore to the crowning heights of the Calton Hill, the High Street, and the Castle Rock!

View of Edinburgh from the castle, engraved by Robert Havell Jr from a painting by E Crawford (see also illustration on p. 39). (Courtesy of Edinburgh City Library)

As a Scot, I feel proud of thee, Edina, thou Queen of cities! See how the elements conspire to adorn the picture: the strong blasts of the east wind have ruffled the bosom of the Frith; a fleet of small vessels has taken shelter in the lee of Inchkeith; a huge grey hail-cloud pours down its long winding streams on the valley of Dalkeith; and the smoke of the city spreads to the westward, like a dense autumnal mist.[17]

In 1822 MacGillivray obtained a job as assistant to Professor Jameson, with a salary of 30 shillings a week. His principle duty was to supervise the natural history museum. He kept a detailed account of his daily activities in the museum, and these records are preserved in the archives of the National Museums of Scotland. These daily reports, written in the third person in neat copperplate, record in meticulous detail the hour-by-hour activities, mostly of a very menial nature. This must have been hard to endure by one of MacGillivray's intelligence and sensitivity. His day books and weekly report books register all the objects sent to the museum, their condition, the donor and the correspondence relating to them. The name of every visitor is recorded, and the accounts are kept to the last penny.

The first entry, dated Monday, 9 December 1822, reads:

The Assistant was occupied from nine to ten in dusting the horizontal cases and rubbing

the wood of the side ones in the British Gallery, as well as in cleaning part of the railing in the galleries of the large room. Attended the examination of a cask of petrifaction sent by the Earl of Dalhousie by Custom House Officers. Was sent to inquire after an animal exhibited in town. *Squalus maximus* caught on the Coast of Sussex 9 years ago. Colour when fish caught greenish. No blubber, it weighed 7 tons and liver 22cwt … etc.

His duties were detailed in the entry of 14 December:

1   To call at Circus [21 Royal Circus, where Jameson lived] every morning on way to College.
2   To make a daily Report of everything done whether in writing in College or in afternoon at home, attending classroom, museum, cleaning examining specimens, and to enquire of Prof Jameson if any cases or packages received for Museum, and also at Mr Wilsons.[18]
3   To keep a register of plans, drawings etc wanted for and used in the lectures.
4   To get from John [John Dickie, the door-man] the number of students, visitors to Museum on Wednesdays and Saturdays.

5   To get a general list made out when opportunity offers of cases in Lumber Room.
6   To get glasses with serpents removed from Oldguard hall to British Gallery provided there be room for them.
7   To commence on Thursday the general examination of the Museum. Take the Insects first.
8   To attend to the temperature of the Upper Room in particular and see that it does not get below 55°. When heat not sufficient to see that the fire is renewed.
9   To go over at least once a fortnight to College at seven in the morning and see that the stove is lighted and also look at its state.
10   To ascertain the hour when the stove is lighted with the view of enabling me to determine the expense of fuel, and the rate of its heating the room. Thought to be lighted always at seven in the morning.
11   To give the day book every Saturday evening to enable Prof J to point out the articles for insertion in the Weekly Report Book.
12   The examination of the Museum to be confined to Tues, Thursday & Friday.

Title page from MacGillivray's day book and a typical page from the weekly report book. (Courtesy of National Museums of Scotland Library)

Such was MacGillivray's nature that he applied himself for the next eight years to these duties with meticulous attention. No holiday or recreation is recorded, except on one day, 28 September 1824, when the 'Assistant having been pressingly invited by Mr W. Jameson to spend a day at Roslyn [where Jameson had a second home], and being further persuaded by Miss Jane, and seeing there was nothing very urgent to be done at the Museum, took the liberty of going there'. Presumably Professor Jameson was away at that time and other members of his household sanctioned this day off.

Jameson appears to have treated MacGillivray with scant courtesy. On 5 July 1823, for example, the 'Assistant called at Professor Jameson at half past nine, but there being apparently no notice taken of him, he walked off, after remaining about ten minutes'. His relationship with the rest of the staff was also difficult:

> There is a want of regularity in the under management of the Museum, owing to the undefined nature of the office of the Assistant and Mr. Wilson [the college janitor], the one not wishing to meddle with the business of the other and both being to appearance unacquainted with the extent of the other's commission. The Assistant wishes to know if it be his duty to clean. John cannot clean to perfection because his vision is not of the most acute. Mr. Wilson dusts occasionally but not regularly.
>
> … it is neither agreeable nor becoming to cringe to or flatter an inferior, in order to get one's duty done.

A cleaner, 'the woman', appears to have been appointed after this entry, but for the rest of his time MacGillivray spent long hours at this most wasteful activity for one of his intellect and ability. Another recurring irritation was the central heating boiler, which was one of MacGillivray's responsibilities. It was inefficient and produced offensive sulphurous fumes due to a crack in its casing. The temperatures were recorded regularly and it proved very difficult to maintain the prescribed 55 degrees. A typical record reads: 'outside temperature 44½° and inside 53¾°.' MacGillivray also faced constant problems with leaking roofs and got little help from Jameson in resolving them.

MacGillivray's main bugbear, however, was the war against moths, mice and other pests which constantly threatened his specimens. He had no effective remedy: camphor and arsenical soap were useless, and turpentine was only slightly better. He eventually decided that baking the specimens was the only cure, but did not have the means of doing this.

He was also responsible for preparing the room for the Wernerian Society meetings and was appointed assistant librarian to the society, although he was not permitted full membership until he left Jameson's service. MacGillivray's evenings were regularly spent translating German and French texts for Jameson, particularly the writings of Cuvier.

Jameson queried the time MacGillivray spent on labelling specimens, to which he responded:

> 15 minutes at an average necessary to the determination of a species, unknown to the assistant, supposing the books describing it to be at hand. 8 minutes at an average to the writing of English name, Latin name, synonym, and country or donor in print letters …. In the case of a Bird known, a minute or two necessary to turn up its description in order to be sure. In the case of nondescripts, 20 minutes to find out whether it be described or not in any book at hand – and upwards of an hours examination before one can be fully convinced that it has not been described. Conclusion – no general average can be fixed upon the writing of labels.

The difficulties and frustrations of his job eventually broke his spirit. An entry of 26 January 1827 records:

> Assistant called as usual at Professor Jameson's but ¾ too late for which he was reprimanded – cleaned as usual in the museum – returned minerals to their places. Assisted Prof Jameson in laying out minerals for lecture. Cleaned 2 cases of birds in the Gallery. Finished cleaning of the East side of the Galleries – attended as usual the Society Room and in lecture room before and after lecture, returned same minerals to their places.

In the evening he transcribed 14 pages of text and did 17 pages of translation for Jameson.

'If Assistant was a little late in the morning he also wrought until very late at night.'

Saturdays brought no relief. On Saturday, 11 July 1829 he had to report to Jameson at Royal Circus at 7.30am, go to the museum for a hammer, then to Nicolson Street for a gun, and then to the Chain Pier at Newhaven by 10am to accompany Jameson and students to the Isle of May to obtain rocks and birds.

During 1828/9 the entries in his report books become briefer – often one-liners such as 'The usual business done in the Museum this week' – and the writing appears more casual. On 15 August 1829: 'Assistant gave intimation to Prof Jameson that he intended to discontinue his present occupation at Martinmas first; which intimation he hereby repeats.' (Martinmas, 11 November, was the traditional Term Day when workers in Scotland changed their jobs.)

MacGillivray's last full entry in November 1829 is written in a very untidy manner – totally out of character and clearly revealing his emotion. It records sums of money due to various members of the museum staff and the unsatisfactory coarseness of the towels. His own financial position is detailed: he had received for the half-year £59, his salary should have been £65, and £6 was still outstanding. The next entry of 21 November is written in another unidentified hand:

> The Assistant Mr. MacGillivray from the increasing expense of his Family etc, and the smallness of the salary from the Museum finds it impossible to remain longer in his present situation. Therefore on Saturday 14th inst. after returning the keys etc. he according to an intimation agreed on by previous contract resigned his office and left the Museum.

Henry Hulme Cheek, in his tirade against Jameson to the Royal Commission, stated on 25 January 1830:

> The late underkeeper [MacGillivray] though salary paid out of funds of the Museum, had a variety of duties imposed on him, in his agreement with the Regius Keeper, which were totally unconnected with the affairs of the Museum, to be explicit … making translations etc for Professor Jameson's publications. There is not at present any person in the Museum to undertake these duties, the late

The Chain Pier at Newhaven.

> Assistant having a short time ago resigned, from his inability to perform the numerous duties which were appended to his office, and from the inadequacy of his salary ….[19]

From this it would appear that MacGillivray was an acquaintance of Cheek's and had discussed his grievances with him. MacGillivray published two articles in Cheek's short-lived *Edinburgh Journal of Natural and Geographical Science* that year.[20]

The saga does not, however, end there. The museum day books continue until 3 July 1830, recording only the names of the visitors and the receipts from the ticket money – and these entries are in *MacGillivray's* handwriting. He must have been re-engaged in some capacity, but there is no record of the circumstances. Perhaps poverty forced him to seek reinstatement, or possibly Jameson belatedly recognised the value of his contribution and asked him to return. As will be seen later, MacGillivray appears to have maintained at least a degree of guarded respect for Jameson. He continued his association with the Wernerian Society and donated dissections of birds to the University Museum until he left Edinburgh in 1841.

Others certainly thought highly of MacGillivray during this period. Charles Darwin, in his *Autobiography*, wrote:

> From attending Jameson's lectures, I became acquainted with the curator of the museum, Mr MacGillivray, who afterwards published a large and excellent book on the birds of Scotland. He had not much the appearance or manners of the gentleman. I had much interesting natural-history talk with him,

and he was very kind to me. He gave me some rare shells, for I at that time collected marine mollusca, but with no great zeal.[21]

Darwin cites MacGillivray and Audubon frequently in his book *Descent of Man*.

Little is known of MacGillivray's activities following his eventual departure from the museum, until his appointment as conservator of the museum of the Royal College of Surgeons of Edinburgh a year later, in 1831. In 1830 he was invited to apply for the post of superintendent of the Zoological Society museum in London at a salary of £100 a year, but he uncharacteristically failed to answer the letters, suggesting perhaps that he may have been in a depressed mood at the time.[22] In *Descriptions of the Rapacious Birds of Great Britain* MacGillivray wrote that he 'continued my observation in the fields, supporting myself by labours in the closet'. One of these 'closet labours' was assisting Audubon to write his *Ornithological Biography*, which must have provided welcome funds during this period of unemployment.

The Royal College of Surgeons of Edinburgh at the time of MacGillivray's appointment was housed in Old Surgeons' Hall in Surgeons' Square, but this building was falling into disrepair and was inadequate for its purpose. Accordingly William Playfair, the architect responsible for the building of the Old College of the university and the Royal Institution, was commissioned to build the present Surgeons' Hall, which was opened in 1832.

A large part of the new building was designed to accommodate the museum, which was then, as now, regarded as an essential teaching facility. The museum had been established in 1807 when the college appointed nine of its Fellows as curators. It remained a relatively meagre collection,

however, until 1821 when the anatomist John Barclay (1758-1826) offered his personal collection of specimens on the condition that a hall would be built to receive it. This was eventually created in the new building.

In 1824 Robert Knox, who had succeeded Dr Barclay in his private anatomical school, wrote to the college, 'I have felt … the great want of a proper museum and of an osteological collection, without which researches into comparative and human physiology cannot be carried out'. He offered to bestow his whole time, labour and energy towards this project, provided that the college defrayed the expenses. The college accepted this offer and in 1826 Dr Knox was appointed as the first conservator of the museum at a salary of £100 per annum. He was true to his word and devoted the next few years, with great energy, to the development of the museum – cataloguing, adding specimens of his own, and purchasing the collection of Charles Bell, amounting to over 2000 specimens, on behalf of the college. (Audubon was shown the Bell collection and 'found the sight extremely disagreeable. The venereal subjects were shocking beyond all I ever thought could be.') The inadequacies of the Old Surgeons' Hall to accommodate this collection became increasingly apparent and reinforced the need for the new building.

During this period, although he was not incriminated in connection with the activities of Burke and Hare, Knox's reputation inevitably suffered and his relations with the college became strained. This reached a climax in 1831 when he had a major disagreement with the curators and felt compelled to resign as conservator.[23]

On 12 August 1831 William MacGillivray was appointed as Knox's successor:

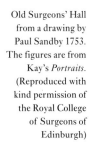

Old Surgeons' Hall from a drawing by Paul Sandby 1753. The figures are from Kay's *Portraits*. (Reproduced with kind permission of the Royal College of Surgeons of Edinburgh)

In 1830 [actually it was 1831] I became a candidate for the conservatorship of the Museum of the College of Surgeons, which somehow, without my being acquainted with three members of that learned and most respectable body, and without soliciting the vote of one individual, I unexpectedly obtained, and continue to discharge the duties, not neglecting the opportunities of improving my anatomical knowledge afforded by the numerous skeletons of birds and other animals in that valuable collection.[24]

Six applicants for the post were considered and MacGillivray won by a narrow margin over his good friend William Craigie. The college laid down certain new conditions which no doubt reflected the disaffection with Knox. The new conservator was not allowed to keep a personal museum, nor could he lecture or leave the city without permission. Knox had been guilty of all these misdemeanours and had continued to run his very popular anatomy classes despite his undertaking to 'bestow his whole time' to the museum.

MacGillivray was to occupy this post for the next ten years. Liberated from the oppressive influence of Jameson and given relatively free rein by the college, this proved to be the most productive period of his life. His literary output was prodigious: in addition to the gigantic task of collaborating with Audubon in the writing of the five-volume *Ornithological Biography*, he translated from the French and edited Richard's *Elements of Botany* (1831) and published *The Travels and Researches of Alexander von Humboldt* (1832), *Lives of Eminent Zoologists from Aristotle to Linnæus* (1834), *Descriptions of the Rapacious Birds of Great Britain* (1836), *An Introduction to the Study of Botany* (1836), a new edition of Smith's *An Introduction to the Study of Botany* (1836), the first three volumes of his *History of British Birds* (1837-52), *British Quadrupeds* (*Naturalist's Library* 1838), *A Manual of Botany* (1840), *A Manual of Geology* (1840) and *A Manual of Ornithology* (1840). In addition, he contributed to the section on ornithology in the seventh edition of the *Encyclopaedia Britannica* and founded the *Edinburgh Journal of Natural History and of the Physical Sciences*, of which he was editor and chief contributor during its lifespan from 1835-9. This journal attempted 'for the first time

The New College of Surgeons, from Grant's *Old and New Edinburgh.*

to combine the lighter character of a popular periodical with the more solid utility of an eminent scientific work', and included in successive instalments Cuvier's *La Regne Animal*, translated by MacGillivray. 'Thus while the views of the lowest classes will be fully met by the cheapness of this work, it is hoped that its beauty and accuracy will render it worthy of the approbation even of the highest.' The journal was illustrated with plates by a variety of artists, some copied from the works of others.

Unfortunately, all these publications did not bring MacGillivray great wealth. He received only £50 for each of the manuals, although they were very popular, each selling several thousand copies. The *History of British Birds* was a labour of love.

> I could write for months without any fatigue; but I cannot make money of them, and have received only £80, for the first volume, and nothing for the second and third; and for books, preparations, fresh specimens, skins, nest and eggs, and paper, I have expended more than the sum received.[25]

It was most unfortunate that at the same time as the first volumes of *A History of British Birds* were being published, his contemporary William Yarrell published his three-volume book of the same name which had greater public appeal and commercial success. It was extensively illustrated with beautiful woodcuts of each species, whereas MacGillivray concentrated more on anatomical drawings of intestines, on which he based his

classification. MacGillivray acknowledged that 'Mr Yarrell's beautifully illustrated and carefully compiled work must come much in the way of mine ...'.[26]

Yarrell, despite the competition which he presented, retained the respect and friendship of MacGillivray, and each author quoted the other frequently in his text. Yarrell was to become one of the supporters of MacGillivray's successful application for the chair of natural history at Aberdeen University.[27] Audubon was also an admirer of Yarrell, with whom he maintained a correspondence and exchanged specimens.

The comparative failure of MacGillivray's *British Birds* was a source of extreme disappointment to him, and no doubt contributed to the delay in the publication of the fourth and fifth volumes which did not appear until 15 years after the first. The reviews of the first volume in Selby and Jardine's *Magazine of Zoology and Botany* criticised both his style and the content, and in particular disliked his system of classification.[28] MacGillivray's justification of his approach is not illogical:

> ... although I have selected the digestive organ as preeminently worthy of attention, I have not done so because I suppose them capable

of affording a key to the natural system, but because the structure of the food determines not only the form and structure of the bird, but also the greater part of its daily occupations.

MacGillivray persuaded Audubon of his belief in the importance of the study of the alimentary tract as a guide to the classification of species, and the later volumes of *Ornithological Biography* include illustrations of such dissections prepared by MacGillivray. MacGillivray was aware, however, that his anatomical approach might not be to everyone's taste. In a letter to his friend James Harley, a wool merchant in Leicester with whom he maintained a voluminous correspondence, he asked, 'Are my technical descriptions too minute or tedious?' Elsewhere he writes:

> Having one night in April laboured very assiduously in correcting these sheets, I became somewhat imaginative about three in the morning, and ... beheld four Hooting-Owls which, having entered by the chimney, alighted on the table in the midst of my books and papers. They had probably been attracted by the odour emanating from a Buzzard's skull which I had recently dissected; for they presently rummaged about in search of something to pick at. Nothing here but dry sapless stuff. 'MacGillivray's Raptors, etc' observed one of the owls; 'Guts and gizzards' quoth another, 'fit only for Turkey-vultures' 'tedious technicalities and objectless digressions,' shrieked the third. 'Besides' said the fourth, 'the fellow ought to imitate us, he has no respect to the majesty of nature ....' Hardly knowing whether to laugh or to cry, I awoke.[29]

With time MacGillivray's *History of British Birds* became recognised as a classic, 'far superior to that of his predecessors and contemporaries',[30] and it is still valued today as a work of reference. In this work he adopted Audubon's device of including interludes or essays on unrelated topics.

> There remains for me, then, only one method of giving a general interest to my descriptions, namely that of occasionally digressing from the subject, to connect it with those to which it naturally bears reference. If in the following pages some slight attempts at ornament may

Left and above: Peregrine falcon and house sparrow from Yarrell's *British Birds*. Yarrell's illustrations were woodcuts done in the style of Bewick by an artist known only as Thompson. Like Bewick, he added vignettes which increased the attractiveness of the book (*above, right*).

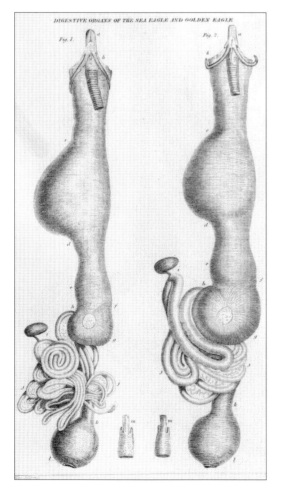

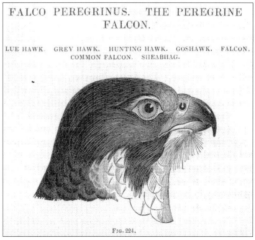

FALCO PEREGRINUS. THE PEREGRINE FALCON.

LUE HAWK. GREY HAWK. HUNTING HAWK. GOSHAWK. FALCON. COMMON FALCON. SHEABHAG.

F<small>IG.</small> 224.

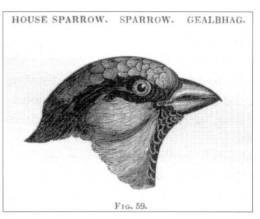

HOUSE SPARROW. SPARROW. GEALBHAG.

F<small>IG.</small> 59.

Left: Illustrations from MacGillivray's *British Birds*. MacGillivray did the drawings from which these engravings were made. The emphasis was on the anatomical details. MacGillivray illustrated the heads of some birds, but never the whole bird although well capable of doing so.

sometimes be made, the reader will not discover in them any fabulous incidents, or any facts so decorated as to lose their proper character [a dig at Audubon?].[31]

Jardine did not like these interludes. 'The writing appears to us an affected attempt to imitate the styles of Isaac Walton and of Audubon, which being extremely peculiar, can only be relished in the originals .... The incidental remarks and digressions liberally dispersed through the volume are (often totally irrelevant to the subject ...).' The fact that MacGillivray was profoundly influenced by Audubon's style, both with regard to his writings and his paintings, is hardly surprising considering the close working association of the two men.

In one of these episodes MacGillivray describes a walk in mid-winter to Peebles, a town to the south of Edinburgh:

In the morning ... of the 26th December 1836, the ground being covered with snow to a moderate height, the wind blowing strongly, and the moon about full, I left Edinburgh accompanied by a young friend. It was only three o'clock when we commenced our expedition, but the moon and the snow together rendered it quite light .... All animated nature seemed buried in sleep or congealed by the frost, the effects of which were very soon experienced .... At Pennicuik we met a man with a lantern, who informed us that it was half-past five ....

By 7am they arrived at an inn twelve miles from Edinburgh where they had a comfortable breakfast, 'which we prefaced and concluded with a glass of whisky, a practice which ... I would strongly recommend as a sovereign remedy against fatigue'. They continued their journey, detailing the varieties of birds encountered, which included grouse. 'Finding the locks of our guns crusted with snow and their muzzles filled, we could only wish the Grouse a merry Christmas.' At length they arrived at Peebles after a difficult walk of 21 miles through thick snow, during which they recorded 25 different species of birds – a remarkable tally in these conditions. The following day they explored Neidpath Castle, about a mile from Peebles on the banks of the River Tweed, in order to study bats. That MacGillivray was prepared to make an expedition in such appalling conditions is a measure of his consuming interest in nature and lack of concern for creature comforts.

In addition to his major works MacGillivray published many articles on a wide range of natural history topics, including geology in the *Memoirs of the Wernerian Natural History Society*, *Quarterly Journal of Agriculture*, *Edinburgh New Philosophical Journal*, *The Naturalist* and elsewhere. During this period he also produced most of his paintings of birds and mammals and fishes which he hoped to publish as a British counterpart to Audubon's *Birds of America*. There are 214 of these paintings now in the keeping of the Natural History Museum in London, having been presented in 1892 by his son Paul Howard MacGillivray. Of these, 121 are bird paintings of 105 different varieties, all painted between 1831 and 1839 while MacGillivray was conservator of the Royal College of Surgeons museum. Many of the paintings are annotated with the source of the bird, many shot by MacGillivray himself or by his son John.

Audubon, who shot several specimens for MacGillivray, said of these paintings:

I think them decidedly the best representations of birds I have ever seen, and have no

Above, left: The 'Great Auk' by Audubon, plate 341 from *The Birds of America*; and by MacGillivray (*above*). Both are drawn from the same specimen. (© The Natural History Museum, London)

hesitation in saying that, should they be engraved in a manner worthy of their excellence, they will form a work not only creditable to you but surpassing in splendour anything of the kind that Great Britain or even Europe has ever produced.[32]

There is little doubt that it was Audubon's inspiration and encouragement that persuaded MacGillivray to follow his example, and he was much influenced by Audubon's style, which can be seen in many of his paintings. It is possible to compare their styles directly, for both painted the same mounted specimen of the great auk which belonged to Audubon.[33]

On 17 May 1831 George Clayton Atkinson visited MacGillivray who was

… engaged in a work on British birds on the scale of Audubon's American Ornithology; in fact Audubon and he are jointly concerned in it: it is to commence in about two years …. When we called he had on his table a drawing for this work which was superior to almost any of Audubon's: it was Razor Bills

and Guillemottes on a mass of rock where they breed …. One of Audubon's great faults, which MacGillivray has fallen into, is representing his birds stepping and stretching with one foot extended.[34]

While maintaining this incredible literary and artistic output, MacGillivray continued to perform his task as conservator, to the entire satisfaction of the college. His first task was to supervise the transfer of the museum contents from the Old Surgeons' Hall to the new building. An entry in the college minutes of 2 August 1832 reads:

Mr Wood [the past president] said there could be but one opinion as to the general assiduity and talent which had been shown by the Conservator in the very arduous task of removing and arranging the Museum, which he had performed so much to the satisfaction of the College. He therefore begged to move that the sum of £50, together with the thanks of the College, be presented to the Conservator for the extra labour he has had in the matter.

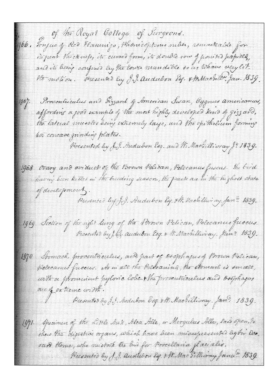

At the next meeting the motion was passed. 'Mr MacGillivray was most deserving of this mark of approbation from the College, especially as the motion proceeded from the curators of the museum, who were best acquainted with the nature and extent of his labours and with the manner in which he had performed his duties.' Clearly MacGillivray had established a better working relationship with his employers than his predecessor had enjoyed.

MacGillivray must have felt much at home in the College Museum as his duties were in many respects similar to those which he had undertaken in the University Museum, including cataloguing, labelling, preserving, cleaning, arranging, dissecting and so on. The specimens donated to the museum were as diverse as those received by the University Museum, including such items as the skeletons of a lion, lioness, tapir and copybara, reindeer horns, a hypertrophied laburnum branch, a cast of Lord Newton's calculus, the diseased spine of a haddock, the skull of a hornbill, a monstrous lamb with six legs, and many surgical instruments. Perhaps the most bizarre specimens were the black vomit from the stomach of a European sailor who died of yellow fever in Jamaica, and the tanned skin of a French officer who had been killed in 1793 in an attack on Breda. MacGillivray made many contributions of natural history subjects and Audubon

was credited with 30 donations of ornithological specimens.

In 1834 MacGillivray reported that the museum held 1085 specimens of human anatomy, 2935 specimens of pathological anatomy, 705 specimens of comparative anatomy, and Dr Barclay's collection of 2512 items which included 400 ornithological specimens that must have been of interest to Audubon. It was truly a wide-ranging collection, and much used by the public as well as students of surgery.

During the rest of his tenure as conservator, the college minutes frequently record satisfaction with his work. The museum was kept in a high state of cleanliness and the specimens were maintained in good preservation. In recognition of his good service the college granted him some dispensations. In 1833 it allowed him to absent himself from the museum on Saturdays, 'for the purpose of enabling him to go into the country and give demonstrations on natural history'. This refers to an additional commitment which MacGillivray had undertaken to teach natural history to the Edinburgh Ladies' Institute, a girls' school in Moray Place which existed from 1834–70. There he gave lectures and demonstrations on Saturday mornings. The prospectus announced that the subjects covered included:

The Nature of the Earth's Surface as adapted for Vegetation. The Distribution of Plants over the Globe. The uses of Botanical Science. The Relations of Plants and Animals. General Idea of the Structure of Plants, their Elementary Tissue, their various Organs, with their principal modifications. Classification Natural and Artificial illustrated by means of quadrupeds and Birds. Linnæan System Etc Etc.

In addition to obtaining permission from the college to engage in these extramural activities, MacGillivray felt bound to seek the consent of his old master Professor Jameson:[35]

Edinburgh, 22 Warriston Crescent
5th March 1832

Sir,

As there was an article in the Contract made between us some years ago, prohibiting me from 'delivering lectures on Natural History, in Edinburgh or its vicinity, during

Professor Jameson's lifetime, without permission from him in writing.' or to that purpose, may I take the liberty of asking if the restriction was meant to apply to me only while acting as 'Assistant and Secretary to the Regius Professor of Natural History in the University of Edinburgh', or if it was intended that it should continue under all circumstances. My reason for troubling you with this request is that I have been urged to prepare lectures or lessons on certain departments of Natural History, to be delivered for the benefit of the rising generation, and my own profit.

I have the honour to be, Sir
Your obedient servant
W MacGillivray

Edinburgh, 12 Graham Street
9th May, 1832

Sir,

I beg leave to call to your remembrance the circumstance of my having requested you by a letter on the 5th March, and by another on the 1st. May 1832, to inform me whether an article of the Contract entered upon by us some years ago, having for its object to prohibit me from delivering lectures in Edinburgh in your lifetime, was meant to bear reference to the period of my assistantship, or to that of my subsequent existence. As I have no copy of that contract, as I never read one line of it, and as I was merely favoured with the perusal of a series of articles which you afterwards said were precisely the same, excepting legal phraseology, may I request that you will have the goodness to furnish me with a copy?

I have the honour to be, Sir
Your obedt. servant
W MacGillivray.

There is no record of a reply by Jameson to these appeals. These letters indicate the strained and formal relationship which existed between the two men. There are also other indications of Jameson's domineering attitude to his sensitive and conscientious erstwhile assistant. In the preface to the third volume of *British Birds*, MacGillivray thanks 'Mr Audubon, to whom I indebted for specimens of several of our rarer feathered visitants … of which I have failed in procuring permission to examine those in

Edinburgh'. This refusal can only refer to Jameson and his museum; however, 15 years later in the preface to the last volume he writes, 'Lastly, to Professor Jameson I am greatly indebted for the liberality with which he laid open to my inspection the valuable materials contained in the beautiful museum of the University of Edinburgh, of which he has long been a distinguished ornament'. His painting of the hawfinch records that it was painted from a specimen supplied by Professor Jameson, so some mellowing of their relationship must have taken place in their declining years.

During 1833 he was allowed leave to visit museums throughout the country. In four weeks he inspected 24 museums – in Glasgow, Liverpool, Dublin, Bristol and London – but in general did not find them superior to his own.

The museum of the Royal College, unlike Jameson's museum, was open to the public without charge between the hours of 12 and 4pm four days a week and attracted a great deal of interest. In 1839 there were 10,256 visitors, of whom 7926 were laymen. MacGillivray, in one of his regular reports to the council of the college, observed on 2 August 1834 that

It has been mentioned to the Conservator, that *low* or *vulgar* persons can derive no benefit from visiting the Museum, but that it is obvious that the inspection of such a collection is calculated to remove many of their prejudices, and that without information all men would be *low* enough. Besides, such persons are the least disposed to handle anything …. Perhaps children under twelve or ten might be excluded with advantage although such as have come have done no harm.

The general public may well have been attracted by morbid interest rather than scientific enquiry, for there were many grotesque and macabre specimens such as the death mask of Burke.

By 1835 he had completed the museum catalogue, which is still extant. A college minute of 3 August 1835 reads:

This work, so creditable to the College and so calculated to increase the usefulness of it, has occupied so much of the Conservator's time and attention, and has been so materially advanced by his assiduity and by his judicious arrangements, as to merit some species of acknowledgment on the part of the College, and with this view the Curators recommend to the College to vote him a gratuity of twenty guineas, which was unanimously agreed to.

His enthusiasm as a museum conservator was described by a contemporary:[36]

He had singular qualifications as Keeper of a Museum. Nothing could exceed his care and patience in preparing an object, except perhaps the delight with which he contemplated the result. His taste in displaying, and his neatness in arranging, were alike remarkable; and both the valuable Museums so long under his care were much indebted to his assiduous labours.

MacGillivray resigned from his post as conservator on his appointment to the chair of civil and natural history at Marischal College, Aberdeen University, in 1841. A minute of 21 April records that the council of the Royal College of Surgeons:

… unanimously resolved to put on record the high sense which they entertain of the value and efficiency of Mr MacGillivray's services as Conservator of the Museum of the College for the last ten years, and to convey to him through their President their sincere congratulations on his appointment to the Professorship of Civil and Natural History in Marischal College, together with their best wishes for his comfort and success in that new department of public duty.

Thus concluded a most fruitful period of MacGillivray's life,[37] which was marked by his election as a Fellow of the Royal Society of Edinburgh in 1834. The extent and breadth of his achievements during this decade is evidence of his remarkable intelligence and industry. His retiral marked the end of a great period of expansion and consolidation of the museum. He was succeeded as conservator by John Goodsir (1814-67),[†] who resigned on his appointment as professor of anatomy in the university, following the retiral of Monro Tertius in 1846. He in turn was succeeded by his brother Harry Goodsir, who after a few months in office was granted leave to join the ill-fated Franklin Expedition in which he perished with the rest of the complement.

Notes

1   MacGillivray, W: *A History of British Birds*, vol. V, p. viii.
2   MacGillivray, W (2): *A Memorial Tribute to William MacGillivray*, p. 60.
3   Cited in Mullens, W H and Swann, H K: *A Bibliography of British Ornithology*, pp. 369-70.
4   *A History of British Birds*, vol I, p. 239.
5   Audubon, J J: *Ornithological Biography*, vol. V, p. 75.
6   MacGillivray, W (2): *A Life of William MacGillivray* (1901).
7   Ralph, R: *William MacGillivray* (1993).
8   Donald MacGillivray in *A Memorial tribute to William MacGillivray* (p. 52) is described as being a much respected member of the island community, and when he died aged 76 he was much missed and sincerely mourned. G C Atkinson in *Expeditions to the Hebrides* (p. 153) paints him in a much less favourable light, stating that he was reviled for having cleared the local population from his lands and having maintained a staunch anti-Catholic stand in a predominately Catholic community. His son Lachlan inherited the family interest in ornithology and supplied specimens to the museum in Edinburgh.
9   It is unclear how the MacGillivray family, who came from a farm in Dunmaglass, Inverness-shire, came to own the prosperous farm at Northton. William Sr appears to have had a financial interest in it which led to a bitter family dispute regarding ownership. His widow Euphemia, who lived on her parent's farm after her husband's death, accused his brothers of having neglected the property. A legal action ensued and eventually the property passed to her son Donald (Jane MacGillivray, personal communication). William Jr referred many years later to 'my father's shepherd', which implies that he considered the farm to have belonged to his father. *The Quarterly Joutnal of Agriculture* (1832), III: 924-9.
10 MacGillivray, W: *A History of the Molluscous Animals*, Preface (1843).
11 *A History of British Birds*, vol. I, p. 175.
12 MacGillivray, W: *Descriptions of the Rapacious Birds of Great Britain*, pp. 93-4.
13 *A History of British Birds*, vol. I, p. 184.
14 William Craigie was one of MacGillivray's very few close friends who shared his interests and was runner-up for the post of conservator of the museum of the Royal College of Surgeons of Edinburgh for which MacGillivray was the successful candidate. Afterwards he emigrated and MacGillivray wrote that he was 'now, in some Canadian wilderness

... making room for himself and his family, beset perhaps with murderous rebels and renegades, my best and most beloved friend William Craigie'. MacGillivray gave two of his children the names Williamina Craigie and William Craigie. His distress on hearing of the death of his friend is described on page 168.

15 *A History of British Birds*, vol. I, pp. 176-9.

16 Ibid, vol. III, p. 550.

17 Ibid, vol. III, p. 543.

18 John Wilson was the college janitor but his duties exceeded those customarily associated with such a post. He also assisted with the museum and was an expert taxidermist, or 'stuffer' as MacGillivray rather inelegantly referred to him. Sir William Jardine stated that his love of ornithology had been aroused by Wilson. Patrick Neill described him as being 'remarkably distinguished for his attachment to natural history pursuits'. He also kept his own museum, which came on the market following his death. MacGillivray, in his new post of conservator of the museum of the Royal College of Surgeons, was authorised to buy specimens from Wilson's museum to the value of £40.

19 *Evidence,* op. cit., p. 629.

20 *Edinburgh Journal of Natural and Geographical Science* (1830), 1: 374-5 and 3: 10-20.

21 *The Autobiography of Charles Darwin*, p. 53 (Collins, 1958). It is of interest that Darwin, during his time in Edinburgh, lived at 11 Lothian Street, adjacent to the University Museum, so he had plenty of opportunity to meet MacGillivray there. His landlady Mrs Mackay, 'a nice clean old body, and exceedingly civil and attentive' according to Darwin, provided a popular students' residence. Subsequent tenants of this same house were John Goodsir, who succeeded MacGillivray as conservator of the museum of the Royal College of Surgeons, and Edward Forbes, who was the unsuccessful applicant for the chair in Aberdeen which MacGillivray obtained. Audubon in 1834 lived nearby in 5 Lothian Street. The houses in Lothian Street up to number 21 were demolished to make way for an extension to the Royal Museum of Scotland. A plaque on the museum wall commemorates Darwin's link with the new building.

22 Letter from N A Vigors to Sir William Jardine in EUL Jardine Correspondence.

23 Tansey, V and Mekie, D E C: *The Museum of the Royal College of Surgeons.*

24 *Descriptions of the Rapacious Birds of Great Britain*, p. 4.

25 Harley, J: *The late Professor William MacGillivray*, p. 133 (1855).

26 Ibid, p. 128.

27 Herrick, H B: *Audubon the Naturalist*, vol. II, p. 225.

28 Anonymous reviews of MacGillivray's *History of British Birds* (vol. I) in *Magazine of Zoology and Botany* (1838), II: 267-9.

29 *A History of British Birds*, vol. III, p. 480.

30 Harley, J: op. cit., p. 389.

31 *A History of British Birds*, vol. III, p. 5.

32 Harley, J: op. cit., p. 119.

33 Neither Audubon nor MacGillivray saw a living specimen of the great auk (*Pinguinus impennis*), which became extinct toward the end of their lives. This large flightless bird was at one time common in the North Atlantic, particularly in the islands off Newfoundland, but with a range extending to the Scottish islands, Iceland and Scandinavia. It was clumsy on land and easy prey to the settlers and fisherman of Newfoundland and Labrador who hunted them relentlessly for their meat, fat and feathers. As they became increasingly rare, private collectors completed the extermination of the species in 1844. Yarrell describes the hunt of one of the last survivors in Orkney which took place in 1813: 'Mr Bullock had the pleasure of chasing, for several hours, in a six-oared boat, but without being able to kill him; for, though he frequently got near him, so expert was the bird in its natural element, that it appeared impossible to shoot him. The rapidity with which he pursued his course under water was almost incredible.' The bird was subsequently killed and presented to Bullock. It was later purchased from his collection by the British Museum. (William Bullock's egg of the great auk was bought by Jameson for the Edinburgh University Museum. See Chapter 7.) John MacGillivray, during his visit to St Kilda in 1840, was told by the inhabitants that the great auk was still encountered around the islands at that time. Audubon recorded that Henry Havell, the brother of his engraver, hooked one when fishing on the banks of Newfoundland and kept it on board for several days before returning it to sea.

34 Atkinson, G C: *Expeditions to the Hebrides in 1831 and 1833*. The whereabouts of this painting is unknown. It is not in the Natural History Museum Collection. Not everyone was so impressed by MacGillivrays' paintings. James Wilson thought that 'His drawings were more accurate than artistical ... the pictorial result was sometimes too like what, in architectural language, might be called the *elevation* of a bird, being deficient in roundness and solidity of form, as well as depth and intensity of colour'. *North British Review* (1853), xix: 5.

35 Jameson Papers, EUL.

36 Thompson, A: *Edinburgh New Philosophical Journal* (1853), 54: 189-206.

37 The Herculean task of combining MacGillivray's museum duties with his vast literary output during this period must have been extremely demanding. The publisher of *British Quadrupeds* in 1838 wrote, 'The public, and we, are well aware, how constantly his time is occupied with his more immediate duties as Conservator of the Museums of the Royal College of Surgeons, as well as his other extensively useful avocations, and therefore excuse the many disappointments we have experienced in the protracted appearance of the British Quadrupeds, which we trust will afford a rich treat in the perusal.' MacGillivray contributed two of the plates used to illustrate this volume.

9 | The Wernerian Society

EDINBURGH had a long tradition of societies and clubs where men of a like mind could foregather and exchange ideas. Many of these existed solely to give opportunity for over-indulgence and debauchery, such as the Spendthrift Club, the Hell-fire Club, the Bonnet Lairds, the Sweating Club, the Dirty Club and the Boar Club. Others had a more serious purpose, such as the Poker Club whose members included Thomas Carlyle, David Hume, William Robertson, Joseph Black and Adam Smith – surely one of the most intellectual gatherings of all times. These clubs provided a meeting ground for a wide cross-section of society where the aristocracy, intellectuals and the literati caroused with lesser mortals. Robert Burns was a member of the Crochallan Fencibles founded by William Smellie, the first editor of the *Encyclopaedia Britannica* which began its existence as an Edinburgh publication. Burns found the society a welcome relief from the more stuffy Edinburgh salons and entertained

its members with some of his more bawdy ballads. The Friday Club, which had among its members the cleric Sydney Smith and the eminent lawyers Francis Jeffrey and Henry Cockburn – both destined to become judges and all noted for their wit and wisdom – must have been a lively gathering. The Aesculapian Club, a medical dining club founded by Andrew Duncan Sr, and the Speculative Club, which had many legal members and discussed such weighty topics as 'The Moral Agency of Man' and 'The History of Imagination', are among the few to survive to this day.

There were two natural history societies in Edinburgh at the time of Audubon's visit, both founded by Professor Jameson. The Plinian Society, an undergraduate body, existed from 1823 to 1841 for the 'Study of Natural History, Antiquities, and the Physical Sciences in General'. At its peak in 1828 it had 184 members. Charles Darwin was elected a member on 28 November 1826, together with William Rathbone Greg (1809-81), the son of Samuel Greg of Quarry Bank Mill near Manchester, where Audubon had enjoyed hospitality earlier that year. William Greg became an acquaintance of both Darwin and Audubon. He invited Audubon to a meeting of the Plinian Society on 12 December 1826 at which he was to speak on the 'Mental and Instinctive powers of Brute Creation', but Audubon was otherwise engaged. Greg was later elected a president of the society. An ardent phrenologist and champion of Combe, Greg staunchly maintained the validity of this philosophy against its critics within the Plinian Society.[1]

Darwin, a regular attender, was stimulated by the quality of debate and discussion on a wide variety of subjects but in particular on the subject of religion, for the Plinian Society had among its members a number of free thinkers who challenged the conventional religious dogmas.

The young Charles Darwin. (Courtesy Ipswich Borough Council Museums and Galleries)

For the first time he heard the accepted biblical teachings on the origins of life being questioned. He was elected to the council of the society a week after he became a member and gave the first public presentation of his career to the society on 24 March 1827 at the age of 17, on original observations which he had made on two marine invertebrates – *Flustra* and *Pontobdella muricata*. (His discoveries were that the larvae of the sea-mat could swim and that black specks on old oyster shells were the eggs of the skate leech.)

Although the Plinian Society was founded by Jameson, he does not appear to have taken much interest in it. His name does not appear in the *Transactions* and he did not intervene when in 1822 the society lost the use of the room in the university in which they had held their meetings since its foundation. The society applied in vain to the Lord Provost and Council of Edinburgh, as patrons of the university, for their support. Eventually Henry Cockburn, in his capacity as Solicitor General, succeeded in persuading the university to provide a room to accommodate several of the undergraduate societies including the Plinian Society.

Thereafter the society went into a gradual decline, the meetings became less frequent and sometimes a quorum was lacking. The last ordinary meeting was held on 19 May 1835. In his evidence to the Royal Commission on the Universities of Scotland on 6 February 1836, Jameson was asked whether the society had possessed a collection of books or manuscripts. He replied, 'They had a collection of both, but a strange set got in amongst them; and one set ran away with the books, and another set ran away with the manuscripts, and the whole property disappeared'. A letter from the secretary of the Plinian Society to the president of the Royal College of Surgeons of Edinburgh, dated 10 February 1841, stated that the society had recently been dissolved and offered its museum collection to the college. The offer was accepted.

Of greater importance was the Wernerian Natural History Society, which was to play such a large part in the lives of many of the personae of this book that it merits this chapter to itself. The society was created by Jameson in 1808 and he remained its president throughout its entire existence. Soon after his death the society was wound up. Membership was highly regarded and keenly sought. Members frequently added

Abraham-Gottlob Werner (1750-1817), reproduced from *The Naturalist's Library*, volume XXXIX.

the letters MWS – Membership of the Wernerian Society – to their fellowships of the Royal Societies and doctorates. The success of the society was due in large measure to the dominant personality of Jameson and its association with the University Museum where it held its meetings. The constant flow of specimens to the museum and the reports from the many journeys of exploration which were being conducted during that period stimulated intense interest. Jameson stated that he had modelled his society on the plan of the Royal Society of Edinburgh and at its peak of influence it did indeed almost match that body in importance.

There were five categories of membership – honorary, resident, non-resident, foreign and corresponding (this last group representing a lower class of membership and not remoteness from Edinburgh). William MacGillivray, for example, became a corresponding member on 29 November 1823, although he was in regular attendance at the meetings and was responsible for arranging the specimens displayed. Corresponding members had to have their papers read by a full member even if they were present at the meeting.

Visitors could be invited and the young Charles Darwin attended during his student days as the guest of his friend and mentor, the zoologist Robert Edmond Grant (1793-1874). Grant was a free thinker who believed that man had evolved from lower forms of life. He was a regular contributor to the society meetings and acknowledged the assistance of Darwin in one of his papers.[2] He became professor of comparative anatomy at the University of London, a post which he held for 46 years. There can be no doubt that although Darwin found the formal university teaching generally dull, and largely abandoned his lectures during his second year, he found great stimulus from the meetings of these societies and the contacts he made there. They laid the foundations of his interest in natural history and contributed to his decision to give up medical studies.

The initial register of the Wernerian Society included three honorary members – Abraham Gottlob Werner, Sir Joseph Banks, then president of the Royal Society of London, and Richard Kirwan, president of the Royal Irish Academy. Among the resident members were several who have figured in the previous chapters, including Patrick Neill, the printer and natural historian who had persuaded Audubon to remain in Edinburgh. Neill was the society's permanent secretary and printer of its *Memoirs*. Patrick Syme, a painter of flowers and fruit, was also a founding member and the society's official artist. James Wilson, elected in 1812, became the society's librarian. The longevity and loyalty of these officers of the society is remarkable. Each was re-elected annually and continued to serve the society almost to the end. Other members who were variously associated with Audubon included Sir William Jardine, Prideaux John Selby, Captain Thomas Brown, Dr Robert Knox, David Brewster and Thomas Stewart Traill. Selby dedicated his *Illustrations of British Ornithology* to the Wernerian Society.

Among the non-resident members was Charles Bell, the artist-surgeon and friend of Jameson then living in London, and the naturalist William Swainson (1789-1855).[†] Foreign members included such eminent natural historians as Baron Cuvier of Paris, Baron von Humboldt of Berlin, and Louis Dufresne. Audubon was thrilled to be elected as a foreign member. Some time later, on Audubon's recommendation, two of his Philadelphia friends and supporters, Richard Harlan MD and Henry MacMurtrie MD, were elected.

The meetings were held monthly during the winter months. Patrick Neill's handwritten minutes of the meetings exist in two volumes in the Edinburgh University Library. The *Memoirs of the Wernerian Society* were published in eight volumes from 1811 to 1839. Some of the papers were printed in full and others summarised or published elsewhere, for example in Jameson's *Edinburgh New Philosophical Journal*, David Brewster's *Edinburgh Journal of Science* or in the *Scots Magazine*. One is struck by the erudition and the artistic ability of the members. Extensive passages were given in French or Latin without the presumption of a translation, and many of the authors illustrated their papers with their own paintings, some engraved by Lizars.

The range of subjects was exceedingly broad and included all aspects of natural history including geology, which was then considered part of natural history.

A typical programme, of 8 March 1823, reveals the diversity of topics:

> The Secretary read an account of a new Species of Pigeon from New Holland, by Sir William Jardine, Baronet, illustrated by a Drawing; likewise Remarks on the Serularia cuscuta of Ellis, by Dr Fleming; and a Notice by Mr L Edmondston, in regard to the Ivory Gull and Iceland Gull.

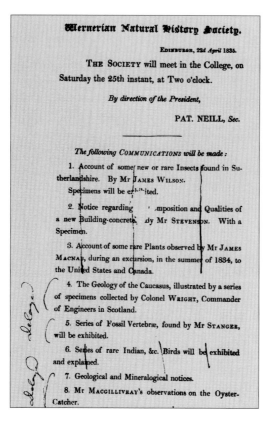

Notice of the meeting of the Wernerian Society on 25 April 1836. (Courtesy of Edinburgh University Library)

Professor Jameson communicated to the Society a Register of the Thermometer, Adie's Sympiesometer, and Leslie's Hygrometer, kept at Corfu, by Mathew Miller, Esq. of the 56th Regiment, with Remarks; likewise a Letter from Mr William Jameson [the president's nephew], dated Lima, descriptive of his Voyage round Cape Horn, and a Chart of the Course, laid down in the mode recommended by Capt Basil Hall.

On 26 April 1826,

Mr Arnott read a paper, by Mr L Edmondson, on the Black-billed Auk and Lesser Guillemot, and Professor Jameson described the specimens exhibited. Dr Knox read a paper on some Peculiarities of the Structure of the New Holland Casuary. A memoir on the Bignoniaceae, by Mr Don, was read; and likewise the first part of Mr Ellis's Account of Dr Rusconi's Observations on the Natural History and Structure of the Aquatic Salamander. Before the close of the Meeting, Professor Jameson gave an account of a series of Models, exhibited at the Meeting, representing the different Indian Castes in Bengal; likewise some Cinerary Urns, lately dug up at Dean Bank near Stockbridge. Some remarkable Javanese Deities, and a complete set of Musical Instruments from Nepaul, were likewise exhibited.

The following papers have been selected from the *Memoirs of the Wernerian Society* because of their interest or relevance to the subjects of this book.

Several describe unusual marine life caught in the Firth of Forth or stranded on its shores, including a swordfish and a variety of whales. In an account by Patrick Neill on 11 February 1808 of a fin-whale stranded near Alloa, he recounted that the '*flenching*' had been carried out before he saw it, making identification difficult. It yielded seven casks of oil, sold to a soap-boiler for £15.

I cannot help here observing, that the carcase might, along with peat-moss, which abounds in the neighbourhood, have produced, on Lord Meadowbank's principle, a quantity of compost manure worth probably a good deal

more than the trifling sum procured with so much labour and expense from the blubber.

The stranding of whales on the shores of the Forth has been a recurrent event, the most recent being in 1997. Dr Robert Knox (the anatomist) and his brother spent three years dissecting a blue whale, or Sibbald's rorqual (*Balaenoptera musculus*), which was washed ashore near North Berwick in 1831. The skeleton, prepared by the Knox brothers, is still to be seen in the Royal Museum in Edinburgh.

There are several papers by William Scoresby, the student protégé of Jameson, describing his explorations of the coastline of Greenland. In a paper describing the different characteristics of ice, read on 11 March 1815, he observed that

Fresh-water ice is fragile, but hard .... The homogenous and most transparent pieces, are capable of concentrating the rays of the sun, so as to produce a considerable intensity of heat. With a lump of ice, of by no means regular convexity, I have frequently burnt wood, fired gunpowder and melted lead, and lit the sailors' pipes, to their great astonishment ....

Below (*top*): The stranded rorqual whale which was dissected by Dr Robert Knox; (*bottom*) the skeleton of the whale. The illustrations, engraved by Lizars, are from Jardine's *Naturalist's Library*, volume XII.

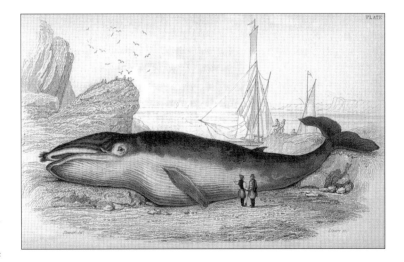

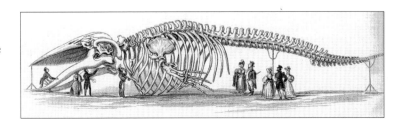

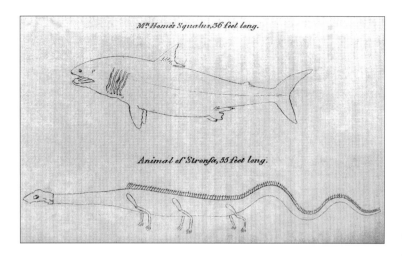

Mr Home's Squalus, 36 feet long.

Animal of Stronsa, 55 feet long.

The Orcadian Curiosity, plate XI from *Memoirs of the Wernerian Society*, volume I (p. 429).

One ship now alone remained, to which the crews of four, and the surviving part of the crew of the fifth … repaired. On the 11th October the last ship was overwhelmed by the ice and sunk. Thus, between three and four hundred men were driven to the ice, and exposed to the inclemency of the weather, almost destitute of food and raiment …. About 140 of the men reached the Danish settlements of the West Coast of Greenland; the remainder, consisting of about 200, perished.

The survivors had to walk about 300 miles in mid-winter without adequate clothing or provisions.

A delightful paper by Dr John Barclay (the eminent anatomist associated with the Royal College of Surgeons of Edinburgh and Robert Knox) described an animal which was cast ashore on the Orcadian island of Stronsay in September 1808. This remarkable animal measured 55 feet in length and 10 feet in circumference according to local observers, who also described three pairs of limbs, variously called 'arms', 'wings' or 'paws'.

Barclay dismissed the suggestion that it could have been a basking shark (*Cetorhinus* [*Squalus*] *maximus*) and regarded it as a new species. In support of this he added a letter from the Rev. Mr Maclean of the Small Isles (Inner Hebrides), who described what he considered was a similar animal seen off the shores of the island of Coll in the same year:

Their astonishment was increased, on observing, that the ice remained firm and pellucid, whilst the solar rays emerging therefrom, were so hot, that the hand could not be kept longer in the focus, than for the space of a few seconds.

In the same paper he described the hazards of sailing in these waters.

… in the year 1777 … the ship Wilhelmina was moored to a field of ice on the 22d of June, in the usual fishing station, along with a large fleet of other whalers. On the 25th the Wilhelmina was closely *beset*. The crew were obliged to work incessantly for eight days, in sawing a dock in the field, wherein the ship was at that time preserved.

On the 25th of July, the ice slacked, and the ship was towed to the eastward, during four days laborious rowing with the boats. At the extremity of the opening, they joined four ships, and all of them were soon again beset by the ice …. On the 15th August, nine sail were collected together; and about the 20th, after sustaining a dreadful storm, and an immense pressure of the ice … two of the ships were wrecked. Two more were wrecked four or five days afterwards, together with two others at a distance from them …. Another was lost on the 7th of September; and, on the 13th, the Wilhelmina was crushed to pieces by the fall of an enormous mass of ice, which was so unexpected, that those of the crew who were in bed had scarcely time to escape on the ice, half naked as they were.

… rowing along the coast, I observed, at about the distance of half a mile, an object to windward, which gradually excited astonishment. At first view, it appeared like a small rock …. Then I saw it elevated considerably above the level of the sea, and after a slow movement, distinctly perceived one of its eyes. Alarmed at the unusual appearance and magnitude of the animal, I steered so as to be at no great distance from the shore. When nearly in a line betwixt it and the shore, the monster directing its head … towards us, plunged violently under water. Certain that he was in chace [*sic*] of us, we plied hard to get ashore. Just as we leaped out on a rock … we saw it coming rapidly under water towards the stern of our boat. When within a few yards of the boat, finding the water shallow, it raised its monstrous head above water, and, by a winding course, got, with apparent difficulty, clear of the creek where our boat lay .... It had no fin that I could perceive, and seemed to me to move progressively by undulation up and down.

Clearly a Loch Ness Monster lookalike!

The monster generated great public interest at the time. The Scottish opinion favoured Barclay's view that it represented a new species, while Sir Everard Home, the eminent English anatomist who examined specimens of the monster which had been sent to London, had the more prosaic opinion that it was just a basking shark. Samples of the cartilaginous vertebrae of the Stronsay monster are preserved in the National Museums of Scotland and are now regarded as being of a basking shark – albeit one of unusually large size, nearly twice as long as the largest basking shark ever recorded.[3]

On the subject of the miraculous, at a later meeting on 22 March 1826, 'The Rev Dr Scot of Corstorphine read a paper on the Great Fish that swallowed up Jonah, and after three days and nights, cast him out on dry land; shewing that it could not be a whale, as often supposed, but was probably a *Squalus carcharias*, or White Shark'. Unfortunately no full account of this fascinating paper was published.

On 25 March 1829 Robert Stevenson (civil engineer and grandfather of Robert Louis Stevenson) gave an account of 'the remarkable instance of a Newfoundland dog, which returned alone from Frankfort [*sic*] to his home in Edinburgh'. Alas no further details are given of this extraordinary journey. Did he somehow stowaway on a boat, and if so how did he know its destination?

The Bible was interpreted very literally and many papers attempted to explain biblical events in contemporary scientific thought. On 5 February 1831

... the Professor read a learned essay, by a Fellow of the Royal Societies of London and Edinburgh, on the Form of the Ark of Noah, as described in the Pentateuch; shewing that the word *tzohar*, rendered *window* in our translation, rather means *tapering upwards*; and that, with this modification, the form of the Ark was not only admirably adapted for

Illustration of the vertebrae of the Stronsay monster by Patrick Syme, plate X from *Memoirs of the Wernerian Society*, volume I (p. 418).

floating, but also for withstanding the shock of waves, although this last quality has been generally denied to it by unscientific commentators.

Dr Thomas Stewart Traill, although living at the time in Liverpool, contributed many papers. He gave an account of an 'Orang Outang' [*sic*], a female procured in the Gulf of Guinea from a native trader. Captain Payne, who brought the unfortunate animal back to Britain, reported that the natives of Gaboon had informed him that orangutans would attack lions and other beasts of prey with clubs and stones, and were reported to have carried off negro girls who were 'for years detained by their ravishers in a frightful captivity'.

When first our animal came on board, (says Captain Payne,) it shook hands with some of the sailors, but refused its hand, with marks of anger, to others, without any apparent cause. It speedily, however, became familiar with the crew, except one boy, to whom it never was reconciled. When the seamen's mess was brought on deck, it was a constant attendant; would go round and embrace each person, while it uttered loud yells, and then seat itself among them, to share the repast.

Traill's jacketed monkey, plate IX from *Memoirs of the Wernerian Society*, volume III (p. 167).

Far right: Section of the mammoth tusk recently found in Edinburgh's Cannonball House. Now in the National Museums of Scotland.

The health of the animal suffered during the voyage. It died soon after arriving at Liverpool and was subjected to a detailed anatomical study described by Traill. Elsewhere he describes other new or unusual species including the jacketed monkey above, which suggests that his artistic ability was less developed than that of many of his contemporaries.

An interesting paper entitled 'Account of the Effects of the Juice of the Papaw Tree (*Carica papaya*), in Intenerating Butcher's meat', by Dr Holder, describes the tenderising property of papaya juice on meat. This property has subsequently been shown to be due to a proteolytic enzyme and use has been made of this agent in recent years in the treatment of the prolapsed intervertebral disc in man.

Robert Bald, a civil engineer, reported the discovery and unfortunate fate of a mammoth's tusk found during the excavations of the Union Canal between Edinburgh and Glasgow. The tusk was well preserved and measured 39 inches in length.

I suggested to Sir Alexander Maitland Gibson [the landowner] to take particular care of it. He accordingly told the workman who found it, to send it to the house of Cliftonhall, where he would give him a gratuity for it. The workman, immediately upon understanding that what he conceived to be a horn, was ivory, and very valuable, went off to Edinburgh with the tooth, and sold it. Sir Alexander, the instant he heard of this went in search of it, and found it in an ivory-turner's, who had given £2 for it; but, most unfortunately … it was sawn across in three places, and part of it prepared for the lathe, to form chess-men; Sir Alexander repaid the money which had been given for it; and he has, in

the most obliging manner permitted me now to exhibit it to the Society.

A section of this tusk was recently rediscovered in a cupboard in Edinburgh's Cannonball House and is now in the Museum of Scotland. It is reckoned to be about 30,000 years old.

On 10 August 1822 an extraordinary meeting was held in order to vote a Congratulatory Address to King George IV on the occasion of his visit to Scotland.[4] This commences:

To the King's Most Excellent Majesty.

May it please your Majesty, We, your Majesty's most dutiful and loyal Subjects, the Members of the Wernerian Natural History Society of Edinburgh, beg leave to approach the Throne with the warmest sentiments of congratulation on the happy event of your Majesty's condescending Visit to this part of the United Kingdom; an event which will be recorded as forming a brilliant and memorable era in the Annals of Scotland.

Amongst the various descriptions of our Countrymen, who are now so eagerly pressing forward to testify their veneration and attachment to your Majesty, we, too, would humbly hope that the tribute of loyalty, gratitude and affection, cordially presented by a Body of Men who have associated for the cultivation of one of the most beautiful and useful of the Sciences, will not be unacceptable to a Prince who, besides possessing the noblest qualifications of a Sovereign, is so eminently distinguished by his knowledge, taste and personal accomplishments, and who is, we believe, himself an admirer of our favourite study.

Above, left: Drawing of Mark Yarwood, plate XIII from *Memoirs of the Wernerian Society*, volume IV (p. 449).

Above: Mark Yarwood's writing, plate XIV from *Memoirs of the Wernerian Society*, volume IV (p. 460).

This eulogy continued for several more paragraphs and was presented to the king by Jameson with a volume of the society's *Memoirs*. The event of the royal visit in 1822 – the first by a reigning monarch since Charles II in 1650 – created an intense interest and excitement. The dissolute and licentious king, reviled in London, was greeted with great warmth and respect by his Scottish subjects. The extravagant address gives some indication of the society's estimation of its own importance on this occasion.

On 11 February 1823, S Hibbert MD FRSE MWS etc. gave an interesting paper 'On the Natural Expedients resorted to by Mark Yarwood, a Cheshire Boy, to supply the Want which he has sustained from Birth, of his Fore-Arms and Hands'.

He told of a boy with congenital amputations of both arms above the elbows, who

… arrived at the age of twelve; and is now a fine, stout, healthy-looking boy, of a lively and cheerful temper, and good disposition …. His stumps are gifted with a sensibility and accuracy of touch, by no means inferior to that degree of delicacy which physiologists have conceived to be peculiar to the structure of the hands.

When I first saw Mark, he was actively engaged at a well-known school-game with the boys of his village. He took up a common marble, and with a conjunct motion of the muscles of the arms, seldom failed to hit, with the greatest dexterity, the mark at which he aimed. He has, indeed, the reputation of being the best marble player in the school.

Hibbert noted that the boy could thread a needle, pick up a sixpence, use a spoon and tie a bow with the assistance of his tongue.

His teacher conceived the possibility of instructing his pupil to write, and the attempt has been crowned with complete success. The paper is fixed to the table by means of a small weight. The boy first seizes the pen with his teeth, from which it is lodged on the soft integuments of the right stump, and retained by the pressure of the left, the pen is drawn along the paper with most remarkable facility. His schoolmaster conceived as a great obstacle his inability to make a pen. This impediment, however, the boy's natural genius has since surmounted. The lad places the quill between his knees, the barrel upwards; and with a knife held between his stumps, cuts off the end, and forcing the blade within the barrel, makes the slit. He next cuts away due portions from each side of the quill until a point is formed. The boy is so proud of this latest acquirement that he has sent me a letter written with a pen made by himself.

Such are the natural expedients resorted to by Mark with the view of obviating a privation, which no one laments less than himself. 'I do not wish to have hands,' said

111

'Egyptian Goose' by
MacGillivray.
(© The Natural History
Museum, London)

species. A drawing was exhibited of the leader of the flock, which had been shot by Captain Sharpe.

An extensive and valuable series of highly finished representations of the indigenous animals of Great Britain, chiefly quadrupeds and birds, by Mr MacGillivray, was also exhibited to the meeting. Professor Jameson pointed out that their peculiar excellence consisted in their combining, with great beauty of pictorial effect, a more accurate representation of the forms of the crania, as always identical in the young and old of the same species, an important particular, greatly neglected by ornithological draughts-men; and also in there being less mannerism in the general treatment of the plumage, the characteristic form and texture of the feathers of each species being particularly attended to by Mr MacGillivray.

Although MacGillivray had ceased to be Jameson's assistant in 1829 and parted from him with a certain amount of ill will, it is interesting that he continued to contribute papers to the society and, as the above entry shows, Jameson continued to hold him in high regard.

By 21 February 1835 MacGillivray appears to have been promoted to ordinary membership and was permitted to read his own paper for the first time.

Mr MacGillivray read some observations on the Dipper (*Cinclus aquaticus*). The peculiarities of form and plumage, adapting it to its amphibious mode of life, were pointed out, and its habits minutely described. The alleged injuries to the salmon-fisheries by this species were rendered doubtful by the results of the author's observations, he having never found any ova or fry of fish in its stomach, which was usually found to contain fragments of coleopterous insects and mollusca ….

On 7 March 1835,

Mr MacGillivray read remarks on varieties of the Fox observed in Scotland. He distinguished four races of varieties …. Dr Traill then exhibited a series of beautiful and correct drawings of British quadrupeds, cetacea, birds, reptiles, and fishes, executed

the contented little fellow, 'as I have never known the use of them, nor have I ever felt the loss of them.'

William MacGillivray was a regular contributor. His first paper to the society was read on 9 February 1822 on two varieties of *Nuphar lutea* found in a lake in Aberdeenshire. He gives the details of these two water lilies in Latin. Subsequent papers covered a wide variety of topics on ornithology, botany, comparative anatomy and geology, revealing the breadth of his interests and knowledge.

In the entry for 23 March 1833,

… a communication by Mr MacGillivray was then read, regarding the occurrence of a flock of foreign water-fowl, the Anas Aegyptiaca, (Egyptian goose) on the eastern coast of Scotland; but the author suggested the possibility of these birds having strayed from Lord Wemyss's pleasure-grounds at Gosford; and the present instance could not therefore, with certainty, be regarded as illustrating the natural migration of the

MacGillivray's painting of the dipper. (© The Natural History Museum, London)

by Mr MacGillivray, and which are intended for his projected work on the vertebrate animals of Great Britain.

Why his paintings had to be presented by Traill is unclear – perhaps he wanted to hear the comments and criticisms of that respected scientist. MacGillivray's ambition to publish his paintings, which alas he was unable to realise, is discussed in Chapter 16, p. 203.

On 8 April 1837, 'Mr MacGillivray then read a paper on the geological relations, and animal and vegetable productions, of the Cromarty Frith [sic], with observations relative to the estuaries and sea-lochs of Scotland'. He had donated his geological collection from this area to the museum. On 7 December 1839 he 'exhibited a specimen of the Butcher bird [great gray shrike, *Lanius excubitor*] which had been shot at Wittinghame and also a beautiful drawing of the same specimen made by himself'.

Although MacGillivray left Edinburgh for Aberdeen in 1841, he continued to maintain an interest in the society. A minute of 18 November 1842 states that he was asked to make a drawing of a pink-footed goose which he had shown.

On 13 January 1844 Mr Torrie (Thomas Jameson Torrie 1808-58, a nephew of the president and assistant secretary of the society) then read an account of an 'ascent of the Peak at Teneriffe in May 1842 by Mr John MacGillivray, at present naturalist to the government expedition under command of Capt Blackwood, the communication having been sent by the author from Sydney, New Holland'. On 10 February 1844 the second part of the ascent was read and 'on a motion of Professor Jameson the thanks of the society were unanimously voted to Professor MacGillivray of Marischal College, Aberdeen for favouring the society with this interesting communication from his son'.[5] This is the last recorded link between MacGillivray and the society which he had supported loyally for more than 20 years.

Audubon was elected a foreign member on 13 January 1827, but prior to his election, on 16 December 1826, 'The secretary read Mr

MacGillivray's drawing of the 'Butcher Bird' (great gray shrike). (© The Natural History Museum, London)

Audubon's account of the Habits of the Vultur Aura, or Turkey Buzzard, in which he exploded the opinion generally entertained of its extraordinary power of smelling'. This paper, which maintained that the vulture was attracted to food entirely by sight and not by scent, was published in the *Edinburgh New Philosophical Journal*[6] and attracted a vitriolic attack from the naturalist Charles Waterton, who had declared otherwise in his *Wanderings in South America*. The furore generated by this paper is described in Chapter 11. Charles Darwin was present as a guest at this meeting and recalled in later life the impression which Audubon made 'with his black flowing locks'.

At this same meeting Audubon displayed his painting of the turkey buzzard and 'afterwards shewed to the Society his mode of fixing recently killed birds in various attitudes, against a board marked with squares or division lines, corresponding to similar lines pencilled on the sheet of paper on which the drawing is to be made'. Audubon published this paper in the *Edinburgh Journal of Science*.[7]

On 13 January 1827 Audubon read a 'Memoir on the Habits of the Alligator', which was published in the *Edinburgh Journal of Science*.[8] At that same meeting 'the members were then invited by the President to view, in another apartment, some live animals, lately brought from Chile, by the Right Hon. Captain Lord Napier, of the Diamond Frigate, particularly the Felix Puma, or American Lion' (see Chapter 7).

On 24 February 1827 Audubon 'read an account of the Natural History of the Rattlesnake (*Crotalus horridus*) illustrated by a beautiful drawing of the animal suffering attacks of mocking birds' (see p. 143). This paper, together with his paper on the vulture, were to land Audubon in the midst of a heated controversy on both sides of the Atlantic which is described in Chapter 11.

On 22 January 1831, 'Mr John James Audubon being present, read an account of the White-headed Eagle of America (*Aquila leucocephala*), and exhibited a splendid engraving of the bird, prepared for his great work entitled The Birds of America'. This paper was presumably taken from the first volume of *American Ornithology*[9] which was published that year. The following is an extract:

The figure of this noble bird is well known throughout the civilized world, emblazoned as it is on our national standard, which waves in the breeze of every clime, bearing to distant lands the remembrance of a great people living in a state of peaceful freedom. May that peaceful freedom last for ever!

Audubon's 'Little Blue Heron', plate 307 from *The Birds of America*. The background is by Lehman. (© The Natural History Museum, London)

He concludes the account with a rather contradictory sentiment:

Suffer me, kind reader, to say how much I grieve that it should have been selected as the Emblem of my Country. The opinion of our great Franklin on this subject, as it perfectly coincides with my own, I shall here present to you. 'For my part,' says he, in one of his letters, 'I wish the Bald Eagle had not been chosen as the representative of our country. He is a bird of bad moral character; he does not get his living honestly; you may have seen him perched on some dead tree, where, too lazy to fish for himself, he watches the labour of the Fishing-Hawk; and when that diligent bird has at length taken a fish, and is bearing it to his nest for the support of his mate and young ones, the Bald Eagle pursues him, and takes it from him. With all this injustice he is never in good case, but like those among men who live by sharping and robbing he is generally poor and often very lousy ....'

On 19 February 1831, 'Mr John James Audubon communicated an interesting and graphic description of a Flood of the Mississippi which he had witnessed during his residence in the western parts of America'. This paper also appears as one of his 'episodes' in *American Ornithology*.[10]

To give you some idea of a *Booming Flood* of these gigantic streams, it is necessary to state the causes which give rise to it. These are, the sudden melting of the snows on the mountains, and heavy rains continued for several weeks .... These delivering their waters to the great streams, cause the latter not merely to rise to a surprising height, but to over flow their banks, wherever the land is low. On such occasions, the Ohio itself presents a splendid, and at the same time an appalling spectacle; but when its waters mingle with those of the Mississippi then, kind reader, is the time to view an American flood in all its astonishing magnificence.

Audubon's 'White-headed Eagle', plate 31 from *The Birds of America*. (Reproduced by kind permission of the President and Council of the Royal College of Physicians and Surgeons of Glasgow)

… I have known, for example, of a cow swimming through a window, elevated at least seven feet from the ground, and sixty-two feet above low-water mark …. But let us return to the Mississippi.

There the overflow is astonishing; for no sooner has the water reached the upper part of the banks, than it rushes out and over-spreads the whole of the neighbouring swamp, presenting an ocean overgrown with stupendous forest-trees. So sudden is the calamity, that every individual, whether man or beast, has to exert his utmost ingenuity to enable him to escape from the dreaded element. The Indian quickly removes to the hills of the interior, the cattle and game swim to the different stripes of land that remain uncovered in the midst of the flood, or attempt to force their way though the waters until they perish from fatigue ….

Even the steamer is frequently distressed. The numberless trees and logs that float along break its paddles and retard its progress. Besides, it is on such occasion difficult to procure fuel to maintain its fires ….

There can be no doubt that MacGillivray and Audubon must have met frequently at these meetings as both men delivered papers to the society during 1827, but their close friendship did not become established until 1830.

Dr Robert Knox, although not one of Jameson's admirers, was also a regular contributor, even after his fall from grace in 1828. His papers displayed a wide range of interests, including 'The Habits of the Hyena of Southern Africa', 'The Anatomy of the Beaver', 'The Foramen centrale of the Retina, as seen in the Eyes of certain Reptiles', 'The Anatomy of the duck-billed Animal of New South Wales, the Ornithorynchus paradoxus' (the specimen had been sent to the University Museum by Sir Thomas Brisbane, the Governor of New South Wales who was a regular contributor to the museum and a member of the society), 'The Origin and Characteristic Differences of the Native Races inhabiting the Extra-tropical Part of Southern Africa', 'The Mode of Growth, Reproduction, and Structure of the Poison-Fangs in Serpents', and 'The *Colymbus septentrionalis*, or Red-throated Diver'. It is a pity that Knox is now remembered only for his association with Burke and Hare and his contributions to the advancement of comparative anatomy are sadly forgotten.

James Wilson, the friend of Audubon and MacGillivray and librarian to the society, was also a regular contributor on a wide range of subjects. These included papers on the common frog, on eagles, on the *Genus mergus* (mergansers), on the museum's puma (see pp. 76–77), on the natural history of the breed of domestic dogs, on glowworms, and on new or rare insects discovered by himself in Sutherlandshire. On 5 February 1831 the Rev. Lansdown Guilding of St Vincents described 'new and beautiful species of West Indian moth, called by him *Attacus wilsoni*, in honour of James Wilson, Librarian of the Society, and a distinguished entomologist'.

In 1833 the society, being in funds, decided to award prizes to individuals who gave the 'best account of a defined district of country in Scotland, including its mineralogy, botany and zoology'. R J H Cunningham received 20 sovereigns for his study of 'The Geology of the Lothians', and Richard Parnell ten sovereigns and a gold medal for his essay on 'The Fishes of the District of the Forth'. Both papers were published in full, filling the entire seventh volume of the *Memoirs of the Wernerian Society*. The limited circulation of this publication ensured that these important works remained largely unrecognised, although there has been a recent revival of interest in Parnell's essay, which has been described as a '*tour de force*'.[11] In this work he maintains the error of regarding the parr as being a distinct species – a view commonly held at that time, notwithstanding the fact that four years earlier James Hogg, the Ettrick shepherd and poet, had reported an experiment which proved convincingly that the parr was a juvenile salmon.[12]

Perhaps because the exclusive nature of its membership attracted envy, the Wernerian Society and its president Jameson became the subjects of an extraordinary vicious attack in the pages of the *Edinburgh Journal of Natural and Geographical Science*.[13] Although unsigned, the author was certainly one of the editors, Henry Hulme Cheek, who was an active member of the Plinian Society. In the first tirade the author, writing in 1830, criticises the scarcity of the society's publications – only five volumes of *Memoirs* in 20 years. He says that despite there being a librarian, James Wilson, the library appeared to be kept under Jameson's control and no one had access to it – and asks what had happened to all the specimens which had been presented to the society?

> … as an active influential Society, of twenty years standing, what is it?… Professor Jameson is calculated to make an excellent President, and in a certain sense he does make such a one. But as it is sufficiently known that he exercises uncontrolled authority over the affairs of the Society, we shrewdly suspect that the editor of a Philosophical and Natural History Journal is not the individual best fitted to regulate the publication of the transactions of a Natural History Society.

In a second lengthy attack[14] on the 'misdirected institution', Cheek again criticises the failure of the council to take appropriate action over the state of the library – the librarian did not even have a key! As a result of the permanency of office of the executive

> … abuses had crept onto the management …. For instance, it was well known that the president, who is the editor of a scientific journal, was in the constant habit of appropriating to his own use the papers which ought to have formed part of the Transactions.

Cheek goes on to hint that because William MacGillivray, Jameson's personal assistant, had been appointed as assistant librarian, 'it shows plainly enough who had access to the books'. A document signed by Patrick Neill the secretary explaining the actions taken by the Library Committee came under minute scrutiny, but Cheek notes, 'he must have been induced or obliged to do it [sign it] by some other person'. He exonerates Neill from any blame, for 'we join the voice of all who know him, in the profession of unlimited esteem for his character and talents'.

Patrick Neill leapt to defend the honour of Jameson and the society by publishing privately a widely circulated pamphlet in which he wrote:

> On reading over the whole article, I was shocked to find, Gentlemen, that it breathed a spirit of rooted enmity and reckless hostility towards Professor Jameson, our distinguished

President, which I did not imagine it possible for an educated person to have entertained, or at least to have published to the world.

He recorded a face-to-face confrontation with Cheek when they talked 'pretty warmly on the subject'. Neill strenuously denied that any pressure had been put upon him to sign the document about the Library Committee: '… that circular having been solely my act and deed, without my being prompted by any one.' He drew Cheek's attention to errors of fact in his second article which had not yet been distributed, and demanded that it be withdrawn. In the event only an errata slip was inserted. An angry exchange of letters followed regarding 'this odious business', in which Neill demanded an apology: 'I shall rejoice to retire from the arena the moment I have done justice to myself and to the Wernerian Society.'

> In Edinburgh, where my character has been pretty well known for a quarter of a century past, the grossest attack which this young stranger could make upon my integrity, was not likely to injure me deeply. But in distant places, so confident an attack on my good name was certainly calculated to do mischief.

In the event no apology was given.

Neill then explains that the infrequent publication of the society's transactions was simply due to shortage of funds, hence it was inevitable 'that papers read before the Wernerian Society should occasionally, at the desire or with the approbation of the author, find a place in our President's scientific Journal, [this] was surely most natural, most proper, and most desirable'. He says it was ludicrous to depict 'our President … as grasping at the use of the few volumes in our possession'.

Patrick Neill's loyal defence of the society, which he had served as secretary for 23 years and which he says 'has been a constant source of solace and pleasure to me', was robust and commendable. However, there was perhaps more than an element of truth in Cheek's attack upon Jameson, who almost certainly abused his position of authority over the society as he did over his museum. Cheek was certainly being fed inside information, no doubt from disgruntled members; however he paid a heavy price, for the

Edinburgh Journal of Natural and Geographical Science (to which both Audubon and MacGillivray had submitted articles) ceased publication soon after these episodes and Cheek faded into obscurity. It did not pay to challenge such men of influence as Jameson and Neill.

The *Memoirs of the Wernerian Society* continued to be published at long intervals until 1839 when it stopped without any explanation. The final volume, eight, is incomplete. Manuscript minutes were continued in Neill's handwriting.[15] The problem was almost certainly financial. A letter from the daughter of the publisher Mr Black to James Wilson dated 8 March 1850 reads:

> My Dear Sir
>
> Regarding the Wernerian Society Transactions, my father told me this afternoon that he has paid for the printing and paper of the Seventh Volume, and taken his note of sale, which has turned out any thing but a good concern.
>
> It seems that we have no account to arrange for the sale of the Books, or for Advertising, so I will thank you to write Prof Goodsir[16] to that effect.
>
> What I wrote before was a mistake, not knowing the arrangements made with my father.
>
> I am yours truly
> Frances Black

Certainly the finances of the society towards the end of its existence appear to have been in a state of considerable confusion. Perhaps also there were too many other competing publications on natural history at that time or perhaps the society was beginning to run out of steam as the reputation of Werner suffered and the energy of Jameson waned. Few new members were enrolled and the old guard became less active. The only honorary member elected after 1837 was the Prince Consort on the occasion of his marriage in 1840. Attendance at meetings seems to have declined and there are several references to meetings being cancelled due to the inclemency of the weather. During the winter of 1847/8 no meetings were held because of the severe indisposition of Jameson.

The last regular meeting took place on 23 November 1850, at which the 'Venerable secretary was prevented by indisposition from attending – a circumstance which had not previously occurred in the history of the society since its foundation in the year 1808'. This minute is signed with a very shaky hand by Jameson and signals the effective end of the society. There are no further minutes until 1856 when the surviving members met to discuss the winding up of the society, which was finally promulgated on 28 November 1857. Its assets were distributed to the Royal Physical Society, the Botanical Society and the University Museum.

There is no doubt that in the early years of the nineteenth century, during Jameson's prime, the Wernerian Natural History Society justified its self-importance. *Blackwood's Magazine*, June 1817, recorded that 'The Society has now existed upwards of twenty-seven years, during which period its records have been graced with the names of all the most distinguished philosophers of Europe and America; and although unaided by the advantages of wealth, it has silently pursued its useful career, and has, both directly and indirectly, contributed most essentially to the well-doing of science.'

For Audubon, membership of this society during its period of greatest influence was a tremendous boost to his self-esteem. Acceptance of his communications by the society and the contacts which he established there did much to establish his confidence and standing in the scientific community. The society was one of the early subscribers to Audubon's *Birds of America*, but discontinued its subscription after paying 18 guineas, which represented the cost of the first six numbers (of five plates each). It is possible that the bound volume of plates in the possession of the National Museums of Scotland are those originally owned by the Wernerian Society.

Notes

1 *Transactions of the Cambridge Bibliographic Society* (1979), VII: 376-90. After completing his studies in Edinburgh, William Greg entered the family business and became a mill manager. He wrote: 'I have the charge of an immense manufacturing concern here, which employs about 600 people, probably as great barbarians as can be found out of Africa and Australia .... I came here full of philanthropic vision and schemes of brightening the intellects and purifying the character of the people committed to my care, but all vanished before the antimagical effect of a fortnights residence among them ....' Later, however, he did take an active part in the establishment of a Mechanics Institution where he gave lectures to audiences of up to 650, the purpose of the lectures being 'less to give *knowledge* to the lower classes than to sharpen their intellects and refine their minds' (quotations from MS A99, pp. 280-1 and 241-2, in the Mitchell Library, Sydney). After the publication of *The Descent of Man* in 1871, Greg renewed his acquaintance with Darwin.

2 Grant, R E: *Edinburgh Journal of Science* (1827), 7: 160-1. In this paper on the ova of Pontobdella, Grant wrote: 'The merit of having first ascertained them to belong to that animal is due to my zealous young friend Mr Charles Darwin of Shrewsbury, who kindly presented me with specimens of the ova exhibiting the animal in different states of maturity.'

3 Geoffrey N Swinney of the National Museums of Scotland has given a reasoned explanation of his conclusion that the monster was a basking shark. Decomposition made recognition of the original animal difficult. The third pair of 'legs' was probably the pair of organs called 'claspers' that are used by the male animal in mating. *Current / the Journal of Marine Education*, pp. 15-17, Winter 1983.

4 George IV's visit to Edinburgh in 1822 attracted enormous interest. It was estimated that 300,000 people lined the streets to catch a glimpse of His Majesty. Sir Walter Scott, who had met the king previously in London and who was the first of his subjects to be created baronet after his accession, orchestrated every detail of the visit. Holyrood Palace, then the 'most depressing and the most irresistibly sepulchral', according to *Blackwood's,* was considered unsuitable for the king's residence and he stayed at Dalkeith Palace, home of the young Duke of Buccleuch. He did, however, hold a reception at Holyrood where he appeared in full Highland garb, including flesh-coloured tights which excited comment and the attentions of the cartoonists of the day. During his two-week visit, which was packed with ceremony and glorified with tartan and fireworks, he visited the castle, attended a ball and a performance of Scott's play 'Rob Roy' at the Theatre Royal. A statue commemorating his visit was erected in George Street in 1831 and remains there today. Audubon must frequently have passed it.

5 An account of John MacGillivray, William's son, is given in Chapter 16.

6 *Edinburgh New Philosophical Journal* (1826), 2: 172-84.

7 *Edinburgh Journal of Science* (1828), 8: 48-54.

8 *Edinburgh New Philosophical Journal* (1826), 2: 270-80.

9 *Ornithological Biography,* vol. I, pp. 160-9.

10 Ibid, pp. 155-9.

11 Swinney, G N and Wheeler, A: 'Richard Parnell (1810-82) and his fish connections', in *Journal of the History of Collections* (2000), 12: 203-19

12 James Hogg (1770-1835) was a remarkable character. Brought up as a shepherd, he developed a talent for poetry which was encouraged by Sir Walter Scott. He became the model for the 'shepherd' in John Wilson's '*Noctes Ambrosianae*' which were regular features in *Blackwood's Magazine.* A keen angler, Hogg was convinced that parr were the young of salmon and carried out an experiment in which he cut a distinguishing notch in the tails of parr and returned them to the water. He then offered a dram to anyone who caught a mature salmon bearing his mark. Two years later 26 salmon were killed 'on the very water where I had marked the pars, all bearing my mark. Here, then, was proof beyond all disputing ....' *The Quarterly Journal of Agriculture* (1831-2), 3: 441-9. Despite this evidence Sir William Jardine, an authority on the salmonidae, continued to maintain that the parr was a distinct species; see *Edinburgh New Philosophical Journal* (1835), 18: 46-59.

13 *Edinburgh Journal of Natural and Geographical Science* (1830), 1: 352-5.

14 Ibid (1830), 2: 269-74.

15 EUL Special Collections (DC 2.56).

16 Professor John Goodsir supervised the winding up of the Wernerian Society.

'Blue Jay' by Audubon, 1825. Plate 102 from *The Birds of America.*
(Reproduced by kind permission of the President and Council of the Royal College of Physicians and Surgeons of Glasgow)

Blue Jay,
CORVUS CRISTATUS,
Male 1. Female, 2, 3.

Drawn from nature by J.J. Audubon F.R.S. F.L.S.

Engraved, printed & Coloured, by R. Havell.

'Rufous-sided Towhee' by Audubon, 1822. Plate 29 from *The Birds of America*.
Blackberry by Mason. (Courtesy of the National Museums of Scotland Library)

'Common Grackle' by Audubon, 1825. Plate 7 from *The Birds of America*, engraved
in Edinburgh by W H Lizars. (Courtesy of the National Museums of Scotland Library)

'Purple Finch' by Audubon, 1824(?). Plate 4 from *The Birds of America*, engraved in Edinburgh by W H Lizars. (Courtesy of the National Museums of Scotland Library)

'Passenger Pigeons' by Audubon, 1824(?). Plate 62 from *The Birds of America*. (Reproduced by kind permission of the President and Council of the Royal College of Physicians and Surgeons of Glasgow)

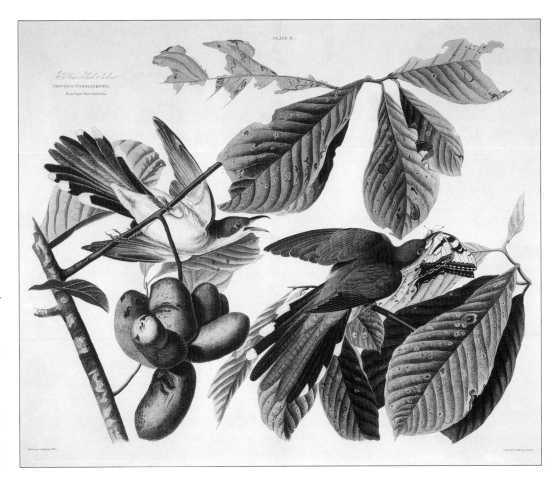

Right: 'Yellow-billed Cuckoo' by Audubon, 1821 or 1822. Plate 2 from *The Birds of America*, engraved in Edinburgh by W H Lizars. Pawpaw tree by Mason. (Courtesy of the National Museums of Scotland Library)

Below: 'Cuckoo with Meadow Pipit' by MacGillivray, 1832. (© Natural History Museum, London)

'Bar-tailed Godwit' by MacGillivray, 'From an individual shot at Musselburgh by Mr Audubon Sept. 1835'. (© Natural History Museum, London)

'Wren' by MacGillivray, 1832. (© Natural History Museum, London)

'Linnet' by MacGillivray, 1834. (© Natural History Museum, London)

'Greater Spotted Woodpecker' by MacGillivray, January 1834. (© Natural History Museum, London)

'Rock Dove' by MacGillivray, autumn 1836.
(© Natural History Museum, London)

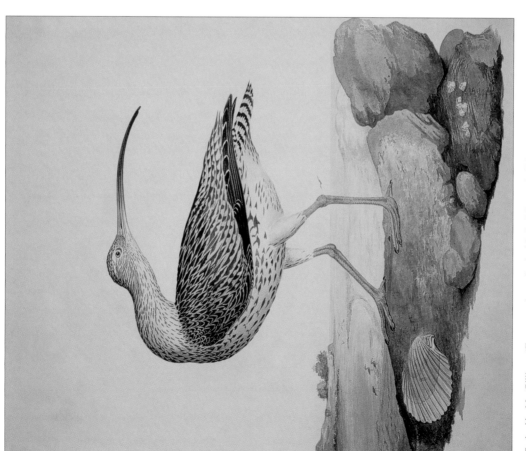

'Curlew' by MacGillivray, 'From a specimen shot by Mr Audubon end of November 1835'.
(© Natural History Museum, London)

'Osprey' by Audubon, 1829. Plate 81 from *The Birds of America*. (Reproduced by kind permission of the President and Council of the Royal College of Physicians and Surgeons of Glasgow)

'Peregrine Falcon' by MacGillivray, from a specimen shot on the Pentland Hills on 24 July 1839. (© Natural History Museum, London)

Right: 'Peregrine Falcon' by Audubon, 1820 and 1824. Plate 16 from *The Birds of America*. (Courtesy of the National Museums of Scotland Library)

Below: 'Long-billed Curlew' by Audubon, 1831. Plate 231 from *The Birds of America*. Background of Charleston by Lehman. (© Natural History Museum, London)

10 | The Second Visit: Travels to England and France

AUDUBON left Edinburgh by coach on 5 April 1827 via Dunbar and Berwick, arriving at Twizel House in Northumberland that same evening. The Selby family made him very welcome. 'We had supper, after which the eagerness of the young ladies made me open my box of drawings; later we had music, and the evening passed delightfully.' He spent some days there, admiring the wildlife in the grounds and painting and giving painting lessons to his hosts. Selby's paintings for his *Illustrations of British Ornithology* seem to adopt more of Audubon's lively style following this visit.

Audubon spent a week in Newcastle-upon-Tyne. He did not like it, commenting what a shabby appearance it had compared with 'the beautiful city of Edinburgh'. The visit was redeemed by obtaining five new subscribers and by meeting and enjoying the hospitality of Thomas Bewick, still involved in producing his incomparable woodcuts such as those used to illustrate his *General History of Quadrupeds* and the *History of British Birds*.

He was a tall stout man, with a large head, and with eyes placed farther apart than those of any man that I have ever seen:– a perfect old Englishman, full of life, although seventy-four years of age, active and prompt in his labours …. Presently he proposed shewing me the work he was at, and went on with his tools. It was a small vignette, cut on a block of box-wood not more than three by two inches in surface, and represented a dog frightened at night by what he fancied to be living objects, but which were actually roots and branches of trees, rocks, and other objects bearing the semblance of men ....

Recollecting … how desirous my sons … were to have a copy of his works on Quadrupeds, I asked him where I could procure one, when he immediately answered 'Here,'

Lithograph of Selby by T H Maguire. (Courtesy of Ipswich Borough Council Museums and Galleries)

Right: 'Bohemian Waxwing' by Selby. (Courtesy of the Trustees of the National Library of Scotland)

Above: Thomas Bewick, from *The Naturalist's Library*, volume XVIII, engraved by Lizars.

Left: Bewick's wood engravings of the 'Common Snipe' (*above*) and 'Kingfisher' (*below*), from his *History of British Birds*.

and forthwith presented me with a beautiful set …. His delicate and beautiful tools were all made by himself, and … his shop was the only artist's 'shop' that I ever found perfectly clean and tidy.[1]

The two men, the leading exponents of their different techniques of depicting birds, mutually admired each other's work. Audubon wrote, 'Thomas Bewick is a son of Nature. Nature alone has reared him under her peaceful care, and he in gratitude of heart has copied one department of her works that must stand unrivalled forever ….' Audubon regarded Bewick as the 'Wilson of England' and named the Bewick's wren

(*Thryomanes bewickii*) in recognition of his contribution to ornithology.

I honoured this species with the name BEWICK, a person too well known for his admirable talents as an engraver on wood, and for his beautiful work on the Birds of Great Britain, to need any eulogy of mine. I enjoyed the pleasure of a personal acquaintance with him, and found him at all times a most agreeable, kind, and benevolent friend.[2]

Bewick visited Audubon in London the following year.

Above: Vignette by Bewick. 'The dog frightened by the ghost-like configuration of tree roots' was the one on which Bewick was working at the time of Audubon's visit. From G R Williams, *Fantasy in a Wood Block*.

Audubon's painting of Bewick's wren, plate 18 from *The Birds of America*. (Courtesy of the National Museums of Scotland Library)

Continuing his journey via York and Leeds, Audubon exhibited his paintings and obtained new subscribers as he went. At Leeds, on the anniversary of his parting from Lucy, he wrote:

How uncertain my hopes at that time were …. Until I reached Edinburgh I despaired of success: the publication of the work of enormous expense, and the length of time it must necessarily take; to accomplish the whole has been sufficient to keep my spirits low, I assure thee. Now I feel like beginning a New Year. My work is about to be known, I have made a number of valuable and kind friends, I have been received by men of science on friendly terms, and now I have a hope of success if I continue to be honest, industrious and consistent … if only I can succeed in rendering thee and our sons happy not a moment of sorrow or discomfort shall I regret.[3]

In Manchester and Liverpool Audubon visited his old friends and reached London on 21 May. His first impressions were unfavourable: 'To me

London is just like the mouth of an immense monster, guarded by millions of sharp-edged teeth, from which if I escape unhurt it must be called a miracle.' He was briefly cheered by meeting his old friend Charles Bonaparte and by a chance meeting with 'young Kidd' (Joseph Bartholomew Kidd), noting his 'youth simplicity and cleverness have attached me to him very much'.

On 13 June he received the shattering news from Lizars that his colourists had 'struck work'[4] and advised him to find new engravers and colourists. The two large projects in which Lizars was then engaged – Selby and Jardine's *Illustrations of Ornithology* and Audubon's *Birds of America* – clearly exceeded the resources of his workshop, and Selby, having the sounder financial resources, won. Audubon became so profoundly depressed that he gave up writing his journal: 'I am quite wearied of everything in London; my work does not proceed, and I am dispirited …. I wish I was out of London.' His mood, however, was lifted by finding a new engraver, Robert Havell Jr (1793-1878) of 79 Newman Street, who undertook to continue the engravings for *The Birds of America*. Kidd, who was returning to Edinburgh, was instructed to direct Lizars to send all unfinished work on Audubon's paintings to Havell.

In a letter to Lucy, Audubon wrote:

I am still here although London is comparatively speaking deserted; it was my intention to have left about 3 weeks ago to travel again to augment the number of my subscribers, but I was prevented from so doing on account of the tardiness of Mr Lizars my Engraver at Edinburgh who nearly exhausted my patience by not supplying the subscribers, for several months after my expectations …. I was forced last week to write him to forward me the *coppers engraved* here to have the Impressions printed and Colored here. I received the whole yesterday in good order and I am truly glad of it, for London affords all sorts of facilities imaginable or necessary for the Publication of such immense work and hereafter my *Principal* business will be carried on here – I have made arrangements with a Mr Havell an excellent engraver who has a good establishment containing Printers - Colorers and Engravers So that I can have all under my eye when I am in London ….[5]

Robert Havell and his father of the same name were for a time in partnership. Until his death in 1832 the elder helped with the printing and colouring, but Havell Jr was entirely responsible for the engraving and latterly for the entire production of *The Birds of America*. He was to prove at least as competent an engraver as Lizars, as well as being cheaper, and over a period of twelve years completed the task, his own artistry contributing much to the success of the final product. The combinations of Audubon with Havell, and Selby with Lizars, are credited with producing the finest books of bird illustration ever published. Audubon held Havell in high regard and presented him with a silver loving cup inscribed, 'To Robert Havell from his friend J.J.A., 1834'. Characteristically, he also named a bird after him. After the work was completed, the Havell family emigrated to America and stayed for a time with the Audubons at their home in New York. Havell retired to Tarrytown on the Hudson River, where he continued to paint and engrave the local scenery.[6]

Audubon had great good fortune in the choice of his associates. Much of the success of *The Birds of America* must be credited to Robert Havell Jr, just as William MacGillivray was a significant contributor to *American Ornithology* and John Bachman to the *Quadrupeds of North America*.

A second event which helped to cheer Audubon up was the subscription of King George IV.

The King!! My dear Book! it was presented to him by Sir Walter Waller, Bart., K.C.H., at the request of my most excellent friend J. P. Children, of the British Museum. His Majesty was pleased to call it fine, permitted me to publish it under his particular patronage, approbation, and protection, became a subscriber on the usual terms, not as kings generally do, but as a gentleman .... The Duchess of Clarence also put down her name; and my friends all spoke as if a mountain of sovereigns had dropped in an ample purse at once – and for *me*![7]

The subscription lapsed on the king's death in 1830.

Audubon left London once more to continue his search for subscribers, which proved discouraging. 'How often I thought during these visits of poor Alexander Wilson. When travelling as I am now, to procure subscribers, he as well

Robert Havell Jr aged 85, from Herrick's *Audubon the Naturalist*.

as myself was received with rude coldness, and sometimes with that arrogance which belongs to *parvenus*.'[8] During these travels, 'Several persons have asked me how I came to part with Mr. Lizars, and I have felt glad to be able to say that it was at his desire, and that we continue esteemed friends'. His paintings were admired wherever he went but the high price of his book was a great drawback. Charles Darwin's sister, Catherine, wrote in a letter to him, 'Papa is also planning buying Audubon's Book on American Ornithology; the author sells it himself, and will not allow any separate number to be sold .... The Plates are magnificent, as they ought indeed to be.' In the event he did not subscribe, having been deterred by the cost.

On 22 October 1827 Audubon returned to Edinburgh and was well received by Lizars who showed his workmen samples of Havell's work and 'observed to them that the London artist beat them completely'. Audubon settled his account and closed his business arrangement with Lizars.

I think he regrets now that he decided to give my work up; for I was glad to hear him say that should I think well to intrust him with a portion of it, it would be done as well as Havell's ... at the same price. If he can fall twenty-seven pounds in the engraving of each number, and do them in superior style to his previous work, how enormous must his profits have been ....[9]

123

Audubon appointed Lizars' brother Daniel as his Edinburgh agent, later to be replaced by Kidd.

He visited his old acquaintances and was particularly pleased with his welcome by Professor John Wilson (Christopher North), who promised to write about him in *Blackwood's*. This took the form of a lengthy scholarly comparison of the works of Alexander Wilson and Audubon in which he emphasises the vitality of Audubon's paintings:

> Audubon's birds fly before you – or you are tempted to steal upon them unawares in their repose, and catch them on the bough they beautify. As one of his falcons goes by, you hear the *sugh* of his wings, and his shrilly cry. There is one picture, particularly, of a pair of hawks dining on teals, on which we defy you to look without seeing the large fiery-eyed heads of the hook-beaks moving as they tear the bloody and fleshy feathers, meat and drink in one, the gore-gouts of carnal plumage dropping from, or sticking in the murderous sharpness of their wide-gaping jaws of destruction … in the drunken delirium of their famine that quaffs and gobbles up the savage zest of its gratified passion.[10]

Audubon would have loved this passage, for he delighted in portraying the harsh reality of nature.

Audubon wrote of John Wilson:

> The more I look at Wilson, the more I admire his originalities, – a man not equal to Walter Scott, it is true, but in many ways nearly approaching him; as free from the detestable stiffness of ceremonies as I am when I can help myself, no cravat, no waistcoat, but a fine *frill* of his own profuse beard, his hair flowing uncontrolled, and in his speech dashing at once at the object in view, without circumlocution; with a countenance beaming with intellect, and eyes that would do justice to the *Bird of Washington*. He gives me comfort, by being comfortable himself. With such a man I can talk for a whole day, and could listen for years.[11]

Wilson confirmed his mutual regard in *Noctes Ambrosiae*, one of his regular informal contributions to *Blackwood's Magazine*:

> We were sitting one night, lately … when a knocking, not loud, but resolute, came to the front door … we felt assured it came from the fist of a friend … and lo! A figure, muffled up in a cloak, and furred like a Russ, advanced familiarly into the hall, extended both hands, bade God bless us …. We were not slow in returning the hug fraternal, for who was it, but the 'American woodsman?' – even Audubon himself – fresh from the Floridas, and breathing of the pure air of far off Labrador!
>
> Three years, and upwards, had fled since we had taken farewell of the illustrious ornithologist – on the same spot – at the same hour; … in less time than we have taken to write it we two were sitting cheek by jowl, and hand in hand … while we showed by our looks that we both felt; … that three years are but as one day! In globe of purest crystal the Glenlivet shone; … and a centenary of the finest oysters, native to our isle … down each naturalists gullet graciously descended.
>
> Audubon … found an opportunity of telling us that he had never seen us in a higher state of preservation – … something about the 'eagle renewing his youth' …. We did not deny that we saw in him an image of the Falco Leucocephalus … it answered his own description of that handsome and powerful bird, viz., 'the general colour of the plumage above is dull hair brown, the lower parts being deeply brown, broadly margined with greyish white' …. And thus blending our gravities and our gayeties, we sat facing one another, each with his last oyster on the prong of his trident ….

At this time Audubon was elected an honorary member of the Scottish Academy (now the Royal Scottish Academy), together with his friends Thomas Sully (1783-1872),† Sir William Jardine, Prideaux John Selby and James Wilson. Audubon showed several paintings at its annual exhibitions.

On 4 November Audubon visited Glasgow for the first time:

> Three inside passengers besides myself made the entire journey without having uttered a single word … all as dull as the barren country I travelled this day. A few glimpses of dwarf like yellow pines here and there seemed to wish to break the dreariness of this portion of Scotland, but the attempt was in vain ….[12]

This was not a successful visit:

> I am off to-morrow morning, and perhaps
> forever will say farewell to Glasgow. I have
> been here *four* days and have obtained *one* sub-
> scriber.[13] One subscriber in a city of 150,000
> souls, rich, handsome, and with much learning.
> Think of 1400 pupils in one college! Glasgow
> is a fine city; the Clyde here is a small stream
> crossed by three bridges. The shipping consists
> of about a hundred brigs and schooners, but
> I counted eighteen steam vessels, black, ugly
> things as ever were built. One sees few
> carriages, but *thousands* of carts.[14]

On 9 November he returned to Mrs Dickie's
in Edinburgh for a few days, during which he had
breakfast with Professor Jameson and climbed
Arthur's Seat again: 'the day was then beautiful
and the extensive view cheered my spirits.' He
then retraced his journey to London, again visiting
Twizel House where Jardine was also a guest. 'In
one of our walks I shot five Pheasants, one Hare,
One Rabbit, and One Partridge; gladly would I
remain here longer ....'

The journey to York was unpleasant:

> ... my companions on the coach of the dormous
> order; eighty-two miles and no conversation
> is to me dreadful. Moreover our coachman,
> having in sight a coach called the 'High-Flyer'
> felt impelled to keep up with that vehicle, and
> so lashed the horses that we kept close to it
> all the while. Each time we changed our
> animals I saw them quite exhausted, panting
> for breath, and covered with sweat and the
> traces of the blows they had received; I
> assure thee my heart ached.[15]

Christmas in Liverpool was very different from
Christmas at home:

> With us it is a general merry-making, a day
> of joy. Our lads have guns, and fire almost
> all night, and dance all day and the next
> night. Invitations are sent to all friends and
> acquaintances, and the time passes more
> gayly than I can describe. Here, *families* only
> join together, they go to church together, eat
> a very good dinner together, I dare say; but
> all is dull—silent—mournful.[16]

Audubon returned to London, the tedium
of the journey being broken by playing whist
with three fellow travellers, 'but only on condition
that they did not play for money, a thing I have
never done'. London depressed him as usual –
he pined for the open countryside where he felt
at home. 'In London, amidst all the pleasures,
I feel unhappy and dull; the days are heavy, the
nights worse … I wish myself anywhere but in
London.' Sir Thomas Lawrence, the famous
portrait painter to whom Audubon had a letter
of introduction from Thomas Sully, received him
kindly and helped him over a financial crisis by
persuading his friends to buy some of Audubon's
paintings.

Lizars reported that some subscribers had
cancelled their subscriptions. Audubon wrote,
'I find on *Experiment* that the Scotch in Scotland
are the same as they are in all parts of the world
where they go, tight dealers, and men who with
great concern untie their purses'.[17] Yet such was
his resilience and faith in himself that he was able
to put these setbacks behind him and continue
his work with increased effort. In a letter to his son
Victor he wrote:

> That Subscribers should die, is a thing we can
> not help, that such fellows as Vigors[18] should
> mortify us, cannot again be countermanded,
> but depend upon it our *Industry*, our *truth*,
> and the regular manner in which we publish
> our Work – this will always prove to the World
> & to our Subscribers, that nothing more can
> be done than what we do, nay that I doubt if
> any other *Family* with our pecuniary means
> ever will raise for themselves such a *Monument*
> as 'the Birds of America' is, over their tomb![19]

Audubon's letters home during this period
indicate considerable confusion and indecision,
although written with great affection. He was
going to stay in Britain for three years or eight
years or for ever, although '… thou must not
think me flighty, and abandoning my dear
America, rough as it is yet; … – No – America
will always be my land. I never close my eyes
without travelling thousands of miles along our
noble streams; and traversing our noble forests.'
Lucy and John would be sent for to join him in
a few months, but the date kept being post-
poned until suitable arrangements could be
made or until his business affairs had stabilised.

John was to come to the University of Edinburgh or Cambridge and help him finish his great work. In no two letters, however, were Audubon's plans the same. Financial problems were a recurring theme – he was clearly leading a hand-to-mouth existence which no doubt contributed to his planning difficulties. Meanwhile he supported himself by selling oil paintings of assorted wildlife at ten to 50 guineas a time. However, he regarded this as a prostitution of his skills and remained unhappy about his technique with oils, periodically resolving to abandon this medium.

Audubon paid visits to Oxford and Cambridge and obtained subscribers in both cities. Cambridge in particular impressed him.

> On entering Cambridge I was struck with its cleanliness, the regular shape of the colleges, and the number of students with floating mantles, flat caps, and long tassels of silk, hanging sideways ... I had a letter for a lodging house where I expected to stay, but no numbers are affixed to any doors in Cambridge. I do not know if it is so in order to teach the students to better remember things .... We walked through the different courts of Trinity, and I was amazed at the exquisite arrangement of the buildings, and when we arrive at the walks I was still more pleased. I saw beautiful grass-plats, fine trees, around which the evergreen, dark, creeping ivy, was entwined, and heard among the birds that enlivened these the shrill notes of the Variegated Woodpecker, quite enchanting .... Since I left Edinburgh, I have not had a day as brilliant as this in point of being surrounded by learned men.[20]

Audubon felt obliged to spend most of his time in London to overlook the engravers, colourers and agents: '... hate it, yes I cordially hate London, and yet cannot escape from it. I neither can write my journal when here, nor draw well ....'

For a change of air he went to visit William Swainson, a naturalist who had travelled extensively in Europe and South America but who was now living at Tittenhanger Green near St Albans.

Swainson had written fulsome praise of Audubon's paintings in Loudon's *Magazine of Natural History*, concluding:

> It will depend on the powerful and the wealthy, whether Britain shall have the honour of fostering such a magnificent undertaking. It will be a lasting monument, not only to the memory of its author, but to those who employ their wealth in patronising genius, and in supporting the national credit. If any publication deserves such a distinction, it is surely this; inasmuch as it exhibits a perfection in the higher attributes of zoological painting, never before attempted. To represent the passions and the feelings of birds, might, until now, have been well deemed chimerical.[21]

Swainson's wife Mary described Audubon's first visit in a letter to her brother John Parkes on 3 June 1828:

> My husband ... returned Friday bringing with him Mr Audubon who left us on Sunday. He is a most agreeable visitor, with guileless simple character which might be expected from first impressions, truly bespeaking a life passed more among birds than men. Mrs Audubon is coming to join him and a son whom he will send to Cambridge. She was the daughter of Mr Bakewell, the great Derbyshire grazier, who went to America from what I imagine political causes of the day and Mrs Audubon was ... very much brought up by Dr Darwin, he told me she was quite a scientific woman, but not a blue stocking. His account of Charles Buonaparte interested us very much. He has finished the continuance of Wilson's Ornithology and has fixed his residence at Florence. He is immensely rich ....[22]

Audubon appears to have been indulging in his habit of elaborating the facts. It is true that Lucy's father William Blakewell had interests in science and was friendly with Erasmus Darwin (1731-1802), grandfather of the more distinguished Charles Darwin, but the family left England in 1802 when Lucy was 14, so it is improbable that Darwins's influence amounted to 'bringing up' Lucy. Erasmus Darwin had been the Blakewell family physician and Audubon, at Lucy's request, had paid homage to Darwin's grave near Derby soon after his arrival in Britain.

Audubon enjoyed the company of the Swainson family and demonstrated his technique of drawing to them. In September 1828 the Swainsons accompanied Audubon on a visit to Paris with a Mr C R Parker, an acquaintance of Audubon but 'a remarkably disagreeable American Artist', according to Mrs Swainson. She described the Channel crossing: '… there never was a set of voyagers more overwhelmed with sickness …. My husband took care of me, till he was too ill to think of anything and poor Mr A took immediate possession of the boards of the quarter deck.' (Audubon always suffered from sea sickness.)

In Paris they received hospitality from the great naturalist Baron Georges Cuvier, to whom Audubon delivered a box of fossil bones on behalf of Professor Jameson. Cuvier described Audubon's paintings as 'the greatest monument yet erected by Art to Nature'. He also met Pierre Joseph Redouté (1759-1840), the famous flower painter. Each admired the other's works and exchanged paintings. Redouté undertook to persuade his friend the Duke of Orleans to become a subscriber. France, however, produced few subscribers, although these were distinguished, including King Charles X, Baron Cuvier, and six sets for the government. Audubon came to realise how lucky or prudent he had been, not to follow Melly's advice to have his paintings reproduced in France.

The year 1829 found Audubon in a quandary. He felt that he should continue to live in Britain to supervise the reproduction of his paintings, which at the present rate of progress was going to take several more years. He also felt the need to check that the fascicles were delivered to the subscribers and to ensure that they paid their dues, while at the same time always seeking out new subscribers. Meanwhile the letters from Lucy were becoming increasingly desperate. She was greatly distressed by the prolonged separation and by Audubon's failure to make satisfactory arrangements for her to join him. Devotion expressed in letters was not enough: 'I love thy letters I adore them – the older I grow the more I feel thy worth and the more I need thy company ….'[23] Such endearments were frequently expressed in his letters, sandwiched between business details. Audubon decided that he must return to America to save his marriage, but that he would keep it secret and travel incognito lest his subscribers became alarmed. (In the event he abandoned this subterfuge.)

Portrait of William Swainson. (Reproduced with permission of Taranaki Museum, New Plymouth, New Zealand)

We will make arrangements *to meet never* to part again! …. I want and must talk to thee, letters are scarcely of use at this great distance when 5 months are needed to have an answer …. Oh my Lucy it will have been a long absence, a great change in my manners but the same sound heart as ever and as ever devotedly attached to thee.[24]

Audubon sailed from Portsmouth on 1 April, together with his spaniel Dash, and arrived back in New York on 6 May 1829 having left his affairs in Britain in the hands of John George Children, librarian at the British Museum, and William Rathbone in London and Joseph Bartholomew Kidd in Edinburgh. He was resolved to return as soon as possible and his first letter to Lucy on arrival delivered an ultimatum; either she would return with him or

… *we probably* never will meet again …. We have been married a good time, circumstances have caused our voyage to be very mottled with Incidents of very different nature but our *happy days* are the only days *I now remember* …. I have no wish to entice thee to come by persuasions; I wish thee to consult thy own-self and that only ….[25]

Lucy, however, by then had become so dis-illusioned by having to take second place to her husband's obsession that she refused to leave her teaching post in St Francisville in order to come to rejoin him even halfway at Louisville. Audubon for his part seemed content to remain in the vicinity of Philadelphia, acquiring further specimens to paint while fretting over the continued hostile reception from his American associates. He had no success in obtaining American subscribers – the Academy of Natural Sciences had declined.

In November Audubon sailed to Bayou Sara, arriving for a tearful reunion with Lucy. They set off by stages for the north, visiting President Jackson in Washington who greeted them kindly. The House of Representatives became Audubon's first American subscriber. Meanwhile his business affairs in Britain were in disarray and he was eager to return. They sailed together to Liverpool in April 1830. Lucy stayed with her sister Ann Gordon in Liverpool while Audubon went on to London to be admitted as a Fellow of the Royal Society of London, his sponsors being John Children and Lord Stanley. Audubon was only the second American to be awarded fellowship of this most illustrious body, the other being Benjamin Franklin. To be thus accepted as a man of science did much for Audubon's self-esteem, and more than compensated for his rejections in his home country.

In a chatty letter to Swainson written in London on 5 May he announced that he was going to write a book. This was an idea which had been at the back of Audubon's mind for some time. Lizars had advised him to publish his illustrations separately from the text in order to avoid having to deposit nine copies of the engravings with the Stationer's Office, which was required for all printed books if a copyright was to be protected. He received a curiously jaundiced reply from his erstwhile friend:

> You think that I do not know that you are an F.R.S. – you are mistaken [Swainson was also a Fellow of the Royal Society], furthermore, you will be surprised at knowing I have been fighting your battles against a rising opposition which originated among some of your *Ornithological friends* (at least so I strongly suspect) for the purpose of your name being *blackballed* ….
>
> The whole of your bundle of young trees [which Audubon had sent him from America]

reached me as withered sticks, not a spark of life in any one of them.

> So you are going to write a book 'tis a thing of little moment for one who is not known, because they have no reputation to loose, but much will be expected from *you*, and you must, therefore, as the saying is, *put your best leg foremost*. I am coming fast round to the prejudice, as you may think it against the Americans …. I am sick of the world and of mankind, and but for my family would end my days in my beloved forests of Brazil.
>
> So Mr Lea did not settle my account with you? I have found *him out*, also, to be no better than he should be. He also is one of your *friends* who would, if he could, cut your throat. Another *friend* of yours has been in England, Mr Ord and has been doing you all the *good* he can: if these are samples of American Naturalists, defend me from ever coming in contact with any of their whole race.[26]

Poor Swainson was clearly in a black mood, and with some justification. His wife was ill and his finances strained. A subsequent exchange of letters appeared to restore more amicable relations to the extent that Swainson contemplated naming a new bird after Audubon. On 22 August 1830 Audubon wrote to Swainson with the following proposal:

> I am desirous to hear from you if you can have the time to spare & the inclination to *Bear a hand* in the text of my work – by my furnishing you with the ideas & observations which I have and you to add *the science which I have not!* – If it would suit you and Mrs Swainson to take us as boarders for few months when being almost always together I could partake of your observations & you mine. – I would like to receive here your ideas on this subject & if possible what amount you would expect from us as remuneration …. I wish if possible to make a *pleasing* book as well as an *instruction* one. In the event of my living with you we will furnish our own wines, porter or ale.[27]

Audubon's approach to Swainson was understandable, for he had the necessary scientific background. He had furthermore given lavish praise to some of Audubon's earlier writings which had appeared in Edinburgh journals, for example:

There is a freshness and originality about these essays, which can only be compared to the animated biographies of Wilson. Both these men contemplated Nature as she really is, not as she is represented in books; they sought her in her sanctuaries. The shore, the mountain, and the forest, were alternately their study, and there they drank the pure stream of knowledge at its fountain-head. The observations of such men are the corner-stones of every attempt to discover the system of nature. Their writings will be consulted when our favourite theories shall have passed into oblivion.[28]

Swainson replied to Audubon's rather extra-ordinary proposal:

First as to boarding with us, you do not know probably, that this is never done in England, except as a matter of necessity or profession, in which case the domestic establishment is framed accordingly. But this consideration, would have no influence with me, in *your* case did other circumstances allow of it. It would however be attended with so many changes in our every-day domestic arrangements, that it becomes impossible ....

Next as to plan. I have always told you that the plan you mention, so far as your own narrative goes, is the very best which could possibly be chosen. *You* have to speak of the birds as they are alive, I to speak of their outward form, structure, and their place in the great System of their Creator .... If my views are correct, every observation you make, *plain, unvarnished,* and strictly *accurate,* will fully and perfectly harmonize. Our parts are totally distinct, and we have no occasion to consult with each other what we should say at every page .... My own remarks had better be kept distinct, in the form of Scientific Notes ... and in this way you will make the work, the *Standard authority* on American Ornithology, which without Science, it certainly would not be ....

He then went on to discuss his financial terms: twelve guineas a sheet of 16 pages with extra for revisions.

It would of course be understood that my name stands in the title page as responsible for such portion as concerns me ....

Our kindest remembrance to Mrs Audubon, and always look upon me as your sincere, but very plain spoken friend, W Swainson.[29]

Audubon must have rejected his terms, for Swainson's next letter reads:

Either you do not appear to have understood the nature of my proposition on supplying scientific information for your work, or you are very erroneously informed on the matter in which such assistance is usually given .... Your friends would tell you ... that even my name would add something to the value of the 'Birds of America'. You pay me compliments on my scientific knowledge, and wished you possessed a portion & you liken the acquisition of such a portion to purchasing the sketch of an eminent painter – the simile is good, but allow me to ask you, whether, after procuring the sketch, you would mix it up with your own, and pass it all to your friends as your production? I cannot possibly suppose that such would be your duplicity and I there-fore must not suppose that you intended that I should give all the scientific information I have laboured to acquire during twenty years on ornithology – conceal my name, – and transfer my fame to your pages & to your reputation .... I am rather glad you did not accept my offer, for I am now assisting in bringing out an Octavo edition of Wilson, by Sir W Jardine which will be arranged according to *my* nomenclature.[30]

No acknowledgement of Swainson's contri-bution appears in Jardine's edition of Wilson's *American Ornithology* publication, although both Jardine and Selby in their publications adopted the quinary system of classification espoused by Swainson. He did, however, write and illustrate three volumes for Jardine's *Naturalist's Library* – two volumes on the *Birds of Western Africa* and one on *Flycatchers* – that show that he was a com-petent artist.

Despite these exchanges the two maintained an occasional exchange of letters of reasonable cordiality for a time and Swainson carried out his intention of naming a bird after Audubon,

a woodpecker *Picus auduboni*, while Audubon responded with the warbler *Limnothlypis swainsonii*. Their relationship gradually soured, however, as each became more critical of the other. Swainson, in a biography of naturalists written in 1840, devoted only one embittered page to Audubon, while giving Alexander Wilson eight and himself the longest entry of 14 pages.[31]

Audubon's rejection by Swainson was to prove fortunate. Swainson was a complex and moody individual who kept falling out with erstwhile friends and colleagues. Furthermore, he was committed to a discredited system of classification, the quinary system,[32] which he would certainly have tried to impose on Audubon's book, and this would have resulted in the book's rejection by the scientific community. Swainson would not have proved a satisfactory collaborator.

Having failed to obtain Swainson's help, Audubon returned to Edinburgh where he succeeded in engaging the assistance of William MacGillivray, which proved to be a fortunate and happy relationship. Before describing this further visit to Edinburgh in Chapter 12, let us dispose of the disturbing affair of the rattlesnake and the vultures.

Above, left: Red-eyed dove by Swainson, from *The Naturalist's Library*, volume XXIII.

Left: Red-billed whidah by Swainson, from *The Naturalist's Library*, volume XXII.

Notes

1 Reminiscences of Thomas Bewick, in *Ornithological Biography*, vol. III, pp. 300-4.

2 *Ornithological Biography*, vol. I, pp. 96-7.

3 *Audubon and his Journals*, vol. I, p. 244.

4 By the time that Lizars' colourists had 'struck work' he had completed 10 engravings: 'Great American Cock', 'Yellow-billed Cuckoo', 'Prothonotary Warbler', 'Purple Finch', 'Bonaparte Flycatcher', 'Great American Hen', 'Young Purple Grakle', 'White-throated Sparrow', 'Selby's Flycatcher', and 'Brown Lark'. Some of these were later reworked by Havell.

5 London 6 August 1827, from *Letters of John James Audubon 1826-1840*, p. 29.

6 Although there is no record that the Robert Havell ever visited Edinburgh, he engraved three paintings of Edinburgh which are reproduced in this book.

7 Buchanan, R: *The Life and Adventures of John James Audubon*, p. 137. See Biographical Profiles (see p. 205) for account of John George Children (not J P Children as Audubon incorrectly labelled him).

8 *Audubon and his Journals*, vol. I, p. 261.

9 Ibid, p. 265.

10 *Blackwood's Magazine* (1831), 30: 278.

11 *Audubon and his Journals*, vol. I, p. 266.

12 Ibid, pp. 266-7.

13 The one subscriber was the University of Glasgow, which still retains the original copy, somewhat water damaged as a result of bombing in World War II.

14 *Audubon and his Journals*, vol. I, p. 267.

15 Ibid, p. 268.

16 Ibid, p. 273.

17 *Letters of John James Audubon 1826-1840*, vol. I, p. 45.

18 Nicholas Aylward Vigors (1785-1840), secretary of the London Zoological Society and editor of its *Journal*, had been a friend of Audubon, who named the Vigors' vireo in his honour. (The bird had previously been described by Wilson and is now known as the pine warbler [*Dendroica pinus*].) The reason for Audubon's later irritation with Vigors is unclear. Vigors had extended an invitation to Audubon to contribute an article to his *Journal* couched in terms which Audubon found offensive, but there must have been some further aggravation (which did not, however, prevent Audubon from accepting membership of the Zoological Society).

19 *Letters of John James Audubon*, vol. I, p. 276.

20 *Audubon and his Journals*, vol. I, pp. 286-7.

21 *Magazine of Natural History* (1828/9), I: 43-52.

22 Swainson, G M: *William Swainson Naturalist and Artist*, p. 17.

23 *Letters of John James Audubon 1824-1840*, p. 64.

24 Ibid, vol. I, pp. 78-80.

25 Ibid, vol. I, p. 83.

26 *Audubon the Naturalist*, vol. II, pp. 97-8.

27 Ibid, p. 102.

28 Swainson, W, in *Magazine of Natural History* (1828/9), 1: 43-52, quoted in the Prospectus of *Ornithological Biography*, vol. I.

29 *Audubon the Naturalist*, vol. II, pp. 104-5.

30 Ibid, pp. 106-8.

31 Swainson, W: *Taxidermy, Bibliography and Biography* in the *Cabinet Cyclopaedia* (1840). This is a most extraordinary book. First, the compilation of two completely disparate subjects – taxidermy and biographies of zoologists – in the one volume is surprising. Second, his treatment of the various zoologists is extremely unbalanced. Some are dismissed with one or two lines while others of equal merit rate several pages. The one page devoted to Audubon is very critical of his *Ornithological Biography*: 'We only suspect that Mr Audubon participates in the almost universal blemish of his country-men, in colouring his narrations (not his paintings) somewhat too highly.' Alexander Wilson gets an enthusiastic eight pages, while James Wilson gets six lines and William MacGillivray only three. Robert Jameson and Thomas Bewick are not included. Charles Waterton, with whom he had so many bitter disputes, is treated with surprising kindness: 'An unscientific, but a very observing naturalist, whose American travels contain many excellent observations on the animals of Guiana and Demerara.' Swainson gives himself the longest entry of 14 pages, which reveals a very disturbed and unhappy man.

32 Knight, D M: *Archives of Natural History* (1986), 13: 275-90.

11 | Vultures and Rattlesnakes

Two of the lectures which Audubon gave to the Wernerian Society in 1826/7 and which were subsequently published in Edinburgh were to land him in bitter controversy and gave George Ord the ammunition with which to pursue his vendetta against him. To assist him Ord recruited an eccentric but willing Englishman, Charles Waterton. Between them these two men were to maintain a sustained assault on Audubon's reputation which lasted several years. These attacks were conducted largely in the pages of Loudon's *Magazine of Natural History*[1] between 1830 and 1833.

Charles Waterton (1782-1865) was a member of an aristocratic Catholic family who lived in Walton Hall in the West Riding of Yorkshire. He was educated at first at home, and then at the age of nine he was sent to a Catholic boarding school where he remained for four years without returning home, even for holidays. He rebelled against this confinement by absenting himself from school to study nature and was frequently beaten for so doing. Waterton finished his education at Stonyhurst College where he was allowed greater freedom and indeed was encouraged to follow his natural history studies. Life there was very spartan, which no doubt helped to prepare Waterton for his later hardships. He acquired a good grounding in classical Latin, which he used with effect in his later writings and caused much amusement after his schooldays by continuing to wear his school uniform of blue tailcoat with yellow buttons long after it was outgrown and out of fashion.

As a Catholic he was denied the opportunity of going to university and aged 20 he left home and remained abroad, with only occasional return visits during the next 27 years. At first he stayed with relatives in Spain where he survived an attack of yellow fever. In 1804 he went to British Guiana where he was to spend 20 years. The colony at that time had a fertile coastal strip where plantations grew sugar cane, cotton and other crops, the labour being provided by large numbers of slaves – a practice of which Waterton disapproved, although for several years he managed such estates owned by his family.

He disliked the vapid existence of the capital Georgetown – his tee-total and religious lifestyle must have distinguished him from the majority of settlers. He was more interested in the customs of the Indians who occupied the unexplored hinterland than in the company of his own kind. Gradually he began to abandon the comforts of civilisation and 'went native'. He started going barefoot and learned to communicate with the Indians and from them how to live off the land. He made two extended journeys of exploration into the wilds of Guiana accompanied by Indian guides, and endured severe hardship and illness for which his panacea was to bleed himself of 30 ounces of blood – a therapy which he practised on himself at least 120 times throughout his long life. On one occasion in which he was accidentally shot in his forefinger when his gun went off as it was being charged, he

> … poured warm water plentifully through the wound, until I had washed away the marks of the gunpowder; then collecting the ruptured tendons, which were hanging down, I replaced them carefully, and bound up the wound, not forgetting to give to the finger its original shape as nearly as possible. After this I opened a vein with the other hand, and took away to the extent of two and twenty ounces of blood.[2]

Waterton regained full function in the finger. On another occasion, at the age of 68, he suffered severe injury to his left arm and concussion when he fell off a ladder. He treated this in his usual way by taking 30 ounces of blood from the arm and a strong aperient. The following day he had a further setback when a servant removed his chair as he was about to sit, with the result that he fell, aggravating his concussion and necessitating the taking of a further 30 ounces by the lancet. The severe injury to his arm, possibly a fracture dislocation of the elbow, was treated successfully by the manipulations of a bonesetter.

In Guiana he received hospitality and friendship from a Scottish timber merchant, Charles Edmonstone, and his half-caste wife, who lived in a remote settlement in the hinterland. Edmonstone was a highly motivated individual who gave shelter to a number of homeless people including two families of freed slaves. He worked hard to protect the native Indians from the worst effects of 'civilisation'. Having made his fortune he returned to Scotland in 1817 with his family and one of the families of freed slaves. Ten years later Waterton became engaged to the 15 year-old daughter of Charles Edmonstone. The unfortunate Anne, brought up in a Presbyterian household, was sent to a Catholic seminary in Bruges for two years to be prepared for the Catholic marriage, which took place in 1829. However she died a year later of puerperal fever shortly after the birth of their son, and two of her unmarried sisters came to live at Walton Hall to care for Edmund and his father. Waterton did not marry again.

He published an account of his travels – *Wanderings in South America* – in 1826, which was widely read and ran to several editions. In this book Waterton describes many encounters with wildlife, including some in which he fearlessly

exposed himself to danger. Two of these episodes, one in which he battled with a boa constrictor and the other in which he helped to capture a large cayman by riding on its back, were greeted with as much scepticism as any of Audubon's tales and tended to make Waterton an object of ridicule in the eyes of many. In Waterton's description of the encounter with the 14-foot boa, he approached it with two 'negros':

> … my own heart … beat quicker than usual; and I felt those sensations which one has on board a merchant-vessel in war time, when the captain orders all hands on deck to prepare for action …. The snake had not moved; and on getting up to him, I struck him with the lance … just behind the neck, and pinned him to the ground. That moment, the negro next to me seized the lance, and held it firm in its place, while I dashed head foremost into the den to grapple with the snake, and to get hold of his tail before he could do any mischief.
>
> … We had a sharp fray in the den, the rotten sticks flying on all sides, and each party struggling for superiority. I called out to the second negro to throw himself upon me, as I found I was not heavy enough …. I had now got firm hold of his tail; and after a violent struggle … he gave in …. This was the moment to secure him … and I contrived to unloose my braces and with them tied up the snake's mouth.
>
> The snake now finding himself in an unpleasant situation, tried to better himself, and set resolutely to work, but we overpowered him …. I stood at the head and held it firm under my arm, one negro supported the belly and the other the tail. In this order we began to move slowly towards home, and reached it after resting ten times; for the snake was too heavy for us to support him without stopping to recruit our strength.

Waterton kept the snake overnight in a bag in his bedroom. 'Had Medusa been my wife, there could not have been more continued and disagreeable hissing in the bedchamber that night.'

On another occasion he overcame a smaller boa by driving his fist, shielded by his hat, 'full in his jaws. It was stunned and confounded by the blow …. I then allowed him to coil himself round my body, and marched off with him as my lawful prize. He pressed me hard ….'

Walton Hall (1831), from Waterton's Essays on Natural History.

During one of his return visits to Europe Waterton arranged an audience with the Pope. He said that while in Rome

I fell in with my old friend and schoolfellow, Captain Jones. Many a tree we had climbed together in the last century; and, as our nerves were in excellent trim, we mounted to the top of St Peter's, ascended the cross, and then climbed thirteen feet higher, where we reached the point of the conductor, and left our gloves on it. After this, we visited the castle of St. Angelo, and contrived to get on to the head of the guardian angel, where we stood on one leg.[3]

At the age of 35 Waterton seems rather old for such schoolboy pranks but it does reveal an unexpectedly frivolous side to his otherwise austere character. He had an abiding passion for climbing trees which continued until his old age. In an essay in which he criticised the fashion of shoes with pointed toes, he observed:

The foot of man does not end in a point; its termination is nearly circular. Hence it is plain and obvious that a pointed shoe will have the effect of forcing the toes into so small a space that one will lie over the other for want of room. By having always worn shoes suited to the form of my foot, I have now at sixty-two the full use of my toes; and this is invaluable to me in ascending trees.[4]

[The author, an orthopaedic surgeon, warmly endorses his comments on shoe design!]

It is remarkable that the eccentric Waterton's feet survived the insults to which he subjected them. Having been accustomed to going barefoot when in Guiana many years before, during a second visit to Rome in 1840 he decided to walk the last 20 miles barefoot. It was frosty morning, which may have dulled his sensation, for he experienced no pain and was unaware of injury until he saw blood on the pavement. On inspection he found 'jagged flesh hanging by a string'. He then deigned to put on his shoes and completed his walk. He had to spend the next two months confined to the sofa before his feet recovered!

On his return to Britain Waterton turned Walton Hall into a museum of natural history and its surrounding park into a sanctuary for wildlife, and would allow no creature to be killed apart from the brown rat for which he had a life-long aversion. He was one of the first to become aware of the destructive effect that the burgeoning Industrial Revolution was making on animal and bird populations and became one of the earliest conservationists. Audubon, too, recognised the adverse impact of man on the environment but did less about it in practical terms. When Audubon visited Labrador in 1833 he observed that 'the aborigines are melting away before a stronger race, as the wild animals are disappearing before them. Nature herself is perishing. Labrador must shortly be depopulated of every thing … which attracts the cupidity of men.' Waterton in his *Travels* wrote, 'Having killed a pair of Doves in order to enable thee to give mankind a true and proper description of them thou must not destroy a third through wantonness, or to show what a good marksman thou art'. What a contrast this attitude is to Audubon's, who took pleasure in slaughtering large numbers.

Waterton spent the latter part of his long life studying the wildlife in his park, sometimes climbing trees for hours at a time, even in his old age, to watch the activities of a nesting bird. His remarkable suppleness enabled him to make his elbows meet behind his back and to scratch the back of his head with his big toe at the age of 77! He led an existence of extraordinary asceticism, sleeping on the floor of an attic room with the windows open in all weathers, wrapped in only a cloak and using a wooden block as a pillow. He rose early, spending an hour at his devotions before commencing his day's activities. He had few friends and was disappointed in his only

Audubon's 'Turkey Buzzard', plate 151 from *The Birds of America*. (Reproduced by kind permission of the President and Council of the Royal College of Physicians and Surgeons of Glasgow)

son Edmund who, in contrast to his father, led a hedonistic existence and eventually squandered his inheritance and sold Walton Hall to pay his debts and support his extravagant lifestyle.

In 1824 Waterton visited the United States, chiefly to pay homage to the memory of Alexander Wilson whose *American Ornithology* he greatly admired. There he met George Ord and established a life-long friendship with him based on their mutual regard for Wilson and a shared dislike of Audubon. While in New York he met Audubon and saw his paintings but made no comment on the visit and Audubon does not mention it.

The origin of the feud between Audubon and Waterton is unclear. The young Charles Darwin, who attended several meetings of the Wernerian Society as a guest, wrote: 'I heard Audubon deliver there some interesting discourses on the habits of N. American birds, sneering somewhat unjustly at Waterton.'[5] This observation is of interest, for Darwin left Edinburgh in 1827, three years before Waterton commenced his public denunciation of Audubon. Clearly the antipathy between the two naturalists had been fermenting over a long period of time, perhaps dating from their meeting in America in 1824. In his 1826 journal Audubon makes a number of snide remarks about Waterton, chiefly with regard to his adventures with a boa constrictor and the cayman, and on 5 November he records that he was visited by the Gregs of Manchester, who brought a '*scrubby*' letter from Charles Waterton ...'.

Darwin's sympathetic attitude to Waterton may have stemmed from his contact with the freed slave who had accompanied Waterton in his travels in Guiana and had come to Scotland with Charles Edmonstone whose surname he adopted. This John Edmonstone lived at 37 Lothian Street adjacent to Darwin's lodgings at number 11. Darwin wrote that 'he gained his livelihood by stuffing birds which he did excellently: he gave me lessons for payment, and I used often to sit with him, for he was a very pleasant and intelligent man'.[6] John Edmonstone prepared specimens for the university natural history museum and would therefore have been acquainted with Robert Jameson and William MacGillivray, and he also worked for a time as a servant to Andrew Duncan Sr. Thus this unlikely individual had met with and been of assistance to four of the personae who feature in this book. Indeed it is probable

that he would also have met Audubon who lived for a time in 5 Lothian Street and was a frequent visitor to the museum.

Waterton had taught John Edmonstone the craft of taxidermy. He described him as having 'poor abilities, and it required much time and patience to drive anything into him'. Waterton was himself an extremely skilled taxidermist who, in addition to preserving the specimens he encountered during his travels, used to amuse himself by combining parts of different animals to make bizarre composite creatures for his museum. One of his creations was a 'Nondescript' – a figure with the appearance of the head of a man made out of the hindquarters of a howler monkey, an example of his curious sense of humour which led some people to doubt the veracity of his writings.

The first of Audubon's articles to come under attack from Waterton was an 'Account of the Habits of the Turkey Buzzard (*Vultur aura*)'[7] in which Audubon maintained that the vulture found its food by sight rather than smell – an observation which contradicted Waterton's views published the same year in his *Wanderings in South America*.

Waterton as usual commenced his criticism in Loudon's *Magazine of Natural History* with a Latin quotation from the Aeneid, '*Et truncas inhonesto vulnere nares*', which he translated as 'and nose demolished by a shameful blow'.

> I never thought I should have lived to see this bird deprived of its nose .... I grieve from my heart that the vulture's nose has received such a tremendous blow .... I have a kind of fellow feeling ... for this noble bird .... We have passed many nights among the same trees ... and saw a great deal of each others company.[8]

He proceeds to give examples of behaviour which he considered evidence of the bird's sense of smell and mocks Audubon's observations.

Waterton's next polemic was against Audubon's account of the rattlesnake, which seems so incredible that it is not surprising that it gave rise to some critical comment. Audubon was not one to allow strict accuracy to interfere with a good story and one wonders whether this was not an example of this tendency. Part of the rattlesnake lecture will be reproduced at length to allow the reader to make up his own mind.

... I shall, therefore, draw your attention more directly to the habits of that species, and begin by enumerating the many real and extraordinary faculties bestowed upon it. These consist in swiftness; in powers of extension and diminution of almost all their parts; in quickness of sight; in being amphibious; in possessing that wonderful and extraordinary benefit of torpidity during winter; and long continued abstinence at other periods, without, however, in the mean time losing the venomous faculty, the principal means of their defence. I shall proceed to elucidate, by well authenticated examples, all those different faculties.

Rattlesnakes hunt and secure for their prey with ease grey squirrels that abound in our woods therefore they must be possessed of swiftness to obtain them. Having enjoyed the pleasure of beholding such a chase in full view in the year 1821, I shall detail its circumstances. Whilst lying on the ground to watch the habits of a bird which was new to me, previous to shooting it, I heard a smart rustling not far from me, and turning my head that way, saw, at the same moment, a grey squirrel full grown, issuing from the thicket, and bouncing off in a straight direction, in leaps of several feet at a time, and, not more than twenty feet behind, a rattlesnake of ordinary size pursuing, drawn apparently out to its full length, and sliding over the ground so rapidly that, as they both moved away from me, I was at no loss to observe the snake gain upon the squirrel. The squirrel made for a tree, and ascended to its topmost branches as nimbly as squirrels are known to do. The snake performed the same task considerably more slowly, yet so fast, that the squirrel never raised its tail nor barked, but eyed the enemy attentively as he mounted and approached. When within a few yards, the squirrel leaped to another branch, and the snake followed by stretching out full two-thirds of its body, whilst the remainder held it securely from falling. Passing thus from branch to branch, with a rapidity that astonished me, the squirrel went in and out of several holes, but remained in none knowing well that, wherever its head could enter, the body of his antagonist would follow; and, at last, much exhausted and terrified, took a desperate leap, and come to the earth with legs and tail spread to their utmost to ease the fall. That instant the snake dropt also, and was within a few yards of the squirrel before it had begun making off. The chase on land again took place, and ere the squirrel could reach another tree, the snake seized it by the back near the occiput, and soon rolled itself about it in such a way that, although I heard the cries of the victim, I scarcely saw any portion of its body. So full of its ultimate object was the snake, that it paid no attention to me, and I approached it to see in what manner it would dispose of its prey. A few minutes elapsed, when I saw the reptile loosening gradually and opening its folded coils, until the squirrel was left entirely disengaged, having been killed by suffocation ... it then took the end of the squirrel's tail, swallowed it gradually, bringing first one, and then the other of the hind legs parallel with it, and sucked with difficulty, and for some time, at them and the rump of the animal, until its jaws became so expanded, that, after this it swallowed the whole remaining parts with apparent ease.

This mass of food was removed several inches from the head in the stomach of the snake, and gave it the appearance of a rouleau of money brought from both ends of a purse towards its centre; for, immediately after the operation of swallowing was completed, the jaws and neck resumed their former appearance. The snake then attempted to move off, but this was next to impossible; ... I then killed it, and cut it open to see how the squirrel lay within. I had remarked, that, after the process of swallowing was completed, singular movements of the whole body had taken place, – a kind of going to and fro for a while, not unlike the convulsive motions of a sick animal, as a dog for instance, about to vomit.[9]

This account of rattlesnake behaviour was greeted with derision by Audubon's enemies. It was republished without Audubon's consent in a journal in Philadelphia in 1828[10] and in a later issue that same year the editor of the journal, Thomas P Jones, commented:

It is a tissue of the grossest falsehoods ever attempted to be palmed upon the credulity of mankind, and it is a pity that any thing like countenance should be given to it, by reproducing it in a respectable Journal. The romances of Audubon rival those of Munchausen, Mandeville, or even Medez de Pinto, in the total want of truth, however short they may fall of them in the amusement they afford.

Thomas Sully had written to Audubon telling him of the critical response in Philadelphia to the papers which he had read and published in Edinburgh. Audubon was clearly stung by these criticisms and wrote back on 22 December 1827:

My dear Mr Sully

… I am not much astonished that in Philadelphia, remarks such as you allude to, should have been made respecting some papers on the habits of objects of Natural History, read by me to different institutions in this country, but I am grieved at it.

The greatest portion of my life has been devotedly spent in the active investigation of Nature …. This arduous task I have followed with unremitting diligence, and with a degree of industry that has caused to my family and to myself more troubles than any person in Philadelphia can be aware of …. You have read some portion of this journal, and have also been an eye-witness of many of the occurrences, and to this I now owe the gratification of possessing your esteem, but, My dear Mr. Sully, you are not the only evidence. Mr. Joseph Mason, who is now, I believe, an artist in your city, accompanied me on a hunting excursion … which lasted 18 months. He drew with me; he was my daily companion, and we both rolled ourselves together on bufaloe robes at night ….

The papers alluded to in your estimable letter, are merely copies from those journals; … I read these papers to the different societies, of which I have the honor to be a member, and read them with a sensation of pleasure that nothing but a full persuasion of their truth could bestow.

Those persons in Philadelphia that have felt a desire to contradict my assertions cannot, without lowering themselves very much indeed affect to conceive that the members of the Wernerian Society would have listened to my 'say so' without investigating the subject even if they had not been well versed in the habits of the objects I treated of. Neither can they believe that all my acquaintance and particular friends would permit me to proceed in relating *Tales of Wonder*, which if untrue, would load me with disgrace, ruin my family, nay prove me devoid of all honor! Could I suffer myself to be so blinded at the very moment when I am engaged in the publication of a work of unparalleled magnitude, of which the greatest naturalists and best judges both in America and in Europe have given the fullest praise and firmest support, and from which my very means of pecuniary comfort are to be drawn? …. '*Le temps découvrira la vérité*' …. I feel assured that the pen that traced them [the criticisms] must have been dipped in venom more noxious than that which flows from the jaws of the rattlesnake![11]

The account of the rattlesnake was eagerly seized upon by Ord and Waterton with perhaps more justification than some of their other attacks. Waterton was certainly familiar with rattlesnakes. In an experiment carried out in Leeds, he compared the toxic effects of rattlesnake venom with that of curare. Waterton had become an authority on the effects of curare, the woolari poison which native Indians used as blowpipe poison. Before an audience of 40 doctors he

… gently introduced *his naked hand within the case*, keeping his eye intently fixed on the snake he intended to secure, and in this unprotected state and with the utmost composure, he gently, and yet firmly grasped the venomous monster by the neck immediately behind the head, and deliberately removed him from his neighbours, which were loudly hissing and springing the rattle all around his hand.[12]

During the experiment one of the rattlesnakes almost escaped, but was fearlessly grasped by Waterton and returned to its case. Nearly all the audience fled, even rushing into the street 'without their hats'! Waterton's fearlessness was indisputable. His biographer Richard Hobson, describing this incident, adopts the style of his subject by inserting an appropriate Latin tag – *Fortissimus ille est qui promptus metuenda pati, si cominus instent* ('he is the bravest who is prepared to encounter danger on the instant'). Waterton recorded that the animals injected with curare died more quickly than those bitten by the snakes.

In Loudon's *Magazine* there is a robust defence of Audubon submitted by 'R.B.' (Robert Bakewell, a geologist and a cousin of Lucy's who lived in London):

> … Mr Charles Waterton's remarks on Mr Audubon's account of the habits of the turkey buzzard … occupy 7 pages, evidently written to throw ridicule on Mr Audubon's statements … though they contain no facts or arguments whatever to invalidate the descriptions of Mr Audubon, but are filled with a series of quizzing interrogatories that are undeserving of serious refutation … how would Mr Waterton's *Wanderings in South America* appear, if subjected to the test of ridicule … or solemn criticism ….
>
> Without making any comparison between the merit of Mr Waterton and Mr Audubon as writers or travellers, I cannot but remark that in some things they present a remarkable contrast. Mr Waterton travelled from his own rich plantations in Demarara, surrounded with his own slaves and attendants. Mr Audubon was a solitary wanderer in the forests of America, often dependent on his gun for support. While Mr Audubon is exposed to dangers and privations, and looks forward to the patronage of the public for his sole support and reward, Mr Waterton is tranquilly seated in a magnificent English mansion, surrounded by paternal acres, and endeavouring to deprive the solitary wanderer of that patronage ….
>
> … It is much safer to put the foot into a hornet's nest, than provoke a swarm of naturalists. I could not see … great injustice done to a highly meritorious character, without endeavouring to repel it.[13]

Bakewell's comparisons between Waterton and Audubon are unjust for there is no doubt that Waterton in his travels in British Guiana suffered hardships every bit as severe as any that Audubon was exposed to, and Audubon was not above making use of the help of slaves when the occasion offered.

Victor, who was in London during 1833, also wrote in defence of his father's reputation

Waterton's rattlesnake demonstration, from *Charles Waterton* by Richard Hobson.

in Loudon's *Magazine*. Audubon wrote to him from Charleston on 4 November of that year:

> … I am sorry that you should trouble yourself about the attacks of Mr Waterton, and more so that you should answer to any of these attacks. – depend upon it, the World will Judge for itself and I conceive, that the regular publication of our Work, accompanied with well ascertained facts will sooner or later cast aside any such animadversions, and the true cause of their appearance through such person as Mr Waterton will very soon be properly understood ….
>
> … I feel greatly proud of our Work, I feel greatly proud that I am the happy possessor of a most excellent Wife and Two Sons whom I can view as my dearest and best attached Friends – I am greatly proud that I possess the knowledge that every word I have published or shall publish is truth and nothing but the result of my own observations in fields and forests where neither of my enemies have or ever will tread ….[14]

In December 1833 he wrote to Victor again:

> The copy of your reply to Mons Waterton is excellent; that from Swainson[15] ought to prove a death blow to the Demerara Gent! I hope that these letters are now before the world, for my mortification has been great enough respecting the blackguardism of G. Ord and others, and yet I am heartily glad that I never paid personally any attention to them through the press or otherwise.[16]

Inevitably Waterton reacted at length, pointing out that he had never possessed a slave. He had engaged local Indians and a negro belonging to an uncle to accompany him on his travels. He did not own the plantations; he had only managed them on behalf of his relatives. He goes on to describe in detail the various hardships which he experienced in his travels and there can be no doubt that they were extreme and almost cost him his life. He returned to one of his favourite attacks on Audubon – that he had failed to get recognition in his own country and had been turned down for membership of the American Philosophical Society. However, by that time this accusation was no longer valid.

Victor Audubon again responded by explaining why his father's first scientific honours were received in Liverpool rather than in America. He quoted from Featherstonhaugh's *Monthly American Journal of Geology and the Natural Sciences* published in Philadelphia in 1831:

> Some of the friends of Wilson did not view with the most cordial spirit those evidences of transcendent merit which others willingly accorded to Audubon's drawings. Then arose the spirit of party, and with it malevolence. A few small minds, who knew little or nothing of nature, and who had officiously intruded themselves into this matter, endeavoured to make up for their want of knowledge on the subject by excess of bad zeal.
>
> This bad feeling like all others … triumphed but a short time; for the American Philosophical Society, Philadelphia, at a full meeting of its most respectable members … elected him an associate, and subscribed for a copy of his magnificent work; and the Society from which he had formerly been rejected paid him the same tribute of respect.

Waterton again responded to Victor's letter.

> How forgetful it was in this gentleman … never to have alluded … to the momentous descent of a large American squirrel, tail foremost, down the rattlesnake's throat …. Nobody doubts that rattlesnakes swallow squirrels; but every body must condemn Audubon's account of a rattlesnake chasing a squirrel and then swallowing it tail foremost. Tail foremost! Why, as long as this

foul stain … remains unblotted out, of what use is it in his son to tell me that his father has explored the 'Floridas, the Keys and the Tortugas Islands.' The story of the rattlesnake will always appear against him, as a phantom of bad omen, and it will warn me how I put confidence in other narratives which may come from Mr Audubon's zoological pen.

> I will now proceed to give Mr Audubon Jun., proof sufficient that I can detect a fable from genuine ornithology …. I myself, with mine own eyes, have seen Wilson's original diary, written by him in Louisville; and I have just now on the table before me the account of the Academy of Sciences indignantly rejecting Mr Audubon as a member, on that diary having been produced to their view.[17]

He then goes on to criticise in minute detail various passages from *Ornithological Biography* which he regarded as incredible, including the account of an eagle robbing a vulture of its food in mid-flight, the young of the ruby-throated humming bird flying a week after hatching, and the Virginian partridge being capable of swimming.

Waterton shows inconsistency when he comments on the improbability of Audubon's rattlesnake swallowing it prey tail first, for in his *Wanderings in South America* he records as fact an even more unlikely event.

> A Dutch friend of mine … killed a Boa … with a pair of stag's horns in his mouth: he had swallowed the stag [presumably tail first], but could not get the horns down: so he had to wait in patience with that uncomfortable mouthful till his stomach digested the body, and then the horns would drop out.

Audubon's friend the Rev. John Bachman (see Chapter 15) also wrote to support him:

> Although from my profession and habits, I feel no disposition to enter into controversy, yet, having had opportunities which few others possess of becoming acquainted with the occupations and literary acquirements of Mr Audubon, and being prompted, not alone by feelings of private friendship, but by a desire that full justice should be awarded him for those expenses, sacrifices, and privations which he has undergone, I take the liberty

of stating what I know on this subject; and I have reason to believe, from the characters of the writers who have doubted his veracity and the authenticity of his works, and that with the generosity of feeling so distinctive of these who are engaged in liberal and kindred pursuits, they will be gratified to assign him the meed of praise which he so undoubtedly needs.[18]

After this lengthy and convoluted sentence, Bachman goes on to suggest that Audubon may have ascribed to the rattlesnake some of the habits of the common black snake (*Coluber constrictor*), although he quotes a number of authorities who have observed rattlesnakes to climb trees and feed on squirrels and rabbits. He then describes a number of experiments which he had carried out or observed which proved that vultures found their food by sight and not by smell, including one gruesome experiment in which a vulture was blinded and then offered putrid food which it failed to consume. The account of this experiment filled Waterton with 'distressing emotions'.

(It is of interest that Audubon's friend Robert Knox read a paper to the Royal Society of Edinburgh in 1823 – four years before this controversy commenced – in which he stated that 'it is by sight only that the vulture is led to discover his prey, and not by the sense of smelling'.[19])

Audubon wisely keeps out of these exchanges, at least in public, but inwardly he seethed and his private letters contain frequent remarks that reveal his burning hatred of his would-be discreditors (he described Ord as the 'venomous tallow chandler of Philadelphia'). In letters to Bachman from Edinburgh he wrote, 'The Reviewers here are all agog waiting for my Volume [the second volume of *Ornithological Biography*] ... on the watch for general defence or attack on Waterton, Ord & others. – what shocking disappointment! – not a word is there in the whole book even in allusion to these beetles of darkness!' And later, 'I think and trust that Ord and that fool Watterton will be greatly punished by my contemptuous silence'.[20]

Waterton's final riposte reveals the real basis for his antipathy to Audubon, which centres on Wilson's famous diary entries made during his visit to Louisville and which, as presented by Ord, was one of the reasons for the original rejection of Audubon for membership of the American Philosophical Society. The validity of these entries

has been fully discussed in Chapter 3. Waterton claims to have seen this diary, which could have happened either during his visit to Philadelphia in 1824 or when Ord came to stay in Walton Hall in 1831, but his account differs in detail from that given by Ord. The truth of these diary entries will never be known, but it is curious that Waterton should not only have had the opportunity of seeing them but that he should have troubled to transcribe them and that his transcription should differ from Ord's version. The very fact that Ord must have gone to such trouble to acquaint Waterton of the contents of the diary is a measure of the obsession of the two men. Waterton shared Ord's admiration of Wilson and was so biased against Audubon that he could see no good in him. Of Wilson he wrote:

> His descriptions are consistent, his observations instructive, his plans heroic, and his exertions unequalled. I admire him in life, and mourn with unfeigned sorrow, over his untimely end.
>
> In looking into Audubon's writings I fully agree in Dr Jones opinion .... I condemn the narrative of the passenger pigeon; I find Audubon's account of himself at variance with itself, and at variance with the account which his friends give of him, and I pronounce his *Biography of Birds* to contain errors which any moderate ornithologist may easily detect.

He goes on to mock at length Audubon's account of the passenger pigeon without acknowledging the fact that Audubon's account owed much to Wilson's observations. Waterton's last published attack on Audubon was contained in his *Essays on Natural History* (1839) in which he covers the same ground again with sustained venom. William MacGillivray was also at the receiving end of Waterton's barbs because of his association with Audubon. Sarcastically MacGillivray was thanked 'for the store of tainted food which he has helped to place in the *Biography of Birds*, for the benefit of us needy ones of rapine and ill omen'.[21] This attack was precipitated by rather uncharacteristic remarks of MacGillivray in which he compared the raven, whose noble characteristics he likens to Audubon, with the carrion crow which 'has its analogue in some other wanderer, who is fond of kicking alligators' ribs, and strangling rattle-snakes' – a thinly veiled jibe at Waterton.[22] Both Waterton and MacGillivray subsequently regretted this intemperate exchange. A mutual friend, James Harley of Leicester, acting as an intermediary wrote:

> Possessing the friendship of the intrepid and adventurous Waterton, whose guest we had recently been at Walton Hall, we told him of the indignity so incautiously bestowed on his researches in the wilds of Tropical America, and the unseemly comparison between the dark-winged raven and its congeners … and the kind-hearted squire himself.
>
> No one could express more justly the comparative worth of MacGillivray's anatomically accurate, and otherwise invaluable labours in the cause of Zoology, than Charles Waterton, when he described to us … the ill-timed indignity just adverted to.
>
> The subject of this memoir doubtless had been 'too severe, too harsh, too unchristian' and on reviewing his labours closely, he felt it to be so.[23]

This was not the end of the rattlesnake controversy. At the same meeting of the Wernerian Society at which Audubon gave his rattlesnake lecture, he exhibited his painting showing a rattlesnake which had climbed a tree attacking a nest of mocking-birds (see opposite page).

Audubon gives a detailed description of his drawing of the rattlesnake in his journal of 25 August 1821. 'Anxious to give it such a Position as I thought would render it most interesting to Naturalist, I put it in that which that Reptile generally takes when on point to Inflict a Most severe wound ….' He continues to describe the anatomy of the fangs.

He concludes this entry:

> My Drawing I Hope Will give you a good Idea of a Rattle Snake although the Heat of the weather Would not permit me to Spend More than 16 hours at it – My amiable Pupil Miss Eliza Perrie also drew the same Snake; it is With Much pleasure that I now Mention her Name expecting to remember often her sweet disposition and the Happy Days spent near her.

His cordial relationship with Eliza was not to last. On 20 October 1821 he wrote:

> Three months out of the 4 we lived there Were Spent in peaceable tranquillity; giving regular Daily Lessons to Miss P. of Drawing, Music, Dancing, Arithmetick, and Some trifling acquirements such as Working Hair etc and Hunting and Drawing My Cherished Birds of America …. This Daughter Eliza of age 15 Years of a good form of *Body*, not Handsome of face, proud of her Wealth and of herself cannot well be too Much fed on Praise ….[24]

This rather spoiled but cherished Eliza took ill and was confined to her room and bed for several weeks on the advice of her physician, the '*Man she Loved*'. Audubon had very restricted access to her during this period and 'perceived … during this While that a remarkable Coolness had taken place from the Ladies toward us'. He and young Joseph Mason who accompanied him were finally dismissed from the family home in circumstances which clearly upset him greatly. Not for the first time Audubon's weakness for attractive young ladies was to land him in trouble. Later, when they encountered each other by chance in a street in New Orleans, Eliza chose to ignore him.

But to return to the controversy regarding the rattlesnake as drawn by Audubon. Waterton derided the fact that Audubon had painted the fangs curved upwards at the tip, whereas he maintained that they should have pointed downwards. It seems a trivial issue, but it generated several scornful diatribes published by Waterton. By a curious coincidence a paper read to the Wernerian Society on 24 January 1824 by Robert Knox on the 'Structure of the Poison-Fangs of Serpents' might have resolved the argument. He observed that the poison fang is fixed to a small moveable bone in the upper jaw. This bone was controlled by two muscles which 'give motion to the fangs'. Clearly it was possible for the fangs to have a different attitude when at rest or during an attack, a fact of which Waterton was aware.

The effect of the concerted campaign of Ord and Waterton was the reverse of what they hoped and simply rallied support for Audubon from many quarters. Favourable reviews of his work appeared in *Blackwood's Magazine*, the *American Journal of Science*, *The Athenæum*, the

'Mocking Birds
Attacked by a
Rattlesnake', plate 21
from *The Birds of
America*. (Courtesy of
the National Museums
of Scotland Library)
(Curiously the reviewer
of this painting in
The Scotsman of
15 November 1826
thought that the
mocking birds were
attacking the
rattlesnake, which was
threatened with
blindness and death
by their onslaught!)

Robert Knox's drawing of the fangs of the rattlesnake, from *Memoirs of the Wernerian Society*, volume V (p. 422).

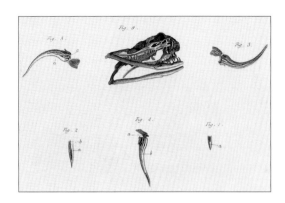

North American Review and many others. Featherstonhaugh, in his *Monthly American Journal*, referred to the 'true history of a conspiracy, got up to utterly break down and ruin the reputation of one of the most remarkable men America ever produced'. An article in Jameson's *Edinburgh New Philosophical Journal* read, '… is Audubon to be held up as an impostor, because he instituted experiments on the power of smelling in vultures, which experiments have been repeated by trust-worthy persons, and found to produce precisely the same results. O candour, whither hast thou fled? – surely not to Walton Hall.'[25] Certainly Audubon had his faults and sometimes allowed his imagination to embellish his writings, but it is noticeable that those with whom he was most closely associated, such as the shrewd observers William MacGillivray and John Bachman, became and remained his staunchest supporters, while his detractors were those who had little or no personal acquaintance with him.

Modern readers must be astonished that such trivial disagreements should generate such heat and occupy so many pages of learned journals, but such disputes were characteristic of the scientific world of the nineteenth century. Audubon had once observed, 'It is really amusing and distressing at the same time to see how inimical to each other men of science are, and why are they so?'[26] Perhaps the last word on these petty issues should be given to Alexander Wilson, who in his poem 'The Foresters' wrote of the rattlesnake:

> Fierce from the centre rose his flatten'd head,
> With quivering tongue, and eyes of fiery red,
> And jaws distended vast, where threatening lay
> The fangs of death, in horrible array;
> While poised above, invisible to view,
> His whizzing tail in swift vibration flew.

There was another remote link between Audubon and Waterton in the person of their mutual acquaintance, Charles Bonaparte. In 1841 the Waterton ménage sailed from Italy in a paddle-steamer which was sunk in a collision with another vessel in which Bonaparte was a passenger. Bonaparte played a crucial role in the rescue operation and is credited by Waterton with saving many lives.[27]

Notes

1   John Claudius Loudon, a landscape gardener, became a very successful publisher of popular journals. His *Magazine of Natural History*, commenced in 1828, flourished on controversial issues such as the Waterton/Audubon dispute.

2   Waterton,C: *Essays on Natural History* (1839), first series, lxviii.

3   Ibid, p. lxxi.

4   Ibid, p. 178.

5   *The Autobiography of Charles Darwin* (Collins, 1958), p. 51.

6   *The Life and Letters of Charles Darwin* (1888), vol. I, p. 40. In an earlier letter to his sister Susan, Darwin wrote, 'I am going to learn to stuff birds, from a blackamoor I believe an old servant of Dr Duncan ….'

7   *Edinburgh New Philosophical Journal* (1826), 2: 172-84.

8   *Magazine of Natural History* (1832), 5: 233.

9   *Edinburgh New Philosophical Journal* (1827), 3: 21-30.

10   *Journal of the Franklin Institute and American Mechanic's Magazine* (1828), II: n.s. 32-7.

11   Cited in *Audubon the Naturalist*, vol. II, pp. 68-71.

12   Hobson, R: *Charles Waterton his Home, Habits, and Handiwork*, pp. 68-73.

13   *Magazine of Natural History* (1833), 6: 369-72.

14   *Letters of John James Audubon 1826-1840*, vol. I, pp. 263-4.

15   Swainson had been wrongly identified by Ord and Waterton as Audubon's collaborator and had written to Loudon's *Magazine* to refute that suggestion, also affirming that he had seen Audubon's manuscripts and was convinced of their genuineness. He commented on the pettiness of these exchanges. He regarded Waterton as 'mad – stark, staring mad' (Letter to Audubon, 18 January 1829).

16 *Letters of John James Audubon 1826-1840*, vol. I, pp. 272.

17 *Magazine of Natural History* (1834), 7: 67-74.

18 Ibid, pp. 164-75. Charles Darwin, during his voyage in the *Beagle*, carried out a similar experiment with the South American condor and found that this carrion vulture also depended on sight rather than smell to find its food.

19 *Transactions of the Royal Society of Edinburgh* (1826), X: 44.

20 *Letters of John James Audubon 1826-1840*, vol. II, pp. 54 and 56.

21 Waterton, C: *Essays on Natural History*, second series, vi.

22 MacGillivray, W: *A History of British Birds*, vol. I, p. 481.

23 *The Literary and Philosophical Society of Leicester* (1855), pp. 107-64.

24 *Journal of John James Audubon 1820-1821*, pp. 190.

25 *Edinburgh New Philosophical Journal* (1835), 18: 136.

26 *The 1826 Journal of John James Audubon*, p. 325.

27 *Essays on Natural History*, second series, cxii-cxviii.

12 | The Third Visit: Collaboration with MacGillivray

ON 13 October 1830 Lucy and Audubon arrived in Edinburgh and lodged with Audubon's previous landlady, Mrs Dickie, at 2 George Street. His main objective was still to write his *Ornithological Biography* and he remained acutely aware of the need for a scientific collaborator after his failure to reach an agreement with Swainson:

> I know I am a poor writer, that I scarcely can manage to scribble a tolerable English letter and not a much better one in French, though that is easier to me. I know I am not a scholar, but, meantime, I am aware that no man living knows better than I do the habits of our birds; no man living has studied them so much as I have done, and, with the assistance of my old journals and memorandum books, which were written on the spot, I can at least put down plain truths which may be useful and perhaps interesting, so I shall set to at once. I cannot, however, give scientific descriptions and here must have assistance.[1]

Audubon approached his old friend and admirer, James Wilson,

> … to ask if he knew of any person who would undertake to correct my ungrammatical manuscripts, and to assist me in arranging the more scientific part of the 'Biography of the Birds'. He gave me a card with the address of Mr W. MacGillivray, spoke well of him and his talents, and away to Mr. MacGillivray I went. He had long known of me as a naturalist. I made known my business, and a bargain was soon struck. He agreed to assist me, and correct my manuscripts for two guineas per sheet of sixteen pages, and I that day began to write the first volume.[2]

MacGillivray was the ideal individual for Audubon's purpose. At the time of their introduction in the autumn of 1830, MacGillivray had resigned his position as Jameson's assistant and was eager for work and in need of financial support. His scientific training and love of natural history, his industry and his literary gifts, were just what Audubon needed. Furthermore his financial demands were much more reasonable than Swainson's and he did not insist that his name should figure in the authorship. An agreement was reached and so commenced a harmonious and effective working partnership that was to continue for nine years, during which the five-volume *Ornithological Biography* was produced.

Title page from the first volume of Ornithological Biography.

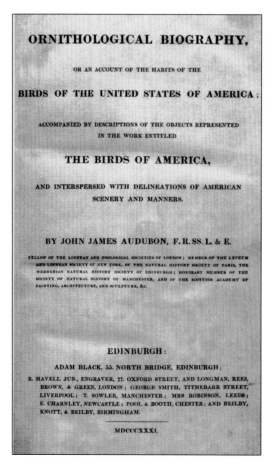

ORNITHOLOGICAL BIOGRAPHY,

OR AN ACCOUNT OF THE HABITS OF THE

BIRDS OF THE UNITED STATES OF AMERICA;

ACCOMPANIED BY DESCRIPTIONS OF THE OBJECTS REPRESENTED
IN THE WORK ENTITLED

THE BIRDS OF AMERICA,

AND INTERSPERSED WITH DELINEATIONS OF AMERICAN
SCENERY AND MANNERS.

BY JOHN JAMES AUDUBON, F.R.SS.L.&E.

FELLOW OF THE LINNEAN AND ZOOLOGICAL SOCIETIES OF LONDON; MEMBER OF THE LYCEUM
AND LINNEAN SOCIETY OF NEW YORK, OF THE NATURAL HISTORY SOCIETY OF PARIS, THE
WERNERIAN NATURAL HISTORY SOCIETY OF EDINBURGH; HONORARY MEMBER OF THE
SOCIETY OF NATURAL HISTORY OF MANCHESTER, AND OF THE SCOTTISH ACADEMY OF
PAINTING, ARCHITECTURE, AND SCULPTURE, &c.

EDINBURGH:

ADAM BLACK, 55. NORTH BRIDGE, EDINBURGH;
R. HAVELL JUN., ENGRAVER, 77. OXFORD STREET, AND LONGMAN, REES,
BROWN, & GREEN, LONDON; GEORGE SMITH, TITHEBARN STREET,
LIVERPOOL; T. SOWLER, MANCHESTER; MRS ROBINSON, LEEDS;
E. CHARNLEY, NEWCASTLE; POOL & BOOTH, CHESTER; AND BEILBY,
KNOTT, & BEILBY, BIRMINGHAM.

MDCCCXXXI.

Although MacGillivray's name does not appear as co-author, his major contribution was acknowledged by Audubon in the Introductory Address in the first volume of *Ornithological Biography* (p. xviii).

There are persons whose desire of obtaining celebrity induces them to suppress the knowledge of the assistance which they have received in the composition of their works. In many cases, in fact, the real author of the drawings or the descriptions in books on Natural History is not so much as mentioned, while the pretended author assumes to himself all the merit which the world is willing to allow him. This want of candour I never could endure. On the contrary, I feel pleasure in here acknowledging the assistance which I have received from a friend, Mr William MacGillivray, who being possessed of a liberal education and a strong taste for the study of the Natural Sciences, has aided me, not in drawing the figures of my illustrations, nor in writing the book now in your hand, although fully competent for both tasks, but in completing the scientific details, and smoothing down the asperities of my *Ornithological Biographies.*

Once the agreement had been reached the two men set to their task with enormous energy, which Audubon described in a letter to his sons:

Writing now became the order of the day. I sat at it as soon as I awoke in the morning, and continued the whole long day, and so full was my mind of birds and their habits, that in my sleep I continually dreamed of birds. I found Mr. MacGillivray equally industrious, for although he did not rise so early in the morning as I did, he wrote much later at night (this I am told is a characteristic of all great writers); and so the manuscripts went on increasing in bulk, like the rising of a stream after abundant rains, and before three months had passed the first volume was finished. Meanwhile your mother copied it all to send to America, to secure the copyright there.[3]

James Wilson wrote that MacGillivray's revisions were 'executed to the improvement of the work, his own personal benefit, the original

author's entire satisfaction and the undoubted advantage of the reading public'. W H Fries wrote that Audubon's 'technical knowledge of the science of ornithology increased rapidly under the tutelage of his friend and collaborator, William MacGillivray. So effective was this Scottish savant in imparting technical knowledge to Audubon that he served essentially as a substitute for formal higher scientific education.'[4] MacGillivray, while accepting that his name should not appear as co-author, was understandably incensed when Jameson suggested to Audubon that there was no need to acknowledge his assistance at all. In a letter to Audubon 7 April 1831, he wrote:

… Prof Jameson sent a flaming eulogy of my translation of Richard [Achille Richard's *Elements of Botany and Vegetable Physiology*, Blackwood, Edinburgh 1831] and wishes me to undertake the translation of a Latin work on Zoology, for the use of his class; nothing that has happened to me for ten years has surprised me more than his having said to you that I did not deserve to be mentioned in your book …. My translation of Richard has been recommended by Prof. Jameson to his pupils, adopted by Dr Graham [Robert Graham, professor of botany] as his text book, and praised, as I am informed, in the newspapers …. Mrs MacGillivray and the children are in good health. I am just about to commence a series of desperate jobs which will occupy me till winter. As I understood your proposals respecting the Birds of Britain to have ended in nothing, and as you do not allude to the subject, I shall suppose all our ideas to have dispersed, and shall think of the matter myself. At the same time I do not think large and expensive works commendable, as they are beyond the reach of those who are most deserving, and most likely to profit by the inspection of them ….

This letter is of interest on several accounts. It indicates that MacGillivray still felt under obligation to Jameson although he had left his service, and indicates also that he must have had discussions with Audubon regarding a joint publication on British birds. In the event MacGillivray did write his five-volume work by himself, but failed to get his paintings published.

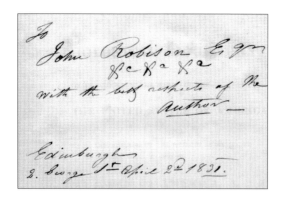

The first volume of Audubon's *Ornithological Biography* was published by Adam Black in Edinburgh in 1831.

The format of the book worried MacGillivray. He preferred a smaller format and suggested this to Audubon. Audubon's rejection of this advice highlights one of the differences between the two men – MacGillivray cautious and conservative in his outlook, while Audubon favoured the grand concept and was prepared to take risks. He wrote: 'The fashionable size of books just now is in Inches 4 by 2½ *so modest*, so empty of novelty and devoid of facts that it is enough to sicken one to look at their pompous coverings – but "never you mind" my Dear Fellow I shall go on just as I began to the last and my Work shall not be a *Beacon* but a Tremendous *Light*house!'[5]

The book consists of descriptions of each bird, starting with a discursive and anecdotal account of the habitat, feeding habits, and general behavioural characteristics, often with tales of successful kills described with considerable pride or at least detachment. Then follows a detailed account of the bird's features. Interlaced at intervals are short 'episodes' on unrelated topics such as 'Improvements in the Navigation of the Mississippi', 'A Flood', or 'Kentucky Sports', in which Audubon tells of events from his experience which he thinks might interest the reader. An extract from 'The Earthquake' gives a sample of these:

> Shock succeeded shock almost every day or night for several weeks, diminishing, however, so gradually as to dwindle away into mere vibrations of the earth. Strange to say, I for one became so accustomed to the feeling as rather to enjoy the fears manifested by others. I never can forget the effects of one of the slighter shocks which took place when I was

at a friend's house, where I had come to enjoy the merriment that, in our western country, attends a wedding. The ceremony being performed, supper over, and the fiddles tuned, dancing became the order of the moment. This was merrily followed up to a late hour, when the party retired to rest. We were in what is called, with great propriety, a *Log-house*, one of large dimensions, and solidly constructed. The owner was a physician, and in one corner were not only his lancets, tourniquets, amputating-knives, and other sanguinary apparatus, but all the drugs which he employed for the relief of his patients, arranged in jars and phials of different sizes. These had some days before made a narrow escape from destruction, but had been fortunately preserved by closing the doors of the cases in which they were contained.

As I have said, we had all retired to rest, some to dream of sighs and smiles, and others to sink into oblivion. Morning was fast approaching. when the rumbling noise that precedes the earthquake began so loudly, as to waken and alarm the whole party, and drive them out of bed in the greatest consternation. The scene which ensued it is impossible for me to do justice to it. Fear knows no restraints. Every person, old and young, filled with alarm at the creaking of the log-house, and apprehending instant destruction, rushed wildly out to the grass enclosure fronting the building. The full moon was slowly descending from her throne, covered at times by clouds that rolled heavily along, as if to conceal from her view the scenes of terror which prevailed on the earth below. On the grass-plat we all met, in such condition as rendered it next to impossible to discriminate any of the party, all huddled together in a state of almost perfect nudity. The earth waved like a field of corn before the breeze; the birds left their perches, and flew about not knowing whither; and the Doctor, recollecting the danger of his gallipots, ran to this shop-room, to prevent their dancing off the shelves to the floor …. However before the shock was over he had lost nearly all he possessed.

The shock at length ceased, and the frightened females, now sensible of their dishabille, fled to their several apartments …. These 'episodes' were discontinued after the third volume due to lack of space and in later editions Audubon was persuaded to delete these passages as being irrelevant, which is unfortunate as they give an interesting insight into his life and times. Audubon may have been correct about the inadequacies of his scientific knowledge, but he had no reason to feel that he lacked literary ability, for letters, journals and passages such as the above show that he could write with style and clarity in his second language, albeit with some idiosyncratic spelling. MacGillivray's writing tended to be more constrained and economical and he considered that one of his functions was to tone down Audubon's more extravagant descriptive passages, which may not always have been necessary. Charles Bonaparte, in a letter to Sir William Jardine, commented on the first volume of *Ornithological Biography*: '… I had advised Audubon to get scientific help. Now Audubon appears to have flown with his own wings, or at least Mr MacGillivray did not furnish him with powerful feathers.'[6]

Inevitably the publication of this volume was an occasion for another outburst from Waterton, who was incensed by a favourable review by a Professor Rennie.[7] His tag from Virgil on this occasion was quite apt: '*Quis novus hic nostris successit sedibus hospes?*' – 'Say who advances to our door with face unknown from foreign shore?'

> Professor Rennie … having desired the public to read those works; I beg permission to say a word or two on the light in which I see them …. A gentleman of his never ceasing application to books cannot fail to be a competent judge of literary merit. Still I own that I do not see Mr Audubon's merit as a writer exactly in the same light as that in which the professor sees it; and, if I have drawn my conclusions from false premises, I trust that … someone from the extensive circle of Mr Audubon's admiring friends, will kindly show me where my error lies.
>
> Without leaving behind him in America any public reputation as a naturalist, Mr Audubon comes to England, and he is immediately pointed out to us as an ornithological luminary of the first magnitude.
>
> … Were the Biography of Birds really the production of Mr Audubon's own pen, I should not be tardy in praising its *literary* merit, notwithstanding its *ornithological* faults.

But having compared the style with that of the article on the habits of Vultur Aura, I came to the conclusion that these two productions could not have been written by the same person …. The first is that of a finished scholar; the second that of a very moderately-educated man.

He goes on at length to justify his belief that Audubon could not have written the *Ornithological Biography*. Victor Audubon, then in London, leapt to his father's defence.[8]

> Mr Charles Waterton having asserted that Mr Audubon was not the author of *Ornithological Biography*, I … do not feel willing to permit such an assertion to pass uncontradicted during my father's absence from England.
>
> I have the authority of the gentleman Mr Waterton refers to, in stating that 'Mr Audubon's proposal to him was to obtain his assistance in the scientific details, and in no other part of the work whatsoever;' and further, I have the authority of this gentleman, for stating his 'firm conviction arising from personal intercourse and the perusal of the original manuscripts, that Mr Audubon, and no other person, is the bona fide author of *Ornithological Biography*'.
>
> I shall not notice Mr Waterton further, except to express my thanks for his generous conduct, in withholding his attacks on Mr Audubon for 2 years after the book in question was published, and during the time the author was in England, and bringing these charges forward when my father has returned to the forests of America and is unable to answer for himself.

In the same issue of Loudon's *Magazine*, Robert Bakewell, Lucy's cousin, wrote:

> … one fact of great importance is … overlooked. Mr Audubon is the son of French parents: he was educated in France until the age of 17; at that time he could not speak the English language. It cannot, therefore, be the least disparagement to Mr Audubon, if … he should wish to receive the assistance and corrections of a native. Mrs Audubon is a lady of distinguished merit, and possesses great intellectual cultivation and mental

John Bachman, by his son-in-law John Woodhouse Audubon. (Courtesy of Charleston Museum, South Carolina, USA)

power ... and is well qualified to correct her husbands manuscripts ....[9]

Audubon's friend John Bachman also rallied to support him:

I come now to notice the most important enquiry ... whether Audubon is the real author of ... *Ornithological Biography*.

For the last two years and a half, I have been intimately acquainted with Audubon: he has resided in my family for months in succession. From a similarity of disposition and pursuits, he was my companion in my rambles through the woods and fields, and the entertainer of my evening hours .... His journals have been regularly submitted to my inspection; his notes and observations were made in my presence; and a considerable portion of the second volume of *Ornithological Biography* was written under my roof .... From all these opportunities ... I do not hesitate to state that Audubon is the author of the book to which his name is attached.

... Some details of the habits and presents of this gentleman ... will account for the manner in which he has been enabled successfully to carry on so large, expensive, and laborious a work as which is now in progress of publication.

He rises with the earliest dawn, and devotes the whole of the day, in intense industry, to his favourite pursuit. The specimens from which he makes his drawings are all from nature; carefully noting the colours of the eye, bill, and legs; measuring ... every part of the bird .... He keeps a Journal, and regularly notes down every thing connected with natural history....

Let the literary world but award to Audubon the justice which he merits; ... this work cannot fail to prove a very important acquisition to the Natural History of America, nor to reflect the highest credit on the liberality of the British public, that has hitherto so efficiently aided him in the publication of it, nor to establish an abiding monument to the fame of its author.[10]

Professor Jameson and William Swainson, who wrote favourable reviews of the early volumes of *Ornithological Biography* in which there were criticisms of Waterton, also came under the lash of Waterton's pen. (In fact the review in Jameson's *Edinburgh New Philosophical Journal* was unsigned and may have been by another, but Waterton attributes it to Jameson.) In a series of letters to his friend Ord he maintained his obsessive hatred of Audubon and of anyone who supported him. In a letter dated 3 July 1835 he wrote:

Master Jameson sees his folly in attacking me. My two letters to him have given universal satisfaction in the country, and nobody pities him. He has not answered them and as far as I can learn, he does not intend to answer them. Indeed, what can he say? The public must now clearly see that the Scotch philosophers have supported Audubon at the expense of truth; and I have run them so hard, that they can no longer defend him .... He is, indeed, an arrogant fool! Only think of heaven imposing upon such a fellow the task of writing the history of your birds! Father Morris sends you his blessing. He is here to-day and says he prays for you continually.

In a letter to Ord dated 1 December 1840 Waterton wrote:

I will review Audubon's biography of birds, in about a twenty or thirty pound pamphlet, in which Swainson, and Jameson, and MacGillivray, and all his other supporters shall have their ignorance brought home to them. I will prove their consummate ignorance in clear terms, by showing that they have held up, almost to public adoration, a man whose book of birds contains unpardonable errors in every page ....

He had published one of his letters to Jameson in a lengthy pamphlet, from which this is an extract:

A Letter to Robert Jameson, Regius Professor of Natural History; Lecturer on Mineralogy and Keeper of the Museum in the University of Edinburgh; Fellow of the Royal Societies of London and Edinburgh; of the Antiquarian, Wernerian, and Horticultural Societies of Edinburgh; Honorary Member of the Royal Irish Academy, and of the Royal Dublin Society; Fellow of the Linnean and Geological Societies of London, &c., &c.

Sir .... You have aimed a severe blow at me, which I did not expect from you; nor do I think I have deserved it, as I am not aware that in all my life I have ever written or spoken one unfriendly word against you. Too often it happens that many a poor humble bee is trodden under foot which never stung the passing traveller. Through Audubon you have aimed a blow at me; through Audubon I will lever a shaft at you in my turn, with an aim so just and true, that it will be utterly out of your power to ward it off.

Waterton continues with a scathing (and seemingly justified) criticism of a passage in the second volume of *Ornithological Biography* which Jameson had quoted in his review. In this passage Audubon relates a tale in which a farmer died after being bitten through his boot by a rattle-snake. A year later his son put the boots on and died as a result of a scratch from the fang which had been left in the boot, and two years later a similar event happened to a second son. Waterton stated that the story

... of this depopulating Munchausen boot, which you have swallowed without straining, was current when I was a boy ... and was

considered a good joke some fifty or sixty years back ... AN ARRANT YANKEE-DOODLE HOAX .... you are no better qualified to review a work on birds than you are to lecture on the poisonous fangs of snakes. Cervantes formerly exclaimed, 'Para mi solo necio Don Quixote, y yo para el. El supo obràr, y yo escrivèr.' (Don Quixote was born for me, and I for him. He knew how to manufacture and I to write.) ... You are a regius professor, with above forty honorary titles after your name; I, am a private individual, scarcely known, whose care it is through life never to be the aggressor, but who will always resist to the utmost any attack made upon him, come from what quarter it may.[11]

Jameson's response – if any – to this letter is not known, but he was not one to be upset by criticism as shown by his handling of the university commissioners and by his stance in the Huttonian/Wernerian controversy.

To Swainson, Waterton also sent a published letter:

... When a man who is not sufficiently well armed espies a lynx slumbering in the woods, he immediately takes himself off, as quickly and as quietly as possible, lest by approaching too near he may disturb the animal, and thus be treated to an awful exhibition of his teeth and claws.

Though, from the place of my repose, I have more than once seen you bewildered and lost in the quinary labyrinth of your fond conceit of circles, and have had you completely in my power, still I have never thought of springing at you; because you did not appear to show symptoms of an attempt to break in upon my retreat.

But now, that you have not only aroused me from my slumber, but have even been incautious enough to take me by the beard neither yourself nor your friends ought to be surprised if I lay a vengeful and a heavy paw upon you.

Pray, how can you venture to pronounce my personalities against Mr Audubon *un-justifiable*? In the same volume in which you have read the personalities you must have seen that his infatuated admirers never hesitated to indulge in personalities against me.

He goes on at length to justify his claims to be considered an expert naturalist and gives a detailed critique of his views regarding Swainson's and Audubon's competence. 'How cruelly has this American snake … bitten our wise men of London and of Modern Athens!'[12]

It is easy to dismiss Waterton as an idiosyncratic crank as many have done, but there is certainly some substance in many of his criticisms. There is no doubt that Audubon's writings were accepted uncritically by his acquaintances in Britain, who were perhaps over-impressed by his romantic personality and the enthusiastic conviction with which he expressed himself. Waterton's mistake was to latch onto trivial and isolated instances of dubious accuracy and infer from these that Audubon's entire output could be discredited. He also laboured his points so trenchantly and repetitively that his audience grew weary and ceased to take him seriously.

It was unfortunate, for he and Audubon had much in common, and had not George Ord triggered his consuming hatred of Audubon the two men might have been good friends. Waterton, although eccentric with regard to his dismissal of the conventions of dress, his fondness for childish pranks and his asceticism, had many positive attributes including his profound knowledge of the classics, his love of nature, his awareness of the need for conservation, and his generosity to the under-privileged.

There are no illustrations in the earlier volumes of *Ornithological Biography* as the book was designed to supplement *The Birds of America*, but in the fourth and fifth volumes there are a number of woodcuts of anatomical features such as the intestines and respiratory passages of birds. Audubon notes in *Ornithological Biography*:

Dissections of (*left*) the American white pelican and (*right*) the American widgeon. Woodcuts from volume IV of *Ornithological Biography*.

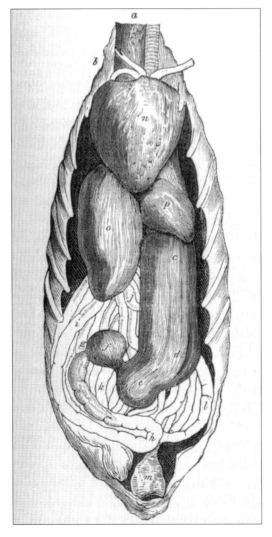

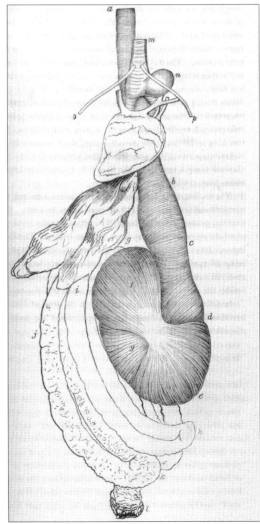

These anatomical descriptions, as well as the sketches by which they are sometimes illustrated, have been executed by my learned friend William MacGillivray, who in the most agreeable manner consented to undertake the labour, by no means small of such a task, and to whom those who are interested in the progress of Ornithological science, as well as myself, must therefore feel indebted. These details I had resolved to present to you, because I have thought that no perfect knowledge of the affinities of species can be obtained until their internal organization is known. I believe the time to be fast approaching when much of the results obtained from the inspection of the exterior alone will be laid aside: when museums filled with stuffed skins will be considered insufficient to afford a knowledge of birds ....[13]

Audubon, influenced by MacGillivray, also did some anatomical dissections, 17 of which he presented to the museum of the Royal College of Surgeons, and for which he received a letter of thanks from the president.[14]

While in Edinburgh and after his return to America, Audubon subjected Robert Havell in London to a constant stream of letters. These contained peremptory instructions urging him to speed the production of the engravings, to purchase canvases for Kidd's paintings, to deliver messages to his friends and subscribers in London and many other duties which seem hardly the responsibility of an engraver. Occasionally a more conciliatory note was added: in a letter to Havell on 10 April 1831 he writes:

Push on with your work, take early walks and enjoy as much as may be in your power that Nature of which you say I speak of with a purpose. – Who knows but what you and yours may not visit the majestic woods off my beloved Country? We are quite well and a happier time have seldom experienced in this fairest of Cities – give our kindly regards to your Dear Wife ....[15]

On 15 April 1831 Audubon and Lucy left for London. On the way they stopped at Liverpool where they 'travelled on that extraordinary road called the railway, at the rate of twenty-four miles an hour'. This was the Liverpool and Manchester Railway, which had opened six months before.[16] It was the first railway designed to carry passenger traffic. Fellow Wernerian William Scoresby had been present at its opening in 1830 and had witnessed the first fatal railway accident in which the local Member of Parliament, William Huskisson, was killed by a passing train.

At this time Audubon looked back on what he had achieved since coming to Britain.

I have balanced my accounts with the Birds of America, and the whole business is really wonderful; forty thousand dollars have passed through my hands for the completion of the first volume. Who would believe that a lonely individual, who landed in England without a friend [Audubon frequently used 'England' as a synonym for Britain] ... and with only sufficient pecuniary means to travel through it as a visitor, could have accomplished such a task as this publication.[17]

It had not been easy or without frustration – 50 of Audubon's original subscribers had discontinued their subscriptions and the effort of seeking new subscribers while supervising the printing and publication over a four-year period had been fatiguing and vexatious. Nonetheless he said, 'I will continue to trust in that Providence which has helped me thus far'.

After brief visits to London and Paris to attend to his business affairs, the Audubons returned to America, landing on 3 September 1831 'after a remarkably fine passage of 33 days' on the *Columbia*. He killed many birds on the crossing, but the boat was going too fast to enable them to be recovered; however, 'vive la joie, no taxes on shooting or fishing'.[18]

Two months later some excitement was caused by the report of Audubon's death in the London *Literary Gazette* and in the Edinburgh *Caledonian Mercury*, which his correspondents in Edinburgh hastened to correct.

During this visit to Edinburgh, Audubon had entered into an agreement with Joseph Bartholomew Kidd to copy 100 of his paintings in oils for the purpose of sale, the proceeds to be divided equally between them.[19] Kidd worked in a desultory manner until 1833. Audubon had high hopes for the joint enterprise and wrote frequently to Victor in London urging him to try to motivate Kidd, but at the same time appears to have been dilatory in paying him for his efforts. In a letter from Kidd to Audubon he wrote, 'You talk of making some regular arrangements to have me paid *punctually*. I thank you for this promise and I hope you will be as good as your word, as it will stimulate me the faster. The reverse is apt to have the opposite effect.' Eventually, towards the end of 1833, the arrangement appears to have been concluded.

On 16 March 1833 Kidd suffered a curious accident which may have affected his productivity. He was attending the auction sale in 16 Picardy Place of the late Lord Eldin's pictures, which included the 'Adoration of the Magi' attributed to Titian,[20] when the floor of the crowded room gave way. Kidd, among many others, fell through to the floor below, their fall being partially arrested by the carpet which sagged through the opening in the floor. Two were killed and 35 suffered injuries, including Kidd who dislocated an arm and sustained multiple bruises, for which he was treated with cupping and blisters, the panaceas

of the time.[21] Kidd had to ask Audubon for a loan of money to support him while convalescing.

A more compelling reason for the conclusion of the agreement with Audubon was that Kidd, as a result of his association with Audubon, had obtained a commission to do the illustrations for *The Miscellany of Natural History*, edited by Thomas Dick Lauder and Thomas Brown (1833). The prospectus reads:

The numerous illustrations, which form a prominent feature in a publication of this kind will be executed in the first style of art. To secure this important advantage, the Editors have associated with themselves Mr J B Kidd, member of the Scottish Academy etc, an artist whose attainments enable him to impart to his subjects that accuracy to be expected from those alone who are acquainted with the Physical Sciences; and when it is mentioned that the celebrated Audubon, the best delineator of birds who has hitherto

Kidd's painting of the blue and yellow macaw, from *The Miscellany of Natural History* (compare with Edward Lear's more elegant parrots on p.163).

Far right: Kidd's painting of the Carolina parrot, from *The Miscellany of Natural History* (compare with illustrations on p. 24 – Kidd's parrot is a copy of Wilson's in reverse).

appeared, has employed Mr Kidd to execute oil paintings of all his subjects, of the same size as the splendid originals …. the Editors hope this fact will be considered a sufficient sanction for the choice they have made.

In fact this introduction grossly overstates Kidd's talents. He may have been a good landscape painter and copier of Audubon's paintings, but his own talent for bird illustration was limited. Compare for example his painting of the Carolina parrot with the renderings of this bird by Wilson and Audubon (see p. 24).

(see p. 24)

The Miscellany of Natural History published a crude engraving of John Syme's portrait of Audubon without obtaining Audubon's permission, which angered him considerably. *The Miscellany*, which had been intended as a rival to Jardine and Lizars' popular *Naturalist's Library*, was not a success and only one volume, on the subject of parrots, was published.

Waldemar Fries has collated the information on the Kidd copies. Audubon received 94 for which he paid £113. These are now scattered in many collections and institutions and 58 have been located. They are hard to identify as they are unsigned and Audubon and his sons also did some copies in oils.[22]

This was not the end of Kidd's links with Audubon. In 1834, while Audubon was in America, William Fletcher, an Edinburgh carver and gilder, took out a summons against him for unpaid debts for the provision of picture frames. Letters of arrestment were raised against Kidd and a bookseller, Alexander Hill, who had 'custody of effects' belonging to the absent Audubon and they were instructed to hand over 'all and sundry goods, gear, corns cattle, money … and all other moveable goods'. The messenger-at-arms 'lawfully fenced and arrested' from Kidd and Hill the sum of £100.[23] The money was repaid by Audubon when he returned to Edinburgh later that year. The picture frames were those which had been used by Kidd for his reproductions of Audubon's paintings.

During the following two and a half years Audubon travelled extensively, from Florida to Maine and Labrador, adding to his portfolio and seeking new subscribers. While in Charleston, South Carolina, in 1831, he met and received hospitality from the Reverend John Bachman, who was to become one of Audubon's greatest friends and supporters. Such was Audubon's personality that Bachman wrote to Lucy that the month during which Audubon stayed at his house 'was one of the happiest months of my life …. How gratifying was it, then, to become acquainted with a man, who knew more about

Far left: Audubon's painting of the Henslow's bunting, plate 70 from *The Birds of America*). (Reproduced by kind permission of the President and Council of the Royal College of Physicians and Surgeons of Glasgow)

Left: Kidd's copy of Audubon's painting of the Henslow's bunting. (Courtesy of the John James Audubon Museum, Henderson, Kentucky, USA)

birds than any man now living – and who, at the same time, was communicative, intelligent, and amiable ....'

Bachman's vigorous defence of Audubon over the vulture controversy and the authorship of *American Ornithology* has been previously described (see Chapter 11, pp. 140–41 and Chapter 12, p. 150). Bachman is possibly the only person who knew intimately and admired both Alexander Wilson and Audubon. It is of interest that he took no part in the debate about the relative merits of the two men which was conducted largely by those who knew only one or the other or neither. From his boyhood Bachman was keenly interested in natural history, and was befriended by Wilson whom he joined in field excursions and for whom he collected specimens. On Wilson's recommendation he succeeded him as a teacher at Elwood School in Milestown, Pennsylvania, where he taught for a year when he was aged 15. He subsequently studied theology and became pastor to the Lutheran church in Charleston where he presided for 55 years. Bachman's collaboration with Audubon in the writing of the text of the *Quadrupeds of North America* is described in

Chapter 15. Both of Audubon's sons were to marry daughters of Bachman.

In October 1832 Audubon sent Victor to Britain to supervise the engravings and look after his business affairs. 'We all hope that your Journey to Scotland and your stay at Edinburgh will prove as gratifying to you as it always was to me and to your Dear Mother. I regret the Death of Walter Scott [on 21 September 1832] as much on your account as I do on mine, but John Wilson [Christopher North] must supply his place.'[24]

In later letters to Victor, Audubon described his ideas about publishing a popular edition of his *Birds* in smaller format once his grand initial plan had been completed.[25] Victor, now aged 24, had clearly become a key figure in the business side of the family enterprise and took an active part in the decision-making, while John, aged 21, was increasingly helping his father with the paintings. 'John has drawn a few Birds as good as any I ever made, and ere a few months I hope to hive this department of my duty altogether to him.'[26]

On 16 April 1834 Audubon returned to Britain accompanied by Lucy and John.

Notes

1   Sim, G: *Life of William MacGillivray*, p. 35.
2   *The Life of John James Audubon the Naturalist*, p. 205. In fact James Wilson records that Audubon first asked him if he would undertake that task of assisting him with his writing, but Wilson refused because he had 'too many irons in the fire'. *North British Review* (1852), vol XIX, footnote p. 10.
3   Ibid, pp. 205-6.
4   Fries, W H: *The Double Elephant Folio*, p. 133.
5   *Letters of John James Audubon 1826-1840*, vol. II, pp. 59-60.
6   Dated 20 November 1831, in the Jardine Archive in EUL. This letter also draws attention to what Bonaparte regarded as incorrect identification of birds by Audubon and urges Jardine to speed up the publication of his edition of Wilson's *American Ornithology* in order to set the record straight.
7   *Magazine of Natural History* (1833), 6: 215-8. This dig at Rennie relates to a previous outpouring by Waterton against Rennie's edition of *Montague's Ornithological Dictionary* in which he wrote: 'the errors it contains can only be accounted for on the score that our Professor, like many other naturalists of high note and consideration, has spent more of his time in books than in bogs. His deficiency in bog-education is to be lamented; for such an education would have been a great help to him in his ornithological writings.' (*Magazine of Natural History* 4, p. 517.)
8   Ibid 6, p. 369.
9   Ibid 6, p. 372.
10   Ibid 7, pp. 164-75.
11   Waterton's *Essays on Natural History* (1871 edn), pp. 585-90.
12   Ibid, pp. 511-23. The 'quinary system' to which he refers was a reference to Swainson's adoption of a bizarre system of classification of animal species which enjoyed a brief vogue during the 1820s but was scorned by most naturalists and soon went out of fashion.
13   *Ornithological Biography*, vol. IV, pp. xxiii-xxiv.
14   Ibid, vol. V, pp. xxiii.
15   *Letters of John James Audubon*, vol. I, p. 135.
16   The Liverpool and Manchester Railway was the first to be designed for passenger travel. The very first railway, the Stockton and Darlington, had been opened five years earlier in 1825 but was largely designed for coal transport and

passengers were a secondary consideration. The Liverpool and Manchester had three classes of passengers. First class rode in closed carriages built in the style of stage coaches, second class in roofed carriages with open sides, and third class in open trucks. It was designed by the engineer George Stephenson, whose *Rocket* engine could reach 24 mph.

17   *Life of John James Audubon*, p. 207.

18   Cited in *The Miscellany of Natural History*, p. 32.

19   In November 1830 Kidd made the following contract with Audubon: 'I the undersigned do agree to copy in oil one hundred of Mr. J. J. Audubon's drawings, being that portion of his collection now engraved and published, under the title of "Birds of America," and to deliver the same into his possession or to his order on or near the first day of May next, being facsimiles of said Drawings – for the sum of One Hundred pounds Sterling money ... Mr. J. J. Audubon furnishing at his expense the canvases and mill boards, and myself the colours, varnishes, and brushes .... J. B. Kidd [signed].'

20   The 'Adoration of the Magi' was sold on that occasion for £262.10s. It is in the collection of the National Gallery of Scotland but is now considered to be a work of Bassano. Lord Eldin (John Clerk), 1757-1832, was a notable collector of paintings.

21   Gordon, E: *The Royal Scottish Academy of Painting, Sculpture and Architecture 1826-1976* and *Audubon the Naturalist*, vol. I, p. 447.

22   *The Double Elephant Folio*, Appendix C, pp. 360-7. Joseph Bartholomew Kidd and the oil paintings of Audubon's *Birds of America*.

23   Scottish Record Office, Edinburgh CS/237/F.10/2.

24   *Letters of John James Audubon 1826-1840*, vol. I, p. 199.

25   Ibid, vol. I, pp. 247-9.

26   Ibid, vol. I, p. 274.

13 | The Fourth Visit: Family Life in Edinburgh

AUDUBON, Lucy and John landed at Liverpool on 7 May 1834 and joined Victor, who had been in London for the previous three years attending to the business side of the publications. As usual Audubon did not enjoy London.

The Town is now what is called 'Empty' that is the Grandies are off shooting Partridges, Grous hares & Pheasants – Parliament is pro-rogued and there is in fact not more than a Million and half of People in town … half of whom are Beggars, thiefs & Blagguards of all sort – We have an unaccountably hot summer – indeed just such a[s] I might have expected in New York …. The Queen of these Realms had returned in perfect safety, she was hissed at her departure and groaned at on her return – the Irish are fighting like Devils and I hope their rows will open the Eyes of their merciless Landlords.[1]

On the other hand, he enjoyed having the entire family together. 'Our Dear sons are study-ing every day.– My Old Friend mends our socks Makes our shirts, Reads to us at Times, but drinks no brandy now a days – she has cast off her purchased sham curls [and] wears her own dear grey locks and looks all the better.'[2]

MacGillivray greeted him with a letter dated 28 May 1834:

Dear Sir

I am glad to hear of your safe arrival, which I did not expect so soon, and pleased to find you in good health and high spirits. As you have the kindness to inquire respecting myself and family, I am happy to inform you that we are all very well, contented and busy. My head and hands are quite full – abundance of work, and sufficient pay – time to ramble now and then for the purpose of hammering rocks, pulling plants, and shooting birds.

You say you have accumulated a mass of materials which you are desirous of seeing in print, and propose that I should revise it as before. I shall be glad to do so, if you please, and willing that you confer the benefit on another, if you find it expedient. As to the terms, let them be such as you please with respect to money; but as time is valuable to me I should like that arrangements be made so as to prevent unnecessary loss of it, by letting me have manuscripts, books, etc. in due array.

The skins of which you speak I appre-hend cannot be disposed of here to any great extent; but I believe shells might be sold to advantage, and bring higher prices than in London.

You ask if I draw Birds yet, with a view to publish. My answer is that I dissect, describe, and draw Birds, Quadrupeds, whales, reptiles, and fishes, with view of astonishing the world, and bettering my condition. I have about a hundred drawings, all the size of life, except-ing two dolphins. But I have determined no-thing as yet respecting publication. Some time ago a friend of mine called on Mr Havell with a letter in which I desired that person to engrave for me a few of my drawings, for the purpose of being exhibited at the meeting of naturalists. I had no answer, and so Mr Havell may go to Jericho, or elsewhere, as he lists; but further your correspondent saith not.

I am decidedly of opinion that, although you should continue the publication of the Ornithological Biography, you might bring out various other works which should not fail to be popular; for example, a biography of yourself, and sketches of American scenery. But of these matters it is impossible to speak to purpose unless I had the pleasure of seeing you, a pleasure which I hope I shall have at the time of the general assembly of the naturalists.

With best respects to Mrs. Audubon, and best wishes for the prosperity of all who bear that name, I have the Honour to be etc.[3]

The 'mass of materials' was the draft of volume two of *Ornithological Biography* which Audubon had written while staying with the Bachmans. MacGillivray wrote to Audubon:

Edinburgh,
11 Gilmore Place, 16 June 1834

Dear Sir

I received your letter yesterday and have the pleasure of answering it. If you send me twenty or twenty-five articles, I can revise them without the books to which you refer, and without your own presence, provided your descriptions be full, and the drawing or plates sent to me …. With respect to printing it seems to me very doubtful that you can get it done in London better or cheaper than here. The best way is to get estimates. If the work were post 8vo., I imagine it would sell much more extensively, but I suppose you have determined to continue it of the same size. You ask about lodgings here. Two doors from me there are good accommodations; but I am sorry, that my own nest which is in a garden, among pear-trees, is rather small. I am sorry that you have resolved to reside in London, that ugly forest of brick buildings swarming with vermin of all genera, species, and varieties, and should like much to see you, that you might condemn one half of my drawings and approve of the rest ….[4]

Edinburgh,
11 Gilmore Place, 18 July 1834

Dear Sir

I received from Mr Neill yours of the 9th along with a parcel of 25 descriptions of birds, and now report progress. I commenced my operations on the 1st July, and have transcribed and corrected eighteen articles, one for each day, but not one on each, the work of Sunday being transferred to Monday. This volume will certainly be much richer and more interesting. It will also be larger. You wish to know my opinion as to the improvement of your style. It seems to me to be much the same as before,

but the information which you give is more diversified & more satisfactory.

Your first volume is only beginning to be known …. Had it been of the post 8vo size, in two volumes it would have gone off in style; but your imperial size and regal price do not answer for radicals of republicans either. Could you sacrifice the first volume, reprint it of a small size and continue the series so to that end? In suggesting this, I firmly believe that my only object is to let the book have fair play. Lizars has sold five or six thousand copies of some of his ill written compilations and if you were to issue yours in a similar style – not of writing but of printing – with 20 wood cuts or engravings in each volume, I am certain it would spread over the land like a flock of migratory pigeons ….

I have often thought that your stories would sell very well by themselves, and I am sure that with your celebrity, knowledge and enthusiasm, you have it in your power to become more popular than your glorious pictures can make you of themselves, they being too aristocratic and exclusive. Excuse me for putting down my thoughts just as they occur, and for wandering from my subject, which was the progress of the manuscript.[5]

The 'ill written compilation' of Lizars refers to *The Naturalist's Library*, edited by Jardine and published by Lizars. It consisted of 40 volumes issued between 1833 and 1843, written and illustrated by several authors and painters. The illustrations were engraved on steel by Lizars and hand coloured. The text in general does not justify MacGillivray's criticism and he himself was to become the author of the volume on *British Quadrupeds* (1838). Many of the illustrations are of very high quality. The books were published inexpensively in the small format which MacGillivray wished that Audubon would adopt, and were very successful.

Audubon was also very critical of *The Naturalist's Library*, which he described as 'trash'. His relationship with Lizars and his brother-in-law Jardine had cooled since Lizars abandoned working on his engravings, and there was possibly an element of jealousy over the financial success of the publication. The final insult was the copying of two of Audubon's paintings without his permission. The first was a vignette based on

The long-tailed African tody by Swainson; and (*far right*) the peacock and Camberwell beauty butterflies – examples of the quality of illustrations in *The Naturalist's Library*.

Far right: The vignette of wood pigeons engraved by Lizars, from *The Naturalist's Library*, volume XIX (compare with original, p. 55).

Audubon's 'Wood Pigeons' which at that time was in Lizars' possession (see Chapter 6, p. 55), and the second the 'Female Turkey and Chicks'.

This provoked an angry letter from Victor to Jardine: '… As my Fathers agent and representative I have to advise you that in case any other plate or plates … copied from the "Birds of America" be published in the "Naturalists Library" or Elsewhere, I shall at once bring an action to recover damages, in behalf of my Father ….' Audubon wrote in a letter to Bachman, 'I do not *treat* with him any more since he took it upon himself to republish some of my plates without leave'. Later editions of the offending volume contained an apology.

Audubon's 'stories' were eventually published as MacGillivray suggested, in a separate volume by Herrick in 1926 under the title of *Delineations of American Scenery and Character*.

MacGillivray wrote to Audubon:

Edinburgh,
11 Gilmore Place, 28th July 1834

Dear Sir
… I called on Mr Kidd & did not find him

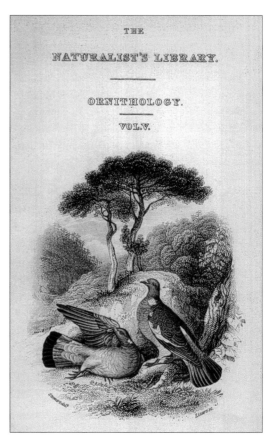

Left: The pirated copy of Audubon's turkey hen and chicks, plate 2 from *The Naturalist's Library*, volume xx (p. 117); and (*below*) Audubon's original, plate 6 (see also illustration on p. 47). (Reproduced by kind permission of the President and Council of the Royal College of Physicians and Surgeons of Glasgow)

at home. Today however, I succeeded, but he informed me that he could not deliver the drawings as they were yet unfinished ....

Can you inform me where Mr. Gould has described a Wagtail formerly confounded with the Yellow Wagtail, and which I am informed he has named moracilla neglecta? I have found the bird here in abundance in some meadows near the town, and thought at first that I had discovered a new species ....

Now that your American birds are completed I suppose you will have at the European or the British. In the latter case what will become of mine? However, I have resolved, God willing, to go through with my task. I have at least 20 drawings superior to anything in the way ever seen by me, excepting always 'The Birds of America,' and so good that one might look at them without disgust even after seeing yours.[6]

It was out of character for MacGillivray to praise his own works but examination of his paintings reproduced in this book will show that his high regard for them was well justified and they do bear comparison with those of Audubon.

Another letter from MacGillivray to Audubon:

Edinburgh,
11 Gilmore Place, 19th August 1834

Dear Sir

... I have seen Mr Kidd twice today, and informed him of your wishes.

The College of Surgeons are so urgent with me to have the Catalogue of the Museum printed by the 1st of November that it will be quite impossible for me to go to London before December, because after the catalogue is done, the registration of students which occupies three weeks commences .... I will see Mr Kidd in a day or two.'[7]

[MacGillivray's catalogue is preserved in the College Museum.]

The references to Kidd are probably connected with Audubon's concern at Kidd's slowness in producing the copies of his paintings in oils as arranged.

The Audubons arrived in Edinburgh in October 1834 and took lodgings in 5 Lothian Street. In a letter to Bachman of 5 November

1834,[8] Audubon describes how the two men worked feverishly to get volume two completed:

Look at the place and date of this most amiable letter and see me from morn to darkness inclosed into night ... at revising, correcting, and sending forth for 'Press' each successive sheets of the 2d Vol. of my 'delightful' Biographies of birds, and then you will have 'a pretty tolerable Idea I guess' of what I am about. My good old friend [Lucy] is at my side dashing away at the same work – Not labour, but most agreeable avocation!

Two weeks later, Audubon wrote: 'Here I am with my old friend [Lucy] and MacGillivray. Rather more than half of my 2d Vol of Biographies are Printed ....' Audubon was beginning to tire of this relentless labour: '... I would rather go without a shirt or any inexpressibles through the whole of the florida swamps in musquito time than labour as I have hitherto done with the pen.' In December volume two was published. A review in the *Athenaeum* (1835) read:

If only considered as evidence that it is in the power of man to achieve whatever he wills, and that no obstacles are too great to be overcome by energy and devotion of purpose, it would claim our good will and best wishes.

He has told what he has seen and undergone ... with unstudied freedom, rising at times to eloquence, not been ashamed to utter the thousand affectionate and benevolent feelings which a close and enthusiastic communion with nature must nourish. The work is full of the man.

Reviews by his erstwhile friend Swainson were less enthusiastic.

With volume two completed, Audubon immediately pressed on with the remaining volumes with relentless energy. In a letter to Bachman of 10 December 1834:[9]

I am quite sure I never have been half so anxious as I am at this moment to do all in my power to compleat my Vast enterprise, and sorrowful indeed would be my dying moments if this Work of mine was not finished ere my eyes are for ever close ... there is something

Far left: Great green maccaw and (*left*) tricolour crested cockatoo by Edward Lear, from *The Naturalist's Library*, volume XVIII.

within me that tells me that should I be so fortunate as to see the close of my present publication, my name will be honourably handed to posterity and the comforts of my sons and their families much augmented through this means.

MacGillivray renewed his contract to continue to revise the next two volumes at the same rate – two guineas per sheet of 16 pages – and all three continued to work with extraordinary energy to produce volume three, which followed in the next year. Lucy wrote:

Nothing is heard but the steady movement of the pen; your father is up and at work before dawn, and writes without ceasing all day. Mr MacGllivray breakfasts at nine each morning attending the Museum four days in the week, has several works on hand besides ours, and is, moreover, engaged as a lecturer in a new seminary on botany and natural history.

Volume three received a fulsome review by Christopher North in *Blackwood's*. Audubon

responded with a letter to him (John Wilson) on 1 January 1836:

My dear Friend:
    The first hour of this new year was ushered to me surrounded by my dear flock, all comfortably seated around a small table in middle-sized room, where I sincerely wished you had been also, to witness the flowing gladness of our senses, as from one of us 'Audubon's Ornithological Biography' was read from your ever valuable Journal. I wished this because I felt assured that your noble heart would have received our most grateful thanks with pleasure, the instant our simple ideas had conveyed to you the grant of happiness we experienced at your hands. You were not with us, alas! but to make amends the best way we could, all of a common accord drank to the health, prosperity, and long life, of our generous, talented, and ever kind friend, Professor John Wilson, and all those amiable beings who cling around his heart! May those our sincerest wishes reach you soon, and may they be sealed by Him who granted us

John Gould by T H Maguire. (Courtesy of Ipswich Borough Council Museums and Galleries)

Far right: The graceful 'Train Bearer Hummingbird by H C Richter. Professor Jameson gave Gould a specimen of this bird.

existence, and the joys heaped upon the 'American woodsman' and his family, in your hospitable land ....[10]

While appreciating the favourable comments on his publications, Audubon was constantly goaded by the criticisms of his long-standing enemies Ord and Waterton, which he affected to ignore while frequently referring to them in his letters. 'As to the rage of Mr Waterton ... I really care not a fig – all such stuffs will soon evaporate being mere smoak from a Dung Hill.'[11] He was also very critical of the work of rivals in the field – especially those who achieved financial success, such as John Gould and William Jardine. In a letter to Bachman of 20 April 1835:[12]

Here there are at present three Works publishing on the Birds of Europe – one by Mr Gould and the others by no one knows who – at least I do not know – Works on the Birds of all the world are innumerable – Cheap as dirt and more dirty than dirt – Sir William Jardine will encumber the whole of God's creation with stuff as little like the objects of the Creator's formations as the moon is unto cheese – but who cares? as long as these miscellanies bring forth 5 shillings per Vol to the pocket bag of the one who produces them ....

I have agreed to exchange a copy of my work with Mr Gould, for his publications .... I have also purchased a monograph of parrots from a Mr Lear, how pleasing it will be to us to look at these together to quiz them all ... and pass our Veto upon them!

In fact the parrot paintings of Edward Lear (1812-88),[†] who was one of several artists contributing to both Gould's and Jardine's works, are generally regarded as being among the best ornithological paintings. Selby regarded Lear's parrots as 'very good beautifully coloured & I think infinitely superior to Audubons in softness & the drawing as good'.

John Gould's work differs from that of Audubon in many respects. His talents as a painter were limited and the great majority of illustrations in his books were done by others, although many were based on rough sketches prepared by Gould. The paintings and the preparation of lithographs were done by his wife Elizabeth until her untimely death at the age of 37, and by such eminent artists as Edward Lear, H C Richter, Joseph Wolf and William Hart.

Most of the paintings were done from skins or stuffed specimens, unlike Audubon's which were generally painted from specimens observed in their natural setting and freshly killed by himself. Audubon and MacGillivray were critical of

Far left: Victor Gifford Audubon and (*left*) John Woodhouse Audubon; from miniatures by F Cruikshank (1838) and reproduced from *Audubon and His Journals* 1900 edition, volume I (pp. 384, 412). Frederick Cruikshank (1800-68) was a Scottish painter who exhibited portraits of J J Audubon and Lucy Audubon in the 1835 Royal Academy exhibition in London. (J J Audubon's portrait was later engraved by Havell.)

the 'closet' naturalists. Gould did, however, do considerable fieldwork in compiling his seven-volume *Birds of Australia*, which is generally recognised as his most outstanding publication. Audubon mocked Gould's elaborate preparation for his travels, which contrasted with his own simple requirements: 'He takes his wife and Bairns with him, a Waggon the size of a Squatters Cabin, and all such apparatus as will encumber him not a little – he has never travelled in Woods, never salted his rump stakes with Gun Powder ….' Gould also differed from Audubon in the success of his publishing ventures, which brought him considerable wealth when compared with Audubon's hand-to-mouth existence until late in life. Perhaps there was a touch of envy in Audubon's comments. In his preface to *Birds of Europe*, Gould thanks Audubon and others 'for the warm interest which they have at all times taken in the present work'.

Despite their differences, Gould and Audubon had much in common. They met several times during Audubon's visits to London and exchanged specimens and publications. Gould presented Audubon with a fine pointer bitch which he sent to his friend John Bachman in the United States.

During the first few months of 1835 the Audubons returned to London, but by summertime they were back in Edinburgh, living in 5 India Street. 'Our sons spend many of their

evenings at Professor Wilsons who has a delight-ful family, Learned & Amiable as well as accom-plished.' They also became good friends with the MacGillivray boys and frequently visited each other's houses. In one of these visits young John MacGillivray accidentally broke the glass case of one of Audubon's specimens much to his annoyance, and on another occasion John MacGillivray and John Audubon were caught

Sir Walter Scott by John Woodhouse Audubon, copied from Raeburn's portrait. (Courtesy of the John James Audubon Museum, Henderson, Kentucky, USA)

John Woodhouse Audubon's portrait of the doorman of the Star Hotel, Princes Street, Edinburgh. (Courtesy of the John James Audubon Museum, Henderson, Kentucky, USA)

poaching in Ravelston Woods and had their guns confiscated.[13]

Both the Audubon boys spent much of their time painting: John made a particular study of the works of the eminent portraitist Sir Henry Raeburn.

John is making Rapid progress in Portrait Painting, he works now for money and has abundance to do here.– on an average Five setters a day, which keep at the easel for Eight hours …. had I been as much so at his age, I might have become a great man, but I had no one to point out the way to me – I left my Father too early or too late and unfortunately had too much money at my command in those days. I am now trying hard to make amend honorable by labouring from morn to night …. Victor Paints fine Landscapes and Works hard also! – My old Friend Knits socks for us all ….We are a Working Familly ….[14]

Among John's sitters were the Lord and Lady Provost of Edinburgh, Sir James and Lady Spittal.

This time spent in Edinburgh was one of few opportunities for the entire Audubon family to remain together for an extended period. It appears to have been one of the happier interludes in Audubon's life, judging by the tenor of his letters. Nevertheless, Audubon was becoming acutely aware of his advancing years and the urgency of completing his work: 'I am almost mad with the desire of publishing my 3d Vol this year. I am growing old fast and must work at a double quick time ….'[15] Within the space of a year, with the help of MacGillivray and his 'Working Familly', he completed the second and third volumes of *Ornithological Biography*, each over 600 pages in length.

Despite this intense concentration on his writings he found time for the occasional recreational outing. On 19 August 1835 Audubon paid a visit to the Bass Rock in the Firth of Forth, 'in the agreeable company of my learned friend William MacGillivray and his son'. The Rock, then as now, had one of the largest breeding colonies of gannets in the world. MacGillivray estimated in an earlier visit that there were 20,000 birds on the island: 'Every part of the mural faces of the rock … was more or less covered by them.' Alexander Wilson described the annual cull of birds (see p. 8) and this continued at the time of Audubon's visit, with up to 2000 birds being taken for food and feathers. MacGillivray described the bird and botanical life of the Rock in detail.[16] Both Audubon and MacGillivray give vivid descriptions of the gannets' technique of catching fish, usually herring or mackerel, by diving on them from a height. MacGillivray's son John, in his account of a visit to St Kilda,[17] describes an incident which he believed to be true, in which a gannet dived with such force on a fish in the bottom of a boat that it passed through the planks, plugging the hole with its body so that the boat was able to reach shore! MacGillivray recorded that some considered that the gannet's call was *grog grog*, 'but neither Mr Audubon nor myself interpreted their notes so, otherwise we could have satisfied a few at least, as we had a bottle of whisky and a keg of water'.[18]

In addition to these activities, Audubon maintained an active correspondence. He wrote constantly to his friend Bachman and frequently chided him about the infrequency of his replies.

> Our Dear Child Maria [Bachman's daughter and fiancée of John] has written 52 Letters to my Dear Boy John.– her Father the Revd John Bachman, has written 7 Letters to his friend J. J. A. in the Mean Time! only think of the disparity between Lovers of the one Sort and those who call themselves Lovers of *Science*.[19]

The letters to Bachman were full of peremptory instructions to shoot, preserve and despatch birds and deal with his business affairs in America. It is perhaps not surprising that the replies were infrequent and provoked Audubon to write, not altogether in jest,

> I think you extremely Lazy! Frightful – horrible – Disgraceful! Why dont you Know then that the older we become the more busy we ought to be for the sake of our Dear children whom I Know are truly busy themselves! fie fie ….

Bachman's friendship must have been tested to its limits, but despite many such injunctions it survived. The repeated request for preserved birds of all kinds was the result of MacGillivray's influence and persuasion that the classification of birds was best determined by their internal anatomy. Audubon had adopted this idea with enthusiasm and required specimens for dissection, the results of which appear in the last two volumes of *Ornithological Biography*. Bachman's reward was to receive many acknowledgements in the book. One curious enigmatic request contained in one of these letters reads, 'MacGillivray would like to see the Heads of Negroes and alligators very much. What do you say?' (They were not sent!)

Although he was finding great difficulty in obtaining new subscribers for his *Birds of America*, and *Ornithological Biography* – despite receiving splendid reviews – was not competing with Gould's or Yarrell's more popular works, Audubon's faith in himself and his project remained undiminished. In a letter from Edinburgh to his great American friend and benefactor Edward Harris, without whose benevolent generosity he 'must have walked off from one

Gannet by MacGillivray.
(© The Natural History
Museum, London)

of the fairest of our Cities like a beggar does in poor Ireland …', Audubon wrote:

> … my work will I hope be finished ere I leave this world, and must be appreciated in years to come, when perhaps my childrens' children will feel proud of their gone ancestor, 'The American Woodsman.' You see my Dear Friend how far enthusiasm and a portion of the like for standing fame carries even your humble servant a man with no other means than his industry and prudence as a means of support, and one with scarce the motive of education. There are moments … when thinking of my present enormous undertaking, I wonder how I have been able to support the extraordinary amount of monies paid for the work alone, without taking cognizance of my family and my expeditions, which ever and anon travelling as we are

from place to place and country to country are also very great.[20]

A letter to Bachman, 1 December 1835, says:

… We are all well and intend leaving this fairest of Cities for Dirty London in about a fortnight …. Our Sons are Improving in their different ways of painting at a surprising rate – John has finished about 50 Portraits for which he has been paid, and he could Maintain Two very decently in Edinburgh through his art, he has made excellent copies of beautiful Pictures, from the originals of Sir Henry Raeburn – 2 of Walter Scot – One of Sir H Raeburn – and 2 beautifull Children.– he is now at the Royal institution copying a beautiful Murillo. Victor paints Landscapes, Battles, and other subjects and comes on equally well. – They visit the best and most learned Society of Edinburgh, passing their evenings alternately at Professors Wilson, Jameson, Trail, and others.[21]

The Audubons returned to London in December 1835 together with their servant Betzy and spent a few months there painting and encouraging Havell. The two boys went on a tour of France and Italy where they were guests of Charles Bonaparte. Maria in America became increasingly upset at the prolonged absence of her beloved John and required placatory letters of explanation. Audubon as ever was keeping in touch with his friends. MacGillivray's response to one of these letters shows him in deep depression due to the death of his 'best and most beloved friend', William Craigie. MacGillivray had a rather reserved nature and made very few close friends. The loss of Craigie affected him deeply:

Edinburgh,
11 Gilmore Place, Tuesday July 1836

My dear Friend

Your letter, which I received on Saturday evening, afforded me very great pleasure. I have been thinking of you ever since, but have scarcely had time to write until this moment, when I have just arrived from Leith, where I have been delivering a Botanical lecture.

I have two lectures there weekly, one at the Young Ladies' Institution, and an excursion on Saturday from twelve till eight. The composition of these lectures, and the drawings necessary for illustrating them, occupy nearly the whole of my time at present, but they will all be over before the end of the month. I have done very little otherwise since I saw you, although I have been generally, in very good health. Craigie's death had a strong effect upon me, and I believe my views of life and its occupations have been a good deal changed by it. It was upon him especially that I had set my hopes. However I am reconciled to my condition. The girls have ever since been particularly anxious to do what they could to assist or please me. My drawings of birds have been stationary for sometime past. I have no one now that you are away, to show them to, or to stimulate me to go on with them …. I shall long for your return, but the thought that you will be here several years will I am assured, keep up my spirits ….

You desire to know how I am 'going on with the world.' The world and I are not exactly as good friends as you and I, and I am not particularly desirous of being on familiar terms with it. I have got rather into difficulties this year, but I do not exactly know the state of my affairs, and must take a few days among the hills by myself before I can understand how I am situated. I cannot write more at present. Present my best regards to Mrs. Audubon and the young gentlemen and accept for yourself and them the best wishes of Mrs MacGillivray.[22]

On 2 August 1836 Audubon set sail for America with John, taking with them 260 live birds including starlings, larks, wild pigeons and jays which Audubon wanted to introduce to America. Alas only 15 survived the journey. Lucy stayed behind in London at 4 Wimpole Street to be near her sister, Ann Gordon, who was now living in London. Victor also stayed behind to supervise the continuing production of *The Birds of America* and to deal with the financial matters which were becoming increasingly complex.

Notes

1   *Letters of John James Audubon 1826-1840*, vol. II, p. 31.
2   Ibid, vol. II, pp. 30-1.
3   Cowes, E: *Bulletin of the Nuttall Ornithological Club* (1880), 5: 123-204.
4   Deane, R: *The Auk* (1901), 18: 241-2.
5   Ibid, p. 243.
6   Ibid, pp. 244-5.
7   Ibid, pp. 245-6.
8   *Letters*, op. cit., vol. II, pp. 47-8.
9   Ibid, p. 58.
10   Cited in *Audubon the Naturalist*, vol. II, p. 139.
11   *Letters*, op. cit., vol. II, p. 77.
12   Ibid, p. 67.
13   *Memorial Tribute to William MacGillivray*, pp. 39-40.
14   *Letters*, op. cit., vol. II, p. 79.
15   Ibid, p. 62.
16   MacGillivray, W: *A History of British Birds*, vol. V, pp. 403-20.
17   *Edinburgh New Philosophical Journal* (1842), 32: 47-70.
18   Audubon, J J: *Ornithological Biography*, vol. IV, p. 234.
19   *Letters*, op. cit., vol. II, p. 89.
20   Cited in *Audubon the Naturalist*, vol. II, p. 143.
21   *Letters*, op. cit., vol. II, pp. 104-5.
22   Deane, R: *The Auk* (1901), 18: 246-7.

14 | The Fifth and Last Visit

ON his return to America, Audubon felt that for the first time he was beginning to get the recognition and acceptance from his own countrymen which he regarded as long overdue. Erstwhile critics or opponents such as Titian Peale began to give him support, although his old enemy Ord kept up his relentless vendetta. With the help of his son John and Maria Martin, the sister-in-law and later wife of the Reverend John Bachman, he was busily involved in painting the birds of the Rockies from skins provided by T Nuttall and J K Townsend.[1] Being unable to travel there himself he was compelled to break his rule of only depicting freshly mounted specimens.

Audubon and John made a final journey to the southern states. Confirmation of his acceptance in his own country came as an invitation from the President, General Andrew Jackson, to dine in the White House.

> The dinner was what might be called plain and substantial in England; I dined from a fine young turkey, shot within twenty miles of Washington. The General drank no wine, but his health was drunk by us more than once; and he ate very moderately, his last dish consisting of bread and milk. As soon as dinner was over we returned to the first room, where was a picture … of our great Washington …. It is the only picture in the whole house ….[2]

It is interesting that Audubon's portrait is now among those in the White House Collection.

Jackson arranged for the party to be provided with government transport and protection because of unrest among the native Indians during their travels to the Gulf, but they found no new birds. On their return to the north they encountered groups of captured Indians being driven from their homeland:

> We overtook two thousands of these once free owners of the Forest, marching towards this place under an escort of Rangers … destined for distant lands … where alas, their future and latter days must be spent in the deepest of Sorrows, afliction and perhaps even phisical want – this view produced on my mind an afflicting series of reflections more powerfully felt than easy of description – the numerous groups of Warriors, of half clad females and of naked babes, trudging through the mire … all formed such a Picture as I hope I never will again witness ….[3]

At the end of this trip John married his patient sweetheart Maria Bachman and they went on their honeymoon to visit the Niagara Falls, from which they returned as 'Happy as if Angels in heaven'. Apart from this happy family occasion, the return visit to America had been rather unproductive. Few new birds had been obtained. The country was in economic depression and as a result there had been few new subscribers. Audubon was keen to return to Britain and his Lucy who had remained in London with Victor, who together with MacGillivray had been left with the task of completing volume four of *Ornithological Biography* from Audubon's notes.

MacGillivray wrote to Lucy from his new address at 16 Minto Street on 4 November 1836:

> Dear Madam
>   At the same moment that Mrs MacGillivray received your very welcome letter of the 27th ulto. I received one not less welcome from Mr Audubon, dated New York, Oct 8th. We have removed from Gilmore Place to Newington, which is a much more pleasant situation in every respect. My young baby, who has received the name of Audubon, is thriving and the other children are in good health, as is Mrs MacGillivray …. We had

a very unexpected fall of snow last week, which however remained only three days. Provisions are expected to be dear this winter, on account of the badness of the summer and autumn ….

I have in hand just now a work on British birds on a larger scale than that on the Rapacious species …. There will be several plates representing the digestive organs and a few skeletons with a multitude of wood-cuts …. I have scarcely done anything in the way of money making since you left this, but must brush up, otherwise I shall be gazetted as an indolent book-maker. In the meantime I have plenty of offers, indeed if I had three heads and six hands, I have work enough for all.

I must endeavour to get through as much as possible before Mr Audubon comes back, which I hope will be about this time next year … by the bye, it will certainly be necessary for him to take a small house for the express purpose of dissecting, otherwise the odour of the rum will bring the excise men upon us.

Please present my best regards to Mr Victor, and be assured that, negligent as I am as to writing, I ever cherish a lively remembrance of you all, being perfectly assured that with him after whom my dearest William Craigie was named, you are my best friends. Pray God to keep you all and send us a happy meeting first in Edinburgh and finally in Heaven.[4]

On 17 July 1837 Audubon and the newly-weds set sail once more for Britain on the steam packet *England*. Among their fellow passengers were the daughter and granddaughter of Benjamin Rush. They arrived at Liverpool after a rapid crossing of 18 days. They travelled to London by the new Liverpool to Birmingham railroad and then by the stagecoach *Tally O*. That evening he was 'in the Arms of My Lucy! – Dear old Friend she was not very well, our arrival produced a great revolution of her nervous sistem, but after a while all was gayety and Happiness at our House in Wimpole Street.'[5]

The Audubons spent several months in London. Audubon himself was busily occupied with painting, writing his book and maintaining his prolific correspondence with Bachman and others, requesting specimens and information to complete his task. He had hoped to restrict his *Birds of America* to 80 fascicles of five pages, but as ever-increasing numbers of new birds

came to his notice he had to cram more and more birds on to each page, to the extent that much of the artistic setting of his earlier paintings was abandoned. Even so, he had to increase the number of fascicles, much to the annoyance of some of his subscribers. These later plates are not his best. The birds lack the vitality of his earlier work and the plants on which they are displayed are not always appropriate to the territory of the subjects.

Audubon's letters during this period became increasingly preoccupied with criticisms of other ornithologists over the identification of birds and who should be given the credit of discovery. If any commented unfavourably on his works they were themselves subjected to severe criticism. Charles Bonaparte, for example, with whom Audubon had endured a rather strained relationship for some time, visited him while in London with apparent friendly overtures and extracted much information in the process. In a letter to Bachman of 14 April 1838, Audubon wrote:

Charles Bonaparte has treated me most shockingly – he has published the whole of *our* Secrets, which I foolishly communicated to him after his giving me his word of honour that he would not do so, and now I have *cut him*, and he never will have from me the remaining unpublished Numbers of my Work. (which by the bye he calls a poor thing) …. So much for a *Prince*!

The family news was better, however. Lucy's health seemed to improve and Maria had become pregnant: 'My Dear Bachman, it may be possible that ere this reaches you, both of us will be Grand Fathers! Nay Mr Phillips thinks that the Chance maybe a double, and if so how blessed I will feel to have a pair of them borned Audubons.'[6]

The last of the engravings of *The Birds of America* was completed and published in June 1838, bringing to completion the labour of twelve years. In all there were 435 engravings containing 1065 life-sized figures of 489 species. The exact number of copies of each plate is unknown but probably did not exceed 300. Many of the subscribers did not maintain their payments and only about 200 complete sets are believed to have been issued – about half in Europe and half in the United States. Of these, 119 are known to exist to this day and have been catalogued.[7] Four complete sets are known to be in Scotland, but none alas in Edinburgh, the city in which it all began. In 1992 Edinburgh University, being temporarily short of funds, felt obliged to sell its folio for the sum of $4.1 million at auction in New York. It was one of the few copies still in the possession of the original subscriber and the only complete set remaining in the city of its origin – a sad loss indeed. Audubon, alas, did not benefit from the high prices which his paintings subsequently realised. The publication brought him fame but not fortune; the production cost of $115,640 was barely covered by the sales during his lifetime. (Appendix III gives details of the Scottish subscriptions.)

During the summer of 1838 Audubon returned to Edinburgh, lodging at first at 7 Archibald Place, conveniently near to the museums of both the university and the Royal College of Surgeons. Some time later he moved to 6 Alva Street, which was 'extremely comfortable'.

His efforts were now concentrated on the completion of volumes four and five of *Ornithological Biography*. During this time his friend John Bachman, who was in poor health, travelled to Europe to convalesce. He also went there partly to attend a natural history conference in Freiburg, but chiefly, one supposes, to see his beloved daughter Maria and his new grandchild who was born on the day of his arrival in London. During this visit, in July, he came to Edinburgh with Audubon and spent three weeks visiting the sights of the city. 'The tour through a healthful, interesting and romantic country, with such a companion, did much to restore Dr Bachman to his wonted health of body and spirit.' Unfortunately Bachman's journal of this visit was destroyed in a fire, but his impression of Edinburgh is given second-hand in a letter by his daughter Eliza to her sister Harriet:

The Audubon's are delighted with Edinburgh. If the city equals the description I have so often read, it must, both in point of natural scenery and agreeable society, be far superior to the far famed London, with all its bustle and humbug. The latter may better suit the rich and the gay, but for those whose circumstances are moderate, and whose pleasures are rational, Edinburgh must be far preferable as a place of residence. The Audubon's house [probably 7 Archibald Place] is delightfully located and exceedingly convenient.[8]

After Bachman left, Audubon settled down once more to his writing.

August came in course, and in that month my beloved wife and the rest of my family joined me. My friend MacGillivray and myself were up to the elbows among the birds which I had brought in spirits with me from America, I acting as secretary, he as prime minister. Under his kind tuition, I think I have learned something of anatomy, which may enable me, at some future period, to produce observations that may prove interesting even to you good Reader, for I promise that no sooner shall I have returned to America, and procured specimens of any of the species, whose digestive and respiratory organs have not been described in this work, than I will try to examine them in detail, and publish the results in the Journals of some of our scientific institutions.[9]

[No such publications were produced.]

The coronation of Queen Victoria was celebrated soon after his arrival in Edinburgh. Audubon was not impressed:

Here the festivals were poor beyond description, and although scarcely anything was to be seen, the whole population was on foot the entire day, and nearly the whole night, gazing at each other like lost sheep.– No illuminations except at two shops …. The fireworks at the castle consisted merely of about one hundred rockets, not a gun was fired from the batteries. MacGillivray & I went to see the fireworks at 10 p.m, and soon returned disgusted.— His museum and the Edinburgh Museum were thrown open *gratis*, and were thronged to excess upwards of 20,000 in the first, and about 25,000 in the other; all was however quite so orderly.[10]

The *Edinburgh Evening Courant* of 30 June 1838 suggested that all was not quite orderly:

The principal point of attraction was of course our splendid Natural History Museum, and here the greatest practical inconvenience occurred, for there being only one door for entrance and exit, the crowd on the outside … pressed round the entrance, and would

Photographs of the surviving houses in Edinburgh in which Audubon lodged: (*far left*) 6 Alva Street; (*right*) 7 Lauriston Place; and (*below*) 5 India Street.

not give way, even to allow those retiring to pass through ....

Eventually another door was opened and some order was restored.

At the Royal College of Surgeons the crowd was also great, and on the door being opened a considerable rush took place which filled the hall and staircase etc, but through the exertions of some active citizens, regularity was speedily restored. Neither the specimens or the public suffered injury at either venue!

Other activities included civic and workhouse banquets. 'The fireworks were on a magnificent scale, and afforded much interest ... and loud cheering.' Lights on Calton Hill and a huge bonfire on Arthur's Seat added to the festivities. Despite the big crowds, 'overindulgence in liquor' was not observed. 'Everyone seemed anxious to enjoy himself on the auspicious occasion ....' Perhaps Audubon and MacGillivray were too exhausted by controlling the crowds at the College of Surgeons to enjoy the occasion, for the door-keeper of the College Museum at that time was not much help, having behaved with 'incivility and improper conduct to ladies visiting the Museum aggravated by a charge of inebriety'.

He was dismissed!

This was to be the last visit of the Audubons to Edinburgh and they seized the chance to visit the parts of the country romanticised by Walter Scott in his Waverley novels. This tour had become an essential feature of the itinerary of American visitors. One wrote:

... and for whom should Nature mourn, if not for him, who has made her dear to many hearts, – who has thrown a charm over all the scenery of his native land, which shall

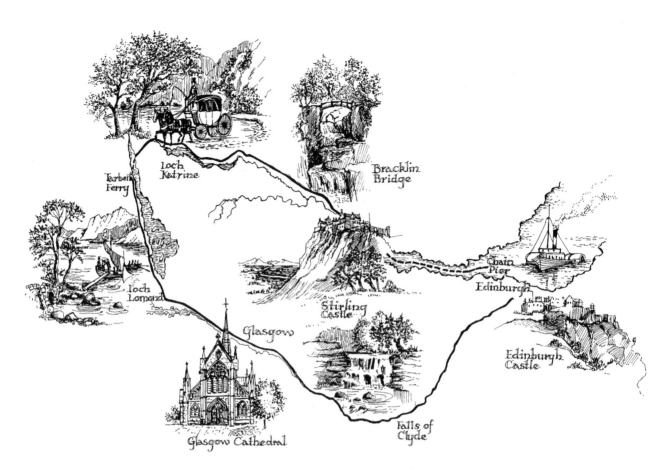

Labels on map:
Tarbert Ferry
Loch Katrine
Bracklin Bridge
Loch Lomond
Chain Pier
Edinburgh
Stirling Castle
Glasgow
Edinburgh Castle
Glasgow Cathedral
Falls of Clyde

Places visited on Audubon's tour of Scotland. (Drawing by Anne Gardner)

live when ages shall have passed away? On every one of her mountains he has set a crown of glory, like that which is flung upon them by the morning sunbeam; he has converted her valleys into a holy land, towards which the footsteps of the literary pilgrim tend ....[11]

Audubon's account of the tour[12] gives such a vivid description of the country and the times that it is cited here almost in full:

When September had mellowed the general aspect of nature, the long-cherished desire of obtaining a glimpse of the highlands of Scotland filled our hearts anew, and we resolved to visit the mountains and lakes so beautifully described by the illustrious Scott. The weather was as fine as we could wish. My good friend MacGillivray, by way of obtaining a holiday, accompanied us, and, independently of the pleasure derived from his conversation, we found him useful in pointing out objects with which he was familiar, and of which we might otherwise not have learned the history.

[MacGillivray had made this same tour previously in 1826 during the course of an expedition to collect geological specimens for the museum.] Early one morning we started, seven in number, for I took with me my dear little grandchild [Lucy], not above two month old, with the desire, perhaps, of letting her breathe the mountain air. [The others in the party were his wife Lucy, his sons Victor Gifford and John Woodhouse with his wife Maria and their maid.]

Every one acquainted with Edinburgh, knows the Chain-Pier[13] at Newhaven [see Chapter 8, p.93]. There, then at eight o'clock we were, walking along its tremulous planks with a feeling of giddiness, and presently after found ourselves seated in the stern of a small steamer, bound for Stirling. There was no wind, the skies were serene, and the smooth waters were alive with shoals of young herrings over which hovered gulls of various species. On some bare rocks near Aberdour, on the opposite coast, stood numerous cormorants, while along the shore, guillemots and auks dived or flew, as our boat approached them.

After passing many beautiful spots, we entered the narrow passage of the 'Queen's Ferry,' and presently obtained a view of the distant hills. At length we reached what I thought a very remarkable place for Scotland, a considerable extent of land embanked, and so much resembling some portions of the shores of the lower Mississippi, that, had the thermometer been at 86°, I should have looked upon it as well adapted for the cultivation of sugar, cotton, or tobacco. But the steamer, slow as was its progress, moved too fast for me; and if ever I again visit the Highlands, it shall be on foot, for no man, with nerve and will, and an admirer of the beauties of nature, can ever truly enjoy the pleasures of travelling, unless he proceed in that manner. After a while, we entered what I should call a singular narrow and tortuous bayou, winding amongst green meadows and cornfields, and on whose margins some herons walked with measured steps, while groups of lapwings flew over us so merrily that we thought they had a holiday too. From the willows and ash-trees on the banks 'cushats' [pigeons] started in great numbers, alarmed by the noise of our paddles. Narrower and more shallow became the bayou, and at length our boat stuck in the mud. After a while, however, the sound of oars came on our ears, and, ere half an hour elapsed, the party from Edinburgh was, amidst much mirth and some sorrow, exchanged for the party from the hills of the north, as anxious apparently to reach their home as we were to leave it further behind. Now see us packed in two great boats, rowed vigorously for a while, then towed along the margins, just in the way the Canadian boatmen still proceed, by means of a wordelle, or as Kentuckyans were wont to do thirty years ago on the Ohio and Mississippi. But, Reader, here we all are at Stirling.

Nature must, I think, at one time have felt, as I would call it, 'quite pleasant;' for in this place she has produced a marvellously close imitation of one of her own works. At least, such was my impression when I found myself walking around the walls of Stirling Castle, so much did the rock at first resemble that of Edinburgh: although in the details the two crags are very different. With delight we gazed on the beautiful valley beneath us,

Stirling Castle, from Beattie's *Scotland Illustrated.*

until our eyes meeting with the wall of dark-blue mountains in the distance, we wished that Claude Lorraine had transferred the landscape to canvass, as he had done hundreds of others far less beautiful or grand.

At Stirling we had a good dinner, for which a good price was paid. Soon after we were on our way to the hills, comfortably enough stowed into a large post-chaise. Before we arrived at the village of Doun, however, darkness overtook us, so that we did not until nine reach Callender. There, we found a good house, kept by a good woman of the name of Stewart. Our friend, MacGillivray had stopped there before; and, although there may be equally good taverns or hotels in Callender, we found no reason to regret our having taken his advice, for in Mrs. Stewart's we spent the night very comfortably.

If travellers are sluggards, I pity them in my heart; for, depend upon it, nature is never more beautiful than whilst she bathes herself, in the morn, in her own dewy waters. Then, traveller, whoever you may be, arouse yourself, leave your couch, emerge from good Mrs. Stewart's house, walk to the bridge opposite, and gaze upon the magnificent landscape around; then lean over the parapet, and trace the nimble trout balancing itself in the pure stream that here slowly moves toward the rapids below. The meadows, though it was autumn were yet green, the hills purpled with heather; and, as the sun's rays dispelled the mist that lingered on the summits of the mountains, I thought that, in all my life, I had never beheld scenery that interested me more.

175

The Falls of Bracklin, from Beattie's *Scotland Illustrated.*

Delightful country! said I, how I should like to spend a summer here, amid clouds and mists, sunshine and pleasant showers! Fresh eggs, new milk, excellent ham, capital Scotch 'porridge,' with bread, butter, and tea, constituted our breakfast, after which we marched in a body to the Falls of Brachlin, guided by a rosy-cheeked Highland lassie, stopping now and then by the way to pick up a wild flower, a blue bell, a 'gowan', or dog rose, or to listen to the magpies and titmice. Pretty high we have climbed to a piece of moorland, where, no doubt, had we dogs and guns with privilege to shoot, we might maim perhaps a grouse, perhaps a black-cock.

But list! The roar of the cataract comes faintly on the ear; there is the very stream which descending turbulently into the ravine, hurries to join the river below. Descend that narrow rocky pass with care, and trip lightly along that crazy bridge, wind to the right, reach the jutting angle of that rock, and now gaze upon the scene! I have looked at hundreds of streamlets in America equally turbulent, but I doubt if, after all, I have seen one so curiously confined within its rocky shores, or so abrupt in its various jets. Clusters of the bright-red berries of the mountain ash hung over the rocks, which were crusted with lichens;

and, as I looked around on that sequestered spot, I thought what a secure retreat it might afford on occasions to some of the wild Celts of the olden times, who lived at variance with their Saxon neighbours in the valley below. I felt as if I were amongst them, enjoying the pleasure of living in the wilds, and then bethought me of the many similar spots yet belonging to our own Sons of the Forest.

Returning towards Callender, and emerging from the wood, we were surprised to see some hundreds of cows, all belonging to the village below, grazing on what might well be called the finest of fore-grounds. The sun, now high, had considerably enriched the tints of the distance, which were mellowed into a hue bordering on the softest of modest purple; the small birds were rejoicing in the trees, the blue peat smoke of the village curled in spiry streams, and all nature seemed as happy as ourselves. But now, here we all are, on board our post-chaise, bound for the Pass of Leny and Loch Lubnig. On proceeding, we found on the left side a brook, hurrying along to reach the level of the meadows of Callender vale, and passed some curiously grouped masses of blocks, amongst which, as our con-ductor informed us, badgers and foxes had often been bayed and worried. At the top of this beautiful pass, which is covered with brushwood, the country opens a little, and we saw on the creek the pretty Dipper, now skimming along, now perched on a stone in the water, in which it plunged at intervals in search of the food best suited to its appetite. On the opposite side the hills rose to a consid-erable height, here and there pleasantly sprin-kled with black-faced sheep, and at length the lake opened to our view, flanked by an abrupt crag on one side, and long ferny slopes on the other. Beautiful miniature of grander objects of the same nature, how pleasant to me seem-ed, from the spot where I stood and gazed upon you, the green valley around, and how singularly well adapted to the scene was the white lodge in the distance, as contrasted with the pure tints of the sky above and the waters beneath! Were I wealthy enough, I should spend at least a month here every summer. The lake, we were told, abounds in fine trout, the hills around afford grouse of different species, and the neighbouring forest is well stocked with roe and red-deer. Here we took our lunch; and, while we were refreshing ourselves with the water of the lake, and a few drops of mountain-dew, our friend MacGillivray pointed out to us the ridges on which we had rambled the previous winter when they were covered with snow.

Retracing our way, we again approached Callender, and crossing the stream, drove through a lane in the direction of the Trosachs. Finding it rather tiresome to ride all day, some of us threw off our coats, and footed it pleasantly. Two small lakes were passed, and we were admiring the purple blossoms of the heather, when we overtook an artist and his beloved on foot, both from London. Putting their extra luggage in our carriage, we continued our march and reached, nearly all at the same moment, the tavern of the Trosachs.

Here we met with many people from different parts of the world: Cockneys, Irishmen, and 'Blue-noses', some very thin, others over thick, some low, and some high in figure and manners. It was quite strange to me to hear a group of Englishmen talking, not of the scenery, but of the precious qualities of their wines in Middlesex. Some who had navigated Virginia Water, wondered whether Loch Lomand and Loch Katherine, were to be compared with Lake Huron and Lake Superior. They sucked their cigars in front of the tavern, walked nowhere, and thought of little else than their dinner ….

The Trosachs are admired by the many, chiefly or entirely on account of Scott's description of them and I am far from being sorry for this. To me, the peep of Loch Katherine obtained from the landing-place, after running and frisking along, and rolling myself among the heather, was absolutely delightful. With that most curious innate desire which there is in us of becoming older, for the purpose of enjoying the morrow, I went to rest anxious to see the morn, and discover what existed beyond the crags that had bounded my view.

Thus, Reader, we spent half a day and a whole night at the inn of Loch Achray, and rose betimes expecting an early breakfast and an early departure; but no, the breakfast was late and hurried, the whole house, one might have thought, had just caught fire, every one called for the waiter, for his luggage, his bill and the boat; and when the bustle was over you might have seen a long procession issue from the hostelry. Giving way to the anxious, we lagged a little behind, and thus had a nice boat to ourselves, while the rest were uncomfortably crammed into another.

Loch Katherine, in my humble opinion, is a beautiful sheet of water. We were told that some parts of it are of extreme depth; but what rendered it so pleasingly welcome to me, was the prospect ever-changing, enlarging, and becoming more and more grand, as the ridges of hills came successively into view. Would I could once more gaze on the beauties of Loch Katherine! Our rowers, however, indifferent to all save the shillings looked for, pulled uncommonly well, and in due time brought us to a very dirty landing, crowded with small ponies, ready-saddled, and standing by the side of a smoky hut, in which they who had not eaten enough at the Trosachs gorged themselves anew.

Now our ladies, the maid, and our sweet babe are all mounted, while my friend MacGillivray, my sons, and your humble servant, are going ahead on foot. The road is rough enough, but the sun shines brightly, and all are merry. When heated, we drink leaving behind a very fat Englishman, we laugh, and seeing a broad-shouldered and sturdy Celt ahead, we strive to make up to him. Of the Gaelic language I know nothing, and yet it gives me great pleasure to hear it spoken by our friendly companion and the mountaineers, as we trudge along. Now down a very steep and narrow pass we wind, and unexpectedly as it were find ourselves on the rocky shores of the famed Loch Lomond. How beautiful those three rugged and peaked mountains opposite those green and wooden slopes and that placid blue lake that stretched out before us, narrowing to the westward and expanding in the opposite direction.

Here we found a few small stone cabins, some fat bairns, abundance of ale, and a sufficient of capital whisky. The artist and his beloved were sketching a little cataract that tumbled over a crag into the lake. Pony after pony, and one pedestrian after another, are seen descending the pass, and in the rear, puffing and melting is the rubicund and ample

Above: Loch Katrine, from Beattie's *Scotland Illustrated*.

Below: The ferry crossing of Loch Lomond, from Beattie's *Scotland Illustrated*.

'Pull away from the opposite shore, good men, and you John Woodhouse, take the tiller.' Now we proceed slowly but steadily toward the land-place of Tarbet.

Friend MacGillivray and I are put ashore, and we stride along a beautiful turnpike road to the house. It is a commodious house, and I should be well pleased to reside here a while every summer. We had scarcely been comfortably settled, when the steamer's cargo of wayworn travellers came in thick upon us, excepting the Burgundy-wine admirer, who somewhere gave us the slip. For the better part of two days we enjoyed ourselves in walking, riding and visiting the neighbouring inlet of Loch Long, with the romantic valley of Glen Coe.

Our voyage to the head of Loch Lomond, and subsequently to its lower extremity, was very pleasant. From Balloch we were carried in crowded coaches to Dumbarton, where we arrived just in time to be hurried on board of a Glasgow steamer, which for half an hour stuck in the mud at the mouth of the Leven, affording us more time than was necessary to see the strangely abrupt crag on which Dumbarton Castle is built. At length we arrive at the far-famed Broomielaw.

Next day it rained, but we were assured that rain is of no importance in Glasgow, and we congratulated ourselves in the beautiful weather which we had in the Highlands. Having visited the Museum of the University, and that of the Andersonian Institution, in both which we were treated with kindness, as well as the Cathedral with its multitudinous tombs, the necropolis, the bridges, and the principal streets, not forgetting the Salt Market, for the sake of honest Baillie Nicol Jarvie, we left the mercantile metropolis of Scotland, and posted toward Lanark. The scenery of the beautiful and fertile valley of the Clyde is of a very different nature from that of the hills which we had just visited, and the contrast was agreeable; but, excepting the celebrated Falls,[14] which have so often been described, and in the Cave in which the Patriot Wallace concealed himself from his many foes, this tract did not present objects on which I love to dwell. Still less does the barren moor that occupies the heights between Lanark and the plain of the Lothians, over

admirer of Burgundy wine …. We eat, we drink, we laugh, and now Rob Roy is talked of, and we all know that there is one of his hiding-places close by.

Here then we are, on this craggy point, from which a heap of great blocks has fallen, and now we ascend toward a small triangular hole, which seems more fitted for the retreat of a badger than of 'an honest man' like the Red Rob. Ladies can hardly venture here, but men may easily ascend, and now, 'one after another, gentlemen, if you please', says the guide, this advice being here quite as necessary as for a person to tell another that a goose is not a turkey. With the aid of a very old and crazy ladder we descend into the hole … all is darkness, damp, and slime. Were I the keeper of this celebrated spot, I would have it quite different before next September.

which we passed, until the beautiful city of the north, with its picturesque 'Craigs', again gladdened our sight.

Pleasant as our trip had been, it seemed not to have benefited the health of my good wife, for in a few days after our return to Edinburgh, she was again taken ill. There is no lack of excellent physicians in that city, and we had the good fortune to fall upon one who not only restored her to health, but who has become a truly excellent and most valued friend. To this gentleman, Dr. John Argyle Robertson,[15] of 58 Queen Street, for his most efficient aid, and most kind and gentle treatment, we can never cease to cherish the most lively feelings of affection. It is a curious part of my history, that during the whole time of my sojourn in Britain, none of the principal medical advisers whom we have occasion to employ would receive any recompense from us. In London, Mr. Bell, and in Edinburgh Mr. Nasmyth, the most dextrous and celebrated dentists of their respective cities, thus afforded us their aid …. To all these excellent friends, whose liberality we have thus experienced, and whose professional aid has been so beneficial to us we shall ever prove most grateful.

On 1 May 1839 the fifth and final volume of *Ornithological Biography* was completed, ending nine years of intense labour. Audubon, who had no doubts about his ability as a painter, had always been diffident regarding his ability as a writer and his inadequacies as a scientist. With MacGillivray's help, however, *Ornithological Biography* received generally favourable critical comment both for its literary style and scientific content. MacGillivray's presentation copy was inscribed: 'These volumes are presented to William MacGillivray with sentiments of the highest esteem and best wishes by his truly and sincerely attached friend John J Audubon.'

Darwin refers to the book frequently in the *Descent of Man*, the *Origin of Species* and the *Variation of Animals and Plants Under Domestication* – surely evidence of scientific respectability. Indeed Darwin cites Audubon's description of the frigate bird's partially webbed feet as evidence of evolutionary development.

To celebrate the completion of their mammoth task, Audubon, MacGillivray and MacGillivray's son John took a walk through the Pentland Hills south of Edinburgh. MacGillivray gives a detailed description of this walk in which William MacGillivray refers to himself as *Ornithologus* and his son as *Physiophilus* – he seemed to have found it easier to express his thoughts when writing in the third person. Some extracts are reproduced, for it highlights many aspects of the relationship between Audubon and MacGillivray and gives insight into their characters. Although the conversation as written appears stilted and excessively formal, there can be no doubt that it reflects the gist of what passed between the three men. Their warm friendship and mutual respect is apparent.[16]

Above: 'Glasgow Cathedral' by William Wilson (1818). (Courtesy of the Edinbugh City Library)

Below: Stonebyres Linn on the Clyde, from Beattie's *Scotland Illustrated.*

179

Ornithologus. A more beautiful morning, or one giving promise of a brighter day, we could not have desired. I am glad that is so, for this may be our last excursion, and I am anxious that the favourable impression made upon you by our Highland mountains and lakes, which we visited together last September, may not be diminished by the sight of our Lowland hills, of which the Pentlands on our right hand are not the least celebrated.

Audubon. What you say as to the weather is true indeed, for a finer May-day I have never seen in any country. The thermometer was at 54° when we left Edinburgh, but the unusual heat is tempered by this gentle breeze from the west. As to your Highland scenery, I freely confess that it is in some respects unrivalled, and your Lowlands are generally very beautiful, while your capital is certainly not equalled by any city that I have seen in Europe or America.

Physiophilus. There is Woodhouselee,[17] the residence of a celebrated historian. There are some Titmice in the trees, Golden-crested Wrens and …. List! did you not hear the Willow Wren?

Aud. I see it, on the top twig of that ash-tree. Do you wish to have it?

Orn. I do but it is off; so, let us proceed ….

Aud. It is wonderful to see how far behind the hawthorn hedges are compared with those about Edinburgh, although these have the advantage of a southern exposure. There are several Willow Wrens, and a single Swallow. What summer birds have arrived?

Phys. On the 25th I shot two Wheatears in the King's Park and on the 29th two Yellow Wagtails, five Chimney Swallows, and a Window Martin, and a Bank Swallow at Colt Bridge.

Aud. These green hills are very pretty. I suppose this narrow pass leads to the glen of which you have spoken.

Orn. It is Glencorse. How few larks we hear to-day! I suppose they are busily occupied in forming their nest. See! there are two Whinchats on the bushes by the brook. Let me try one of them. Not killed. I suppose the gun is in bad trim, or the shot too large, or the powder bad ….

Aud. Let Physiophilus take the gun, while you and I clear our eyes with a pinch. There must be some birds among these thickets.

Orn. The lambkins are basking in the sun, and there stands a most lovely Pied Wagtail with a tuft of wool in its mouth. It must have its nest in that quarry. Here are two fishers. They must have poor sport, the water being so very low and clear, and the sky so bright. Go to them, Physiophilus, and say, Gentlemen, Piscatores, how fares it with you this fine May morning? I hope you have had several glorious nibbles. It gives me pleasure to see two fools, each at one end of a rod, and sham fly at the other.

Phys. Nay go thyself. I am no admirer of 'quaint old Izaac'. A Wheatear! two of them on the top of the wall. They have alighted by the edge of the pond.

Orn. We cannot shoot them, as the Water Company threatens all intruders. This is the reservoir that supplies Edinburgh.

Aud. It is a fine sheet of water, considered as such, but as a lake it is more remarkable for the bareness of its banks than for any other quality; and there seem to be no birds upon it, not even a Heron. In such a place in America there would be Ducks or Coots, or Water Hens. How amazingly like our Red Lark are these Pipits. If I had met with them in a prairie I should certainly have taken them to the same as ours. Are there no Dippers here?

Orn. The only bird to be met with on the margins of the lake is the Sandpiper, but the Dipper I have often seen on the brook below, as well as in the glen before us, although we have not met with it to-day. Here, however, is a pair of Ring Ouzels, which are migratory birds, arriving in the end of April, and dispersing themselves over the hilly and mountainous tracts, as far as the northern coasts.

Aud. Beautiful birds! their cry is very like that of our Robin, the Turdus migratorious, and so is their flight.

Phys. Another pair. Hear the Red Grouse! 'Cok, cok, cok, go-back, go-back.' There he bounces away; down he comes on the side of the hill, where he runs and struts with his tail raised and his wings drooping. Whirr! off goes the hen. How easily I might shoot her!

Orn. Down with that gun of thine! Thou mighst be tempted to fire, and then we should be breakers of the game-laws, and disturbers of the peace of this sequestered valley. These birds are Mr. Robertson's not ours. Here is a shepherd. How far is it to Currie?

Shepherd. Six miles. Did the game-keeper see you?

Orn. I suppose not, at least we did not see him. We shoot no game.

Shep. They dinna alloo folk wi' guns here. I dinna misdoubt ye, but I wad advise ye no to shoot ava, but pass on quietly. [ava: at all]

Orn. Well, we promise. Now, Mr. Audubon, here is a pretty valley, with heathery hills on both sides, grass in the bottom, and a clear brook, tempting to the mouth in this hot weather. More grouse, one, two, three.

Aud. I did not think there had been any so near town. There must be good shooting on these hills. Your Grouse never alights on trees, does it? All ours do, even the Willow Grouse in winter, when it comes southward, as well as our Partridge.

Orn. Neither of our Ptarmigans perches on trees, but the black Grouse does. Here are three more Ring Ouzels, and Pipits in abundance. This is a famous place of resort for the Cuckoos, but it does not seem that they have arrived yet.

Phys. A hare on the hill, scudding along! I see a Sandpiper by the brook in that hollow.

Aud. Let us sit down a few minutes then. There is a small stripe of water coming down the rock.

Orn. Yes, that is the celebrated waterfall, Niagara in miniature, and this Habbie's Howe,[18] for the history of which, and its connection with Allan Ramsay, I refer you to the Society of Scottish Antiquaries, or your friend Mr. Maclaren. Here comes a shepherd. A fine day, friend! Is the lamb dead?

Pastor. No, but its no like to live; the drouth's o'er sair, an' the sheep can get little to eat. [drouth: drought; sair: severe]

Aud. Physiophilus comes with the Sandpiper. It is amazingly like our Totanus chlorophygius. Five miles to Currie, and nothing till then but water. Let us be off. Ah! – a rattle-snake!

Orn. Lacerta agilis – Who would have thought to find it here? I have it, and will keep it as a memorial.

Phys. A dead crow. It is not Corvus Corone? It will make a good skull.[19]

Opposite page, top: Distant view of Edinburgh, engraved by Robert Havell Jr. (Courtesy of Bruntsfield Golf Club, Edinburgh)

Opposite page, bottom: Audubon's painting of 'The Magnificent Frigate Bird', plate 271 from *The Birds of America*, showing the details of the feet to which Darwin refers in his *Origin of Species*. (© The Natural History Museum, London)

Drawing of
Habbie's Howe
(artist unknown).

Aud. See that little Hawk, how beautifully it glides along in its rapid slanting descent. What a splendid figure the small thing cuts! It very much resembles our Pigeon Hawk. What is it?

Orn. The Merlin, so like your Pigeon Hawk, as you say, that some individuals of both species can hardly be distinguished. Indeed I think the authors of the Fauna Boreali-Americana have mistaken the one for the other. There goes its mate. Their cries very much resemble those of the Kestrel. Hear the Curlews respond to them. These birds are very numerous on the hills and moors of this part of the country, as you may have observed .... But now we have gained the ridge of the hills, and there before us is a long moor covered with carices, rushes, and heath. How beautifully the Lapwings fly! It is strange that a bird so nearly allied to the Plovers and Tringas should have the wings so broad and rounded, while theirs are so pointed. Have you no birds in America analogous to this?

Aud. Not one. It is a beautiful and gentle creature, not-withstanding its peevish wail. Don't shoot it Physiophilus; it has a nest, and if you kill it you probably destroy five birds, or prevent four from being hatched. I hate to see birds shot when breeding.

Phys. By any person but yourself. Well, I desist, although I am anxious to have the skull of one, being, as you know forming a series for the purpose of comparing the alleged phrenological indications with the known habits of the birds.[19] The many American

skulls with which you have presented me will prove of great interest in this respect. Come now, a smart walk of half an hour on this road, and we shall be at Currie.

Orn. Hot weather, gentlemen! Get up this back stair if you can; and now, here is the house, 'at whose friendly door the weary traveller loves to call'. Walk in. Which way? Rest is pleasant to the weary, drink to the thirsty, food to the hungry, and we three are all these.

Aud. What shall we have? Whisky and water, porter, bread and cheese, cold meat, and something besides.

Phys. Gentlemen, with your permission, I take the porter.

Aud. Do. Dull drink! Hand me the noggin. Come, here's to our better acquaintance. We have had a very pleasant day. I have not seen so much game in Scotland before.

Orn. Here's to all lovers of nature, and especially to all true ornithologists .... Gentlemen, excuse me, I hope they will yet equal those of England, and trust me, I have seen no history of the birds of that country, not any representations of them, that I think may not, under favourable circumstances, be surpassed by your humble servant.

Phys. Bravo! To excel, a man must not undervalue himself. But I must qualify this drowsy stuff with a little of your pure aqua. Now for the soup and oat bread. The expenditure of so much fluid by cutaneous transpiration must be counterbalanced by absorption.

They continued their walk, discussing and noting the plants and bird life encountered. Physiophilus shot a willow wren at the behest of Ornithologus who observed that no mechanic in Edinburgh will match in real knowledge of nature a shepherd from Yarrow Braes or Tweedsmuir.

Phys. Here are two Willow Wrens. I shot what I thought was a Blackcap, but it fell into a thicket of sloes and brambles, and I could not find it.

Orn. Now, take the gun, Mr. Audubon, and shoot me a bird or two to be kept as memorials of this day's excursion, that, when you are basking in the warmth of your American sunshine, under some flower-clad Magnolia, listening to the notes of the Mocking Bird, and enjoying the repose so sweet after protracted labours like yours, I may call to mind the many happy days we have spent together in cold Scotland.

Aud. With good will. There is a lovely male Yellow Bunting on the very tip of the fir-tree. Now for it. Come not a miss yet! The first shot I have fired since I came to England last.

Phys. Here is Colinton. Shall we go by the road, or through the woods?

Orn. Take the woods by all means. But let us first quench our thirst. Here is a public house ....

Aud. May you prosper, and may I live to see engraved your drawings of the Birds of Britain, which I sincerely declare to be the best representations I have yet seen.

Orn. You have so often said so, that I must believe your partiality to the man has not deceived you into a belief that his productions are better than they really are. I wish all the world, excepting of course the authors of similar works, may agree with you. Who knows but the day may come?

Aud. Be assured more strange things have happened. How little did I think when I commenced my drawings that they should ever form a series of engravings occupying more than four hundred sheets of double elephant folio. Hope for the best, and put me down as your first subscriber.

Orn. It is done. Now, Physiophilus, move a-head, and give room for tacking. There are Dr. Walker's cedars of Lebanon[20] on the bank opposite, and here a most beautiful male Chaffinch, worthy of being shot by the American Ornithologist.

Aud. Down it comes. A lovely creature it is indeed. Stop here now, and let us gather a hatful of these wild flowers for my daughter that she may dry them, to keep in remembrance of Scotland.[21]

They completed their walk to Edinburgh via the village of Slateford, Ornithologus complaining that the corn on his sixth toe ached!

Phys. Farewell, I must leave you here, and hasten home to finish an essay on the organs of destructiveness in ornithologists, and on the

The village of Currie, from Grant's *Old and New Edinburgh.*

impossibility of determining the analogous parts in the brains of birds.

Orn. A very pleasant day we have had, and now having rested two hours with Americanus Ornitherinus, and enjoyed his hospitality, I go home to prepare for repose by writing half a dozen pages or so.

In these times of ecological awareness it is difficult to reconcile their manifest love of birds with their readiness to kill specimens in great number. Audubon thought little of killing many birds in order to obtain an ideal specimen for painting, while the MacGillivrays, father and son, required specimens for dissection and scientific study. They were all excellent shots and seemed to take pride and pleasure in their prowess. Elsewhere Audubon wrote, 'You will doubtless be surprised when I tell you that our first fire among a crowd of Great Godwits laid prostrate 65 of these birds', and in an account of trumpeter swans he wrote that killing 50 was 'a feast for a sportsman'. The prevailing attitudes and the acceptance of the practice from their early lives must have made it seem a perfectly natural activity. Later Audubon expressed regret for such 'murders ... as I do now while peaceably scratching my paper with an iron pen, in one of the comfortable and quite cool houses of Old Scotland'. He shows some sensitivity when he asks that the female lapwing be spared for the sake of her young, and in *Ornithological Biography* he wrote:

The most melancholy ornithological exhibition that I remember to have witnessed, was that of a wounded Dipper which was shot

183

through the lungs, above Cramond bridge, near Edinburgh. It stood still, without attempting to fly off, apparently insensible to all external objects, its legs bent, its wings drooping, its head declined … in that state the sufferer stood for five minutes until I got over the stream to it when it expired in my hand.[22]

Clearly he had a very ambivalent attitude towards the killing of his beloved birds. In his later life, however, he became acutely aware of the dire effects of man's exploitation of other species. Describing the commercial egg collectors of Labrador he wrote:

So constant and persevering are their depredations that ducks, guillemots, puffins, gulls etc., which, according to the accounts of a few settlers I saw in the country, were exceedingly abundant twenty years ago, have abandoned their ancient breeding places …. Nature having been exhausted and the season nearly spent, thousands of these birds left the country without having accomplished the purpose for which they had visited it. This war of extermination cannot last many years more.

Alas, although this lesson has been learned time and again since Audubon's day and despite the pioneering efforts of the Scotsman John Muir, who recognised the importance of preserving natural habitat, many species continue to be hunted or starved almost to extinction.

In 1996 the author, together with the ornithologist Mike Phillips, repeated the walk through the Pentland Hills at the same time of year. It was colder than in 1838: 41° compared with 54° then. Woodhouslee has been replaced by a more modern house although some of the original stabling survives and Habbies Howe is submerged under a new reservoir, but otherwise the topography had changed little from Audubon's day. Of the birds mentioned by MacGillivray, all but three – the whinchat, ring ouzel and merlin – were seen in 1996 (and these still commonly occur in this area). Many more were seen which were not mentioned by MacGillivray including the dunnock, wren, robin, rook, greenfinch, wood pigeon, grey wagtail, starling, magpie, mallard, pheasant, greylag goose, redpoll, lesser black-backed gull, common gull, cuckoo, dipper, kestrel, snipe, oyster-catcher, tree creeper, tufted duck,

and little grebe. It is probable that many of these species were encountered by MacGillivray and his companions and not mentioned, for there is no indication in his account that they were recording all that they saw. Elsewhere MacGillivray records most of these birds as occurring in the vicinity of Edinburgh at that time.[23] It is gratifying, however, that 158 years later the range of bird life and the habitat remain largely intact.

The Pentland walk was the last recorded activity of Audubon in Edinburgh. Audubon had grown to love Edinburgh and Scotland and his talents flourished in that warm and stimulating environment. One commentator wrote: '… let him not forget that … when America refused the unknown wanderer of the woods a seat among her naturalists, Scotland unhesitatingly conferred on him honours which his zeal, his enthusiasm, and the success of his labours, so well merited ….'[24] Audubon recorded his feelings on leaving the city in the introduction to volume five of *Ornithological Biography*.[25]

When I presented you with the fourth volume of this work, I was in fair Edina; and now, when I offer you the fifth, I am in Edina still. What beautiful walks there are, Reader, around that superlatively beautiful city! The oftener I have rambled along them, the more I have thought with deep regret, that now at last I am on the eve of bidding those walks, and the friends whom I know I possess there, a last adieu. No man, methinks, can ever leave a country where he has been kindly treated, without a deep feeling of sorrow. When I left England, and all my dear friends there, that feeling was as pungent as it is at this moment, when I am about being thrust into a coach, to travel as fast as horses can speed towards Bristol, there to place myself on board that leviathian of the Atlantic, 'the Great Western,'[26] to be paddled to my own native shores. But then, Reader, the remembrance of much kindness, and the gratitude resulting from it, will ever warm my heart. Whether far or near, I will ever try to communicate with those dear friends, and with you too, good Reader, should you be desirous of my doing so ….

To Professor Traill and the Curators of the Library of the University of Edinburgh, for the liberality of which they have allowed me the use of many valuable works not otherwise to be procured, I offer my sincere thanks; as well as to Professor Jameson for the specimens sent to him by the late Dr. Meredith Gairdner, which he has had the kindness to lend me from the rich Museum under his charge. Allow me also to mention the names of a few friends to whom I shall ever feel most deeply indebted. The first on the list is William MacGillivray, and I wish

that you, Reader, and all the world besides, knew him as well as I do ....

I have pleasure in saying that my enemies have been few, and my friends numerous. May the God who granted me life, industry, and perseverance to accomplish my task, forgive the former, and for ever bless the latter!

Audubon left Britain for the last time on 25 June 1839.

Notes

1 Thomas Nuttall (1786-1859) was an Englishman who travelled extensively in North America in order to follow his interest in natural history in all its aspects. He, like Alexander Wilson, was inspired and encouraged by William Bartram. In 1832 he and Audubon met and became good friends and shared their knowledge in their respective publications, for Nuttall was writing his *Manual of Ornithology* at that time. During 1834/5 Nuttall, together with his friend John Kirk Townsend, went on an overland expedition to the Pacific coast making many new discoveries of plant and animal life. Audubon who had been unable to fulfil his ambition to make a similar journey, was thrilled to be able to purchase, through the generosity of his friend Edward Harris, 93 skins of birds from Nuttall and Townsend which he used to complete 76 plates, helping to make his work representative of the entire United States rather than of the eastern states to which his own explorations had been confined.

John Kirk Townsend (1809-51), a young American natural historian, was invited by Nuttall to join him in his western expedition. The pair made an effective duo, Townsend being chiefly interested in zoology while Nuttall was primarily a botanist. Townsend was somewhat aggrieved that Audubon should have the credit of publicising his finds, although Audubon readily acknowledged their origin. In particular he objected to Audubon's naming of the MacGillivray warbler, which he had previously named 'Tolmiei' after the friend who had provided the specimen. Nevertheless he later provided, somewhat reluctantly, several of the specimens used by Audubon in his *Quadrupeds*. Some of Townsend's bird skins eventually found their way into the extensive collection of Sir William Jardine, Audubon having sold them to a dealer in Edinburgh.

2 Audubon, L: *The Life of John James Audubon*, p. 398.

3 *Letters of John James Audubon 1826-1840*, vol. II, pp. 145-6.

4 Deane, R: 'Unpublished letters of William MacGillivray to John James Audubon', in *The Auk* (1901), 18: 239-49.

5 *Letters*, op. cit., vol. II, p. 175.

6 Ibid, pp. 199-200.

7 Low, S M: *Catalogue of the new Birds of America Section of the Audubon Archives* (1993).

8 Letter of Eliza Bachman dated 11 December 1838 to her sister Harriet, from *John Bachman*.

9 *Ornithological Biography*, vol. V, pp. xi-xii.

10 *The Auk* (1894), 11: 309-13.

11 Hook, A: *Scotland and America 1750-1835*, pp. 179-80.

12 *Ornithological Biography*, vol. V, pp. xii-xxii.

13 The Chain Pier at Newhaven had been built in 1821 at a cost of £4000. It was located opposite the Peacock Inn, which still exists; famed then and now for its fish dishes. The pier was used by the steam packets plying between Newhaven and the ports in the Forth estuary including Queensferry, Grangemouth, Alloa and Stirling. The fisherfolk of Newhaven were very excited when it was proposed that George IV should land on their pier on his celebrated visit to Edinburgh in 1822 and were disappointed when, at the last moment, the royal landing was changed to Leith. It became a favourite base for sea bathers when this became a popular pastime in the 1850s. The illustration shows its construction – a series of bridges suspended from chains linked stone pillars. It was destroyed by a storm in 1898. (McGowran T: *Newhaven-on-Forth, Port of Grace*, p. 100 (John Donald, Edinburgh, 1985.)

14 The four picturesque falls of the River Clyde – Bonnington, Corra, Dundaff and Stonebyres Linns – occured in quick succession and powered a series of water mills. They are now obscured by a hydroelectric development.

15 John Argyll Robertson was the father of a more famous son, Douglas Argyll Robertson (1837-1909), an ophthalmic surgeon in Edinburgh who acquired an international reputation. A particular abnormality of the pupil of the eye, known by his name, is familiar to all medical students.

16 MacGillivray, W: *A History of British Birds*, vol. II, pp. 462-71.

17 MacGillivray refers to Alexander Fraser Tytler, Lord Woodhouselee 1742-1813, a Scottish judge who in 1780 was appointed professor of universal history at Edinburgh University. Lord Cockburn described him as 'a person of correct taste, a cultivated mind, and literary habits, and very amiable; which excellences graced, and were graced by,

the mountain retreat whose name he transferred to the bench. But there is no kindness in insinuating that he was a man of genius, and of public or even social influence, or in describing Woodhouselee as Tuscaulum.'

18   Habbie's Howe refers to a scene described in Alan Ramsay's pastoral comedy *The Gentle Shepherd* (1725):

Jenny   The shining day will bleach our linen clean,
The water's clear, the light unclouded blew
Will make them like a lily wet with dew.

Peg   Gae far'er up the burn to Habbie's How,
Where a'the sweets o'spring and summer grow:
Between twa birks, out o'er a little lin,   (birk: birch; lin: cascade)
The water fa's, and maks a singan din;
A pool breast-deep, beneath as clear as glass;
We'll end our washing while the mornings cool,
And when the day grows het, we'll to the pool'
There wash our sells – 'tis healthfu now in May
And sweetly cauler on sae warm a day.

Peg   Daft lassie, when we're naked, what'll ye say
Gif our twa herds come brattling down the brae'
And see us sae? That jeering fallow Pate
Wad taunting say, 'Haith, lasses, yer're no blate!'

The exact location of this pleasant spot was the subject of intense debate, although it is not known whether Ramsay had a specific location in mind. The waterfall in the Logan Burn in Glencorse referred to by MacGillivray was one of the sites accepted as the real Habbie's Howe. In the event Peg and Jenny spent so much time discussing their swains, the 'herds', that they remained 'blate' (clothed).

19   John MacGillivray's interest at that time was the study of birds' skulls to see if he could find evidence to support the theory of phrenology. To this end he acquired a vast collection, which he eventually sold to Robert Jameson for his museum for £5 after much negotiation (see Chapter 16).

20   The Rev. John Walker, who preceded Jameson as professor of natural history, created a notable garden at his manse in Colinton. The cedars, which were referred to by MacGillivray, still stand in the vicinity of the garden. In the garden itself there is still a massive old yew tree which must also have been seen by Audubon. This tree is notable, as Robert Louis Stevenson, whose grandfather Dr Lewis Balfour was then the incumbent, played in the manse garden as a boy and refers to it frequently in his writings:

Below the yew – it still is there –
Our phantom voices haunt the air
As we were still at play,
And I can hear them call and say:
'How far is it to Babylon'

21   This must refer either to Audubon's daughter-in-law Maria, or to his grandchild Lucy, as Audubon's own two daughters died in infancy.

22   *Ornithological Biography,* vol. IV, p. 498.

23   *A History of British Birds,* vol. II, pp. 302-6.

24   Anon: *Edinburgh New Philosophical Journal* (1835), 18: 143.

25   *Ornithological Biography,* vol. V, pp. x-xi and xxiiv-xxv

26   The *Great Western* was the first paddle steamer to provide a regular crossing of the Atlantic. Conceived and designed by the great engineer Isambard Kingdom Brunel (1806-59), she had her maiden voyage on 8 March 1838. Her average journey to and from New York took 14 days and in her first 18 months she made 20 crossings. In the event, for unknown reasons, Audubon did not sail on the *Great Western* although his son Victor did in 1839. Audubon made his last Atlantic crossing in the same year on the sailing ship *George Washington*, a journey which took 39 days – although even this was an advance on his first crossing on the sailing schooner *Delos* in 1826 which had taken 65 days.

Audubon after Edinburgh | 15

IT would have been understandable if Audubon had rested after completing his Herculean task, but his return to America was anything but relaxation. The Audubons settled at first in New York, where John Woodhouse and his father set about producing a new popular edition of *The Birds of America* in a reduced octavo size. John used the camera lucida technique which Audubon had learned from Dr Brewster in Edinburgh.[1] The paintings were lithographed by J T Bowen, an English settler. This edition appeared in seven volumes from 1840 to 1844 and met with great financial success, leading to seven further editions. In these the text and illustrations were combined and further illustrations added as new species were identified.

During 1839 a second daughter, Harriet, was born to John and Maria, and Victor became engaged to Maria's sister Eliza, much to Audubon's pleasure, but Bachman's distress at the prospect of losing another daughter. Alas, Maria's health declined after Harriet's birth and she died of tuberculosis in 1840 at the age of 23. Eliza suffered from the same disease and died the following year aged 22. Both brothers married again, John in 1841 to Caroline Hall by whom he had seven children. Victor married Georgiana Mallory in 1843 and they had six children.

Audubon wearied of city life – he could not live in any city, except 'perhaps fair Edinburgh'.[2] In 1842 he moved into a new house on a 24-acre estate which he called Minnie's Land, Minnie being his term of endearment for Lucy. This lay in the country, a few miles upstream from New York on the Hudson River. This was the first real home for the Audubon family since their time in Henderson 19 years earlier.

Maria, Audubon's granddaughter, recollected that

… Minniesland with its large gardens and orchards, especially celebrated for peaches,

its poultry yards and dairy which added to the comfort of the home and of the many guests who always found a welcome there, had an interesting side in the elk, deer, moose, foxes, wolves and other wildwood creatures which were kept for study and pleasure; and still another in the books, pictures and curios within the ever hospitable house, but more than all was the charm of the tall gray-haired old man, who by talent, industry, and almost incredible perseverance won it for those he loved.[3]

The publishing enterprises continued. Concurrently with the production of the popular version of *The Birds of America* the Audubon family set about their next project, *The Quadrupeds of North America*, designed to complement the original *Birds*. John Bachman agreed to write the text of the new book, leaving the Audubons, father and sons, free to concentrate on the illustrations.

Minnie's Land, from *Audubon the Naturalist.*

One of Audubon's surviving journals covers part of this period. It records that he spent much of his time travelling in the eastern states and Canada, selling his books with considerable success, particularly of the smaller edition of *The Birds of America*. While in Washington on 25 July 1842 he sardonically writes, 'Heard for the first time of the death of my beloved good friend *Charles Waterton* (God grant him pardon for all his sins)'.[4] In fact Audubon had been misinformed – Waterton did not die until 1865, outliving Audubon by 14 years. There are many references in this journal to fatigue and trouble with his bowels, in contrast to the robust health and vigour revealed in his earlier journals. Age and overwork were beginning to tell.

In March 1843 a Scottish businessman, Andrew Coates, from Alexander Wilson's home town of Paisley, visited the Audubons at Minnie's Land and described the ménage:[5]

It was only after reaching the house that I learned we had chosen a very trying time for the family, because, on the following morning, Mr. Audubon was to take his departure for the Rocky Mountains, on his last excursion in pursuit of his favourite study …. It was a bold and perilous adventure, such as might well have tried the courage of young men capable of enduring the greatest hardships …. But such was Audubon's restless nature and love of adventure … that no influence that could be brought to bear upon him was found strong enough to dissuade him from his purpose. And yet, with all his boldness and daring, he was one of the gentlest of men. As a husband, a father, and a friend he had a heart overflowing with kindness. Indeed his character was written on his countenance, on which might be read kindness, courage, and genius. He had a sharp eye, regular and finely-formed features, and a noble and expansive forehead, from which his silvery locks flowed back in graceful folds. If I were to picture to myself the ideal of a patriarch I would choose Audubon as my type. His conversation was both interesting and instructive. There was an emphasis and meaning in every word he uttered. He had a strong French accent – so strong, indeed, that one would have imagined he had newly left the country in which he had spent his early years …. But his French accent, so far from being a drawback, gave an additional charm to his conversation ….

The family consisted of Mr. and Mrs Audubon, their two sons and their wives and children. [His sons later built their homes nearby.] In this happy family it would be difficult to find a more perfect example of everything that can render home beautiful and attractive. One soul seemed to animate every member from the oldest to the youngest. Mrs. Audubon was some years younger than her husband, but age did not seem to have told upon her. She must have been beautiful when young, and still retained a pleasing and beautiful expression of countenance. She was natural and simple in her manners, and, indeed, a fine example of well-bred, sensible English lady …. Their two sons were fine-looking men, highly cultured, and kindly and genial in their manners ….

The house in which Audubon lived was in keeping with the character of its occupants. It was plain and unpretentious, but wanting in nothing that was necessary to comfort. It was surrounded by grassy parks and natural wooding, but unadorned with parterres or other evidences of elaborate gardening …. His sons, who took charge of the publication [of *The Birds of America*], told me that there now only remained three copies unsold. One copy they kept for themselves, but that, they told me, was an expensive luxury which they meant to part with. I afterwards purchased the whole three copies, one for myself and the others for my two brothers in Paisley.

[One of these was afterwards presented to the Paisley Free Library, where it now is.]

On the day after this visit, 11 March 1843, Audubon set out on a 'perilous adventure' – his last ambition – a journey to the western states. This he did by steamboat down the Ohio River and up the Missouri as far as the Yellowstone River, where he and his companions remained for two months at Fort Union collecting, measuring and painting new birds and quadrupeds. His last journal covering this period is full of interest and keen observation; clearly his return to the wilderness life he loved best had revived his spirits. Inevitably this account details the daily killings of birds and animals, which were encountered in abundance, usually for the purpose of study and painting or for the pot, but sometimes apparently just for 'sport'. Audubon as usual displayed his ambivalence to such activity in which he participated fully. At times he writes with admiration of the prowess of the hunters while at the same time recognising the long-term ecological consequences. He was distressed by the slaughter of buffaloes which were killed for their tongues alone, the rest of the carcass being left to rot.

> One can hardly conceive how it happens, notwithstanding these many deaths and the immense numbers that are murdered almost daily on these boundless wastes … so many are yet to be found …. But this cannot last; even now there is a perceptible difference in the size of the herds, and before many years the Buffalo, like the Great Auk, will have disappeared.[6]

Audubon felt too old to take part in the buffalo hunts himself. His companion Edward Harris gave vivid descriptions of these which involved riding at full gallop after the fleeing animals while firing and recharging their muzzle-loading rifles. Even he had pangs of conscience after the kill. 'We now regretted having destroyed these noble beasts for no earthly reason but to gratify a

sanguinary disposition which appears to be inherent in our natures. We had no means of carrying home the meat and after cutting out the tongues we wended our way back to camp, completely disgusted with ourselves and with the conduct of all white men who come to this country.'[7]

Audubon returned home after eight months with long untrimmed hair and beard, making a striking figure. The following year he concluded his ornithological studies by adding 61 new birds and increasing the number of plates to 500 in a new octavo edition of *The Birds of America* from specimens obtained during his Missouri expedition. Thereafter he concentrated on paintings for *Quadrupeds*.

During 1846 Audubon's mental faculties began to fail. A visitor wrote that he had

> … greatly changed since I had last seen him. He wore his hair longer, and it now hung in locks of snowy whiteness over his shoulders. His once piercing gray eyes, though still bright, had already begun to fail him. He could no longer paint with his wonted accuracy and had at last, most reluctantly, been forced to surrender to his sons the task of completing his Quadrupeds of North America.

'Tawny Weasel' by John Woodhouse Audubon; background by Victor Gifford Audubon. Plate 148 from *The Quadrupeds of North America*.

'Oregon Flying Squirrel'
by J J Audubon, plate
15 from *The Quadrupeds
of North America*.

Surrounded by his large family including his devoted wife, his two sons, and their wives, his enjoyment of life seemed to leave little to him to desire. He was very fond of the rising generation, and they were as devoted in their affectionate regards for him. He seemed to enjoy to the utmost each moment of time, content at last to submit to an inevitable and well earned leisure, and to throw upon his gifted sons his uncompleted tasks.[8]

The plate size of *Quadrupeds* was imperial folio (28 by 22 inches), somewhat smaller than the double elephant folio of *Birds*. Lithography had superseded copper engraving. One hundred and fifty plates were produced and published in three volumes between 1842 and 1848. Audubon completed about half the plates and the rest were painted by his son John, who spent 18 months in England in 1846/7 to get access to zoological specimens held in the British Museum and elsewhere in Europe which were not readily available in the United States. John's talents were such that it is difficult to distinguish his paintings

from those of his father. Victor painted many of the backgrounds.

The three-volume set cost $300 and about 300 complete sets were sold. Edinburgh University was one of the early subscribers to *Quadrupeds* and still retains its copy.

John Bachman, meanwhile, laboured under great difficulty to complete the accompanying text. Living in Charleston he had little access to the main libraries of the country. The Audubons, who had undertaken to supply him with the sources that he required, were very dilatory in responding to his requests and at times relationships became strained. During this period his wife died. Two years later he married his wife's sister, Maria, who had previously been involved in assisting Audubon with his paintings for *Birds* (see Chapter 1, note 12). She provided valuable service in acting as Bachman's secretary and editorial assistant when his own health and eyesight were failing. Eventually the text of *Quadrupeds* was completed and published between 1846 and 1854. Bachman received no financial return. 'I have cheerfully given my own labors without any other reward

'Black Rat' by J J Audubon; background by Victor Gifford Audubon. Plate 23 from *The Quadrupeds of North America*.

than the hope of having contributed something toward the advancement of the cause of Natural History in our country.'⁹

In fact there was little financial return to anyone from the imperial edition of *Quadrupeds*. George Ord, Audubon's eternal enemy, wrote with some prescience to his friend Waterton: 'In a pecuniary point of view it will prove a failure. No expensive works of the kind will succeed in this country; and the author of the imprudent project ought, from his experience, to know it. But you can do nothing with an enthusiast, to whom everything appears *couleur de rose*.'¹⁰

Audubon in his later years suffered from progressive dementia. He contributed less and less to the completion of *Quadrupeds* and did not live to see the final volumes. A further octavo edition, combining both text and paintings, was subsequently produced under the editorship of Victor. John had reduced the size of the illustrations as he had for *Birds*, by means of the camera lucida. Although *Quadrupeds* was the first attempt at a comprehensive account of North American animals and many of the paintings in *Quadrupeds* compare favourably with those of *Birds*, it never achieved the same popularity or financial success. It undoubtedly suffered from the premature death of its chief author, whose dynamic personality and powers of persuasion had been its inspiration. Perhaps birds have a wider appeal.

Bachman, who visited Minnie's Land in 1848, wrote:

> Mrs. Audubon is straight as an arrow, and in fine health, but sadly worried .... Audubon has heard his little song sung in French, and has gone to bed. Alas, my poor friend Audubon! the outlines of his countenance and his form are there, but his noble mind is in ruins.¹¹

He lingered in this state, cared for by his devoted family until his death on 27 January 1851, aged 66.

Audubon's great contributions to art and to natural history received due recognition in his lifetime and many obituaries appeared. The Academy of Natural Sciences of Philadelphia, which had initially refused him membership, recorded his death in their minutes of 4 February 1851:

> That the Society has heard with profound regret of the death of their esteemed and

venerable colleague John James Audubon .... That by the demise of this truly great man, Science has lost one of her most zealous and gifted disciples of the Arts, a master of the branch he cultivated .... That we recognise in Mr Audubon a man who has happily lived to fulfill his destiny as an explorer of the great field of American Zoology, while the splendid volumes which are the fruit of his labors, will diffuse the knowledge and love of science to the latest generations.

The *Illustrated London News* wrote: 'As a delineator of birds, Audubon never had an equal; his subjects breathe of all the freshness, character, and vigour of living nature. His attitudes are of the most spirited description, infinitely varied and all appearing as in their native haunts ....'

Eighteen years earlier a reviewer of Audubon's work wrote, with great foresight, 'like all remarkable men, Mr Audubon has had his share of vituperation; but the time will be, although it cannot benefit him, when his works will be referred to as among the most perfect productions of our time'.¹² With the passage of time his fame and reputation have increased and his name has become linked with a host of organisations and societies concerned with natural history. His weaknesses – his vanity, tendency to romanticise, his flirtations and occasional neglect of Lucy in the single-minded pursuit of his objective – are usually forgotten or outweighed by his achievements. Sacheverell Sitwell gives a recent assessment:

> ... there is nothing in the world of fine books quite like the first discovery of Audubon. The giant energy of the man, and his power of achievement and accomplishment, give to him something of the epical force of a Walt Whitman or a Herman Melville. The *Birds of America* is a heroic undertaking; and that one man should have endured the hardships and ardours of so many long and lonely journeys, painted the pictures, written the text, and contrived the publication upon so gigantic a scale, puts him among the immortals .... Audubon is the greatest of bird painters; he belongs to American history, and as a writer he described things that human eyes will never see again.¹³

Despite his fame, Audubon's publications had not brought great wealth and his two sons, who had devoted their lives to assisting their father in the production of his works, were left with limited funds and without alternative careers.

In 1848 gold was discovered in California and gold fever swept the United States. At that time travel to the west was extremely arduous, whether by tedious sea voyage around the Horn or by overland routes through country which had been little explored and was occupied by hostile Indians and even more dangerous outlawed whites. There were two routes – the Oregon Trail which had been opened up by Lewis and Clark in 1803, and a southern route, the Santa Fé Trail. John Woodhouse was persuaded to join a gold-seeking expedition which left New York in February 1849, choosing the southern route. Ninety-eight men set out under the leadership of a Colonel Webb. The journey was disastrous. Cholera attacked the party on two occasions, killing eleven men in all. John twice caught the disease but survived. The money which they carried was stolen and 20 of the party lost heart and returned to the east. Their leader deserted them when the going became difficult and John was elected to replace him. The remainder of the party completed the journey under his leadership. The enormous hardships under which they travelled are recounted in his journal which was published by his daughter Maria. John's writing reveals considerable literary talent with the ability to describe scenes and situations with great vividness. The following passage provides a sample:

I went to the sick tents; poor young Liscomb worn out and heart broken sat leaning against the tent where his father lay dying, looking as pallid and exhausted as the sick man, and almost asleep; I roused him and sent him to my tent to get some rest. Edward Whittlesey was next, looking as if he had been ill for months; his dog, a Newfoundland, was walking about him, licking his hands and feet and giving evidence of the greatest affection; from time to time smelling his mouth for his breath, but it was gone.

I slowly walked to Boden's tent but there was no change from the stupor into which he had fallen; and I sat down to wait, for what? All exertions had been made to save our brave men, and all had failed. Like sailors with masts and rudder gone, wallowing in the trough of a storm-tossed ocean, we had to await our fate, one of us only at a time going from tent to tent of our dying companions to note the hour of their last breath.[14]

They eventually continued their journey with only 57 of the original party of 98. Despite the difficulties of the journey John managed to record the animal and plant life encountered. Occasionally there was some relief from the gruelling conditions:

Fourth of July. Paso Chapadaro. Calm, misty, silent. The sun soon threw its red light over all we saw to the west, but was hidden by the range of mountains to the east which we had passed, till mastering at an effort, as it seemed, the highest ridge, it burst forth in all its splendor. In the bottom of my saddle-bags, rolled in a handkerchief, was a flag given me by poor Hamilton Boden, and by the time the haze had gone, it floated in the breeze, from the top of the highest tree near our camp; nature was all in a smile, and we prepared to spend the day according to our various inclinations. Some slept, some basked in indolence, some started off to look for game, some looked to their saddle-bags and blankets; all was rest, at least from travel, and I unpacked my paper and pencils and make a sketch of the 'Fourth of July Camp'.

Wild cattle were abundant, and noon saw our camp in possession of a fine heifer shot by Rhoades. Steaks were broiled and fried, ribs roasted, brains stewed in the skull; delicacies under such circumstances unequalled by the cuisine of a palace.[15]

They reached the Pacific after a journey of nearly ten months and found that they had arrived too late. They explored the gold fields but found them fully occupied and exploited. John returned home by sea in July 1850, having suffered considerable financial loss instead of making his fortune as he had hoped. His resolution, and qualities of leadership and compassion, deserved better.

John and Victor spent the rest of their lives at Minnie's Land, working on the estate and eking out a living on the proceeds of subsequent editions of *Birds* and *Quadrupeds*. Victor, the more businesslike of the two, injured his back in a fall in 1856 and became progressively more disabled until his death in 1860 at the age of 41. John, who had inherited many of his father's traits including his love of music, natural history and painting, also inherited his lack of business acumen and suffered further financial loss in an unsuccessful publishing venture. His daughter Maria wrote:

> Never a 'business man,' saddened by his brother's condition, and utterly unable to manage at the same time a fairly large estate, the publication of two illustrated works ... the securing of subscribers and the financial condition of everything – what wonder that he rapidly aged .... After my uncle's death matters became still more difficult to handle, owing to the unsettled condition of the southern states where most of the subscribers ... resided. Worn out in body and spirit, overburdened with anxieties, saddened by the condition of his country, it is no matter of surprise that my father could not throw off a heavy cold which attacked him early in 1862.[16]

After playing on his violin some 'Scotch airs of which he was so fond', he lapsed into delirium and died two days later, aged 49.

In 1861 Lucy had been compelled to sell the family folio of *Birds* for $600 in order to pay off debts incurred by John Woodhouse in his last unsuccessful publishing project. The long-suffering Lucy, having survived the deaths of her dearly loved husband and sons, was obliged to live with relatives as her finances did not allow her to maintain Minnie's Land, which she first rented and then had to sell. For a time she resumed teaching at the age of 70 to supplement her income. In 1870 she sold the copper plates of the engravings of *Birds*, which had survived an earlier fire in a New York warehouse, to a scrap-metal dealer for a small sum. Fortunately a few were saved and about 78 still survive.[17] Audubon's original paintings she sold, after much hard bargaining, for $4000 to the New York Historical Society where they remain on display. During 1867 Lucy wrote a biography of her husband based largely on his journals, which she edited and expurgated quite extensively to remove passages which she thought distasteful.

Lucy died in 1874 aged 86. Despite the long periods of separation from her husband and the neglect and hardship which she sometimes suffered as a result of his obsession, her love for him endured to the end. A visitor to their home had written:

> The sweet unity between his wife and himself ... her quickness of perception, and their mutual enthusiasm regarding these works of his heart and hand, and the tenderness with which they unconsciously treated each other, all was impressed upon my memory. Ever since, I have been convinced that Audubon owed more to his wife than the world knew ....[18]

Notes

1   Audubon, M R: *Audubon and his Journals*, vol. I, p. 209.
2   Ibid, p. 71.
3   Biographical Memoir by Maria R Audubon, in *Western Journal 1849-1850*, p. 27.
4   *Journal of John James Audubon 1840-1843*, p. 83.
5   Coates, A: 'Personal Reminiscences of Audubon', in *Proceedings of the Perthshire Society of Natural Science* (1893-5), 2: xxiv-xxix.
6   *Audubon and his Journals*, vol. II, p. 131.
7   Harris, E: cited in *Up the Missouri with Audubon, The Journal of Edward Harris*, p. 149.
8   Brewer, T M: cited in *Audubon the Naturalist*, vol. II, pp. 286-7.
9   Quoted in *John Bachman*.
10 Letter from Ord to Waterton, 22 June 1845, cited in *John James Audubon in the West*, p. 151.
11 Bachman, J: cited in *Audubon the Naturalist*, vol. II, p. 292.
12 Anon: *Edinburgh New Philosophical Journal* (1835), 18: 144.
13 Sitwell, S and Buchan, H: *Fine Bird Books*, p. 28.
14 John Woodhouse Audubon: *Western Journal 1849-1850*, p. 63.
15 Ibid, pp. 116-7.
16 Ibid, p. 37.
17 The romantic history of the surviving copper plates is related in Fries, W H: *The Double Elephant Folio*.
18 Audubon, L: *The Life of John James Audubon*, p. 439

MacGillivray after Edinburgh | 16

IN 1841 MacGillivray applied for the regius chair of natural history in Marischal College,[1] Aberdeen, and prevailed against powerful competition. Among the other applicants were John Fleming and Edward Forbes. The Rev. Dr John Fleming (1785-1857) was one of Scotland's leading naturalists and geologists and an enthusiastic Wernerian. His *Philosophy of Zoology* (1823) gave him international recognition that was enhanced by his discovery of fossilised fish remains in Fife, which can still be seen on display in the Museum of Scotland. He read a paper on this topic before the Wernerian Society in 1830, and argued that his discoveries were contrary to the theories of Hutton. In 1845 he was appointed to the chair of natural science in the Free Church Theological College in Edinburgh. Edward Forbes, a marine biologist of distinction, was strongly supported by Professor Jameson whom he was to succeed to the chair of natural history in Edinburgh following Jameson's death in 1854 (see Chapter 7).

This last chapter in MacGillivray's life promised welcome stability to his family, who had been accustomed to frequent moves from one rented house to another while in Edinburgh.

It appears that I have at length found a temporary refuge from the storm …. Being fond of rural shades and solitary rambles, and having always in mind the health of my family, I have chosen for my habitation a house in the midst of a large garden, a mile and a half distant from Marischal College, and half a mile beyond Kings's College …. In the last six weeks I have walked more than in the whole previous year, and have slept less than at almost any time of life; so that, although in excellent health, I am getting so thin that my clothes are quite loose about me. Nothing can be more pleasant than my locality. The house and garden are bounded on two sides by two lanes … on which are a few similar houses inhabited by the aristocracy of the village; proud enough people, as village nobles generally are. Just opposite is a fine old Cathedral.[2] I love to sit in the old church and listen to the reading of the Scripture, and the exposition of their doctrines. Many times have I been struck by passages which bore reference to my own case. I have never been very regular in my church-goings, but here I find difficulty in staying away.[3]

MacGillivray entered into his new career with his customary enthusiasm and dedication. His lectures attracted a wide audience in addition to his assigned students. One of his former pupils wrote: 'He was exceedingly *loveable* and undoubtedly the first ornithologist in Europe, and we were all proud of his fame. One thing always made a great impression on me: he treated his

St Machar's Cathedral, Old Aberdeen, as it would have appeared in MacGillivray's time. From *The Baronial and Ecclesiastical Antiquities of Scotland* by R W Billings, William Blackwood & Sons, Edinburgh (1852).

Inscription in the author's copy of *The Natural History of Deeside and Braemar.*

Right: Knock Castle by MacGillivray's daughter Isabella, from *The Natural History of Deeside and Braemar.*

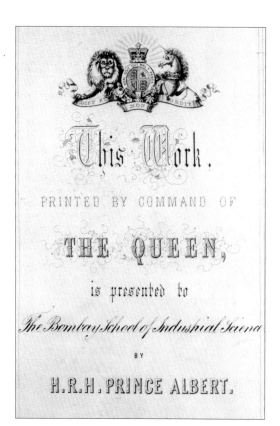

class as men and gentlemen, and we reciprocated his action. It was far otherwise with some of the professors.'[4] In 1844 his old alma mater, King's College, awarded him an honorary LL D (Doctor of Laws).

Much of his teaching consisted of fieldwork which involved long journeys with his classes. Another of his students commented that 'he could walk the most active of them into limp helpless-ness, and remain as fresh as at the outside of the march'. Aberdeen University had no natural history museum at that time, and having spent the previous 20 years intimately involved in the running of two museums, MacGillivray appears to have enjoyed the freedom to return to the nat-ural living world in which to teach and conduct research in the open air. He took the opportunity to add a study of shellfish to his already encyclo-paedic knowledge of natural history and two years after his appointment he published a *History of the Mollusca of the North-East of Scotland* which contained descriptions of 20 species new to science.

Alas, even the salary of a regius professor did not bring MacGillivray the financial security which he must have craved. A love of natural history did not guarantee a good income, as

Audubon and Swainson could testify. Raising the ten surviving children was a heavy burden, and the family had to move several times into smaller homes. Throughout his life he was beset by financial worries, which no doubt contributed to his periods of depression as well as denying him the opportunity of having his paintings published.

In 1850 he made his last walking excursion – a month's exploration of the valley of the Dee, together with his son Paul and daughter Isabella. His observations from this trip formed the basis of his last book *The Natural History of Deeside and Braemar*. This was published for private circulation after his death by the command of Queen Victoria who shared MacGillivray's love for this part of her kingdom and built her holiday retreat at Balmoral near Braemar.

In the preface to this book he writes: 'If the Valley of the Dee had many times been traversed by the wise and the learned, the man of science and the man of wit, the poet, the painter, and the tourist, it is equally instructive to the naturalist, who ought in his own person to represent all these characters.' Certainly in his own life and work he demonstrated most of these attributes to a high degree. His poetic gift of expression, his keen observation and his deep love for his native Scotland are revealed in a word picture in which he describes the view from the bridge over the Dee at Invercauld:

Before we pass on, let us pause once more – not because we are weary of travel, or of the world. Here the bed of the Dee is obliquely intersected by a broken ridge of slaty rock, passing from south-west to north east. The stream is broken by it into a succession of

Lochnagar by
MacGillivray, from
*The Natural History of
Deeside and Braemar.*

little falls and rapids, and then glides away over its stony bed to wind afar amidst pine-clad hills. Beautiful scene! I almost weep when I look upon thee; for tears flow from the pure fountain of happiness as well as from the troubled springs of sorrow. How unlike, in thy quiet loveliness, to the fierce rudeness of human nature! Not a living creature is to be seen but a lad whipping the water. The western sun shines in full splendour in a sky unobscured, although scattered flakes of white vapour glide slowly eastward in its upper region. Long shadows are perfected from the tall pines, while the hill top, purpled with flowering heath, or grey with lichen-crusted stones, are lighted with the blaze. Far away up the wooded glens is still seen the scarred ridge of Lochnagar. Not a breath stirs the tiny leaf of the Birch, not a sound is heard but from the waters. Ought not he to whom Providence has allotted all this to be happy?[5]

MacGillivray's health declined after this excursion to such an extent that he felt unable to continue teaching, and in 1851 he went to Torquay accompanied by one of his daughters in the hope that the better climate might improve his health and lift the depression from which he also suffered. While there his wife Marion, who had remained in Aberdeen, died in February 1852 of 'disease of the brain'. MacGillivray remained in Torquay and a month after his wife's death published the fourth volume of the *History of British Birds*. In the preface he wrote:

As the wounded bird seeks some quiet retreat where, freed from the persecution of the pitiless fowler, it may pass the time of its

anguish in forgetfulness of the world, so have I, assailed by disease, betaken myself to a sheltered nook where, unannoyed by the piercing blasts of the North Sea, I had been led to hope that my life might be protected beyond the most dangerous season of the year. It is thus that I issue from Devonshire the present volume, which, however, contains no observations of mine made there, the scenes of my labours being in distant parts of the country …. It is not until disabled that the observer of the habits of wild animals becomes sensible of the happiness he had enjoyed, in exercising the faculties with which his benign Creator has endowed him. No study or pursuit is better adapted for such enjoyment, or so well fitted to afford pleasures not liable to be repented of, than Natural History.

His failure to return to Aberdeen at the time of Marion's death was not due to any estrange-ment or lack of feeling. MacGillivray does not expose his feelings for his family in his writings as freely as Audubon did, but the few references he makes in his surviving letters reveal a deep affection. His own state of health at that time must have prevented the journey. Aware of his own imminent death, his visit to Torquay had been for the purpose of giving him time and opportunity to finish his *magnum opus*. Just as Audubon had found, such a compulsion could at times conflict with family responsibilities.

The fifth and last volume of *A History of British Birds* was published in July of that year, completing MacGillivray's life's work and his major contribution to natural history which had started with the publication of the first

William MacGillivray's headstone in the New Calton Cemetery, Edinburgh. Inset is a bronze relief reproducing MacGillivray's painting of the golden eagle (see illustration on p. 86).

volume 15 years earlier. The conclusion to this last volume reads:

> I have been honest and sincere in my endeavour to promote the truth. With death apparently not distant before my eyes, I am pleased to think I have not countenanced error through fear or favour. Neither have I in any case modified my sentiments so as to endeavour thereby to conceal or palliate my faults. Though I might have accomplished more, I am thankful for having been permitted to add very considerably to the knowledge previously obtained of a very pleasant subject.

A reviewer of the last volume of *British Birds* wrote:

> The publication of the first three volumes proved a bad speculation, involving the author in pecuniary liabilities and compelled him to severe labour in support of a large family .... As a valuable writer in geology, botany, and some departments, especially mollusca, of zoology, he is very favourably known, but it is as the author of *British Birds* that his name will go down in posterity.

His dying effort was to finish it … to put the keystone to a long career of zealous devotion to science, bequeathing to the naturalist a legacy of which his country may well be proud – to all men the precious example of an earnest life.[6]

The fate and financial failure of *A History of British Birds* has been described in Chapter 8. If only MacGillivray had had the resources and opportunity to publish his own splendid paintings together with his text, how different its reception might have been. Perhaps had he lived longer and taken time off from his professorial duties he might have achieved his frequently stated objective of publishing his paintings, which would surely have brought him fame if not fortune.

MacGillivray died in Aberdeen at the age of 56 in September 1852, seven months after the death of Marion and a year after the death of his friend Audubon. He was buried in the family plot in the New Calton Burial Ground in Edinburgh, where Marion and two of their children, who had died in infancy, had been interred. Because of the impoverished circumstances of the family no headstone marked the plot. In 1898 'A meeting of several gentlemen who specially cherished his memory was held in Edinburgh … with a view to promoting a suitable memorial of him'. A headstone was erected in 1900, decorated with a bronze plaque modelled from MacGillivray's painting of the golden eagle, while at the same time a memorial tablet was erected in Marischal College, Aberdeen.

The MacGillivrays had 12 children,[7] two of whom died in childhood. One of these, named William Craigie after his father's great friend, died aged eight of 'inflammation of the brain'. Of the remaining ten, at least five are known to have emigrated to Australia.

The eldest, John, who was born in 1821, followed in his father's footsteps, first studying medicine[8] and then changing course for natural history. His name has cropped up from time to time in the previous chapters.

In 1840 John visited the island of St Kilda, 60 miles off the west coast of Scotland. His account of the flora and fauna of the island reveals a remarkable depth of knowledge of natural history for a lad of 18, and his description of the lifestyle of the natives and of his journeys to and from the island make fascinating reading.[9] Even today the journey to St Kilda can be hazardous in a small boat. His outward journey was obscured by thick fog. Lacking a compass, they followed the flight paths of the seabirds returning to the island and made a successful landfall. The return journey in a rowing boat accompanied by two St Kildans was even more exciting. They set off towed by a larger vessel, but as night came on,

… the wind had been gradually increasing, and now blew a heavy gale, breaking the tops of the huge billows which rolled in majestically from the Atlantic. The small leaky boat … proving rather troublesome was abandoned by our friends in the other, who would tow us no longer. We were thus left to our fate, in a dark night with a storm blowing off land, to reach which we had a miserable boat half filled with water, and two oars, one of them broken. After rowing incessantly during the night, without making progress, and barely escaping from being drifted out to sea, at day break we found ourselves off the Sound of Harris, and after a long continued struggle, contrived to make the uninhabited island of Shellay ….

Their troubles were not over. After breakfasting on brackish water and raw limpets they made a further journey to the nearest inhabited isle of Pabbay, almost foundering on hidden rocks on the way.

In 1840 John published the results of his studies of birds' skulls, in which he eloquently debunked the theory of Vimont that the 'science' of phrenology could be applied to avian species.[10] Ever short of funds, he tried to sell the skulls used in this study to Professor Jameson.

Sept 22 1846

Sir,

Being about to leave this country for a period of four or five years, I am desirous of parting with my collection of skulls of Birds, the purpose for which I formed it in 1839-41 having been accomplished. It consists of 161 skulls of 132 American Species, 148 of 97 British Species, 10 of 8 Foreign and Domesticated species and 11 American specimens of which I have also British examples—in all 330 specimens of 237 species. They have been,

John MacGillivray, woodcut from *A Vertebrate Fauna of the Outer Hebrides*.

with scarcely an exception prepared by myself, and are in good condition, with names and [qualities?] the sex also being noted in very many instances. The American birds were brought over in visits by Mr Audubon, and I procured the heads after dissection by my father. Many of these are very rare as are also some of the British species. The price is £15 and my father suggested that perhaps you might purchase the lot for the University Museum. I shall also add about 20 skulls of British Quadrupeds. Should you wish to see the collection I can send it whenever you please, it being ready for being packed.

I have been promised the appointment of Government Naturalist to a vessel soon to be commissioned by Capt Owen Stanley (son of the Bishop of Norwich) to continue the Fly's survey. I expect to sail in about two months. We shall probably see most of the [Clinois?] neighbouring islands, also of the south coast of New Guinea, and the voyage promises to be much more interesting zoologically and botanically than the last.

I have the honor to be yours obediently John MacGillivray[11]

Laurence Jameson (who succeeded William MacGillivray as assistant to his uncle Robert Jameson) replied that the condition of the specimens was bad and the catalogue full of mistakes. 'My uncle regrets that his bad state of health and residing in country, prevents him from visiting the Museum to inspect your collection.'

John declared in a rather testy letter to Laurence, '… you will find that the Catalogue is correct …. I am confident there is not the slightest inaccuracy in this point', and in a further letter dated 17 September 1846 he wrote:

Dear Sir

By this time you have I dare say thoroughly inspected the collection of skulls and are able to form a correct estimate of its value. The agreement with Professor Jameson was that it would be purchased for £15 provided the specimens were in good condition and correctly labelled. The former of these conditions you do not find fulfilled – the latter putting aside the circumstance of 2 specimens occasionally being the same number – is I believe fulfilled …. you or any one acquainted with ornithology can readily make out which is which. Transmission from Edinburgh to this place and the two subsequent removals have caused the loss of many of the small bones …. I had neither time nor inclination to overhaul the temporary catalogue or relable the specimens having no further use for them as I used them in Phrenological purposes imperfect specimens were just as useful as perfect ones.

You are I suppose dissatisfied with the price. I shall leave that entirely to yourself and will accept whatever you think is a fair price. My desire to be independent of my father, and the great expense I shall shortly incur in fitting out for a 5 years voyage prevents me from gratuitously presenting the collection to a public Museum as I should have liked to do. My father does not appear to care for them else I would have given them to him.

At any rate I hope you will come to a speedy determination about the matter as I wish the subject to be closed having already more on my hands than I can well accomplish prior to my departure.

I remain Yours very truly
John MacGillivray

Laurence replied with an offer of £5 which John accepted, but that was not the end of the matter. A further letter from Laurence dated 7 November 1846 appeared:

Dear Sir

I shall feel much obliged if you will acknowledge by the enclosed receipt the five pounds you received for the Collection of Skulls. Being Public money it must be particularly accounted for otherwise I would not have troubled you.

My Uncle desires me to say that he expects your papers for the Journal soon.
Yours very truly
Laurence Jameson

The receipt was eventually delivered. The papers referred to were on the Aboriginal language of western Australia.

The museum of the Royal College of Surgeons in London must also have been interested in John's skulls, for a letter from John to Professor Owen[12] dated 15 October 1841, Old Aberdeen, reads:

Sir

In answer to your letter of the 13th I have to state that I do not think the collection of birds skulls alluded to would answer the purposes of the Museum under your charge. This I do from a consideration of your question regarding the presence of the lower jaw, hyoid bone and sclerotic plates of the eye, none but the first of which have been preserved. The skulls were collected for phrenological purposes … and the result was a complete conviction of the absurdity of this system so far as it related to birds ….

During my nigh intended voyage (as naturalist on HMS Fly) to Australia, Torres St, New Guinea etc. I shall be but too happy to attend to any recommendations from you to collect objects of Comparative Anatomy, and when I visit London shall take the liberty of speaking to you upon the subject …. I have no doubt but the Admiralty would sanction my presenting any such that I might collect to the Museum of the Royal College of Surgeons.

Between 1842 and 1856 John MacGillivray was engaged as naturalist on three voyages of exploration to the southern Pacific. First he was employed by the Earl of Derby[13] to collect specimens on the expedition of HMS *Fly* (1842-6). His second voyage was as government naturalist

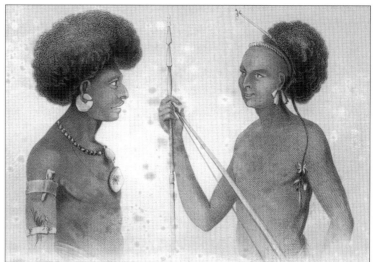

aboard HMS *Rattlesnake* (1846-50). Also on this voyage, as assistant surgeon, was Thomas Henry Huxley (1825-95), who later achieved fame as an eminent biologist, president of the Royal Society and defender of Darwin's theory of evolution. The two men at first became good friends and worked well together; however, towards the end of the voyage, for reasons unknown, their relationship became strained.

In 1852 John MacGillivray published his major work the *Narrative of the Voyage of H.M.S. Rattlesnake* to favourable reviews, even by the

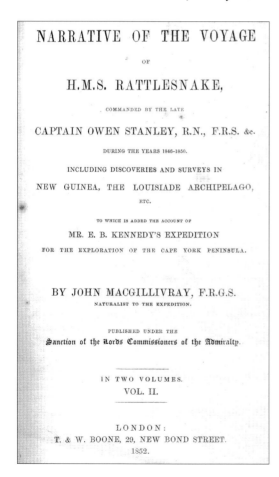

NARRATIVE OF THE VOYAGE

OF

H.M.S. RATTLESNAKE,

COMMANDED BY THE LATE

CAPTAIN OWEN STANLEY, R.N., F.R.S. &c.

DURING THE YEARS 1846-1850.

INCLUDING DISCOVERIES AND SURVEYS IN

NEW GUINEA, THE LOUISIADE ARCHIPELAGO,

ETC.

TO WHICH IS ADDED THE ACCOUNT OF

MR. E. B. KENNEDY'S EXPEDITION

FOR THE EXPLORATION OF THE CAPE YORK PENINSULA.

BY JOHN MACGILLIVRAY, F.R.G.S.

NATURALIST TO THE EXPEDITION.

PUBLISHED UNDER THE

Sanction of the Lords Commissioners of the Admiralty.

IN TWO VOLUMES.

VOL. II.

LONDON:

T. & W. BOONE, 29, NEW BOND STREET.

1852.

estranged Huxley whose drawings had been used by John MacGillivray to illustrate his book.

Huxley's diary of the voyage was published by his grandson Julian Huxley in 1935, from which the illustration of HMS *Rattlesnake* above is taken.

The third voyage was on HMS *Herald* (1852-6), which ended unhappily for John MacGillivray. He was dismissed from the ship in Sydney in 1855 as a result of a disagreement with the captain, Denham, resulting in a court of inquiry. What his offence was is unknown, but there are hints that alcoholism may have been a factor. A colleague on the *Herald*, the medical officer T M Tayner, named a newly discovered petrel *Pseudobulweria macgillivrayi* after John. This bird was not recorded subsequently until its recent rediscovery.[14] It must be unique for both father and son to be remembered in the names of birds.

During these voyages John MacGillivray obtained a vast number of specimens, some of which are still to be seen in the Royal Museum in Edinburgh and the Derby Collection in Liverpool Museum.[15] Others were sent to the British Museum.

While in Sydney in 1848 on the *Rattlesnake* expedition, John MacGillivray had married an Aberdeen lady, Williamina Paton Gray, who returned home with him on the ship. John treated her very shabbily, leaving her in Britain with her three infants in conditions of extreme poverty, dependent upon the charity of friends. In 1856 she set off with her children to join him in Sydney after his dismissal from the *Herald* but died of consumption during the voyage.

Above, left: HMS *Rattlesnake* from T H Huxley's *Diary of the Voyage of H.M.S. Rattlesnake* (*1935*).

Above, right: Natives of Redscar Bay, New Guinea by T H Huxley, from volume 2 of the *Narrative of the Voyage of H.M.S. Rattlesnake* by John MacGillivray.

Left: Opening page of the *Narrative of the Voyage of H.M.S. Rattlesnake*, volume II.

Three sisters of John also emigrated to Australia and may have cared for the children.

John MacGillivray spent the rest of his days in Australia writing a few scientific and newspaper articles and 'lecturing gratis for the purpose of enlightening and elevating the Working Classes'. He continued to travel around Australia collecting specimens which he sent to collectors in Britain including Edward Forbes, John Gould and Sir W J Hooker.

In 1862 he applied for the post of curator of the museum in Sydney and sought the support of Richard Owen, superintendent of the Natural History Museum of London, to whom he wrote from Sydney on 21 June 1862.

Sir

Believing that the appointment of a Curator to the Museum here will be referred to you in conjunction with Sir Charles Nicholson and Professor Huxley, I take the liberty of soliciting your good offices on my behalf, should you think me a suitable person for that appointment. I had been absent about 3 years in the SW Pacific and Torres Strait, when on reaching Rockhampton I heard of the vacant curatorship, and proceeded at once to Sidney, where, in pursuance of an advertisement inviting candidates to send in applications, I sent mine, a copy of which I enclose ....

Although I do not entertain more than the slightest prospect of success, yet I have thought it best to take the liberty of making this formal application to you ....

His application was not successful and he continued to support himself as a professional collector of natural history specimens for museums in Australia and Britain, and for the Melbourne Exhibition to which he sent 130 species of birds in 1866. John's activities during these last years of his life are recorded in a series of letters to E P Ramsay of Sydney University.[16] Together with James Fowler Wilcox, a friend and fellow naturalist from his *Rattlesnake* days, John spent two years in the Grafton area collecting and annotating the wildlife of the region and discovering a number of new species.

They travelled long distances, camping in the bush, often with aborigine guides, and shooting (as was the custom of the times) almost anything that moved. John was a first-class shot and had a three-barrelled gun which he used with great effect: 'I suddenly started 2 fine big ones [wallaroos] .... So I pitched into them, right and left, and if there had been a third I believe I would have killed it also with my third or rifle barrel, because snap shooting is that in which I feel most confidence in myself.'[17] But in the same letter he wrote: 'I don't care much about shooting *now*'.

If there had been a problem with alcohol it certainly was no longer evident, for his enthusiastic letters are full of achievement in the collecting, recording and preparation of specimens under very trying conditions – even water was in short supply. John's letters contain a number of references to his deteriorating health and to a chronic cough and breathing difficulties, although he did not allow this to restrict his collecting or his travels. He records riding 30 miles in three and a half hours to visit a friend's station for dinner. A letter from Grafton at this time (1 July 1866) contains the following curious passage: '... I leave this house never to return for I would not live a day longer than necessaray under the same roof as an inquisitive. prying and unscrupulous woman, the maker, begetter, and inventor I believe in many instances, of all of this scandal ....' What the alleged scandal was is not recorded.

In 1867 John returned to Sydney and obtained lodgings in an '*attic* retreat with its windows, which I can keep open at night and sleep without danger of aggravating my dyspnoea – I feel quietly inclined ....' He was engaged in preparing a paper on conchology with a Dr Cox and was planning a further collecting trip to Cape York which was to last a year or two. This trip was to be expensive, but he would manage with his own resources and what he could 'get from others, especially my brother [Paul]'. Alas, John did not live to fulfil this ambition. He died of his illness on 6 June 1867, aged 46.

John MacGillivray died in poverty leaving only a quantity of papers which his landlady, to whom he owed three weeks 'B and R', regarded as worthless. To Mrs Macdonald, the landlady of the Forth and Clyde Public House in Cumberland Street in Sydney where MacGillivray spent his evenings, he had given his copy of the *Voyage of the H.M.S. Rattlesnake* but had borrowed it back from her in order to lend it to his patron E P Ramsay. The *Sydney*

Morning Herald noted the death of the 'distinguished naturalist', which indeed he was, although his contributions did not do justice to his potential. His writings reveal that he had inherited from his father a wide general knowledge of natural history and a considerable literary ability. Perhaps the fact that, like his father, he did not concentrate in depth on any one field, accounts for the fact that he is less remembered than his younger brother Paul who became an authority in the narrow field of polyzoa.

One of John's sons, John William MacGillivray (born 1853), is known to have been given employment in the Australian Museum by his father's friend E P Ramsay.

Paul Howard MacGillivray (1834-95) studied medicine and also emigrated to Australia in 1855 where he practised surgery in Bendigo, Victoria, not far from his sisters who had settled in Ballarat. He was elected president of the Medical Society of Victoria. He also achieved distinction as a naturalist and collected many specimens which were given to the Museum of Natural History in Melbourne. In 1880 he was elected a Fellow of the Linnean Society of London in recognition of his contributions to natural history, an honour which was never granted to his father or his brother John. In 1892 Paul presented his father's paintings to the Natural History Museum in London. It is known, however, that some of William's paintings were dispersed after his death and their fate is unknown.[18]

The youngest son, William, is also recorded as having inherited 'a strong predilection for natural science and, had he lived, might, it was believed, have rivalled his two distinguished brothers'.[19] Alas, he died aged 17.

The love of natural history led both Audubon and MacGillivray along similar paths. Both men produced beautiful paintings of the birds of their own countries and wrote multi-volume ornithological texts which remain valuable sources of reference to this day. Both men inspired their sons to follow in their footsteps. Neither gained financial reward from his publications and both they and their families endured periods of great hardship although, this never destroyed their faith in their ultimate objectives.

The fact that Audubon, by dint of extraordinary effort and single-mindedness, managed to have his paintings published and so brought to the notice of a wide public, ensured recognition in his lifetime and ever-increasing fame to this day. It is interesting to speculate that if MacGillivray had been able to achieve his ambition of publishing his paintings, his name might be as well known today as that of Audubon. However, the writings of both men, although of considerable merit, lack the wide popular appeal of a beautiful illustration and there is little doubt that Audubon's name would have been largely forgotten today were it not for his paintings. I hope that the reproduction of some of MacGillivray's illustrations in this book may help to redress the balance and lead others to believe, as I do, that MacGillivray merits belated recognition as 'Scotland's Audubon'.

Notes

1   At that time there were two universities in Aberdeen: Marischal College, to which MacGillivray was now attached, and King's College, his old alma mater. There was much rivalry between the two. Both are now merged in the University of Aberdeen.
2   St Machar's Cathedral remains today much as it would have been in MacGillivray's time.
3   Harley, J *Leicester Literary and Philosophical Society*, pp. 152-6, 1855.
4   *Life of William MacGillivray*, pp. 100-1.
5   *The Natural History of Deeside and Braemar*, pp. 56-7.
6   Attributed to a Dr Fleming, cited in *Life of William MacGillivray*. Manuscript in Aberdeen City Library.
7   Manuscript of John MacGillivray in Mitchell Library, Sydney, lists the children of William and Marion MacGillivray:

   1   John 18.12.1821 – Aberdeen, Chapel Street.
        †6.6.1867 Sydney Australia of respiratory illness.
   2   Isabella 5.9.1823 – Edinburgh, Raeburn Place.
        †16.10.1865 Ballarat Victoria, Australia of consumption.
   3   Williamina Craigie 4.12.1825 – Edinburgh, 21 Cheyne Street.
   4   Marion MacCaskill 10.12.1826 – Edinburgh, 21 Cheyne Street.

    5 William Craigie 6.10.1828 – Edinburgh, 21 Cheyne Street.
          †1836 of inflammation of the brain. New Calton Burial Ground.
    6 Anne 8.5.1830 – Edinburgh, 21 Warriston Crescent.
          †1831.
    7 Anne Dorothea 1.10.1832 – Edinburgh, Graham Street.
    8 Paul Howard 3.5.1834 – Edinburgh, 11 Gilmore Place.
          †1895 Australia.
    9 Audubon Felix 8.7.1836 – Edinburgh, 11 Gilmore Place.
  10 Caroline Mary 12.5.38 – Edinburgh, 1 Wharton Place.
          †8.2.1865 Ballarat, Consumption.
  11 Margaret Christina 6.3.1840 – Edinburgh, 1 Wharton Place.
  12 William Norman 19.1.1842 – Old Aberdeen, Chanonry.
          †1859 Consumption.

    Marion MacCaskill, who was twice married, emigrated to Australia to live in Ballarat where her sisters Isabella and Caroline also lived. Anne Dorothea married the Rev. Patrick Beaton, chaplain to the forces, and lived in Mauritius and later in Paris. She died in 1910.

8   The minute book of the council of the Royal College of Surgeons of Edinburgh records on 12 November 1836 an application from Dr Thomas Johnston Aitken for leave to enter into indentures with Mr John MacGillivray for five years. This may have been William's son, although he would have been only 15 years old at the time. Apprenticeship to an established surgeon was the means of acquiring surgical training at that time.

9   *Edinburgh New Philosophical Journal* (1842), 32: 47-70.

10   *The Edinburgh Academic Annual* (1840).

11   This letter and the subsequent correspondence is filed with the Edinburgh University Museum report books, held in the library of the Royal Scottish Museum of Edinburgh.

12   Sir Richard Owen (1804-92) matriculated at Edinburgh University in 1824 and was one of Jameson's pupils. He completed his medical training in London. Owen became conservator of the Hunterian Museum of the Royal College of Surgeons of London, and in 1856 superintendent of natural history at the British Museum. In 1881 he opened the present Natural History Museum in South Kensington, for the design and planning of which he was largely responsible.

13   Lord Edward Smith Stanley (1775-1851) became the thirteenth Earl of Derby in 1834 and created at his estate Knowsley Park an extensive menagerie, a natural history museum and library. He employed a number of collectors, including John MacGillivray, to provide him with specimens, and the leading bird and animal painters of the day, including Edward Lear, Henry Constantine Richter, Josef Wolf and John Gould, recorded his collection. At his death the menagerie was dispersed but the museum collection was given to Liverpool to found the Liverpool Museum. His priceless collection of illustrated natural history books remains in Knowsley Hall. Several of the mammalian specimens in the Liverpool Museum have been identified as being collected by John MacGillivray for the Knowsley Museum.

14   Watling, D: *Birds of Fiji, Tonga and Samoa* (Wellington, New Zealand, 1982) (Dougal MacNeill, personal communication). John MacGillivray also had a molluscan genus named after him.

15   Largen, M J and Fisher, C T: *Archives of Natural History* (1986), 13: 225-72.

16   Iredale, T: 'The last letters of John MacGillivray', in *Australian Zoologist* (1937), 9: 40-63.

17   Ibid, p. 43.

18   Sim, G: *Life of William MacGillivray*, p. 114.

19   *Memorial Tribute to William MacGillivray*, p. 51.

BIOGRAPHICAL PROFILES

Mᴀɴʏ of the individuals who played a part in the lives of Audubon and MacGillivray have been mentioned briefly in earlier chapters. Some, such as Sir Walter Scott, Sir Henry Raeburn and Charles Darwin, are so familiar as to need no further mention, but others who may be less well known are also personalities of considerable interest and merit fuller treatment. Brief biographies of a selection of these are given in this chapter.

Reverend John Bachman (1790-1874) is a central figure in this book and was probably the only person who knew both Alexander Wilson and Audubon well. As a boy he became keenly interested in natural history and accompanied Wilson on his excursions and provided him with some of his specimens. On Wilson's instigation he followed him as teacher at Elwood School in Milestown, Pennsylvania, at the age of 15, in order to be able to support himself in his theological studies. While a student he developed the first symptoms of the tuberculosis that was to be a recurring disorder throughout his long life. Through Wilson he met Baron Alexander von Humboldt, the leading German scientist of his day, who was visiting America. In 1815 he was appointed pastor at St John's Lutheran Church in Charleston, South Carolina, which he served faithfully for 55 years. For a period of three years he combined his ministry with the chair of natural history at Charleston College. In 1816 he married Harriet Martin by whom he had 14 children, five dying in infancy. In 1831 he met Audubon in Charleston and the two men became close friends and collaborators in the writing of *The Quadrupeds of North America*. The marriage of the two Audubon sons with two Bachman daughters is noted in Chapter 15. Both young wives died soon after of tuberculosis. Harriet's sister Maria, having been taught to paint by Audubon, assisted him by painting the backgrounds of a number of his paintings. Following the death of Harriet in 1846, Bachman married Maria who acted as his amanuensis as his eyesight failed and thus made a major contribution to the production of *Quadrupeds*. To convalesce from one of his recurrent bouts of illness, Bachman made a trip to Europe in 1837 at the suggestion of Audubon. During this trip he visited Audubon in Edinburgh and renewed his acquaintance with von Humboldt in Berlin. Unfortunately the journal of his travels was destroyed in a fire. Audubon named two birds after his friend: the black oystercatcher (*Haematopus bachmani*) and the Bachman's warbler (*Vermivora bachmanii*), which is now probably extinct.

John Bartram (1699-1777) was the father of William. He was a distinguished botanist, regarded as a pioneer of modern science by no less a person then Linnaeus. King George III appointed him as his official American Botanist at a salary of £50 a year. He was one of the founder members, together with Benjamin Franklin, of the American Philosophical Society which was launched in 1743. He sent the seeds of American plants to many correspondents in Europe and was said to have 'enriched the eastern world with the vegetables of the West'. He established on the banks of the Schuylkill River a botanical garden of note and it was here that his son William offered Alexander Wilson friendship and hospitality.

William Bartram (1739-1823) inherited his father John's interest in natural history and developed a considerable skill in painting plants and animals. Many of his illustrations are now in the Natural History Museum in London and some have been published. He travelled extensively in the south-eastern states and wrote *Travels* *through the North and South Carolina, Georgia, East and West Florida, the Cherokee Country …* which attracted great popular interest. A copy of this book came into the hands of Samuel Taylor Coleridge who considered it 'a work of high merit', and both he and his friend William Wordsworth adopted many of the images from this book in their own works. Coleridge's 'Ancient Mariner' and 'Kubla Khan' and Wordsworth's ballad 'Ruth' and other poems contain ideas and passages from Bartram's work. George Ord, the scourge of Audubon, thought highly of Bartram: 'He was a source of reference to many naturalists of his day, and there was scarcely an American or Foreign writer who attempted the natural history of this country but applied to him for information on their relative treatises ….' The Bartram home and a fragment of their garden still survive within the city of Philadelphia.

Sir Charles Bell (1774-1842) was one of four brothers who distinguished themselves in medicine and law. He studied medicine at Edinburgh University, during which time he and Robert Jameson became good friends. In 1804 he moved to London where he practised surgery and taught anatomy. Bell was an excellent artist and published *On the Anatomy of Expression* – a book intended as a guide for artists. His paintings of wounded soldiers from the Napoleonic Wars can be seen in the Royal College of Surgeons of Edinburgh. Bell was appointed professor of anatomy and surgery at the Royal College of Surgeons of England and did research of outstanding importance and originality on the functioning of the peripheral nerves – a contribution which has been ranked with the work of William Harvey on the circulation. In 1835 he returned to Edinburgh to occupy the chair of surgery.

Thomas Bewick (1753-1828) was a farmer's son who from his earliest days developed an interest in art and nature. He was apprenticed to Ralph Bielby, an engraver in Newcastle, and acquired skills in engraving on copper and wood. He is remembered chiefly for his mastery of wood engraving, then a dying art which he revived. He illustrated many books and published two – *The General History of Quadrupeds* and the *History of British Birds* – that achieved wide popularity. An agreeable feature of these books is the addition of vignettes of country scenes,

which display a keen sense of humour and give an interesting view of contemporary customs. After his death the Bewick's swan (*Cygnus bewickii*) was so named in his memory.

Charles Lucien Bonaparte (1803-57) was the Prince of Musignano, and son of Napoleon's brother Lucien. He travelled to America at the age of 20 to further his interest in ornithology and remained there for four years, during which he updated Alexander Wilson's *American Ornithology* with the approval and assistance of Wilson's executor, George Ord. Bonaparte identified the storm petrel and named it in honour of Wilson (*Procellaria wilsonii*). He was one of the few people in Philadelphia at that time who befriended Audubon and admired his paintings. He introduced Audubon to the Academy of Natural Sciences where his paintings were condemned by Ord and others. Bonaparte was responsible for naming and describing about 20 species of birds found in eastern America. On his return to Europe he settled in Rome where he continued his ornithological studies. Later he became involved in the politics of the country and had to flee from Italy to the Netherlands where he continued his work on ornithological classification. He spent his last years in Paris, having reconciled his political differences with his family.

Sir David Brewster (1781-1868) was an eminent optical physicist who did much original work on the polarisation of light. He was the inventor of the kaleidoscope and developed refracting lenses. Brewster was one of the founders of the British Association. He was a co-editor of the *Edinburgh Philosophical Journal* together with Robert Jameson from 1819-24, but following a disagreement with Jameson he established the rival *Edinburgh Journal of Science*. He was a leading contributor to the seventh and eighth editions of the *Encyclopaedia Britannica*, and became principal successively of St Andrews and Edinburgh universities. Audubon wrote of Brewster: 'He is a great optician, and advises me to get a camera-lucida, so as to take the outline of my birds more rapidly and correctly. Such an instrument would be useful in saving time, and a great relief in the hot weather.'

Sir Thomas MacDougall Brisbane (1773-1860) was born in the Scottish town of Largs. He studied mathematics and astronomy at Edinburgh University and then entered the army. He took part in the Flanders campaign of 1793 and later fought in the Peninsular War of 1812, suffering wounds in both. He was appointed governor of New South Wales in 1821 and sent many natural history specimens back to Jameson's museum from that country. He encouraged immigration and introduced grapes, sugar cane and tobacco, but the economy of the country was poorly managed and his appointment was terminated after four years. He established an observatory at his home in Scotland and made a number of original astronomic discoveries. He succeeded Sir Walter Scott as president of the Royal Society of Edinburgh and held that office for 28 years.

John George Children (1777-1852) befriended Audubon during his first visit to London in 1827. He was secretary of the Royal Society and had been appointed keeper of the zoology department of the British Museum in 1822, thanks largely to the patronage of Sir Humphrey Davy. Children's interests were chiefly geological and William Swainson, the unsuccessful candidate, was justifiably very upset, for his wider natural history interests would appear to have made him better qualified. Others thought so to, for Thomas Stewart Traill wrote an anonymous article in the *Edinburgh Review* in which he strongly criticised the appointment of an 'unqualified person' to run the natural history department. Children introduced Audubon to the Linnean Society, at which he exhibited his paintings to general acclaim. Children was instrumental in making the contacts which resulted in King George IV becoming a subscriber to *The Birds of America*. He acted as Audubon's agent and liaison with Havell when Audubon returned to America in 1829 and in 1831. Audubon felt that his election to the Royal Society of London was largely due to Children. Typically, Audubon named a bird the Children's warbler in honour of his friend, but this was later recognised to be an immature yellow (Rathbone's) warbler.

Sir Robert Christison (1797-1882) became professor of medical jurisprudence in Edinburgh in 1822 and acquired a European reputation as a medical expert in criminal trials for poisoning.

He was the forensic expert for the Crown in the trial of Burke and Hare and did not share Lord Cockburn's views regarding Knox's innocence: 'My own opinion at the time was that Dr Knox … had rather wilfully shut his eyes to incidents which ought to have excited the grave suspicions of a man of his intelligence.'

In 1832 Christison was appointed professor of materia medica, and he held that post for 45 years. 'When lecturing on curare … he used to come to the University … before the class met, to practise with the blowpipe, so that … he might demonstrate how the natives made use of it. A target having been placed he … took aim and in a moment it was quivering in the bull's eye, and he returned to his desk amidst the rapturous applause of his class.' Christison became president of the Royal College of Physicians and of the Royal Society of Edinburgh.

Henry Cockburn (1779-1854), Lord Cockburn, was one of Edinburgh's leading lawyers at the time of Audubon's visits. Although neither mentions the other in his writings, there can be no doubt that their paths must have crossed. Audubon attended many social occasions at which Lord Cockburn would have been present and they had many acquaintances in common. He was born into a wealthy family, closely related to Henry Dundas, Viscount Melville, the Lord President (the most senior judge) in Scotland. He practised as a successful advocate for many years. Cockburn was involved in the trial of Burke when he successfully defended Helen MacDougal who had been charged as Burke's accomplice. He stoutly defended the reputation of Robert Knox as being 'spotlessly correct' over the matter of Burke and Hare. A whig, Cockburn was appointed Solicitor-General for Scotland in 1830, and was responsible for drawing up the first Reform Bill for Scotland. In 1834 he was raised to the Bench and continued to serve as a judge until his death at the age of 74. Cockburn's *Memorials of His Time* gives an interesting account of the people and politics of Scotland. His town residence at 14 Charlotte Square was at the other end of George Street from Audubon's lodgings with Mrs Dickie. Cockburn commented on his pleasure at the call of the corncrake which could be heard from Charlotte Square at that time. Alas, one now has to go to the remote fringes of Scotland to hear its call.

George Combe (1788-1858) was one of a family of 17 children. He became a successful lawyer. In 1816 he met Spurzheim, the founder of the concept of phrenology, and was so influenced by him that he became the leading protagonist of this new 'science' and established the Phrenology Society and its *Journal*. His books *A System of Phrenology* and *Constitution of Man* were enormously successful and influential. He married a daughter of the actress Sarah Siddons who brought a considerable dowry. He travelled extensively in America and Europe to spread his beliefs, and stoutly defended himself and phrenology against powerful criticism from many quarters.

Baron Georges Cuvier (1769-1832) was France's most distinguished natural historian, who had held high office both under Napeoleon and during the subsequent Bourbon regime. Among his many influential publications was the four-volume *Règne animal distribué d'apres son organisation*, which MacGillivray was translating into English at the time of Audubon's meeting with Cuvier.

Andrew Duncan Sr (1744-1828) was professor of the Institutes of Medicine. He was president of the Royal College of Physicians for two terms and was physician to His Majesty the King in Scotland. Duncan founded the Richmond Street Dispensary for the poor and opened the first lunatic asylum in Edinburgh in 1807 (now the Andrew Duncan Clinic), having been affected by the death of the poet Fergusson in appalling conditions in a madhouse. For these two endeavours he was awarded the freedom of the city of Edinburgh. He also founded many medical clubs and societies including the Medico-Chirurgical, the Harveian, the Aesculapian and the Royal Caledonian Horticultural societies, all of which survive to this day. He was still alive at the time of Audubon's visit and in his 80s bathed regularly in the Firth of Forth and climbed Arthur's Seat each May morning. On reaching the summit on 1 May 1826, at the age of 82, he read a poem addressed to the Duke of Gordon, then the oldest living peer:

> Once more, good Duke, my duty to fulfil,
> I've reached the summit of this lofty hill,
> To thank my God for all his blessings given,
> And by my prayers, to aid my way to heaven.

> Long may your Grace enjoy the same delight,
> Till to a better world we take our flight.

To which the duke replied:

> I'm eighty-two as well as you,
> And sound in lith and limb;
> But deil a bit, I am not fit,
> Up Arthur's Seat to climb.

> In such a fete I'll not compete –
> I yield in ambulation;
> But mount us baith on Highland shelts,
> Try first who gains the station.

> If such a race should e'er take place,
> None like it in the nation;
> Nor Sands of Leith, nor Ascot Heath,
> Could show more population.

Clearly a couple of spirited old men!

Andrew Duncan Jr (1773-1832) became professor of medical jurisprudence at Edinburgh University. He founded the *Annals of Medicine* with his father and was its first editor. It became the *Edinburgh Medical and Surgical Journal* in 1805, of which he was also editor. He isolated the drug cinchonin from Peruvian bark. (Cinchonin was used for the treatment of febrile disorders including malaria.)

Edward Forbes (1815-54) was born and spent his childhood in the Isle of Man, where he developed his interest in natural history. He came to Edinburgh in 1831 to study medicine and was much influenced by professors Jameson and Graham and by Robert Knox. During this period he founded the Maga Club and its magazine *The University Maga*, which was illustrated with his own cartoons of his teachers. After a few years Forbes abandoned his medical studies in order to pursue his vocation as a naturalist, just as his mentor Jameson had done before him. His interests were wide and he published more than 200 papers, his main contributions being on marine biology. He identified the varying forms of life which characterised different ocean depths and gave these zones the names by which they are still known. Having, to his surprise, failed to obtain the post of professor of natural history in Aberdeen to which MacGillivray succeeded, Forbes was appointed to the chair of botany at King's College in London and curator of the museum of the Geological Society. He later became palaeontologist to the Geological Survey. His ambition, however, had always been to fill the chair of natural history in Edinburgh, and following Jameson's death in 1854 his ambition was realised. Alas, he died within six months of his appointment at the age of 39. In contrast to Jameson, Forbes was an extrovert genial man with a wide range of interests, an open mind and a sense of humour. T H Huxley, whom Forbes had helped to become established as a naturalist, wrote of him that he 'has more claims to the title of the Philosophical Naturalist than any man I know of in England. A man of letters and an artist … he has sympathies for all, and an earnest truth-seeking, thoroughly genial disposition which wins for him your affection as well as your respect.' It is perhaps a measure of the two men that Jameson, despite his long period of power and influence, has attracted no biographer, while Forbes' short life is remembered by several biographies, the most complete being the *Memoir of Edward Forbes* (1861) written by two contemporaries, George Wilson and Archibald Geikie. His premature death denied Edinburgh University the opportunity of becoming a leading centre of marine biology.

John Goodsir (1814-67) was a pupil of Robert Knox and became an outstanding anatomist. He was a good friend of Edward Forbes and shared lodgings with him in 21 Lothian Street. He succeeded William MacGillivray as conservator of the museum of the College of Surgeons in 1841, and then succeeded Alexander Monro Tertius as professor of anatomy at Edinburgh University in 1846. He was an active and contributory member of the Wernerian Society and after Jameson's death supervised the winding up of the society. While conservator of the museum he studied the structure of bone, using the compound achromatic microscope recently developed by Lord Lister's father, and was the first to recognise that bone was a living tissue, formed and resorbed by cells rather than by the blood vessels as John Hunter had postulated.

John Gould (1804-81) shared Audubon's obsession with ornithology. Like Audubon, he had limited education and no artistic training. At the age of 14 he followed his father's occupation as a gardener but spent his spare time acquiring a skill at taxidermy, which led to his appointment in 1827 as 'Curator and Preserver' to the museum of the recently founded Zoological Society of London. It was a period of intense interest in natural history. As the Empire expanded, travellers were fascinated by the new forms of animal and plant life which they encountered, and avidly collected specimens which were sent back to Britain. In this post Gould had the opportunity of examining closely these exotic bird and animal specimens and was astute enough to recognise their potential as a source of illustrations for books on natural history. His museum was one of the few which came in for favourable comment by William MacGillivray during his tour of British museums in 1833. Gould's first work was *A Century of Birds hitherto unfigured from the Himalaya Mountains*, published between 1830 and 1833, and the success of this encouraged him to produce a succession of popular books on birds and animals for the remainder of his long life. Unlike Audubon his publications brought him considerable wealth. His extensive collection of birds and eggs was bought by the Natural History Museum in London after his death. Many of the specimens in his collection had been supplied by John MacGillivray, with whom he had corresponded regularly.

Robert Graham (1786-1845) qualified in medicine and became professor of botany first at Glasgow University and then in Edinburgh. He was physician to the Royal Infirmary of Edinburgh and conservator of the Botanical Garden. He was responsible for organising the transfer of the Royal Botanical Garden from its old location on Leith Walk to its present site at Inverleith.

Sir James Hall (1761-1832) studied geology and chemistry and became a good friend of and collaborator with James Hutton, whose theories he endorsed and confirmed by laboratory experimentation. He became president of the Royal Society of Edinburgh and from this position of influence was instrumental in tilting the Huttonian/Wernerian debate in favour of Hutton.

He was a founder member of the Caledonian Horticultural Society and its first vice-president. Sir James Hall, who was deaf, was noted for wearing 'Wellington ears', which consisted of cups made out of papier maché that were tied over the ears with ribbons, the Duke of Wellington having resorted to a similar device. The Hall family offered Audubon friendship and support during his stay in Edinburgh.

Captain Basil Hall (1788-1844), the son of Sir James, assisted his father in his geological studies. He entered the navy at the age of 14 and rose to the rank of captain. His account of his travels, *Fragments of Voyages and Travels* (1831), was very popular and established his reputation as an author. He became a close friend of Sir Walter Scott and through his naval connections was able to arrange for Scott to convalesce in the Mediterranean. Scott noted that he 'takes charge of everyone's business without neglecting his own, and has done a great deal for me in this matter'. Captain Hall was a pivotal figure in Edinburgh society and opened many doors for Audubon. His wife was the daughter of Sir John Hunter, consul general of Spain. Lady Hunter also gave Audubon hospitality at her home in Edinburgh. 'Hall's Ledge' on Britain's remotest island of Rockall commemorates the first landing on that island by Basil Hall when serving as a lieutenant on HMS *Endymion* in 1811.

James Hutton (1726-97) was a polymath and one of the distinguished band of intellectuals who became recognised as leaders of the Scottish Enlightenment. Hutton qualified in medicine but never practised. He developed a process for the manufacture of sal ammoniac, which gave him financial independence and enabled him to pursue his other interests, which included geology and the improvement of farming practices. He was one of the leading figures in the development of the Forth and Clyde Canal, serving on its executive committee for seven years. Hutton's *Theory of the Earth* and other contributions have led him to be regarded as the father of the science of geology. His studies anticipated Darwin's theories of variation and natural selection. Together with his close friends Joseph Black and Adam Smith, he founded the Oyster Club which became a popular forum for the leading members of the Enlightenment. He was an active member of the

Royal Society of Edinburgh, established in 1783. On Hutton's death, his family, advised by his friend Joseph Black, donated his valuable collection of geological specimens to the Royal Society of Edinburgh. The society had no option but to transfer it, reluctantly, at a later date, to the keeping of the University Museum, having been specifically precluded by its charter from establishing a museum. Thus it came under the custody of Jameson, who disagreed with Hutton's theories. Pleading shortage of space, Jameson relegated Hutton's collection to a storeroom to which he denied access even to members of the Royal Society. When in 1827 a Royal Commission asked David Brewster, then secretary of the Royal Society, 'Do you know anything of Dr Hutton's collection?', he replied laconically, 'I do. I believe that I am one of the curators of that collection, but I have never had any access to it.' The collection eventually was lost without trace.

Sir William Jardine (1800-74) was born in Edinburgh and studied medicine but never practised. He married Jean Home Lizars, the sister of William Home Lizars, Audubon's first engraver. He was an enthusiastic naturalist and author. At his home, Jardine Hall in Applegirth, Dumfriesshire, he created a museum which contained 6000 specimens of birds, some of which were acquired by the National Museums in Edinburgh after his death. He admired Alexander Wilson and edited an edition of Wilson's *American Ornithology* in which he wrote a biography of the author. Jardine had many contacts with Audubon, from whom he received some instruction in painting. Audubon was invited to Jardine Hall but never managed to fit in a visit. Jardine published a book on *British Salmonidae* illustrated by himself, and together with his brother-in-law Lizars edited the very popular 40-volume *Naturalist's Library* which was published to make the 'Great Works of Creation available to the masses at a reasonable price'. Other publications included *Illustrations of Ornithology* in conjunction with his friend P J Selby. He was vice-president of the Wernerian Society and a Fellow of the Royal Societies of Edinburgh and London.

Francis Jeffrey (1773-1850) studied law and was called to the Bar in 1794. Together with Sydney Smith he founded the *Edinburgh Review* in 1802 and was its editor for 26 years. The *Edinburgh*

Review became enormously influential as the organ of liberalism throughout Britain and the dominions. Cockburn said that it 'elevated the public and literary position of Edinburgh to an extent which no one not living intelligently then can be made to comprehend'. Jeffrey's first wife having died, he married an American, Charlotte Wilkes, in 1813. When the whigs came into power in 1830, Jeffrey was made Lord Advocate while his friend Henry Cockburn became Solicitor-General. In 1834 he was promoted to the Bench and served as a judge until his death at the age of 77. Lord Cockburn, his biographer, wrote: '… head and heart included, his was the finest nature I have ever known. In him intuitive quickness of intellect was combined with almost unerring soundness, and the highest condition of reasoning powers with the richest embellishments of fancy …. His love lapped others so naturally in its folds that his mind was probably never chilled by harsh emotion, even towards those he was trying to overpower.' Audubon, in his brief meeting with Jeffrey, did not share this opinion – Jeffrey was one of the few people whom he immediately disliked.

Joseph Bartholomew Kidd (1808-89) had an undistinguished career as an artist. He was a pupil of the Rev. John Thomson of Duddingston, a notable landscape painter who was one of the early subscribers to *The Birds of America*. Kidd was a founder associate of the Scottish Academy in 1829 (later the Royal Scottish Academy) and exhibited landscape paintings regularly at its annual exhibitions until 1836, when he joined his brother in Jamaica. There he continued to paint and published a volume of his Jamaican illustrations. In 1843 he moved to London to become a drawing master at Greenwich. He painted a portrait of Queen Victoria for the Royal Hospital School in Greenwich. Kidd died aged 81. He is chiefly remembered for his association with Audubon.

Robert Knox (1793-1862) was a bright student and dux of the High School of Edinburgh. He enrolled as a medical student at Edinburgh University in 1810, although had to resit his anatomy examination! He attended the wounded in Brussels after the Battle of Waterloo and later served in South Africa during the Kaffir Wars. In 1820 he returned to Edinburgh and became a very popular teacher of anatomy in a private extra-mural school. Students flocked to his classes (504 in 1828) in preference to the dull teaching of the university professor Monro Tertius. Bodies for dissection were hard to obtain, leading to his unfortunate and unwitting(?) involvement with Burke and Hare (see comments by Cockburn and Christison, above). The public were not convinced of his innocence and a popular ballad of the time went:

> Doun the close and up the Stair
> But and ben wi Burke and Hare
> Burke's the butcher, Hare's the thief
> Knox the man that buys the beef.

Knox had a keen interest in comparative anatomy and contributed many papers to the Wernerian Society and the Royal Society of Edinburgh, to both of which he had been elected. He served as conservator of the museum of the Royal College of Surgeons of Edinburgh from 1826 until 1831 when he was succeeded by William MacGillivray. During the 1830s his popularity as a lecturer declined and his applications for several university posts were unsuccessful. His fellowship of the Royal Society of Edinburgh was cancelled and he fell into debt. Knox decided to leave Edinburgh to seek his fortune elsewhere, first in Glasgow and then in London where he achieved a modest living from lecturing and an appointment as pathological anatomist at the Brompton Cancer Hospital.

Alexander Lawson (1772-1846), a Scotsman, learned his craft as an engraver in Britain before emigrating to America and settling in Philadelphia, which was then the centre of printing and publishing in the United States. There he established a family business and became an influential member of society, noted for his free thinking. Lawson engraved the paintings of Alexander Wilson and became a close friend. The two maintained a regular correspondence. Lawson gave Wilson advice on painting and added his own 'improvements' to the final product. After Wilson's death he joined with Ord in the furtherance of Wilson's memory and influence, and in this role was largely responsible for preventing the publication of Audubon's paintings in America. Audubon in his journal referred to him as the 'Philadelphia brute'.

Edward Lear (1812-88), chiefly remembered for his books of nonsense verse, was an outstanding bird painter. He was the youngest of 21 children of a wealthy London stockbroker, who later became bankrupt leaving the family in poverty. He was a self-taught painter who, at the age of 18, embarked on the ambitious *Illustrations of the family of Psittacidae or Parrots* for which he lithographed his own illustrations. He subsequently contributed extensively to the books published by John Gould and was engaged by Lord Stanley to paint the animals and birds of his menagerie at Knowsley Hall. Lear also painted the illustrations for Selby's contributions on pigeons and parrots for Jardine's *Naturalist's Library*. Although his work was viewed unfavourably by Audubon, many of his paintings bear close comparison with those of Audubon. Lear's eyesight deteriorated and by the age of 25 he had to abandon bird illustration and spent the remainder of his life restlessly travelling in Mediterranean countries where he made a living from landscape painting and writing. He described himself in a poem written shortly before his death, part of which reads:

How pleasant to know Mr Lear,
    Who has written such volumes of stuff;
Some think him ill-tempered and queer,
    But a few think him pleasant enough.

His mind is concrete and fastidious,
    His nose is remarkably big;
His visage is more or less hideous,
    His beard it resembles a wig.

William Home Lizars (1788-1859) was the son of an engraver. He studied art and two of his paintings, 'Scotch Wedding' and 'Reading of the Will', were exhibited at the Royal Academy in London and are now in the National Gallery of Scotland. (His fellow student David Wilkie was to paint these same subjects a few years later.) He was one of the first members of the (Royal) Scottish Academy. The early death of his father meant that Lizars had to give up his painting in order to support the large family by continuing the engraving business, at which he showed much greater talent than his father. His initial endorsement of Audubon's paintings and the first engravings of his work was undoubtedly one of the main reasons for Audubon choosing

Edinburgh as his base in Britain. Many of Lizars' engravings have been used to illustrate this volume, including scenes of Edinburgh from Ewbank's *Picturesque Views of Edinburgh*, and natural history subjects from the works of Audubon, Selby and the *Naturalist's Library*. This last production, which was the brainchild of Lizars, was published together with his brother-in-law Sir William Jardine and was financially very successful. Audubon, particularly in his early days in Edinburgh, was a frequent guest at the Lizars' home at 3 St James Square, adjacent to his lodgings in 2 George Street. Both of these properties have since been replaced by modern buildings.

Alexander Monro Tertius (1773-1859) was the last in a dynasty of professors of anatomy at Edinburgh University which occupied the chair for 126 years. Nepotism was commonplace in the university at that time. The first two Monros were men of distinction, but Tertius, who held the chair for 48 years, was notoriously idle and lectured from his grandfather's notes. He was noted for his massive build and slovenly manners: '... his magnitude confers a sort of corporeal dignity on sloth.' Edward Forbes described him as being 'parsimonious in knowledge as well as cash, though abounding in both', and Charles Darwin said 'he made his lectures on human anatomy as dull as he was himself'. Tertius did very little practical dissecting but is remembered for a public dissection of the body of Burke, the resurrectionist, before a large and clamorous crowd. Although his chair was combined with the professorship of surgery, he never operated. Despite the poor conduct of his professorial duties he was popular with the students, 'to whom he is invariably affable and communicative and lenient ... as an examiner'. He was elected a Fellow of the Royal Society of Edinburgh and of the Royal College of Physicians of Edinburgh. Audubon was flattered to be invited to dinner at the Monro house. John Goodsir succeeded Monro Tertius as professor of anatomy.

George Ord (1781-1863) was born into a wealthy family who owned a ship chandler and rope-making business. Although he became head of the firm he appears to have spent his life as a sportsman and hunter. Embittered by the death of his child and the mental illness of his wife, he became a disputative individual who made few friends. Nevertheless he was an influential figure and was one of the founding members of the Academy of Natural Sciences in Philadelphia. Largely as a result of his work with Alexander Wilson, he was elected to the Philosophical Society of which he became secretary and later president. Little is known about him apart from his association with Wilson and his opposition to Audubon.

William Henry Playfair (1789-1857), the son of an architect, was born in London. At the age of five he was brought to Edinburgh to live with his uncle John Playfair, the eminent mathematician and geologist who championed Hutton's theory of the origin of the Earth. Young William Playfair followed his father as an architect and was responsible for the design of many of Edinburgh's principle buildings including the New Quadrangle of Edinburgh University, the Royal College of Surgeons of Edinburgh, the Royal Institution (later the Royal Scottish Academy and now to become part of the National Gallery of Scotland, which he also designed). His characteristic classical style was largely responsible for giving Edinburgh its soubriquet – 'Modern Athens'. Audubon was familiar with many of Playfair's buildings, which remain largely unchanged to this day.

William Rathbone (1787-1868) was born in Liverpool, the son of a wealthy merchant of the same name. He became a prominent educationalist and philanthropist; his 'munificence was as delicate as widely spread'. Rathbone was a patron of the arts, hence his admiration of Audubon. He married Elizabeth, the eldest daughter of Samuel Greg of Quarry Bank near Manchester to whom Audubon was introduced by Rathbone. Elizabeth's brother William Rathbone Greg befriended Audubon in Edinburgh. The Rathbone family became generous benefactors of Liverpool University.

Benjamin Rush (1745-1813), an American, came to Edinburgh to study medicine, graduating MD in 1763. While in Edinburgh he was called upon by his alma mater, Princeton College in New Jersey, to persuade John Witherspoon to come to America as president of the college. Rush became a prominent physician in Philadelphia and helped to develop the medical school of that city as the leading medical school of its day in America. He was a tireless reformer and, like Witherspoon, was a signatory of the Declaration of Independence. He is regarded as the father of American psychiatry.

William Scoresby (1789-1857) was the son of a whaler based in Whitby. He made his first voyage to Greenland with his father at the age of ten, and aged 17 he was made first mate. Such was his proficiency that at the age of 22 he was given command of his own ship. The whaling voyages were conducted in the summer months in Arctic waters, and the Scoresbys, father and son, were among the most successful at their trade. During the winters young Scoresby received such education as was available in Whitby, but at the age of 17 he decided to attend Edinburgh University where he lodged with a Mrs Schearer. 'Excepting a little deficiency in *cleanliness*, an article for which lodging-houses in Edinburgh are not famous, and abating a small want of *conscientiousness* in my hostess regarding her right to my stores, I found my quarters … exceedingly comfortable.' There he came under the influence of Professor Jameson, who was fascinated by this young student who had already experienced so much polar travel. The two men became firm friends and Jameson encouraged Scoresby in his scientific studies, which he combined with his whaling expeditions. In 1806 the Scoresbys, father and son, reached the most northerly point then achieved by boat – 81° 31'n. In 1815 he speculated on the possibility of man reaching the North Pole, concluding that it was feasible, and detailed with remarkable prescience the requirements and difficulties of such an expedition. (This achievement was first accomplished nearly a century later by the American Robert E Peary in 1910.) Scoresby's stature as a scientist increased and led to his election to the Royal Societies of Edinburgh and London, and earned him the respect and friendship of such eminent men of science as Sir Joseph Banks, Sir Humphrey Davy, André-Marie Ampère and Baron Alexander von Humboldt. Thomas Stewart Traill became a close friend, with whom he wrote a paper on electro-magnetism. Scoresby's two books on the Arctic regions and on whale fishing were widely praised.

Deeply religious, Scoresby abandoned his successful and profitable career as a whaler in 1825 and became ordained into the Church of England, spending the rest of his days as a clergyman, although he continued his scientific studies. He gave a paper on magnetic induction at the first meeting of the British Association for the Advancement of Science in York in 1831. Although there is no record that Scoresby met Audubon, they had many friends in common, and as both were members of the Wernerian and Royal Societies it is almost certain that their paths must have crossed.

Prideaux John Selby (1788-1867) was born into a wealthy land-owning family. He lived at Twizel House near Belford in Northumberland, where he pursued his interests in natural history. Twizel House was on the road from Edinburgh to London and was a staging post for many travellers, particularly those with similar interests who were always welcome. At the time of Audubon's visits he was engaged in completing his *Illustrations of British Ornithology* and was working on the joint project with Jardine, *Illustrations of Ornithology*. Selby etched and engraved his own paintings which were then printed by Lizars. After Audubon's visits his paintings became more animated. He also wrote two volumes for the *Naturalist's Library* and with Jardine founded the *Annals or Magazine of Zoology, Botany and Geology*. He became High Sheriff for Northumberland. Audubon named the Selby flycatcher after him but later realised that the bird was the female hooded warbler (*Wilsonia citrina*), so the attribution to Selby was abandoned.

Reverend Sydney Smith (1771-1845) was a celebrated preacher, essayist and wit. While acting as a tutor he came to Edinburgh with his charge in 1798. There he studied moral philosophy and medicine and delivered popular sermons. He became very attached to Edinburgh. 'Never shall I forget the happy days spent there, amidst odious smells, barbarous sounds, bad suppers, excellent hearts and most enlightened and cultivated understandings.' He enjoyed the 'large healthy virgins, with mild pleasing countenances and white swelling breasts; shores washed by the sea; the romantic grandeur of ancient, and the beautiful regularity of modern buildings ....' With reference to the 'total want of faecal propriety' that was a feature of Edinburgh at that time, he wrote:

> Taste guides my eye, where'er new beauties spread,
> While prudence whispers, 'Look before you tread'.

During this period Smith was one of the originators of the *Edinburgh Review* together with Francis Jeffrey, and was editor of the first issue in 1802. He continued to contribute regularly after he left Edinburgh on subjects such as the slave trade, the ill-treatment of chimney sweeps' climbing boys and the emancipation of Catholics. His whig politics denied him the opportunity of advancement in the Church, but he served a country parish in Yorkshire faithfully for 20 years. A brilliant conversationalist, he was a welcome guest who could reduce any company to helpless laughter. He said of Lord Macaulay, the 'book in breeches', that his conversation was made delightful 'by his occasional flashes of silence'. (Macaulay, author of the *History of England*, was a close friend and a fellow contributor to the *Edinburgh Review*.) In a lengthy and sympathetic review of Charles Waterton's *Wanderings in South America*, Smith commented on the passage about the sloth which 'moves suspended, rests suspended, sleeps suspended, and passes his whole life in suspense, like a young clergyman distantly related to a bishop'. He noted that the boa swallows a tortoise, shell and all, and consumes it slowly in the interior, 'as the Court of Chancery does a large estate'. During his return visit to Edinburgh in 1827 when he met Audubon, he took the opportunity of visiting Jameson's museum.

John Stokoe (1775-1852) was a naval surgeon who was posted to St Helena from 1817-19 during the time of Napoleon's exile to that island. Although not officially one of Napoleon's doctors, he was befriended by the emperor who demanded that Stokoe should attend him during the illness which afflicted him during his last years. Stokoe's behaviour so incensed the governor, Hudson Lowe, that he was court-martialled on spurious charges and dismissed from the navy with a much-reduced pension. Joseph Bonaparte, the emperor's elder brother, was so upset by the unfair treatment of Stokoe that he made him one of his *pensionnaires*. In this capacity he was employed to escort Joseph's daughters in their journeys to join their father, then domiciled in America. One of these daughters, Zenaïde, married her cousin, the naturalist Charles Bonaparte, who became Audubon's friend and it was through this connection that Audubon first met Stokoe in Philadelphia in 1824. Stokoe continued to serve as an agent for the Bonaparte family when he returned to Edinburgh and acted as a link between Audubon and Charles Bonaparte during Audubon's stay in Edinburgh.

Thomas Sully (1783-1872) was born in England and went to the United States at the age of six. He became one of America's first portrait painters of note and in 1820 returned to London to study under Sir Thomas Lawrence. In 1824 Audubon had lessons from Sully in oil painting, and Sully subsequently became one of Audubon's chief supporters. It is probable that Audubon recommended him for membership of the Society of Artists of Edinburgh. On being notified of his election, Sully replied to the secretary that he was 'peculiarly grateful at the suffrage of a Society composed entirely of my own profession and from a city endeared to me by my earliest recollection'. Audubon wrote to Sully: 'Edinburgh, this Queen of cities, has greeted me with a welcome far superior to that experienced in Liverpool …. The newspapers, the people, the nobility, all have paid me homage due only to very superior men …. What will my friend Ord say to all this when he … hears of all those wonderful events?' Sully replied that his success had charmed all of his friends in America and that it would soon silence his few remaining enemies: 'Be true to yourself, Audubon and never doubt of success.'

William Swainson (1789-1855) described himself as having an 'impediment of speech, resulting from a peculiarly nervous temperament'. His education ceased at 14, which left him 'wayward and unhappy'. He inherited his father's interest in natural history and while still in his teens obtained a job in Sicily that gave him the opportunity to explore the wildlife of the Mediterranean, which improved his morale and determined his future career. He then travelled extensively in Brazil but was discour-

aged by Robert Jameson's critical reception of his article describing his travels.

On his return Swainson mastered the newly developed technique of lithography and produced his *Zoological Illustrations* from 1820 to 1823. Other publications include the *Fauna Boreali-Americana*, and three volumes of Jardine's *Naturalist's Library* which were illustrated with his paintings and engraved by Lizars. He struggled to make a living from his writings but was chronically impoverished and suffered a further blow when his wife died in 1835, leaving him with five young children to raise. In later life he became embittered and critical of many of his erstwhile colleagues including Audubon. 'He can shoot a bird, preserve it, and make it live again, as it were, upon canvass: but he cannot describe it in scientific, and therefore in perfectly intelligible terms.' Swainson emigrated to New Zealand in 1841 and tried his hand unsuccessfully as a farmer. He then obtained a post as Botanical Surveyor in Victoria, Australia, but returned to New Zealand a year before his death.

John Thomson (1765-1846) was the first occupant of the chair of surgery of the Royal College of Surgeons of Edinburgh, established in recognition of the fact that systemic surgery in the university had been taught by the Monro dynasty of anatomists who were neither practising surgeons nor Fellows of the college. His appointment met much opposition from the university and the town council. The Lord Provost sent a message 'expressing a hope that he would not persevere in his intention of lecturing … otherwise the Magistrates and Council would feel it to be their duty to interrupt him and dismiss his audience'. Thomson replied: 'Present my compliments to the Lord Provost and say that the lecture is prepared and that it is my intention to deliver it on the morrow to the students of Edinburgh although I should read it through the bars of a prison.' In the event, no action was taken and after many years of opposition the university relented and Thomson was appointed to the newly created regius chair of surgery within the university. Later he resigned this chair and was appointed to the newly founded chair of pathology – the first in this field in Scotland.

Thomas Stewart Traill (1781-1862) was born in Orkney. He studied medicine in Edinburgh and practised in Liverpool for 30 years. There he became a founder of the Royal Institution of Liverpool and of the Literary and Philosophical Society. He maintained a lifelong interest in natural history. He was a friend of William Scoresby and collaborated with him in several publications. Traill gave Audubon much support and encouragement on his first arrival in Liverpool. In 1833 he returned to Edinburgh as professor of medical jurisprudence and continued to teach until his death at the age of 80. He was an active member of the Wernerian Society and was editor of the eighth edition of the *Encyclopaedia Britannica*. Audubon named the willow flycatcher '*Empidonax traillii*' in his honour. He became president of the Royal College of Physicians of Edinburgh

Reverend John Walker (1734-1804) became a minister of the Church and eventually obtained a charge in the village of Moffat. He was noted for the care that he took over his appearance and was said to have spent two hours a day at the hands of his hairdresser in marked contrast to his successor, Robert Jameson, who was noted for his unruly hair. Throughout his life he studied botany and on 1779 was appointed to the chair of natural history at Edinburgh University, which post he held for a time in conjunction with his parish duties 50 miles away. Later he was appointed to a church in Colinton near Edinburgh, which made it easier for him to attend to his dual responsibilities. There he created a notable garden. He initiated the natural history museum at the university but it did not survive his death and Jameson had to recreate it from scratch.

William Yarrell (1784-1856) was born in London and followed his father into the trade of a newspaper agent. In middle age he gave up the business to devote time to his lifelong interest in natural history. He became a member of the Linnean Society and was a founder member of the Zoological Society. He published a *History of British Fishes* in 1836 and his *History of British Birds* in 1843. This last book was written and illustrated to appeal to the general public and enjoyed great success, attaining several editions. MacGillivray's book of the same name, published at the same time, was more technical and failed to achieve wide popularity or financial success. Yarrell corresponded with Audubon and MacGillivray. He was responsible for the naming of the Bewick's swan (*Cygnus bewickii*) in recognition of the contributions of his friend and fellow ornithologist.

Audubon's Publications in Edinburgh

Major Works

- The first 10 plates of *The Birds of America*, engraved by W H Lizars (1826-7).

- *Ornithological Biography*, 5 volumes (Adam Black and Adam & Charles Black, Edinburgh, 1831-9).

Journal Articles

- In the *Edinburgh New Philosophical Journal*:

- 'Account of the Habits of the Turkey Buzzard' (*Vultur aura*), 2, pp. 172-84 (1826).
- 'Observations on the Natural History of the Alligator', 2, pp. 270-80 (1826).
- 'Notes on the Rattlesnake' (*Crotalus horridus*), 3, pp. 21-30 (1827).
- 'Hunting the Cougar, or the American Lion', 11, pp. 103-15 (1831).
- 'The Ohio', 12, pp. 122-6 (1832).
- 'Account of a Hurricane in North America', 12, pp. 278-81 (1832).

- In the *Edinburgh Literary Journal*:

- 'The Flood of the Mississippi', 5, pp. 140-2 (1831).
- 'Improvements in the Navigation of the Mississippi', 5, pp. 194-5 (1831).

- *A Synopsis of Birds of America* (Adam & Charles Black, Edinburgh, 1839) (largely written by William MacGillivray).

- In the *Edinburgh Journal of Science*:

- 'Account of the Carrion Crow or *Vultur atratus*', 6, pp. 156-161 (1826/7).
- 'Notes on the Habits of the Wild Pigeon of America, *Columba migratoria*', 6, pp. 257-65 (1826/7).
- 'Account of the Method of Drawing Birds employed by J. J. Audubon, Esq., F.R.S.E.', 8, pp. 48-54 (1828).

- In the *Edinburgh Journal of Natural and Geographical Science*:

- 'Account of the Habits of the American Goshawk (*Falco palumbarius, Wils.*)', 3, pp. 145-7 (1831).

APPENDIX 2
Dates of Audubon's Visits to Edinburgh

Approximate dates of Audubon's visits to Edinburgh and the addresses of his lodgings
(those marked with an asterisk still exist):

26 October 1826 to 5 April 1827
   2 George Street

22 October to 11 November 1827
   2 George Street

13 October 1830 to 15 April 1831
   2 George Street

October 1834 to December 1834
   5 Lothian Street

June 1835 to December 1835
   5 India Street*

June 1838 to 10 July 1839
   7 Archibald Place* and 6 Alva Street*

The Scottish Subscribers to
The Birds of America

Only the five marked with an asterisk continued their subscriptions to completion of the four volumes,
and of these only the Glasgow University folio remains in the possession of the original subscriber.

The University of Edinburgh*

The University of Glasgow*

Sir William Allsworth Bart, Edinburgh

The Duke of Buccleuch, Dalkeith Palace*

The Rev. E Craig, 59 Great King Street, Edinburgh

Mrs Hamilton Nisbit Ferguson, Edinburgh

The Rev. Mr Gibson, Lochmaben

Lieutenant-General Graham, Stirling Castle

Lady Helen Hall, near Edinburgh

Sir William Jardine, of Jardine Hall, Dumfries

Daniel Lizars, Bookseller, Edinburgh

John Lizars MD, Edinburgh

The Countess of Morton, Dalmahoy near Edinburgh

W Ogilvie, Glasgow

The Society of Writers to her Majesty's Signet, Edinburgh*

The Rev. John Thomson, Duddingston, Edinburgh

The Wernerian Natural History Society, Edinburgh

W H Williams Edinburgh

James Wilson, Edinburgh

Henry Witham, Edinburgh and Durham*

In addition to the above, Andrew Coates (1814–1900), a member of the wealthy thread manufacturing family based in Paisley, bought three of the unsold sets still in the possession of the Audubon family. They were purchased when he visited Audubon in Minnie's Land in March 1843 just prior to the latter's departure on his final journey to the western states. One of Coates's sets was donated to the Paisley Public Library where it is still held.

The Duke of Buccleugh's folio was sold in 1941 to be broken up and resold by a New York dealer in 1942.

Henry Witham's folio was sold by a descendant in London by Christies in 1951 for £7000 to Lord Hesketh.

The Writers to the Signet's folio was sold in London by Sotheby's in 1959 for £13,000.

Edinburgh University's folio – the only copy in the city where the publication started – was sold in New York by Christies in 1992 for £2.3 million.

At time of publication (2003), four complete and three incomplete sets are known to exist in Scotland. Glasgow University holds its original folio in the Hunterian Library.

The Mitchell Library in Glasgow has a folio bequeathed to it by Robert Jeffrey (1827-1902) of Crosslee House, Renfrewshire, who had bought the set together with the five-volume *Ornithological Biography* in 1892 for £345. The copies of *Ornithological Biography* are those presented to Robert Jameson by Audubon. The original subscriber to the engravings is unknown.

The Paisley Library owns a set given to it in 1870 by Sir Peter Coates (1808-90) a brother of Andrew Coates (see above).

A fourth complete set is privately owned.

Incomplete sets are held by the Royal Faculty of Physicians and Surgeons of Glasgow which has the first two volumes, and the University of Aberdeen which has volume 2. It is possible that the set of 29 plates in the possession of the National Museums of Scotland were those to which the Wernerian Society subscribed. The 15 loose plates held by the National Museums of Scotland were acquired from the Free Church College in Edinburgh.

Most of the information here has been obtained from the well-researched *Double Elephant Folio* by W H Fries.

APPENDIX 4
Places visited by Audubon in and around Edinburgh

Those marked with an asterisk are still extant and largely unchanged since Audubon's time.

Edinburgh Castle*
Holyrood Palace*
The Assembly Rooms*
Register House*

Roslin Chapel*
Roslyn Castle*
The Theatre Royal

Edinburgh University Old Quadrangle (then newly built)*
The Royal College of Surgeons of Edinburgh*
The Royal Institution (now part of the National Gallery of Scotland)*

Private House	Occupant
41 Albany Street*	Dr Welbank
30 Abercrombie Place*	James Russell, professor of surgery
32 Abercrombie Place*	John Syme, artist who painted Audubon's portrait
2 Brown Square	George Combe, lawyer and phrenologist
Canaan Lane, Woodville*	James Wilson, natural historian
Canonmills House	Patrick Neill, printer and natural historian
29 Castle Street*	William Nicholson, painter
17 Charlotte Square*	Lord Clancarty
10 Coates Crescent*	Sir David Brewster, scientist and academic
Craiglockhart House*	Alexander Monro Tertius, professor of anatomy
Dalmahoy House*	Earl of Morton
32 Drummond Place*	James B Fraser, explorer and author
27 Dundas Street*	David Bridges, newspaper editor
59 George Square*	William Ritchie, co-founder and editor of *The Scotsman*
80 George Street	John Thomson, professor of surgery
92 George Street*	Francis Jeffrey, lawyer, editor of the *Edinburgh Review*
128 George Street*	Sir James Hall, geologist
11 Gilmore Place*	William MacGillivray, natural historian
6 Gloucester Place*	John Wilson (Christopher North), writer

Private House	Occupant
24 Great King Street*	Henry Witham, natural historian
62 Great King Street*	Robert Graham, professor of botany
63 Great King Street*	Patrick Syme, artist
66 Great King Street*	Miss Patrickson
16 Hope Street*	Lady Hunter
Lothian Road, Brae House	Anne Grant, author
42 Lothian Street	John Stokoe, physician to the Bonapartes
16 Minto Street*	William MacGillivray, natural historian
33 Northumberland Street*	Mr Simpson, advocate
10 Old Fishmarket Close	Patrick Neill's print shop
2 Pilrig Street*	Joseph Moule
21 Royal Circus*	Robert Jameson, professor of natural history
8 St Colme Street*	Basil Hall, sailor and author
3 St James Square	Willam Home Lizars, engraver and publisher
4 St James Street	Mr Heath
10 Surgeons' Square	Robert Knox, anatomist
3 Walker Street*	Sir Walter Scott, author and lawyer
1 Wharton Place	Robert K Greville, botanist; and later William MacGillivray, natural historian
22 Windsor Street*	Samuel Joseph, sculptor
45 York Place*	Andrew Duncan Jr, physician
17 Young Street*	William J Bakewell, cleric, relative of Lucy Audubon

BIBLIOGRAPHY

ADAMS, A B: *John James Audubon A Biography* (London, Victor Gollancz Ltd, 1967).

ALLEN, D E: 'The struggle for specialist journals: natural history in the British periodicals market in the first half of the nineteenth century', in *Archives of Natural History*, 23, pp. 107-23 (1996).

ANON: 'Darwin's Student Days', in *Scotsman Newspaper* (Edinburgh, 29 October 1935).

ANON: 'Review of Audubon's Birds of America and Ornithological Biography', in *Quarterly Journal of Agriculture*, 3, pp. 132-43 (1831).

ANON: 'Review of Audubon's Birds of America Vol II and Ornithological Biography', in *Edinburgh New Philosophical Journal*, XVIII: 131-44 (1834).

ANON: John Wilson's Obituary, in *Gentleman's Magazine*, New Series, 41: 656-7 (1854).

ANON: Robert Jameson's Obituary, in *Gentleman's Magazine*, New Series, 41: 656 (1854).

ASHWORTH, J H: 'Charles Darwin as a Student in Edinburgh 1825-1827', in *Proceedings of the Royal Society of Edinburgh*, 55: 97-113 (1935).

ATKINSON, G C: *Expeditions to the Hebrides in 1831 and 1833* (edited by Quine, D A) (Maclean Press Waternish, Skye, 2001).

AUDUBON, J J: 'A flood of the Mississippi', in *Edinburgh Literary Journal*, 5: 140-2 (1831).

AUDUBON, J J: 'Account of the Carrion Crow, or *Vultur atratus*', *Edinburgh Journal of Science*, 6, pp. 156 (1827).

AUDUBON, J J: 'Account of the Habits of the American Goshawk', *Edinburgh Journal of Natural and Geographic Science*, 3, pp. 145-7 (1830).

AUDUBON, J J: 'Account of the Habits of the Turkey Buzzard (*Vultur aura*)', in *Edinburgh New Philosophical Journal*, 2: 172-84 (1826).

AUDUBON, J J: 'Account of the Method of Drawing Birds employed by J. J. Audubon, Esq., F.R.S.E.', *Edinburgh Journal of Science*, 8, pp. 48-54 (1828).

AUDUBON, J J: *American Ornithology*, volumes I-V (Edinburgh, Adam Black, 1831-8).

AUDUBON, J J: 'Hunting the Cougar, or American Lion', in *Edinburgh New Philosophical Journal*, 11, pp. 103-15 (1831).

AUDUBON, J J: *My style of drawing birds* (Ardsley New York, The Overland Press, 1979).

AUDUBON, J J: 'Notes on the Habits of the Wild Pigeon of America' (*Columba migratoria*), in *Edinburgh Journal of Science*, 6, pp. 257-65 (1827).

AUDUBON, J J: 'Notes on the Rattlesnake' (*Crotalus Horridus*), in *Edinburgh New Philosophical Journal*, 3, pp. 21-30 (1827).

AUDUBON, J J: 'Observations on the Natural History of the Alligator', in *Edinburgh New Philosophical Journal*, 2, pp. 270-80 (1826).

AUDUBON, J J: *Ornithological Biography*, volumes I-V (Edinburgh, Adam Black, 1831-9).

AUDUBON, J J: *The Birds of America* (London, 1827-38).

AUDUBON, J J: *The Watercolors for the Birds of America* (New York, The New York Historical Society, 1993).

AUDUBON, J J and BACHMAN, J: *The Quadrupeds of North America* (New York, 1846-54).

AUDUBON, J W: *J. W. Audubon's Western Journal 1849-1850* (Tucson, The University of Arizona Press, 1984).

AUDUBON, L: *The Life of John James Audubon the Naturalist* (New York, G P Putnam's Sons, 1875).

AUDUBON, M R: *Audubon and His Journals* (New York, Charles Scribner's Sons, 1900).

BACHMAN, C L: *John Bachman* (Charleston, 1888).

BARCLAY, J B: 'Patrick Neill MA LLD FRSE 1776-1851', in *Year Book of the Royal Caledonian Horticultural Society*, pp. 6-11 (1989).

BELL, A: *Sydney Smith, a Biography* (Oxford, Clarendon Press, 1980).

BELL, C: *Anatomy of Expression* (London, Longmans 1806).

BENNETT, J H: Biography of the late Professor Edward Forbes, in *Monthly Journal of Medical Science*, 20: 75-92 (1855).

BEWICK, T: *A General History of Quadrupeds* (Newcastle upon Tyne, Bewick & Hodgson, 1807).

BEWICK, T: *History of British Birds* (London, Beilby & Bewick, 1797).

BEWICK, T: *A Memoir of Thomas Bewick written by himself 1822-1828* (ed Weekley, M) (London, The Cresset Press, 1961).

BIRSE, R M: *Science at the University of Edinburgh 1583-1993* (Edinburgh, 1994).

BLACKBURN, J: *Charles Waterton 1782-1865 Traveller and Conservationist* (London, Bodley Head, 1997).

BLUM, A S: *Picturing Nature. American Nineteenth-century Zoological Illustration* (Princeton, Princeton University Press, 1993).

BOEHME, S E (ed): *John James Audubon in the West. The Last Expedition* (New York, Harry H Abrams, 2000).

BOREMAN, T: *A description of three hundred animals* (London, Baldwin & Craddock, 1833).

BUCHANAN, R: *The Life and Adventures of John James Audubon* (London, Sampson Low, Son and Marston, 1868).

CALDER, J: *The Enterprising Scot* (Edinburgh, Royal Museum of Scotland, 1986).

CANTWELL, R: *Alexander Wilson Naturalist and Pioneer, A Biography* (Philadelphia, B Lippincott Co, 1961).

CHALMERS, J: 'Audubon in Edinburgh', in *Archives of Natural History*, 20: 157-66 (1993).

CHALMERS, P: *Birds Ashore and A-foreshore* (London, Collins, 1935).

CHAMBERS, R: *Traditions of Edinburgh* (Edinburgh, Clark Constable, 1824).

CHANCELLOR, J: *Audubon; A Biography* (London, Weidenfeld and Nicolson, 1978).

CHEEK, H H: 'Wernerian Natural History Society', in *Edinburgh Journal of Natural and Geographic Science*, 1: 352-5 (1830); 2: 269-74 (1830).

CHITNIS, A C: 'The University of Edinburgh's Natural History Museum and the Huttonian-Wernerian debate', in *Annals of Science*, 26: 85-94 (1970).

CLARK, R W: *The Huxleys* (London, Cox & Wyman Ltd, 1968).

CLEARY, M K: *John James Audubon* (Leicester, Magna Books, 1991).

CLEMENT, R: *The Living World of Audubon* (London, Country Life Books, 1975).

COATES, A: 'Personal Reminiscences of Audubon', in *Proceedings of the Perthshire Society of Natural Science*, 2: XXIV-XXIX (1894).

COCKBURN, H: *Journal of Henry Cockburn being a continuation of the Memorials of his Time* (Edinburgh, Edmonston and Douglas, 1874).

COCKBURN, H: *Memorials of his time* (Edinburgh, T N Foulis, 1909).

COLERIDGE, E H: 'Coleridge, Wordsworth and the American Botanist William Bartram', in *Transactions of the Royal Society of Literature*, 27, second series: 69-92 (1907).

COMBE, G: 'M Audubon, M Weiss, Carl. Mar., V Weber', in *Phrenology Journal*, 4: 295-302 (1827).

COMBE, G: Reply to Francis Jeffrey', in *Phrenology Journal*, 13: 1-82, 1827.

CORNER, G W (ed): *The Autobiography of Benjamin Rush* (American Philosophical Society, Princeton University Press, 1948).

CORNING, H (ed): *Journal of John James Audubon made during his trip to New Orleans in 1820-1821* (Boston, The Club of Odd Volumes, 1929).

CORNING, H (ed): *Journal of John James Audubon made while obtaining subscriptions to his Birds of America 1840-1843* (Boston, The Club of Odd volumes, 1929).

CORNING, H (ed): *Letters of John James Audubon 1826-1840* (Boston, The Club of Odd Volumes, 1930).

COUES, E: 'Behind the Veil', in *Bulletin of the Nuttall Ornithological Club*, 5: 123-204 (1880).

CRESSWELL, C H: *The Royal College of Surgeons of Edinburgh. Historical Notes from 1505 to 1905* (Edinburgh, Oliver & Boyd, 1926).

CROMBIE, B W: *Modern Athenians* (Edinburgh, Adam and Charles Black, 1882).

DAICHES, D et al (eds): *A Hotbed of Genius. The Scottish Enlightenment 1730-1790* (Edinburgh, Edinburgh University Press, 1986).

DANCE, S P: *The Art of Natural History. Animal Illustrators and their Work* (London, Country Life Books, 1978).

DARWIN, C: *The Autobiography of Charles Darwin* (London, Collins, 1958).

DARWIN, C: *The Correspondence of Charles Darwin Vol 1 1821-1836* (Cambridge, Cambridge University Press, 1985).

DARWIN, C: *The Descent of Man* (London, John Murray, 1894).

DARWIN, C: *The Origin of Species* (London, John Murray, 1900).

DARWIN, C: *Voyage of H.M.S. Beagle. Journal of Researches etc* (London, T Nelson & Sons, 1896).

DARWIN, F: *Life and Letters of Charles Darwin, including an Autobiographical Chapter* (London, 1887).

DAVIS, P & HOLMES, J: 'Thomas Bewick (1753-1828), engraver and ornithologist', in *Archives of Natural History*, 20: 167-84 (1993).

DAVIS, W E & LeCROY, M: 'A watercolor and notes by Alexander Wilson', in *Archives of Natural History*, 21: 237-42 (1994).

DAVIS, W E & JACKSON, J A: *Contributions to the history of North American ornithology* (Cambridge, Massachusetts, 1995).

DEAN, D R: *James Hutton and the History of Geology* (Ithaca and London, Cornell University Press, 1992).

DEANE, R: 'Unpublished letters of William MacGillivray to John James Audubon', in *The Auk*, 18: 239-49 (1901).

DELATTE, C E: *Lucy Audubon; A Biography* (Baton Rouge, Louisiana State University Press, 1982).

DESMOND, D & MOORE, J: *Charles Darwin* (London, Michael Joseph, 1991).

DOW, D A (ed): *The Influence of Scottish Medicine* (The Scottish Society of the History of Medicine, 1988).

URANT, M and HARWOOD, M: *On the road with John James Audubon* (New York, Dodd Mead & Co, 1980).

EWAN, J: *William Bartram Botanical and Zoological Drawings, 1756-1788* (Philadelphia, The American Philosophical Society, 1968).

EWBANK, J & LIZARS, W H: *Picturesque Views of Edinburgh. Drawings by J Ewbank*, engraved by W H Lizars (Edinburgh, Lizars, 1835).

EYLES, V A: 'Robert Jameson and the Royal Scottish Museum', in *Discovery*, 15: 155-62, 1954.

FEDUCCIA, A: *Catesby's Birds of Colonial America* (Chapel Hill, The University of North Carolina Press, 1985).

FLEMING, F: *Barrow's Boys* (London, Granta Books, 1998).

FORD, A: *The 1826 Journal of John James Audubon* (New York, Abbeyville Press, 1987).

FORD, A: *John James Audubon* (Norman, University of Oklahoma Press, 1964).

FORD, A: *John James Audubon, A Biography* (New York, Abbeville Press, 1988).

FRASER, A G: *The Building of the New College. Adam, Playfair and the University of Edinburgh* (Edinburgh, Edinburgh University Press, 1989).

FREEMAN, R B: *British Natural History Books 1495-1900* (Folkestone, Wm Dawson & Sons, 1980).

FREEMAN, R B: Darwin's Negro Bird Stuffer, in *Notes and Records of the Royal Society of London*, 33: 83 (1979).

FREMEAUX, P: *With Napoleon at St. Helena, Being the Memoirs of Dr John Stokoe* (trans from French, Edith S Stokoe) (London, The Bodley Head, 1902).

FRIES, W H: 'Joseph B Kidd and the Oil Paintings of Audubon', in *Art Quarterly*, 26: 338-49 (Detroit, 1963).

FRIES, W H: *The Double Elephant Folio* (Chicago, American Library Association, 1973).

GILBERT, W M: *Edinburgh in the nineteenth Century* (Edinburgh, J & R Allan, 1901).

GITTINGS, R: *John Keats* (London, Heinmann, 1968).

GORDON, E: 'Audubon's Passion', in *New Yorker*, 28: 96-104 (1991).

GORDON, M: *Christopher North. A Memoir of John Wilson* (Edinburgh, Edmonton & Douglas, 1862).

GORDON, E: *The Royal Scottish Academy of Painting, Sculpture and Architecture 1826-1976* (Edinburgh, Charles Skilton Ltd, 1976).

GOULD, J: *Birds of Great Britain* (London, Eyre Methuen Ltd, 1980).

GRANT, J: *Old and New Edinburgh* (London, Cassell & Co Ltd, 1860).

GRANT, R E: 'Notice regarding the Ova of the Pontobdella muricata, Lam', in *Edinburgh Journal of Science*, 7: 121-5 (1827).

GROSART, A B (ed): *The Poems and Literary Prose of Alexander Wilson* (Paisley, Alex Gardner, 1876).

HALL, B: *Travels in North America in the years 1827-1828* (Edinburgh, Cadell & Co, 1829).

HAMILTON, J: *Memoirs of the Life of James Wilson of Woodville* (London, James Nisbet & Co, 1859).

HARLEY, J: *Leicester Literary and Philosophical Society. The late Professor William MacGillivray* (Leicester, Crossley and Clarke, 1855).

HARWOOD, M: *Audubon Demythologised* (New York, National Audubon Society).

HAWKE, D F: *Benjamin Rush Revolutionary Gadfly* (Indianapolis, The Bobbs-Merrill Co Inc, 1971).

HERRICK, F H: 'Audubon and the Dauphin', in *The Auk*, 54: 476-99 (1937).

HERRICK, F H: *Audubon the Naturalist: A history of his Life and Time* (New York, Appleton-Century Co Inc, 1938).

HOBSON, H: *Charles Waterton his Home, Habits, and Handiwork* (London, Whittaker & Co, 1867).

HOOK, A: *Scotland and America 1750-1835* (Glasgow, Blackie, 1975).

HUNTER, C: The influence of Alexander Wilson upon John James Audubon, in *The Scottish Naturalist*, 101: 85-95 (1983).

HUNTER, C: *The Life and Letters of Alexander Wilson* (Philadelphia, American Philosophical Society, 1983).

HUXLEY, L: *Life and letters of Thomas Henry Huxley* (London, Macmillan, 1900).

HUXLEY, T H: *Diary of the Voyage of H.M.S. Rattlesnake* (London, Chatto and Windus, 1935).

HYMAN, S: *Edward Lears's Birds* (London, Weidenfeld and Nicolson, 1980).

IREDALE, T: 'The last letters of John MacGillivray', in *Australian Zoologist*, 9: 40-63, 1937.

IRWIN, F: 'The Man in the Wolfskin Coat', in *Country Life*, 28: 1104-6 (1977).

IRWIN, R: *British Bird Books, An index to British Ornithology 1481-1948* (London, Grafton & Co, 1951).

JACKSON, C E: *Bird Etchings: The Illustrators and Their Books 1655-1855* (Ithaca and London, Cornell University Press, 1985).

JACKSON, C E: *Bird Illustrators: some artists in early lithography* (London, H F & G Witherby Ltd, 1975).

JACKSON, C E: 'The changing relationship between J. J. Audubon and his friends P. J. Selby, Sir William Jardine and W. H. Lizars', in *Archives of Natural History*, 18: 289-307 (1991).

JACKSON, C E: *Great Bird Paintings* (Woodbridge Suffolk, Antique Collectors Club, 1993).

JACKSON, C E: *Prideaux John Selby a gentleman naturalist* (Stocksfield Northumberland, The Spredden Press, 1992).

JAMESON, L: Biographical Memoir of the late Professor Jameson, in *Edinburgh New Philosophical Journal*, 57: 1-49 (1854).

JAMESON, R: *Mineralogical Travels* (Edinburgh, 1813).

JAMESON, R: Review of Wilson's American Ornithology, in *Edinburgh Literary Journal*, 6: 133-7 (1831).

JAMESON, R: *The Wernerian Theory of the Neptunian Origin of rocks.* A facsimile reprint of Elements of Geognosy 1809 (New York, Hafner Press, 1976).

JARDINE, W: *British Salmonidae* (London, British Museum, 1979).

JARDINE, W: *Naturalist's Library* (Edinburgh, W H Lizars, 1843).

JONES, J: The Geological Collection of James Hutton (*Annals of Science*, 41: 223-44, 1984).

JOYCE, M: *Edinburgh, The Golden Age 1769-1832* (London, Longmans Green & Co, 1951).

KEATS, J: *The Letters of John Keats 1814-1821* (Cambridge, Cambridge University Press, 1958).

KIRKSOP, W: 'W. R. Greg and Charles Darwin in Edinburgh and after – an Antipodean Gloss', in *Transactions of the Cambridge Bibliographic Society*, 7: 376-90 (1979).

KNIGHT, D M: 'William Swainson: naturalist, author and illustrator, in *Archives of Natural History*, 13: 275-90 (1986).

KNOTT, C G *et al* (eds): *Edinburgh's Place in Scientific Progress* (Edinburgh, Chambers, 1921).

LAMBOURNE, M: *John Gould – Bird Man* (Milton Keynes, Osterbon Productions Ltd, 1987).

LARGEN, M J & FISHER, C T: 'Catalogue of extant mammal specimens from the collection of the 13th Earl of Derby now in the Liverpool Museum', in *Archives of Natural History*, 13: 225-72 (1986).

LAUDER, T D: *The Miscellany of Natural History, Vol I Parrots* (London, Fraser & Co, 1833).

LEHMANN, J: *Edward Lear and his world* (London, Thames and Hudson, 1977).

LINDSEY, A A (ed): *The Bicentennial of John James Audubon* (Bloomington, Indiana University Press, 1985).

LOCKHART, J G: *Peter's letters to his kinsfolk* (Edinburgh, Blackwood, 1819).

LONSDALE, H A: *A Sketch of the Life and Writings of Robert Knox* (London, Macmillan & Co, 1870).

LOW, S M: *Catalogue of the New Birds of America section of the Audubon Archives* (New York, American Museum of Natural History, 1993).

LYSAGHT, A M: *The Book of Birds. Five centuries of bird illustration* (London, Chancellor Press, 1975).

McBURNEY, A R W: *Mark Catesby's Natural History of America. The watercolors from the Royal Library Windsor Castle* (London, Merrell Holberton, 1997).

McDERMOTT, J F: *Audubon in the West* (Norman, University of Oklahoma Press, 1965).

McDERMOTT, J F (ed): *Up the Missouri with Audubon, the Journal of Edward Harris* (Norman, University of Oklahoma Press, 1951).

McEVEY, A: *John Gould's Contribution to British Art* (Sydney, Sydney University Press, 1973).

MacGILLIVRAY, J: 'On the mental qualities of birds', in *The Edinburgh Academic Annual 1840* (Edinburgh, Adam and Charles Black, 1840).

MacGILLIVRAY, J: Owen Correspondence (1841) (unpublished).

MacGILLIVRAY, J: 'Account of the Island of St Kilda, chiefly with reference to its Natural History; from Notes made during a Visit in July 1840', in *Edinburgh New Philosophical Journal*, 32: 47-70 (1842).

MacGILLIVRAY, J: *Narrative of the Voyage of H.M.S. Rattlesnake* (T & W Boone, London, 1852).

MacGILLIVRAY, W & JAMESON, L: *Edinburgh University Museum Report Books* (in Library of the National Museums of Scotland)

MacGILLIVRAY, W: *British Quadrupeds. Naturalist's Library*, volume VII (Edinburgh, Lizars, 1838).

MacGILLIVRAY, W: *Descriptions of the Rapacious Birds of Great Britain* (Edinburgh, Maclachlan & Stewart, 1836).

MacGILLIVRAY, W: *A Hebridean naturalist's Journal 1817-1818,* (Stornoway, Stornoway Gazette, 1996).

MacGILLIVRAY, W: *A History of British Birds,* volumes I-V (London, 1837-52).

MacGILLIVRAY, W: *A History of the Molluscous Animals* (London, Cunningham & Mortimer, 1843).

MacGILLIVRAY, W: *Lives of eminent Zoologists from Aristotle to Linnaeus* (Edinburgh, Oliver & Boyd, 1834).

MacGILLIVRAY, W: *A Manual of Botany* (London, Scott, Webster & Geary, 1840).

MacGILLIVRAY, W: *Manual of British Birds* (London, Adam Scott, 1846).

MacGILLIVRAY, W: *A Manual of British Ornithology, Part 1 The Land Birds* (London, Scott, Webster & Geary, 1840).

MacGILLIVRAY, W: *A Manual of Geology* (London, Scott Webster & Geary, 1840).

MacGILLIVRAY, W: *The Natural History of Deeside and Braemar* (London, Queen Victoria, 1855).

MacGILLIVRAY, W: 'On the Habits of the White-tailed Eagle, with an Account of the Modes of destroying Eagles practiced in the Hebrides', in *Quarterly Journal of Agriculture*, 31: 924-9 (1831).

MacGILLIVRAY, W: *Richard's elements of botany* (Edinburgh, Blackwood, 1831).

MacGILLIVRAY, W: *Tribute to the Memory of a Friend* (Edinburgh, Oliver & Boyd, 1820).

MacGILLIVRAY, W: *W. Withering's British Plants* (London, Edward Law, 1858).

MacGILLIVRAY, W (ed): *The Edinburgh Journal of Natural History and of the Physical Sciences* 1835-9).

MacGILLIVRAY, W (2): *A Memorial Tribute to William MacGillivray* (Edinburgh, Private, 1901).

MacGILLIVRAY, W (2): *Life of William MacGillivray* (London, John Murray, 1910).

MASON, A S: *George Edwards the Bedell and His Birds* (London, Royal College of Physicians, 1992).

MEARNS, B & MEARNS, R: *Audubon to Xanthus. The lives of those commemorated in the North American Bird Names* (London, Academic Press, 1992).

MEARNS, B & MEARNS, R: *Biographies for Birdwatchers* (London, Academic Press, 1988).

Memoirs of the Wernerian Natural History Society (Edinburgh, 1812-39).

MULLENS, W H: 'Some early British Ornithologists and their works IX William MacGillivray and William Yarrell', in *British Birds*, 2: 389-99 (1909).

MULLENS, W H and SWANN, H K: *A Bibliography of British Ornithology from the earliest times to the end of 1912* (London, Macmillan and Co, 1912).

NORTH, C: 'Audubon's Ornithological Biography Introduction', in *Blackwood's*, 30: 1-16 (1831).

NORTH, C: 'Audubon's Ornithological Biography. Wilson's American Ornithology. Second Survey', in *Blackwood's*, 30: 247-80 (1831).

NORTH, C: 'Comments on Combe and phrenology', in *Blackwood's*, 21: 106 (1826).

NORTH, C: 'Discussion of Audubon's exhibition', in *Blackwood's*, 21: 105 (1827).

NORTH, C: 'Review of Wilson's American Ornithology', in *Blackwood's*, 19: 661-70 (1826).

ORMOND, R: *Sir Edward Landseer* (London, Tate Gallery, 1981).

PATERSON, J: *Kay's Edinburgh Portraits A series of anecdotal Biographies Chiefly of Scotchmen* (London, Hamilton, Adams & Co, 1885).

PEATTIE, D C: *Audubon's America The narratives and experiences of John James Audubon* (Boston, The Riverside Press, 1940).

PECK, R M: William Bartram and his travels', in *Society for the Bibliography of Natural History*, 2: 35-50 (1983).

PETERSON, R T and PETERSON, V M: *Audubon's birds of America* (New York, Abbeyville Press, 1991).

PITMAN, J: *William Jardine Papers* (Edinburgh, National Museums of Scotland, 1981).

Plinian Society Transactions 1825-1841. MS Edinburgh University Library, Special Collections.

PORTER, C M: 'The Drawings of William Bartram (1739-1823), American naturalist', in *Archives of Natural History*, 16, 289-303 (1989).

PREECE, R C & KILLEEN, I J: 'Edward Forbes (1815-1854)', in *Archives of Natural History*, 22, 419-35 (1995).

RALPH, R: 'A Portrait of William MacGillivray', in *Archives of Natural History*, 19: 265-7 (1992).

RALPH, R: 'John MacGillivray – his life and work', in *Archives of Natural History*, 20: 185-95 (1993).

RALPH, R: *William MacGillivray* (London, The Natural History Museum, 1993).

RICHARDSON, J: *The Life and Letters of John Keats* (London, Folio Society, 1981).

RITCHIE, J A: 'A Double Centenary – Two Notable Naturalists, Robert Jameson and Edward Forbes', in *Proceedings of the Royal Society of Edinburgh*, 66: 29-58 (1955).

RITCHIE, J A: 'The Edinburgh Explorers', in *University of Edinburgh Journal*, 12: 155-9 (1943).

ROSE, M B: *The Gregs of Quarry Bank Mill* (Cambridge, Cambridge University Press, 1986).

ROUKE, C: *Audubon* (London, G Harrap & Co, 1936).

Royal Commission on the Scottish Universities, volume I, University of Edinburgh (1837).

SAUER, G C: *John Gould the Bird Man. A Chronology and Bibliography* (London, Henry Sotheran Ltd, 1982).

SCHUFELDT, R W & AUDUBON, M R: 'The Last Portrait of Audubon, together with a Letter to his Son', in *The Auk*, 11: 309-13 (1894).

SCOTT, W: *The Journal of Sir Walter Scott* (Edinburgh, Oliver and Boyd, 1950).

SCOTUS, Dr Monro, in *Lancet* 1, 391-4 (1828).

SELBY P J: *Illustrations of British Ornithology* (Edinburgh, Lizars, 1833).

SHEPHERD, T H: *Modern Athens Displayed in a series of views; of Edinburgh in the nineteenth century* (London, Jones & Co, 1829).

SHEPPERSON, G: 'Darwinism and the Study of Society', A Centenary Symposium (London, Tavistock Publications, 1961).

SIM, G: *Life of William MacGillivray* (1900) (unpublished MS, Aberdeen City Library).

SITWELL, S (ed): *Audubon's American Birds from Plates by J. J. Audubon with an Introduction and Notes on the Plates* (London, B T Batsford Ltd, 1949).

SITWELL, S & BUCHAN, H: *Fine Bird Books 1700-1900* (London, William Collins, 1953).

SKENE, J: *A series of sketches of the existing localities alluded to in the Waverley Novels* (Edinburgh, Cadell & Co, 1829).

STAMP, T & STAMP, C: *William Scoresby Arctic Scientist* (Whitby, Caedmon of Whitby Press, 1975).

STORER, J and STORER, H S: *Views of Edinburgh and its vicinity* (Edinburgh, Constable & Co, 1820).

STRONG, E: 'William Home Lizars', in *Scotsman Newspaper* (Edinburgh, 11 March 1989).

SWAINSON, G M: *William Swainson: Naturalist and Artist* (Palmerston North, New Zealand, G M Swainson, 1989).

SWAINSON, G M: *William Swainson: Naturalist and Artist Family Letters and Diaries 1809-1855* (Palmerston North, G M Swainson, 1992).

SWAINSON, W: *Flycatchers. Naturalist's Library*, volume x (Edinburgh, Lizars, 1838).

SWANN, E: *Christopher North (John Wilson)* (Edinburgh, 1934).

SWANN, T: *Great Zoological Books A Bookseller's perspective* (Private, 1996).

SWEET, J M: 'The Collection of Louis Dufresne (1752-1832)', in *Annals of Science*, 26: 33-71 (1970).

SWEET, J M: 'Robert Jameson and the Explorers: The search for the North-west Passage, Part 1 I. W. Scoresby Jr, C. L. Giescke, M. Wormskiold and John Ross', in *Annals of Science*, 31: 21-47 (1974).

SWEET, J M: 'William Bullock's Collection and the University of Edinburgh', in *Annals of Science*, 26: 23-32 (1970).

SWEET, J M: 'The University Puma', in *University of Edinburgh Journal*, 27: 218-221 (1976).

SWEET, J M: *The Wernerian Theory of the Neptunian Origin of Rocks by Robert Jameson* (New York, Hafner Press, 1976).

SYME, P: *A treatise on British Song-Birds* (Edinburgh, John Anderson, 1823).

TANNAHILL, R: *The Poems and Songs of Robert Tannahill* (Paisley, Alex Gardner, 1900).

TANSEY, V & MEKIE, D E C: *The Story of the Museum of the Royal College of Surgeons of Edinburgh* (1978) (private publication).

TANSEY, V & MEKIE, D E C: *The Museum of the Royal College of Surgeons of Edinburgh* (Edinburgh, Royal College of Surgeons of Edinburgh, 1982).

THOMSON, A: 'Biographical Account of the late William MacGillivray', in *Edinburgh New Philosophical Journal*, 54: 189-206 (1853).

THOMSON, D: *Raeburn The art of Sir Henry Raeburn* (Edinburgh, Scottish National Portrait Gallery, 1997).

WATERSTON, C D: *Collections in Context* (Edinburgh, NMS Publishing, 1997).

WATERTON, C: *Wanderings in South America* (1825).

WATERTON, C: *Essays on Natural History* (London, Longman *etc*, 1839).

WATERTON, C: *Essays on Natural History* (London, Frederick Warne & Co, 1871).

WHEELER, A (ed): *Contributions to the history of North American Natural History* (London, Society for the Bibliography of Natural History, 1983).

WILLIAMS, G R: *Fantasy in a Wood-block* (Chicago, Caxton Club, 1972).

WILSON, A: *American Bird Engravings. All 103 plates from American Ornithology* (New York, Dover Publications, 1975).

WILSON, A: *American Ornithology* (London, Chatto and Windus, 1876).

WILSON, A and BONAPARTE, C L: *American Ornithology* (London, Chatto & Windus, 1876).

WILSON A & BONAPARTE, C L: *American Ornithology or the Natural History of the Birds of the United States* (Edinburgh, Constable & Co, 1831).

WILSON, G & GEIKIE, A: *A Memoir of Edward Forbes* (Cambridge and London, Macmillan & Co, 1861).

WILSON, J: *Illustrations of Zoology* (Edinburgh, Blackwood, 1831).

WILSON, J: *A Treatise on Insects* (Edinburgh, Adam & Charles Black, 1835).

WILSON, J: *A voyage round the Coasts of Scotland and the Isles* (Edinburgh, Adam & Charles Black, 1842).

YARRELL, W: *A History of British Birds* (London, John Van Voorst, 1839).

YOUNGSON, A J: *The Making of Classical Edinburgh* (Edinburgh, Edinburgh University Press, 1966).

SELECT INDEX

Individuals and organisations with chapters devoted to them are not included in the index:
hence John James Audubon, Robert Jameson, William MacGillivray, Alexander Wilson,
Edinburgh University and the Wernerian Society are not separately indexed.

(Bold denotes a separate entry in Biographical Profiles)